COMMUNICATION AND COMMUNITY
An Approach
to Social Psychology

COMMUNICATION AND COMMUNITY
An Approach to Social Psychology

William M. Berg
Robert Boguslaw
Washington University

Prentice-Hall, Inc., Englewood Cliffs, New Jersey 07632

Library of Congress Cataloging in Publication Data

BERG, WILLIAM M.
  Communication and community.

  Bibliography: p.
  Includes index.
  1. Social psychology. 2. Communication—Social as-
pects. 3. Interpersonal communication. 4. Child devel-
opment. 5. Life cycle, Human. I. Boguslaw, Robert.
II. Title.
HM251.B4543 1985   302   84-23727
ISBN 0-13-153818-7

Editorial/production supervision and
   interior design: Dee Josephson
Cover design: Joe Curcio
Manufacturing buyer: John Hall
Cover Photos: Ken Karp
              Irene Springer

Printed in the United States of America

10 9 8 7 6 5 4 3 2 1

ISBN 0-13-153818-7

Prentice-Hall International, Inc., *London*
Prentice-Hall of Australia Pty. Limited, *Sydney*
Editora Prentice-Hall do Brasil, Ltda., *Rio de Janeiro*
Prentice-Hall Canada Inc., *Toronto*
Prentice-Hall Hispanoamericana, S.A., *Mexico*
Prentice-Hall of India Private Limited, *New Delhi*
Prentice-Hall of Japan, Inc., *Tokyo*
Prentice-Hall of Southeast Asia Pte. Ltd., *Singapore*
Whitehall Books Limited, *Wellington, New Zealand*

Dedicated to
Debbie and Emily Julia
and to
Wanda and our daughters, Chelle, Janet, and Lisa

CONTENTS

PREFACE

For all of us, life is somewhat like being at the controls of a speeding car that has no brakes. We find ourselves moving ahead at an incredible rate of speed—forced to make decisions at every crossroad.

What shall I do with my life? What kind of work should I prepare to do? Whom shall I date? Whom shall I marry? What kind of friends do we want? Should we have children now? Should our baby be breast-fed or bottle-fed? When should our child be toilet-trained? What sort of education ought we provide for our children? What kind of society do we want to have for them and for ourselves as well as for other people? How can we convince people that our product or political position is "better"? How can we move ahead on our jobs? How can the performance of our team (at work or in sports) be improved? How can we be happy? What exactly is "retirement"? At what age should we retire? What should we *do* during retirement years?

The questions are endless. They occur at every stage of what some like to call the "life-cycle." There are countless professions that purport to provide more or less definitive answers to these questions and to an infinite variety of related ones. Clergymen, teachers, social workers, child psychologists, physicians, managers, labor leaders, management consultants, gerontologists—the list goes on and on.

This book, the reader should be warned, does *not* have preprogrammed, computerized answers to these questions. The field of social psychology, however, does address itself to issues of central importance in understanding them.

This volume constitutes one possible introduction to that field. Our approach is not the only one possible. We have arranged most of the material from the perspective of the human life cycle. But even this can be done in a variety of ways.

We have emphasized, at every stage, problems of human communication as well as the phenomenon of human community. We have also tried to provide an understandable introduction to what we regard as the most useful and important methods, theories, and substantive concerns in the field.

We hope all, or at least much of this will be of interest and value, not only to fledgling social psychologists on the way to a career in this field, but to all those who wish to understand themselves and other people somewhat better.

We would like to thank Ed Stanford of Prentice-Hall for his cooperation in the initial formulation of this project. Susan Taylor and Bill Webber continued to provide such cooperation during the latter stages of the project. Wayne Spohr's encouragement and enthusiasm is also greatly appreciated.

A number of people assisted in the preparation of this book. We are indebted to Elsie Glickert and other sociology staff members for their assistance in preparing early drafts of some of the chapters. We are especially grateful to Rebecca Torstrick for her careful attention to details as the manuscript was being word-processed. We also appreciate the careful attention of Dee Josephson, production editor, and the Prentice-Hall copy-editors.

Finally, we are grateful to our reviewers who provided thoughtful and insightful comments throughout the process: Charles Bolton, Portland State University; Clyde W. Franklin, II, Ohio State University; Richard Felson, State University of New York at Albany. As authors, of course, we are responsible for the contents of this book.

COMMUNICATION AND COMMUNITY
An Approach to Social Psychology

CHAPTER ONE
THE FIELD OF SOCIAL PSYCHOLOGY

Many people feel that the study of a new field should properly begin with a definition. But as one highly respected professional insists, "There are almost as many definitions of social psychology as there are social psychologists."[1] For a newcomer to the field, such a statement may be seen as either a threat or an opportunity. It could suggest (1) that the field is characterized by a great deal of disorganization or (2) that it is a field in which a great deal is happening and where an inquiring mind can make important contributions. We happen to believe that the second approach is the more accurate description, although it is probably true that new ideas characteristically germinate in what appears to be the soil of disorganization.

In any event, another author has provided us with what is billed as perhaps the single most widely accepted definition of the field of social psychology: "an attempt to understand and explain how the thought, feeling and behavior of individuals are influenced by the actual, imagined or implied presence of others."[2]

As we progress, it will become clear that social influence is an important focus of this book, although we construe it in a somewhat broader manner than have other social psychologists. Specifically, if people are to influence other people, it would seem that they must "interact." Interaction takes place in a social context. It takes a place between individuals who occupy particular social positions in which they may enjoy a certain status and play specific roles. According to another expert, then, "Social Psychology is [therefore] the study of social interaction as a phenomenon in its own right and as a component of larger social systems."[3] By the time you have finished reading this book, we hope that you will understand more completely what it is you can expect to learn and what you should not expect to learn from definitions.

For example, take the definition we have just given. It is very broad, and it could easily include a great deal of material usually seen as falling within such different disciplines as sociology, anthropology, and psychology. We agree that these disciplines are relevant to social psychology. However, we are not sure that social psychology needs to be restricted to interaction. Moreover, the preceeding definition appears to be a bit unfocused.

Other authors have deliberately refused to define the field of social psychology. For them, it is not a theoretical construct that might require a rigorous definition but simply an historical development that has become a field of study.

Here the point is an interesting one: the boundaries of various intellectual disciplines are seldom defined very precisely. Thus, it is not clear where one must draw the precise boundary between physics and chemistry or precisely how either of these differs from biology and how all of them differ from bio-chemistry, biophysics, and so on. Similarly, it is not clear how one separates in any formal manner the study of literature from the study of linguistics or the study of either of these from the study of languages, psycholinguistics, or ordinary language philosophy. In short, it is possible to refuse to define a field and to ask the beginner to be patient. Tell him or her, "You will understand what the field is all about after you have seen, in some detail, what it has to offer."

In this book we try to adopt a third alternative. We shall *not* attempt to provide an all-encompassing definition of the field of social psychology, nor shall we avoid this responsibility completely by asking the reader to be patient. Rather, we shall identify three major themes in social psychology that guide our discussions in this book.

The first of these we refer to as *communication*. By communication, we mean the interactions and transactions that take place between individuals and larger social collectivities. This includes, but is not restricted to, the processes of social influence. The communication perspective entails a broader conception of how people interact with one another and how they interpret and construct meanings in the course of that interaction. The second theme that guides our approach to social psychology concerns individual self and personality and their development. This involves the question of how the biological organism—so to speak—is transformed into a human being. This entails two subsidiary questions: (1) How does a person come to have a sense of himself or herself as an autonomous individual? and (2) Why do certain types of people evolve in different ways? Our third theme is more macrosocietal in orientation. Communication and individual development do not take place in a vacuum. Rather, they occur in different societal and cultural contexts. This third theme concerns how living in different social, cultural, and historical contexts affects communication and developmental processes—it addresses the problem of human community.

Throughout this book, our discussions of substantive topics in social psychology will be informed by these three themes. The remainder of this chapter is devoted to a discussion of different types of social influence and how they may be related to different social and historical contexts.

CONFORMITY AND OBEDIENCE

Let us begin by visiting a particularly important study—one conducted many years ago by Solomon E. Asch. You enter his laboratory and find yourself in a room with four other people. Someone shows you a straight line (line x) and asks each of you to compare it with three other lines (lines a, b, and c). Your job is to say which of these lines most closely approximates the length of line x. Simple enough?

Now, let us say that it is pretty clear that line x is the same length as line b but that it is considerably shorter than line a and longer than line c. The first person in your group is asked the question, "Which of the lines (a, b, or c) most closely approximates line x in length?" Person 1 responds: "Line a." Persons 2, 3, and 4 give the same answer. What do *you* say?

Asch found that people would agree with the incorrect judgment as often as 35 percent of the time, and subsequent research has established even higher rates of conformity with what "should" be clearly erroneous answers. Interestingly, when Asch and his colleagues interviewed people who gave incorrect answers after the experiment, he found that many had perceived the lines correctly. However, under the pressure of total group unanimity, they gave the conforming but incorrect response to the experimenter.[4]

Studies like Asch's indicate that people can influence other people in dramatic and strong ways. Social psychologists are very much interested in how a person's thoughts and actions are influenced by other people. They are interested in why some people are more influenced than others and what makes some efforts to influence others more successful than other efforts. They have studied processes of social influence with small groups in laboratory situations as well as with large populations through the use of methods like survey research. They have tried to understand the limits of social influence and how it works in everyday situations outside the laboratory in the everyday world.

As an example of social psychologists' attempts to understand the limits of social influence, consider the following scenario. Returning home from work one day, you begin paging through the newspaper. You see an advertisement asking for people to participate in a psychological experiment. You note that participants in the experiment are paid. You can use the money. Moreover, the prospect of participating in such an experiment is intriguing. So you answer the ad.

A few days later you arrive at the laboratory. The experimenter (Dr. Brown) explains the purpose of the experiment to you and to another older subject (Joe) who apparently has also answered the ad in the newspaper. You are told that the purpose of the experiment is to investigate the effects of punishment on learning. More specifically, Dr. Brown wants to know how much punishment is necessary to maximize learning and whether or not the age of either teacher or learner has an effect on the learning process. Dr. Brown explains that one of you is to be the teacher while the other is to be the learner. He flips a coin, and it is decided that you are to be the teacher.

You go next into a room where there is a complex instrument panel attached to a shock generator. A shock electrode is administered. Dr. Brown explains that, although these shocks may seem painful, they can cause no permanent tissue damage. Dr. Brown next takes you to the instrument panel attached to the shock generator. He shows you that each of the switches is clearly labeled with the among of voltage administered if the switch is pulled. You see that each switch increases the shock by an increment of 15 volts. The last switch administers a shock of "450 volts." The switches are grouped into fours. Each group has a label. These range from "slight shock" to "extreme intensity shock" and finally, "danger: severe shock." Beyond this are two groups of switches marked simply "XXX."

As the teacher, you are to read a series of word pairs (e.g., red-apple; run-walk) to the learner. Following a trial run, you are to read the first word of the pair and another four words, one of which is the word originally paired with the first word (e.g., red, mother, syllabus, apple, building). Joe is supposed to repeat the other word of the original pair (e.g., apple). The experimenter explains that you are to administer an increasingly higher level of shock each time Joe (who has been placed in an adjacent room and is now barely visible through a tinted window) gives an incorrect answer. Before delivering the shock, however, you are told to announce the correct word(s) and the level of shock about to be administered. You are to continue this procedure until all the word pairs are learned.

The "learning" experiment begins. Joe makes a number of mistakes and, in a few moments, you are up to 150 volts. You ask Dr. Brown if you are to keep going. Then 165 volts is delivered. You ask Dr. Brown if you are to keep going. Another 165 volts is delivered. You hear the learner cry out in the adjacent room.

"That guy is hollering in there," you say. "He might have a heart condition. You want me to go on?"

Then 180 volts is delivered. You become more concerned.

"He can't stand it. I'm not going to kill that man in there! You hear him hollering? He can't stand it. What if something happens to him? . . . I'm not going to kill him . . . . I'm not going to get that man sick in there. You know what I mean? I mean I refuse to take responsibility. He's getting hurt in there. He's in there hollering . . . I mean, who is going to take responsibility if anything happens to that guy?"

Dr. Brown says he will assume responsibility and you jack the voltage up to 195 volts. The screaming continues.

"You see he's hollering," you say to Dr. Brown. "Hear that? Gee—I don't know."

"The experiment requires that you go on," says the experimenter.

"I know it does, sir, but I mean—ugh—he doesn't know what he's in for. He's up to 195 volts."

210 volts is delivered.
225 volts is delivered.
240 volts is delivered.

"Aw no," you say. "You mean I've got to keep going up with the scale? No sir. I'm not going to kill that man! I'm not going to give him 450 volts."

"The experiment requires that you go on."

"I know, but that man's hollering in there. . . "[5]

You continue to object. But, somehow, you also continue to increase the voltage. At 300 volts, the learner begins to bang on the walls. You question the experimenter again, but push up to 315 volts and ultimately all the way up to the maximum 450 volts. After you have administered the maximum voltage, Dr. Brown explains the real purpose of the experiment to you.

Actually, the experiment had nothing at all to do with learning but rather with obedience. Joe was, in fact, a confederate of Dr. Brown's and was not actually receiving any shocks. The draw by which teacher and learner were selected was fixed so that the confederate would always assume the learner role. The experimenter, a social psychologist by the name of Stanley Milgram, was interested in the extent to which adults in our culture are able to disobey the commands of what seems to be legitimate authority. Milgram was surprised to learn that 66 percent of his subjects would go as far as 450 volts and that the average maximum level delivered was 405 volts.

Milgram was also interested in the factors that would either increase or decrease obedience. He noticed that rates of obedience were highest when the spatial distance between the learner and teacher was the greatest, that is, when the learner was in an adjacent room and voice contact between the two was minimal. Obedience increased as the distance between learner and teacher increased. When they were in separate rooms, as we have seen, 66 percent of the subjects continued until 450 volts had been reached. When the learner and teacher were in the same room, about 40 percent of the subjects went as far as 450 volts. When the teacher physically had to place the learner's hand on a metal plate before administering the shock, about 30 percent went as far as 450 volts.

Obedience was also reduced by reducing the credibility of the authority figure. In one of Milgram's experiments, some subjects were informed that the experimenter was a prestigious Yale psychologist; others were led to believe the experimenter had no university affiliation. Those in the former condition were more obedient. In another set of experiments, Milgram used two teachers. The second teacher was a confederate of the experimenter. When the second teacher refused to continue with the experiments, the subject almost always (90 pecent of the time) also refused to continue. The proximity of the experimenter also affected the rate of obedience. Obedience decreased when the experimenter was in another room (some subjects went so far as to lie about the number of shocks they actually administered).

In this connection, it is interesting to note that Asch and some of his followers have shown that conformity can be reduced by breaking up the unanimity of a group. In one experiment, the researchers had a confederate deviate from the dominant perception of the group (i.e., estimate that the line was much shorter or longer than other group members estimated it to be). In this experimental condition, conformity was reduced considerably. Significantly, conformity was reduced even if the nonconforming confederate disagreed with the group in a more incorrect direction (i.e., if he or she selected a line even farther in length from line a). It is also interesting to note that on matters of opinion (as opposed to perception), dissenters from the group opinion would not reduce conformity unless they dissented in the same direction as the subject.

On the other hand, rates of conformity may be increased in ambiguous situations. If the "facts" are unclear, people will tend to look to others for information and guidance. When subjects in a variant of the experimental design used by Solomon Asch were provided with rulers, conformity was considerably reduced. However, when the lines could not be measured or when the factual state of affairs could not be verified, conforming behavior increased. Conformity also was increased when subjects were presented with matters of opinion rather than perception. Faced with ambiguous social situations, people are more likely to conform to what they perceive to be the expectations of others than to search for the facts themselves.

Studies like those carried out by Asch and Milgram tell us a great deal about some aspects of the nature of social influence. Conformity research illustrates how people may form opinions about critical matters related to national and international affairs. Very few North Americans have direct knowledge of such places as Zimbabwe, Lebanon, the Sudan, or even Nicaragua and Honduras. Rather, our opinions on issues related to such places may be strongly influenced by the statements of others in our immediate environment.

Research on obedience illustrates how authority may justify cruel or unethical behavior. Clearly, the authority and esteem attached to the position of former President Richard M. Nixon provided a part of the basis for John Dean's actions in the Watergate affair. The effects of social influence need not always involve such extreme actions. In a recent experiment, social psychologists arranged a situation in which nurses at a hospital received a call from a doctor requesting them to prepare medication for certain patients. The medication was not on the hospital list of approved drugs, and the dosage to be applied exceeded acceptable levels. Nevertheless, almost all the nurses proceeded to prepare the medication.[6]

ARE SOME PEOPLE MORE SUSCEPTIBLE TO SOCIAL INFLUENCE THAN OTHERS?

Many of the studies we have discussed so far indicate how easily and how strongly individuals can be influenced, especially in ambiguous circumstances. This, for some, may lead to a misleading conception that human beings are completely pliable. Most social psychologists would agree, of course, that human beings are social animals, that is, that the meaning and significance our lives are derived essentially from our social existence. In this sense, social influence processes are fundamental to the nature of human existence and may exert a considerable power over us.

However, to speak of the fundamental nature of social influence processes is not to imply that it is always easy to influence people in desirable or, as in the case of some of the preceding experiments, undesirable ways.

In some senses, it is often very difficult to influence individuals. For example, while Milgram may have succeeded in getting many of the subjects in his experiments to obey the experimenter's instructions, he did not succeed in altering their underlying attitudes or beliefs about obedience or the value of punishment.

Getting people to comply with an instruction or request seems to be a very difficult form of influence than attempting to persuade individuals to change certain basic beliefs or opinions.

There are aspects or qualities of individuals that may mediate or otherwise affect the course of the influence process. Milgram, for example, found that "teachers" who obeyed most readily were more authoritarian than were those who were either reluctant to proceed or refused completely to go on with the experiments. Other research suggests that individuals who have a heightened sense of justice are less likely to proceed as far in administering shocks as are those who are less concerned with others' well-being or with general principles of moral action. (See Chapter 7.)

A number of social psychologists have examined the idea of a conforming personality and have studied particular personality traits that seem to be more or less characteristic of conforming and obedient individuals. One example of research related to conformity entails the idea of fate control. Researchers have shown that individuals who believe that they have a greater mastery of their environment and more control over their destiny are less conformist than are those who believe that they exercise only limited control over their environment and feel that their destiny is determined by factors beyond their own influence.[7]

A good deal of research in the area of conformity has focused on the relationship between behavior and the authoritarian personality. Relying on a Freudian perspective (Chapter 4), certain social psychologists have argued that authoritarianism grows out of child-rearing practices that involve a high degree of strict discipline. Individuals raised by such practices, according to this theory, are unable to deal with ambiguities and tend to rely on instructions from superordinates when dealing with complex and confusing problems. Such individuals are generally less tolerant of others (especially others who are different than themselves) and are more likely to have a high commitment to authority figures.

Other social psychologists have linked conformity with various larger sociological processes.

David Riesman, in his book *The Lonely Crowd*,[8] differentiated three different personality types associated with conformity. The "traditional-directed" individual is one who follows the cultural blueprint passed down from generation to generation. This individual simply adheres to the same rules and standards as his or her parents. "Inner-directed" individuals, according to Riesman, have broken away from the traditions of their parents and grandparents. These individuals are self-motivated. Interestingly, Riesman argues that this personality type was tied to the developing stages of capitalism that required a great deal of individual initiative rather than a simple following of previously established practices. Finally, Riesman points to a third personality type: the "other-directed" individual. Where the inner-directed type is guided by a set of goals acquired early in life, the other-directed individual continues to look to others for guidance and direction. Metaphorically speaking, the inner-directed individual is motivated by an internal gyroscope that pushes him or her in accordance with a previously established course. The other-directed individual gains his or her direction through the use of an internal radar scan, which searches others for signals as to proper and improper behavior. Where the inner-directed personality was appropriate for the developing stages of capitalism, the other-directed personality fits the later stages of capitalism that entail a heavy emphasis on consumption. Consider, for example, the number of women who end up wearing their hair in the same style as a famous Olympic figure skater or the number of men who purchase a particular type of car because it is "sharp" or cool."

In some ways, Riesman's concept of other-directedness was foreshadowed by Thorstein Veblen's notion of "conspicuous consumption."[9] Here, one makes purchases primarily for the sake of demonstrating a certain level of financial well-being. In colonial New England, for example, where nails were both expensive and a high-priority item, wealthy people would often hammer them unnecessarily into their doors, primarily to signify that they could afford such extravagance. "Advertising" one's wealth through conspicuous consumption certainly is not uncommon in our society. Consider the current trend of designer clothing. The "Gucci" label, for example, signals that the purchase of expensive leather goods is not beyond one's means and that the purchaser may feel free to walk unembarrassed through such high-class shopping places as Saks Fifth Avenue or Neiman-Marcus, where similar "labels" may be purchased. These approaches conceptualize conformity as a kind of social behavior that is more characteristic of people in certain types of economic, social, and historical periods. We shall return to this topic later in this volume.

DIMENSIONS OF SOCIAL INFLUENCE

Social influence often operates in strange and enigmatic ways that are only partly understood. For example, experimental social psychologists have examined the phenomenon of *psychological reactance*.[10] In those situations where individuals feel that their freedom is being threatened, they may become motivated to assume a nonconforming position (anticonforming might be a better term) to restore a sense of independence.

Conformity and nonconformity contain a variety of different dimensions. Let us consider nonconformity first. Consider an individual who is submitted to a great deal of social pressure to behave in a particular way. This individual may behave differently for the purpose of nonconforming. Have you ever been in a discussion where you take an opposing opinion simply to be different—to play "devil's advocate"? Have you ever taken a position you do not even agree with simply "for the purposes of discussion"? This type of nonconformity needs to be distinguished from those occasions on which you refuse to conform because "in your heart" you disagree with the majority. Where this latter form of nonconformity reflects your *independence*, the former shows a desire for anticonformity.

Similarly, there are different dimensions of conformity. You may conform to a rule or a norm. For example, you may adhere to the norm that says that students must study hard, even if others do not and even if you can still pass without studying. On the other hand, you may conform to the expectations of others. In this case, you might study hard only if there are others around you who are also studying and who encourage (and maybe even pressure) you do to the same. Or you may study because you want to receive a good grade or impress your professor. In this regard, some social psychologists believe that conforming behavior is largely a function of the rewards that accompany such behavior and the extent to which individuals value those rewards.[11]

Conformity, obedience, and other forms of social influence are complex phenomena that are embedded in an interactional and communications matrix. As we have seen, the success or failure of any attempt at influence depends on a variety of factors, including characteristics of both the individual attempting to exert influence and the individual who is being influenced, the extent to which these individuals are similar or different, their previous histories, and the current circumstances. It is in this sense that the question of the limits of social influence pose an important conceptual and theoretical starting point for social psychologists. Social psychologists, people who have various forms of power, and others often are able to create situations in which they can maximize the influence exerted on others. In some senses, Milgram's experiments were so successful because, in our society, the scientist is accorded a certain degree of authority and with this authority comes a certain degree of power. However, we must keep in mind that not every one went as far as the maximum shock level, and, as we have seen, the rate of obedience could be decreased by a variety of factors.

SOCIAL ROLES AND INFLUENCE

In popular television serials, paperback novels, or motion pictures, "cops" and "robbers" are persons who have arrived at their respective roles as a result of their experiences in the "real world." If the robbers are arrested and confined to a jail or prison, they are watched over by guards who presumably have been more or less adequately trained for their jobs and have learned, at least to some extent, to control whatever sadistic or other violent impulses they may have when interacting with the prisoners. But what happens when persons are suddenly thrust into these roles with no prior experience or training? How will they react?

This matter was studied in an unusual experiment some years ago.[12] Twenty-two subjects were selected from among 75 persons who answered a newspaper advertisement. The advertisement asked for men to volunteer to be subjects in a psychological study of prison life. Those selected would be paid $15 per day.

The experimenters had built a prison in a 35-foot section of a building at Stanford University. It was divided by two walls. One of those contained the entrance door to a cell block; the other contained a small observation screen. Three 6-by 9-foot cells were made by replacing the doors of laboratory rooms with barred steel painted black. The only furniture in the cells consisted of a cot with mattress, a sheet, and a pillow for each prisoner. A small unlighted closet across from the cells was used as a solitary confinement facility.

All subjects were told that they might be called upon to play the role of either a guard or a prisoner. Prisoners were to remain in the prison for 24 hours a day until the study was completed (up to two weeks). Guards worked three-man, eight-hour shifts. They remained in the prison only during their work shifts.

Half the subjects were asked to be prisoners; the other half were to be guards. Prisoners were given little information about what might be in store for them except that they would have little privacy and they might expect to have their basic civil rights suspended while serving as prisoners. They were told, however, that no physical punishment would be used.

The guards were led to believe that the experiments were primarily interested in studying the behavior of the prisoners. They were given few explicit instructions except for being told that they must not use physical punishment or physical aggression.

The Palo Alto City Police Department cooperated with the experimenters and allowed the prisoners to be arrested at their own homes by a police officer on suspicion of either armed robbery or burglary. They were read their legal rights, searched, handcuffed, and taken to the police station in a police car. There, they went through the usual procedures of being fingerprinted, having an identification file prepared, and being placed into a cell. Later, they were driven to the experimental prison at the university. There, they were stripped, deloused, and required to stand naked and alone in the cell yard for a while before being given a prisoner's uniform and having a "mug shot" taken. They were then taken to a cell and told to be silent.

After six days and nights, the experiment was called off by the experimenters. It seemed to be getting out of hand. A former prison chaplain had been invited to speak with the prisoners. He was supposed to help the experimenters evaluate how closely the simulated prison setting approximated the "real thing." In his talk, he scolded the prisoners for not doing anything to get released. He told them they ought to have lawyers to get bail and to argue for the dismissal of charges placed against them. Several of the prisoners took his advice and contacted their parents to obtain legal assistance. Events soon seemed to get beyond control of the experimenters. A visitor convinced them that what they were doing to the subjects in the experiment was cruel and even inhuman. It violated their own moral values. The experiment stopped.

During the course of the experiment, data were collected through the following means:

1. Video and audio tape recordings of interactions between prisoners and guards
2. Questionnaires and mood inventories filled out by all subjects
3. Personality tests taken by all subjects
4. Daily guard shift reports
5. Postexperimental interviews

Among the things the experimenters felt that they learned from this study are the following:

1. There was a sharp difference between the behavior of the guards and the prisoners. Guards did more than simply issue commands. They insulted, threatened, and used both verbal and physical aggression toward the prisoners. The prisoners initially resisted, answered questions when asked, and from time to time asked questions themselves. But as the days passed, the prisoners seemed to do less and less. They rarely did anything at all on their own initiative. If they acted at all, it was in response to what the guards demanded.

2. With each successive day, the behavior of the guards seemed to become more abusive and hostile. Some appeared to be literally sadistic and apparently enjoyed seeing the prisoners suffer.

3. The prisoners seemed to become increasingly depressed and more negative in their approach to other people and even showed indications of wanting to harm others.

4. All prisoners suffered psychologically. Half of them were unable to deal effectively with the mental strain and had to be released because of extreme depression, acute anxiety, or psychosomatic sickness.

5. The prisoners who seemed to be able to cope best with conditions in the prison were those whose test scores indicated a relatively high degree of "authoritarianism" in their personalities.

6. Records of the private conversations of prisoners showed that even when they were alone 90 percent of what they talked about with each other had to do with immediate prison conditions, food privileges, punishment, harassment, parole, and various other complaints. (They did not, very often, speak about their past or future lives even when the guards were not present. The illusion of imprisonment seemed to be maintained consistently.)

7. Five prisoners eligible for parole were asked if they would be willing to forfeit all money earned by participating in the study if they were released. Three of them agreed. The experimenters mention this event as an indication of how much the situation had come to control them. Obviously, if they were not going to receive any money, they had no obligation to remain. Yet when told this deal would have to be discussed with the staff, the prisoners allowed themselves to be escorted back to their cells while awaiting the decision.

8. The experimenters noted that, although the subjects were selected on the basis of being normal and sane, within a few days they were acting in ways that under other circumstances would have to be described as abnormal, insane, neurotic, psychopathic, or sadistic. Their behavior could not be explained in terms of their original traits but was related to the situation in which they found themselves.

The researchers interpret those findings to demonstrate a "tyranny of situation and role." They caution us to look for the causes of human behavior in the environment in which individuals act and not in individuals themselves. Guards are not inherently mean. Rather, they are placed in situations where mean behavior is the norm, and they are given roles that require a certain degree of brutality. These roles are embedded in larger social institutions.

Reflecting on the significance of their research, the authors comment that:

Perhaps of even greater significance is the realization that actual prisons are but a concrete and steel metaphor for society's more subtle yet ubiquitous psychological prisons of the mind. We refer here to those social institutions, conventions, and attitudes which act to bind or restrict a man's freedom, imprisoning him in routinized modes of working and living, in a maze-way of confining and distorting social roles, in definition of self and others which are unnecessarily rigid and narrow.[13]

Individuals may control and influence the behavior of others not only by manipulating them directly but also by manipulating their social institutions. In a broader sense, though, social institutions themselves exert power and influence over our actions. We leave it up to the reader to decide whether this power and influence is as potent as the researchers in the Stanford prison study claim they are.

Once again we have come full circle. The three interrelated themes that form the basis of social psychology endeavors have reemerged. Social psychology studies (1) *people* who (2) *communicate and interact* in (3) a *social* and *cultural context*. From the perspectives of these three themes, we can proceed to examine social psychology and its relevance for our lives. First, however, let us take a more detailed look at communication.

NOTES

[1]Elliot Aronson, *The Social Animal* (San Francisco: W. H. Freeman, 1976), p. 4.

[2]Gordon Allport, "The Historical Background of Modern Social Psychology," in G. Lindzey and E. Aronson, eds., *The Handbook of Social Psychology* (Reading, Mass.: Addison–Wesley, 1968), p. 247.

[3]Robert H. Lauer and Warren H. Handel, *Social Psychology: The Theory and Application of Symbolic Interactionism* (Boston: Houghton Mifflin, 1977), p. 7.

[4]S. E. Asch, "Effects of Group Pressure upon the Modification and Distortion of Judgments," in H. Guetzkow, ed., *Groups Leadership and Men* (Pittsburgh: Carnegie Press, 1951).

[5]S. Milgram, "Some Conditions of Obediance to Authority,' in B. Franklin and F. Kohout, eds., *Social Psychology and Everyday Life*, New York: David McKay, 1973, pp. 73–93.

[6]C. H. Hofling et al., "An Experimental Study in Nurse-Physician Relationships," *Journal of Nervous and Mental Disease*, Vol. 143 (1966), pp. 171–180.

[7]D. P. Crowne and S. Liverant, "Conformity Under Varying Conditions of Personal Commitment," *Journal of Abnormal and Social Psychology*, Vol. 60 (1963), pp. 547–555.

[8]D. Riesman, *The Lonely Crowd* (New Haven, Conn.: Yale University Press, 1961).

[9]T. Veblen, *The Theory of the Leisure Class* (New York: Modern Library, 1934).

[10]J. W. Brehm, *Responses to Loss of Freedom: A Theory of Psychological Reactance* (Morristown, N.J.: General Learning Press, 1972).

[11]J. Dittes and H. Kelley, "Effects of Different Conditions of Acceptance upon Conformity to Group Norms," *Journal of Abnormal and Social Psychology*, Vol. 53 (1956), pp. 100–107.

[12]See Philip G. Zimbardo, "Transforming Experimental Research into Advocacy for Social Change," in Morton Deutsch and Harvey A. Hornstein, eds., *Applying Social Psychology* (Hillsdale, N.J.: Erbaum Associates, 1975), pp. 33–66. Material relating to method and procedure was published originally in C. Haney, C. Banks, and P. Zimbardo, "A Study of Prisoners and Guards in a Simulated Prison," *Naval Research Reviews* (Washington, D.C.: Office of Naval Research, 1973).

[13]Craig C. Haney and Phillip G. Zimbardo, "Social Roles and Role Playing: Observations from the Stanford Prison Study," in E. P. Hollander and R. G. Hunt, eds., *Current Perspectives in Social Psychology* (New York: Oxford University Press, 1976), p. 270.

CHAPTER TWO
THE MEANINGS OF "COMMUNICATION"

One of the themes guiding our approach to social psychology is the concept of communication. Indeed, we have tried to indicate how social influence processes are embedded in communication and social interaction. If we are to influence a person, we must, in one way or another, communicate and interact with that individual. In this chapter, we will investigate the meaning of communication in more detail.

The dictionary meaning of the term is, of course, familiar to everyone and has even become something of a cliché. Communication is a process by which meanings are exchanged between two or more persons through the use of some symbols that both or all of them understand. Communication also refers to various techniques for expressing ideas effectively whether this be by speech, writing, pictures, paintings, dance, or other art forms. In general, it is very often used to refer to the technology used to transmit information.

These definitions may well be necessary to explain the meaning of communication, but they are scarcely sufficient. In this chapter, we examine some of the features of communication that make it especially relevant as a perspective in approaching the field of social psychology. We shall examine various modes, channels, and forms of communication and trace their relevance for understanding interpersonal influence processes.

In general, it is convenient to think of communication as the process through which social influence is exerted. Without communication, groups could not be formed and alliances could not be established or rearranged. Even apparent "noncommunication" may turn out to be a form of communication.

A person's "silence" to a lover may signal some sort of dissatisfaction. On a more global level, breaking off official communications between two nations may well be a prelude to overt hostilities.

In short, communication often occurs even when it is unintended. One social scientist insists that "No matter how one may try, one cannot *not* communicate."[1] Another defines society simply as "people in communications."[2]

One may ask many questions about communication. Are infants communicating "contentment" when they stop crying? What does a gurgle mean? Do children learn to communicate with themselves? Is this how "thinking" develops? A love letter is a communicative act. When an automobile driver signals a left-hand turn, is this a communicative act of the same order? All animals communicate with each other. Is this the same as human communication? How about computers? Does a human computer programmer communicate with his or her computer? Are machines that transmit messages to each other engaged in communications? This book will deal with questions like these and many more. They are not questions that sociologists and social psychologists take lightly. Understanding the impact of existing and potential communications technology on the relationships among individuals in society may well be the most centrally significant challenge of our times. We are just beginning to understand the effects that television has had on a generation of viewers. The emergence of workplaces without human presence in which industrial, office, and even educational processes are directed through consoles at remote locations provides just a hint of what may well lie just ahead. At stake may be the very meaning of what is involved in being a human being.

COMMUNICATION IS SHARING

The term "communication" comes from the Latin words *communis* (common) and *communice* (to share). As one social psychologist has put it, "When we communicate we are trying to establish a 'commonness' with someone."[3]

This is *not* necessarily to suggest that communication involves trying to establish a common basis on which some sort of social transaction can take place.

In face-to-face communication, commonness may include simply the fact that the participants share the same sector of space and time, that they monitor each other's orientation, that they have access to a similar sensory field (i.e., they can hear spoken words, read sign language).

In written or telephonic communication, the participants share the concepts and symbols used to communicate. For communication to be shared, it is not enough to transmit symbols from one individual to another. It is also necessary for the message to have some relevance for the participants. The message need not have exactly the same relevance for all participants, but it is necessary for the participants to share enough of a common frame of reference so that the message has some sense or significance. We do not have to agree on what constitutes the "true" significance of the message; we must, however, agree that there is *some* significance.

All this may seem to conflict somewhat with a notion that we all hold to a greater or lesser extent—namely, the notion that "I" am an individual; I don't have to share anything with anyone else. We all like to think of ourselves as individuals separate from all other creatures on the face of the earth. At the same time, in the silence of our private rooms or at times of crucial decision making in our lives, we may allow ourselves to frame the question: "Who am I?"

Sociologists and social psychologists noted a long time ago that no human being can truly be an individual without at the same time being a social creature. Our very thoughts are framed in the language we learned at our mothers' knees. If we are born and spend our early years on a farm in Kansas, U.S.A., we are unlikely to grow up expressing our thoughts in Swahili, Tamil, or Malaysian. Our "individuality" is shaped at the outset by the messages we receive beginning at the very first moment we emerge from our mother's womb and announce, *Je suis arrivé*, or its equivalent.

So to say that communication is shared is to imply a great deal more. For communication to be shared, the participants must have a common frame of reference. This means that they must have a common or similar culture. The relationship between communication and culture has long been an important subject of investigation in sociology and social psychology. Throughout this book, we shall investigate this matter at some length and try to understand how people in different cultures are affected by language and other communication channels.

COMMUNICATION IS MULTICHANNELED[4]

Much research in social psychology has been based on verbal or linguistic communication. But there are many other possible channels. Some social psychologists are now coming to appreciate the importance of nonverbal communication.

A young man and woman meet for the first time at a discotheque. "Hi," says the man. "Hi," says the girl. "Would you like to dance?" asks the man. The woman smiles and laughs, and the two stroll off to the dance floor.

What has occurred?

A "normal" observer might report (somewhat pedantically) that one person asked another to dance and that the other replied affirmatively, whereupon they left to begin the dance process.

But suppose you are not "normal"—that you happen to be an anthropologist fresh from Tibet and that you want a detailed description of what has just occurred with respect to these two people.

As a good anthropologist, you will have begun your observations earlier in the day and continued them along into the evening. You will have noticed that the two subjects of your investigation are wearing clothes significantly different from those worn during the daylight hours. The evening clothing seems to cling to the skin to a greater extent and in strange sorts of ways seem to highlight various features of the anatomy. Beyond this, both parties (and indeed virtually all others in the room) seem to exude sweet, perfumed odors that were considerably less evident during the daylight hours.

Both parties seem to walk differently inside the discotheque than they did outside. The male person seems to strut somewhat in a manner reminiscent of the male mating strut of some species of birds. You will notice too that both persons seemed to make periodic visual surveys of the room and then return their eyes to the drinks in front of them. Immediately prior to the request for a dance, their gazes had met. This was followed by what appeared to be smiles on the part of both of them.

As you begin to reflect about your observations, you may begin to realize that the request for the dance was a bit more elaborate than you had originally assumed. Indeed, the verbal request may well have been part of a larger communication process. Eye contact between the two individuals began prior to the verbal request. The atmosphere in which the request was made was enhanced by the pleasant aromas emanating from the two participants. As the verbal request was made, you notice that the man making the request extended his hand toward the woman. They touched hands en route to the dance floor.

The preceding communication involves at least six different channels. Most obvious is the *linguistic* or *verbal* channel. To the question, "What did the man do?" an ordinary observer might reasonably respond, "He asked her to dance," To the question, "What did the woman do?" any observer might respond, "She said 'yes.' " The propensity to report the encounter in linguistic terms is so strong that we may be tempted to use linguistic terminology even when it is not correct in terms of what actually occurs. In this event, as we have described it, there was no point at which the woman actually said "yes." Yet we can infer an equivalent response from her behavior. This is because she actually *did* communicate such a response through other channels.

The woman's response consisted in part of what was described as a short, happy laugh. This laugh partially supplanted a verbal response. Somewhat less than a verbal response, such things as laughs and other vocal but nonverbal (i.e., those not made up of complete words) utterances may augment or supplant words in conveying a message. This *paralinguistic* or *subverbal* channel includes the way in which words are vocalized; their pitch, range, and intensity; as well as other nonverbal components of speech. In written form, paralinguistic devices may include such things as exclamation points and question marks.

In this example, the linguistic and paralinguistic actions took place in a visual as well as an auditory field. Smiles were exchanged between the participants. We noticed that these preceded the verbal request. We also noticed that the participants appeared to carry themselves in special sorts of ways, reminding us of how certain birds strut as part of their mating rituals. Through the visual medium of communication, the participants can survey each other's dress and behavior to ascertain if they are appropriate for the occasion. Important information is conveyed through the visual field. This visual communication may be just as important as the auditory aspect. Indeed, had the two participants not "measured up" visually, the verbal request may not have been made or the response might have been an hysterical laugh, rather than a short happy one.

The visual, as well as the auditory, field contains a variety of different channels of communication. Two of these channels are closely related. The *proxemic* mode of communication concerns spatial relations and body orientation. There are cultural rules that regulate how close or far away we stand from each other and how we orient toward each other. These rules regulate gaze and touch. They tell us the occasions on which it is appropriate to look at each other and how we are to look. Clearly, the orientation of two people in a discotheque will be different from that between a professor and student in the classroom, even though unbeknown to the two in the discotheque, one may very well be a professor and the other a student.

The *kinesic* channel of communication is very similar to the proxemic. It includes gross body movements as well as more subtle changes in position. Smiles, raised eyebrows, and biting lips are important kinesic actions; so too are styles of walking or sitting. Kinesics differ from proxemics in the sense that the latter concerns the organization of space among communicating persons, including the use of gaze to segment the visual field. Whereas kinesics is concerned with eye movement to express surprise or questioning, proxemics is concerned with the direction of gaze and the extent of eye contact. In terms of the previous example, kinesics might roughly be said to concern the woman's smile after being asked to dance, whereas proxemics concerns the couple's gaze and spatial orientation prior to the verbal request.

Beyond these there is one further channel of communication evident in the preceding example. Both participants, it was noted, were wearing perfume. Smell may thus have been a subtle but not necessarily unimportant component of the communicative event. This *olfactory* channel of communication though not as thoroughly researched as other channels may play an important role in communication processes among human beings as well as other animals. Clearly, had either person smelled as though he or she had just finished a marathon, the chances that they would have ended up dancing together would have been severely limited.

Social psychologists have studied many of these communication channels and have discovered that nonverbal communication can play an important role in social interaction. In the following pages we shall review some of these interesting studies.

Space and Spatial Relations

Research on spatial relations as a factor in human communication has been guided by two different paradigms that have resulted in different methodological approaches. Ethnologists have been interested in space as a biological phenomena. They have noted how territorial demarcations among nonhuman animals are genetically determined. Robert Ardery,[5] for example, has studied what he terms the "territorial imperative" among human beings, noting the points at which various forms of territorial encursion result in "flight" or "fight."

Ardrey has argued that a territorial imperative operates among human animals as well. Although most social psychologists do not agree that human behavior is genetically determined to the same extent as the behavior of birds and of animals, a number of researchers have explored human spatial behavior in terms of the notion of "flight" through some fairly original natural field experiments.

Many of these experiments have focused on consequences of violating personal space boundaries in public places. In one experiment, for example, the researchers compared the responses of female students who were studying in a library with different forms of territorial encroachment (e.g., sitting next to a person or across from a person at a large table). The most frequent response was "flight" (i.e., the person originally sitting at the table left). The closer the invader moved toward the individual, the more quickly the individual would flee. Very few individuals actually asked the invaders to move, although prior to flight they often emitted hostile gestures (e.g., angry stares) toward the invaders.[6]

Another biologically based approach to spatial relations between human beings concerns the effects of population density and overcrowding. There is evidence from studies of nonhuman animal behavior that extreme overcrowding (high population density as measured by the number of living individuals per unit of space) can have a negative impact on an individual's chances for life. Deer, overcrowded on an island in Chesapeake Bay, died as the population increased. Interestingly, most of the deer did not die of starvation but, rather, from too much adrenalin produced, scientists believe, as a response to stress of high density.[7] Rats raised in a high-density situation exhibited increased rates of distorted behavior. Some rats withdrew from social and sexual intercourse. Most rats became more aggressive as territorial boundaries were violated.[8]

Human beings, however, appear to be more creative in their responses to overcrowding. Although high-density living creates some problems for humans, there is no simple relationship between density and such problems. Social psychologist Stanley Milgram believes that city dwellers have developed certain behaviors that function as coping mechanisms for dealing with stimulus overload in high-density situations. Milgram notes that city dwellers tend to spend less time in interaction (e.g., they tend to have shorter conversations with one another.) and they learn to disregard "low-priority inputs" (e.g., the alcoholic asleep on the sidewalk would not be tolerated in most suburban neighborhoods). These and other behavioral techniques, according to Milgram, enable urban residents to cope better with the large number of sensory inputs evident in high-density situations.[9]

A second approach to the study of the role of space in human communication is based on the assumption that spatial relationships among human beings are socially and culturally established. One of the first social scientists to note the importance of the cultural aspect was the anthropologist Edward T. Hall, who distinguished different types of "personal space":

> intimate distances: actual physical contact to roughly 18 inches; causal-personal distances: one and a half feet to four feet social-consultative (impersonal) distances four to twelve feet; public distances twelve feet and more.[10]

He used these to compare and contrast spatial orientation as a function of the type of setting and the nature of the social encounter in which the individuals were involved. Hall was very much aware of the fact that these distances were based on a sample of upper-middle-class professionals living in the northeastern part of the United States. He suspected that spatial organization would vary in different cultures. Hall has, in fact, presented a number of very suggestive descriptive examples of such variation.[11]

Hall's basic ideas have been explored more systematically through the comparison of spatial relations among different groups of people in natural field settings. For example, two anthropologists compared spatial relations between pairs of Arabs and pairs of North Americans in public places and found that, in general, Arabs moved closer together, confronted one another more directly, and were more likely to touch one another.[12] Other researchers, however, have pointed out that there may be substantial differences within specific cultural groups,[13] and one researcher believes that differences in spatial relations may be as much a function of socioeconomic status as they are of culture.[14] These comparative methodologies have expanded our understanding of human spatial behavior.

Sociologists also have been interested in developing category systems for spatial organization among human beings. Two sociologists[15] view spatial organization in terms of four categories. *Public territories* are areas that are "officially open to all, but . . . expectations . . . modify freedom (of use and behavior)."[16] Examples of public territories include restaurants, beaches, playgrounds, and so on. *Home territories* refer to "areas where the regular participants have a relative freedom of behavior and a sense of intimacy and control over the area."[17] Examples of home territories include club houses, homosexual bars, and street corner turfs. Usage is based on one's identification as a member of the group that designates the area as its domain. *Interactional territories* are in some ways more difficult to define. These refer to "any area where a social gathering may take place."[18] According to the authors, there is an "invisible boundary" surrounding any interactional event. These boundaries are complexly organized and highly fragile. Such a boundary may surround a party or specific interactional and conversational units at the party. Although these boundaries may change rather rapidly, encroachment may often be resisted as well. Finally, body territories refer to the space encompassed by one's anatomical structure and is considered to be the most private and inviolate of spaces. As we shall see in our discussion of touch, definitions of territory may vary as a function of a wide variety of sociological and cultural variables.[19]

Although these territorial divisions have not been experimentally demonstrated, researchers note that different forms of territorial encroachment generate certain kinds of protective reactions. "Turf defense," for example, is cited as one type of reaction.

Posture

The phenomenon of body language is the idea that we may express attitudes and emotions through posture and other body movements. Social psychologists have become interested in this phenomenon and have developed methods for studying it.

According to one researcher, one's posture has "positional cues" that can have important effects for interaction. Body orientation may serve to facilitate or dissuade communication. Indeed, the maintenance of interactional territories is largely facilitated through body orientation. One experiment, for example, showed that in attempting to persuade other persons, those who maintained an open (i.e., reclined, stretched, limbs apart) as opposed to a closed (i.e., limbs crossed or pressed together) position enjoyed greater success.[20]

Touch

Touch is an important channel of communication. As we shall see (Chapter Five), touch is an essential component of the interaction between the mother and newborn infant. As we go through life, touch may serve to convey such varied emotions as love and anger.

Methods for studying touch vary as a function of the researcher's interests. Some researchers have been concerned primarily with the amount of touching that takes place between peoples in Central and South America, noting a discernible trend toward greater amounts of touching as one moves south.[21] Further, some research indicates that touch also may be a function of sex and social status. There appears to be something of an interaction effect here. Men in superordinate positions tend to touch women in subordinate positions.[22]

Simply looking at the amount of touch that takes place between individuals in different groups may not, however, tell us a great deal about the meaning of touch in any specific social situation. This is because any touch behavior can have multiple social functions. Hand-to-hand touching, for example, can signify such diverse meaning as care, fear, play, and anger. Hence, in studying the meaning of touch, it is necessary to consider the interactional context in which touch takes place.

Olfaction

Although difficult to document, the role of olfaction in social life may be significant. According to one researcher, each individual may have his or her own "olfactory signature." He noted, for example, that dogs had difficulty in distinguishing the smells of identical twins.[23] Another researcher believes the olfaction is one of the infant's first modes of sensation that may linger and subconsciously play a role in later life.[24]

Through descriptive accounts, researchers have attempted to account for the ways in which aversive or pleasant odors may influence social interaction in especially spatial distances) different contexts. Edward T. Hall, for example, notes the following:

> Olfaction occupies a prominent place in the Arab life. Not only is it one of the distance-setting mechanisms, but it is a vital part of a complex system of behavior.
> Arabs consistently breathe on people when they talk. However, this habit is more than a matter of different manners. To the Arab good smells are pleasing and a way of being involved with each other. To smell one's friend is not only nice but desirable, for to deny him your breath is to act ashamed. Americans, on the other hand, trained as they are not to breathe in people's faces, automatically communicate shame in trying to be polite.[25]

Given all the money spent on perfumes in our society, it would be hard to conclude that smell does not play an important role in social interaction. One researcher speculates that Americans' concern with covering over natural body odors with perfumes reflects a peculiar ambivalence toward sexuality. Natural sexual odors have become taboo, on one hand, while, on the other, we strive for another form of sexuality with manufactured, artificial odors.[26]

The Face

The face is a very important conveyor of emotions. In fact, even though we have relatively good control over our facial expressions, it may still display emotions we do not necessarily want to be apparent. Imagine, for example, that your professor has just done something that is most embarrassing, causing you to smile. You may feel that you must repress that smile so as not to embarrass her (or him) and possibly suffer some negative consequence in the way of grades. (Some professors may feel they must control their own facial expressions to avoid communicating their sense of frustration or exasperation with some students.)

One of the systems most frequently used to represent facial expression is known as the *Facial Affect Scoring Test (FAST).*[27] This system divides the face into three areas: brows and forehead area; eyes, lids, and bridge of nose area; and the cheeks, nose, mouth, chin, and jaw area. Various emotions may be described in terms of changes in these facial areas. The emotion of surprise, for example, has the following characteristics: jaw dropped open, lips and teeth parted; eyelids opened, showing the white of the eye; horizontal wrinkles across the forehead; and brows raised, curved, and high.

To test the validity of FAST, a number of experiments have been used to see the extent to which subjective judgments of different facial expressions agree with manipulation of the muscle structure of the face. Photographs, videotapes, and live facial expressions representing different muscle configurations were shown to subjects in different cultures. Interestingly, there appears to be considerable consistency among people of different cultures in connecting facial musculature configurations, and emotional states.[28]

Eye Behavior and Gaze

Although the eyes are clearly part of the face, they also have been the subject of independent investigation by social psychologists interested in communication. As we have seen in connection with the face, the eyes are important as a conveyor of emotions. The FAST system contains a way of relating movement of the brows, eyelids, corners, and so on to various emotional states.

Other researchers have examined pupil dilation and constriction as a reflection of different emotional states. Some research indicates that pupils tend to dilate when individuals are in a distressed or negative emotional state and that they tend to constrict when they are in a happy or positive frame of mind. In one experiment, pupils of people shown pictures of concentration camp scenes tended to dilate whereas those shown pictures of pleasant sights tended to constrict.[29] Other research shows that the condition of one's pupils (constricted or dilated) may suggest certain emotional states to others. In one study, identical pictures of the same woman were presented to different audiences.

The pictures were touched up so that in one series the woman's pupils were larger whereas in another they were smaller. Viewers tended to rate the woman whose pupils were enlarged as generally happy whereas the woman with the smaller pupils were rated as sad.[30]

Although this research has addressed some interesting questions about the role of the eyes in expressing different emotional states, its applicability to real-world settings has not yet been established. Pupil dilation and constriction can be affected by a large number of physical factors, especially light. Other studies have had *only partial* success in replicating these early findings, suggesting that pupil dilation and constriction are completely related to emotional and attitude states.[31]

Gaze (i.e., vision direction) is an important part of face-to-face communication. Social psychologists have noted that the position of the head and brows can be an important signal in initiating and/or terminating other forms of communication.[32] Gaze also may communicate emotions or express important aspects about the relationship between persons. Some researchers have noted in correlation between intimacy and the amount of time spent in mutual gaze.[33] Mutual gaze, according to this view, increases in the context of intimacy and close physical proximity.[34]

Individuals may use all of the above as well as other communication channels in constructing a meaningful communicative event. Although each of the above communication channels are analytically separate from the standpoint of the researcher, they are, from the standpoint of the participant in communication, complexly interrelated. Indeed, the supposition is that the meanings conveyed through each channel are complementary in nature. One is not supposed to say "I love you" with one's lips while stating "Stay away" with one's posture. As we shall see shortly, however, human communication is not always so harmonious. Before discussing this, however, it is important to consider the relevance of both meaning and information in human communication processes.

CYBERNETIC COMMUNICATION: COMMUNICATION AS MONOLOGUE

We have been discussing communication as a process by which *meanings* are exchanged between two or more *persons* through the use of *symbols* that both or all of them understand. But communication may also refer to a process in which *information* (as distinct from *meaning*) is exchanged from one *non-human* entity to another with the use of symbols that neither of them understands.

If we stop speaking about people, we seem to be leaving the field of social psychology, which is, of course, very much oriented toward people. But these days, the boundaries between human beings and robots seems to be diminishing—at least in the eyes of many persons. For one author, the basic question of cybernetics has been whether or not machines can be made to think. But, he tells us, in another sense, this does not matter; what matters is that machines can be made to do many complicated things for us. The point being that we might on one hand want to know whether we can design a machine more intelligent than ourselves, or we might want merely to take advantage of whatever help is available in the field of automatic control systems.[35]

When Norbert Wiener introduced the term "cybernetics" in 1948,[36] he thought of it as the name for a new science of control and communication in animals, machines, and human beings. Thus, it seemed to take for granted the notion that human beings, other animals, and inanimate things can all be described with the use of essentially the same methods. Beyond this, it focused on the notion of "feedback" in the form of "information." Cybernetics is derived from the Greek word for "steersman." The steersman or helmsman is the person who watches a compass to determine the difference between the actual course a ship is taking and its projected course. When a difference occurs, the steersman corrects the ship' course in response to this feedback. The principle is identical to that found in an ordinary room thermostat that either heats a room or allows it to cool as the room temperature varies from some preestablished objective or goal (e.g., 68 degrees Fahrenheit). What communication engineers call "feedback" is essentially what system engineers call "servo system" or "closed-loop system," what physiologists call "homeostasis," and what economists call "boom and slump cycle."[37]

Feedback uses signals that report errors to adjust the behavior of a system so that it moves in the direction of its predetermined goal. Additional examples often cited include such things as the physiological processes that keep human body temperature or blood pressure constant and a computer guiding a missile to a moving target in the sky.

Cybernetics has a distinctive orientation with respect to its study of machines or mechanisms. It does not deal with any specific machine by asking how it will behave under any one set of empirical conditions. It asks "What are *all* the possible behaviors that it can produce? . . . Cybernetics envisages a set of possibilities much wider than the actual, and then asks why the particular case should conform to its usual particular restriction."[38]

Communication among mechanisms—between machines rather than between people—has become centrally important in an age of automation or automatic control mechanisms. Such mechanisms are dependent upon feedback for their operation—and feedback must be communicated. To focus upon communication among mechanisms is to raise what appears to be more general questions such as, "What 'thing' is communicated from one machine to another?" "What restricts the amount of that thing it is possible to communicate at any given time?" "How can the rate of communicating the thing be increased (or decreased)?" "How can the quality of the thing be improved?" It should not be surprising that questions of this sort were raised very seriously by engineers and other technologists at such places as Bell Telephone Laboratories and other places where problems of telecommunications were matters of central concern. The work of three men at Bell Telephone Laboratories, H. Nyquist, R. V. L. Hartley, and Claude E. Shannon,)[39] is credited with leading to the formulation of what has become known as the "mathematical theory of communication."

The basic model used in this work seems clearly to be a linear process—it has a definite beginning and a definite end. Shannon's diagram is shown in Figure 2–1.[40]

The *information source* selects a specific message from a set of possible messages. It may consist of written or spoken words, a picture, music, or other things. The *transmitter* changes this *message* into a *signal* that is sent over the *communication channel* from the transmitter to the *receiver*. The channel can be a wire; the signal may be an electric current on this wire; the transmitter can be the set of devices such as a telephone transmitter that changes the sound pressure of the voice into varying electrical current. The transmitter may also be a device that codes written words into sequences of interrupted currents varying in length such as dots, dashes, and spaces as used in telegraphic or some forms of radio transmission. In radio, the channel is space rather than wire, and the signal is an electromagnetic wave. When human beings are viewed as communication systems from this perspective, the information source is the brain, and the transmitter is the voice. This, in turn, is transmitted through air, which in this case is the channel.

FIGURE 2-1

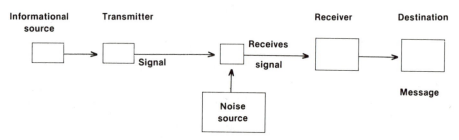

In this model, the *receiver* is essentially a transmitter operating in reverse that converts the transmitted signal back into the original message. (If my brain is the information source and your brain is the destination, my vocal system is the transmitter and your ear is the receiver.)

Things get muddied up somewhat in this process by something called *noise*. This consists of things added to the signal that the information source did not intend to include. These things may include simple distortions of sound in a telephone system, static in a radio, distortions of shade or shape in television, or transmission errors in a telegraph system.

Information, in this model, does not have its ordinary everyday connotation. Specifically, it must not be confused with *meaning*. Thus two messages, one of which is pure nonsense and the other of which is heavily ladened with meaning, can be exactly equivalent in information as used in this model. In short, information here refers not so much to what in fact you do say as to what in theory you might have been able to say. For example, if you are restricted to sending a "canned" greeting message via Western Union, your information capacity depends upon the number of canned messages that are available. If one of those messages refers to the complete text of an encyclopedia, then a good deal of meaning might be conveyed by selecting it, but the information communicated would still depend upon the number of other canned messages available. If there were only one other such message available, then we would have a two-choice situation. This would be referred to as information of unity. Thus the concept of information does not apply to the individual messages as the concept of meaning would. Unit information simply indicates that there is available an amount of freedom of choice that it is convenient to regard as a standard or unit amount. This unit is referred to as a "bit," an abbreviation of "binary digit." (There are two numbers in the binary number system—0 and 1. These two digits can be used to represent any two choices. A binary digit or bit is associated with the two-choice situation having unit information.) Thus, to define the amount of information in a message (again as distinct from meaning), it is necessary to know the total number of messages contained in the repertoire of the information source.

Information sources may be characterized by varying degrees of organization or *entropy* (entropy refers to the extent to which a situation is random—a well-shuffled deck of cards may be said to be characterized by a high degree of entropy). Physical scientists tend to be fascinated by entropy because of the second law of thermodynamics, which says that entropy always increases in nature—physical systems tend to become less and less organized or more and more shuffled. In theory, one can tell whether a movie of a physical world is being run forward or backward by noting what happens to its entropy.

When there is less order, there is more entropy. Much less information is required to describe a condition of low entropy of anything. For example, it requires much more information to describe the position of each card in a well-shuffled deck than it does to say, for example, that the deck is organized by the four suits beginning with the ace, deuce, and so on to jack, queen, king.

Another concept used to describe information is *redundancy*—a measure of interdependence of the signals. The redundancy of English has been estimated to be about 50 percent. That is to say that we are free to choose about half of the letters or words we use in writing or speaking. The other half is controlled by the structure of the language. A language must have at least 50 percent real freedom in the choice of letters if you want to construct satisfactory crossword puzzles in it. Redundancy can be seen as a measure of the fraction of letters that can be deleted at random from a long message without making the message unintelligible.

Information, then, is a measure of the freedom of choice one has in selecting a message. As freedom of choice increases (i.e., as information increases), there is an increase in uncertainty that the message actually selected is a particular one. When noise is introduced, this uncertainty increases. This leads to what appears to be a contradiction: Since information is increased when uncertainty is increased, can we say that noise is beneficial?

The difficulty with this formulation is that, although the received signal has more information, when noise is introduced, some of the noise is "spurious" and "undesirable." To extract the useful information, it is necessary to subtract this spurious portion. This process is facilitated by redundancy in the original message. The more redundancy there is in an information source, the easier it is to deal with problems of noise and other imperfections in transmission without losing meaning.

For communication engineers, considerations such as these and related ideas have been incorporated into formulas that provide quantitative statements for the amount of information, the capacity of a communication channel, the rate at which it is possible to transmit symbols over a communication channel, the spurious part of received signal information that is due to noise, and many other related matters.

There is a sense in which applying such ideas to human beings is offensive. People do not like the idea of being reduced to mechanisms. We all like to feel that there is something more to being human. We feel that there *must* be something more to communication between human beings than can be expressed in formulas derived from an analysis of telephone, telegraph, radio, or television systems. Trying to state precisely what this something more is has been a difficult problem for many serious scholars for many years.

One approach[41] is based on a distinction between information viewed as uncertainty reduction and information as content or meaning. When information is viewed as uncertainty reduction, failures in transmission seem to be more easily reduced to problems of channel capacity, noise, and other factors more directly relevant to mechanical communication systems. Information viewed as content is presumably more relevant to human beings. There is, however, an additional set of difficulties arising from different assumptions held by the receiver and sender of messages. These are taken-for-granted facets, beliefs, or views that may even be "unconscious" but that result in identical messages having different meanings for different persons. Thus it has been observed[42] that all content information is connotative rather than denotative. In logic, connotation is a term used to denote an object and also to imply certain characteristics of that object. If you point to an animal and say, "That is a goat," you have denoted it. The characteristics of the goat may include features such as hardy, sexy, strong-smelling, usually horned, bearded, ruminant, quadruped. If you use the expression "goatlike" in a message, you are not necessarily communicating precisely what it is you have in mind. For one speaker (or listener) the message may connote smell, for another, it may be a beard, and for a third, it may refer to sexual behavior.[43]

Another approach involves making a distinction between two modes of discourse that conflict with each other. For Ashley Montagu and Floyd Matson, the distinction can be expressed simply as one between the mode of "monologue" and that of "dialogue."[44] For them, when a communicative act is in the form of a monologue, it serves the end of power. When it occurs as a dialogue, it serves the end of community. Monologue occurs when one person talks at another; dialogue occurs when two people speak with each other. The point here is simply that monologues are appropriate modes of communication for mechanical devices; dialogues are more appropriate for human beings. Unfortunately, human beings do not always restrict themselves to the dialogue mode of communication. Often, conversation between two human beings consists of a series of alternating monologues. Perhaps the point to be made is that human beings are not beyond treating human beings as mechanisms. Those who do so, we call authoritarian. But the techniques of authoritarianism are intricate. They often come wrapped in the form (but not the reality) of dialogue.

COMMUNICATION AS DIALOGUE

What happens when two people speak with each other? In what way does a dialogue differ from two monologues?

To begin with, people tend to use more than one channel of communication at a time. As Jules Henry has put it, "Every kiss between lovers must carry with it a comment of how it is meant."[45] Henry suggests that after many affairs, some persons may become more expert in interpreting the meaning of kisses and embraces and grade them according to warmth, sincerity, and intensity. These persons may be able to answer such questions as, "Did he kiss you as if he meant it?" "Are her embraces becoming more and more distant?" "When he says he loves you, does he say it as if he really means it?"

It is this "really means it" quality of messages that presumably gets transmitted on channels other than the conventional ones of voice. Messages between any two persons seem to be incomplete unless they contain some sort of signal about how the message is intended.[46]

In a sense, people send editorials along with every message. A "double-bind" can arise when a person receives conflicting messages on different channels. Thus, parents can say "I love you" to a child while his or her touch and eyes communicate "I can't stand you, you make me sick".[47]

Additional difficulties arise when the *real* message is indeed, "I love you," but is read as, "I can't stand you, you make me sick." In short, human beings are very adept at distorting messages on the receiving end as well as transmitting some that are contradictory. The messages themselves include unbelievably subtle ways of doing such things as varying voice inflection to making almost undetectable gestures of various kinds.

We can now, perhaps, begin to discern more clearly the difference between communication as monologue and communication as dialogue. The former consists of simple transmissions of information; the latter is much more like what we have previously defined as communication—all those processes by which people influence each other. This definition is based on the premise that, "all actions and events have communicative aspects, as soon as they are perceived by a human being . . . such perception changes the information which an individual possesses and therefore influences him or her."[48]

And so it is that monologues are not really communicative acts. If I go out to sea on a dinghy and recite the Declaration of Independence at the top of my lungs, I have not engaged in a communicative act unless, perhaps, some part of me is affected by the recitation and I have in some way engaged in what some people might call an internal dialogue. If I tape record my recitation, nothing has changed. If I transmit the record over a radio and someone hears it, I may communicate something, but that something will be heavily influenced by the context of the broadcast—the station; the introductory remarks, if any, that are inserted to go along with the broadcast; and whether these remarks are spoken by a dedicated patriot, a comedian; someone who is asking for the election of a Republican candidate for president or speaking on behalf of women's liberation. Thus,

> Where the relatedness of entities is considered, we deal with problems of communication; where entities are considered in isolation from one another, problems of communication are not relevant".[49]

COMMUNICATION AND INTERPERSONAL RELATIONS

Dialogue, then, is something other than the sum of two monologues. The *unit* of a dialogue is an interpersonal relation. In the words of Harry Stack Sullivan,

> it makes no sense to think of ourselves as "individuals," "separate," capable of anything like definitive description in isolation . . . . No great progress in this field of study can be made until it is realized that the field of observation is what people do with each other, what they communicate to each other, about what they do with each other. When that is done, no such thing as the durable, unique individual personality is ever clearly justified.[50]

Sullivan was a psychiatrist, but he felt strongly that the fundamental problems of psychiatry as well as of social psychology involved interpersonal relations. Concern with communication was the basis of Sullivan's work in psychiatry. He saw the psychiatrist as a "participant observer" rather than as an observer who was external to the person being observed or "treated." Psychiatry, for him, rested on two underlying propositions: "(1) a large part of mental disorder results from and is perpetuated by inadequate communication; and (2) each person in any two-person relationship is involved as a portion of an interpersonal field, rather than as a separate entity, in processes which affect and are affected by the field."[51]

Sullivan has been compared with the unconventional anthropologist, Gregory Bateson.

> Both questioned sharply the American overemphasis on the individual. Both were preoccupied with communication. Both emphasized relationship. . . . Both made original contributions to the treatment of schizophrenia: Sullivan in his whole system and Bateson in his formulation of the double bind as well as other penetrating concepts relating to schizophrenia. . . . Both took their stands on the side of the humanity of the schizophrenic patient."[52]

Bateson was not primarily interested in schizophrenia. For him and his associates, schizophrenia was essentially an illustration of the double-bind. As he noted many years after the original development of the double-bind concept, his research was funded by organizations interested in the need to apply "science" to the field of psychiatry: "and we let ourselves be strongly and disastrously influenced by the need to apply our science to that field."[53]

He apparently was ambivalent about the field of psychiatry because it seemed to him that the very idea of curing someone involved placing power in the hands of the person doing the curing. He was distressed with the existing state of conventional thinking in the field of psychiatry and what he saw as the obsession with power on the part of his psychiatrist colleagues.

The first article to outline the double-bind concept appeared in 1956. It was called, "Toward a Theory of Schizophrenia." It seems to have been suggested by something called the "theory of logical types." This theory was developed by Alfred North Whitehead and Bertrand Russell in their classic work, *Principia Mathematica*. It arose from a need to explain certain logical contradictions that had bedeviled mathematicians and philosophers for centuries. The oldest of these contradictions is the ancient one involving Epimenides the Cretan. Epimenides, it is alleged, asserted that all Cretans were liars. Question: Is this statement by Epimenides a lie? If so, then it can scarcely be asserted that all Cretans are liars since for Epimenides, a Cretan, to call them liars is a lie and, therefore, they must all be persons who tell the truth. If, on the other hand, we assert that Epimenides is telling the truth, then we are in the presence of at least one Cretan who is telling the truth, and the assertion that all Cretans are liars is demonstrably false.

The simplest form of this contradiction is the case of the person who says, "I am lying." As Russell and Whitehead point out, "if he is lying, he is speaking the truth, and vice versa."[54]

The theory of logical types undertakes to demonstrate that apparent contradictions or paradoxes of this sort result from a "vicious circle." This arises from the supposition that a collection of objects may contain individual objects that can be defined only by referring to the collection as a whole.

Thus when Epimenides said, "I am a liar," he was making a statement at a different order or level of abstraction from the statement "All Cretans are liars." Accordingly, no paradox or contradiction exists.

In the field of formal logic, this separation between a class and its members is maintained strictly. Bateson and his associates pointed out, however, that in communications between human beings, this separation is breached inevitably and continually. When the breaching occurs between a mother and child, a pathology attributable to the double-bind occurs. For example,

1. Human beings must continually distinguish between such activities as play and nonplay or between what is meant as fantasy, sacrament, or metaphor. Even among nonhuman mammals, there seems to be a continual exchange of signals identifying some behavior as play and other behavior as nonplay. These signals are of a higher logical type than are the messages that are being classified. Human beings presumably must deal with a much greater degree of complexity in these matters, and our vocabulary for making these discriminations is still very poorly developed. We rely primarily on such nonverbal cues as posture, gesture, facial expressions, and intonations to communicate these messages.

2. Humor may well be a method human beings use to explore themes implicit in a thought or relationship. It seems to depend upon implicit changes in logical types to obtain its effects. ("Who is that lady I saw you with last night? That was no lady. That was my wife.")

3. Human beings often falsify the communication mode or logical type in which they are engaged. They may do this either deliberately or "unconsciously." Among

the former are such behaviors as the artificial laugh, the simulation of friendliness to manipulate someone, the confidence trick, or simple "kidding." (It has been reported that some nonhuman animals engage in similar kinds of activities on occasion.) Among the latter are hostilities that people conceal even from themselves. This may take the form of real hostility disguised as playful metaphors. ("You are a dirty dog.") It may also assume the form of an unconscious distortion in someone's mind of someone else's signals that identify the mode in which the communication is taking place (mistaking shyness for contempt, etc.).

4. Human beings as well as other animals "learn" that certain events carry implicit messages. A rat may learn that "someone up there" is telling him that cheese is to be found inside the left rather than the right door of the maze. A dog who hears a buzzer may start to salivate because the buzzer, in effect, contains a message saying, "meat is on the way." Human beings can receive messages of this sort and presumably can learn to direct much more subtle, complex, or "higher" forms of learned transmissions.

The "well-adjusted" human being has learned to handle different levels or logical types of signals. Bateson and his associates felt that schizophrenics had difficulty in assigning the correct communication modes they receive from or send to other people. Moreover, they had difficulty in assigning the correct communication modes to their own thoughts, sensations, and perceptions. Thus in trying to discover the reason for the onset of schizophrenia in people, searching for dramatic traumatic episodes in the life history of the affected persons may be completely irrelevant. Schizophrenics presumably have lived in an environment in which unconventional communication is the norm.

All the focus on the initial double-bind article was on schizophrenia. It noted that double-bind situations led to breakdowns in the ability of individuals to discriminate between logical types. When caught in a double-bind, however, the most "normal" of persons will tend to react defensively much as schizophrenics do. A double-bind situation is characterized by the following elements:

1. Individuals are involved in intense relationships (an intense relationship is one in which people feel that it is essential to discriminate the kind of message that is being communicated so that an appropriate response can be made).
2. The other person in the relationship is expressing two orders of message, one of which denies the other.
3. The individual cannot inquire (for one reason or another) about the order of message being transmitted (i.e., he or she cannot make a "metacommunicative" statement—a statement about communication).

Situations of this sort abound in everyday life. Some prove to be much more traumatic than others. We shall encounter many of them throughout the remainder of this book. At this point, it is perhaps sufficient to note that dialogues lead us into a world of enormous communication difficulties occurring throughout the entire life cycle of human beings and affecting every facet of interpersonal relations.

THE STUDY OF CONVERSATION

Perhaps one of the most ubiquituous forms of communication is conversation. We probably spend more time engaged in conversation than in any other form of communication. Conversation may be a means for dealing with the smallest details of everyday life as well as for reaching decisions of worldwide importance.

Recently, sociologists have had a renewed interest in the structure and organization of conversation. A good deal of this research has been geared toward identifying and describing some of its formal properties. One of the simplest of these is called *adjacency pairs*.[55] These are sequences of utterances in which the first utterance (the "first pair part") implies that another type of utterance (the "second pair part") should follow. Adjacency pairs include such conversational phenomena as greetings, question-answer sequences, offer-acceptance/refusal sequences, and so on. The first pair part sets the stage, in a sense, for the second pair part.

The organization of adjacency pairs may be relatively simple as in the case of the standard greeting:

A: Hello
B: Hello

In some cases, however, they may be elongated and complicated as in the following:

A_1:	Goodbye.	First pair, part 1
B_2:	When will I see you again?	First pair, part 2
A_3:	Will you be at the meetings in Chicago?	First pair, part 3
B_3:	Yes.	Second pair, part 3
A_2:	Well, then.	Second pair, part 2
B_1:	Goodbye, then.	Second pair, part 1

Conversational analysts have identified a number of different types of adjacency pairs and have related these to other conversational forms such as turn taking.

They are interested not only in identifying and describing such formal properties of talk but also in understanding the conventional ways in which conversation is structured and organized. In so doing, conversational analysts hope to discover the rules that allow individuals to converse. This has generated a variety of research interests including studies of turn taking in conversation, identity negotiations, story telling, jokes, and so on. Analysts also focus on how conversations may vary in different settings (e.g., as in courtrooms or meetings) or how they vary as a function of different participants (e.g., turn allocational processes appear to be different for men and women in our society).[56] An important focus of conversational analysis concerns what analysts call the conversational environment—verbal and nonverbal factors that provide contexts for particular conversational events.

Perhaps the most fully understood of these research agendas is the turn-taking process. Analysts have identified 14 different characteristics of turn taking in conversations. Then, through the analysis of a large compendium of transcribed conversations, researchers were able to show how these 14 characteristics could be explained by two general conversational rules. The authors note, for example, that first pair parts of adjacency pairs may serve as speaker selection devices. The reader may note that B's question, "When will I see you again?" in the previous sequence did not immediately receive an answer, although it did successfully allocate the next turn to A.

The parsimoniousness of the turn-taking model has recommended it to linguists as well as to sociologists. However, the researchers' primary interest is social-psychologically oriented. It is concluded that turn taking is significant because it provides a motivation for attentiveness in conversation independent of interest or other subjective factors. One needs to listen to others' turns at talk either to enter or to leave the conversation. More important, the location of an utterance in a particular turn at talk can have an important bearing on the meaning of that utterance. Turn units are rarely complete grammatical statements. Rather, they are fragments, and fragments such as "today," "how many," and so on make sense only in terms of their relationship either to prior or subsequent utterances.

LANGUAGE AS CREATIVE ACTIVITY

Social psychologists have for some time been concerned with the nature of language and verbal behavior. Indeed, there has been considerable debate as to how one should approach this question.

This debate erupted in the late 1950s following the publication of B. F. Skinner's *Verbal Behavior*.[57] In this book, Skinner set forth the outline for a behavioristic (see Chapter 4) and functionalist theory of language. Skinner contended that verbal behavior was controlled by external factors. As he put it, "A person does not act upon the world. The world acts upon him."[58] According to this theory, the chance that a child will continue to use a particular verbal form is contingent upon the response that he or she receives for using that form. If a child is rewarded with food every time he or she says, for example, "Please, can I have a cookie?" then the child will continue to use that expression whenever he or she is hungry. The critical elements in the production of verbal behavior are (1) the stimulus situation (i.e., hunger) and (2) the history of reinforcement (i.e., the extent to which the child is rewarded with a response that reduces his or her needs).

Linguist Noam Chomsky criticized Skinner's approach to verbal behavior.[59] According to Chomsky, Skinner's behavioristic and functional approach failed to explain how children at very young ages are able to combine different elements of their language (sounds and words) to produce completely novel utterances, utterances that they had not previously made and that, therefore, could not have been reinforced. According to Chomsky, "an essential property of language is that it provides the means for expressing indefinitely many thoughts and for reacting appropriately in an indefinite range of new situations."[60] This property, it is argued, cannot be completely understood within the behaviorist framework.

For Chomsky, the variety and novelty of language use means that children must possess some kind of inherent or innate language capacity that helps them to understand the very complex set of rules ("grammar") through which they create novel utterances. This is not to suggest that children can articulate the rules of grammar. It is to suggest that they have a sufficient understanding of those rules to produce intelligible sentences. For example, a young child may be able to deduce the question, "Is the cat on the mat?" from the declaration, "The cat is on the mat," without being able to explain that this transformation entails placing the verb in the question form before the subject of the declarative sentence. Similarly, a child may learn that a banana is yellow. He may then be able to apply that characteristic to other yellow objects (e.g., the sun) without being able to explain the relationship between nouns and adjectives. A child thus possesses the ability to use grammar without necessarily being able to articulate the rules governing grammatical expressions.

In addition, Chomsky contended that reinforcement is inadequate as an explanation of language learning. He cited evidence of problem-solving among animals that occurs without any extrinsic reward and argued that such processes are even more evident in human behavior.

The idea that the ability to learn and produce novel utterances must be explained in terms of an innate language capacity has been criticized from a behavioral perspective. Albert Bandura[61] has advanced the idea that the rate at which children learn new utterances may have a behavioral basis, albeit one that is substantially broader than the purely Skinnerian perspective. Bandura argued that children learn not only through direct reinforcement but also through imitating and modeling observed behavior. Bandura's approach differs from a purely Skinnerian view in that it posits the existence of cognitive processes that provide for observational learning (see Chapter 4). It is consistent with a purely Skinnerian view in that it considers reinforcement to be a central component of the learning process. According to this view, children observe others who use particular linguistic utterances, and they observe that such usages can be functional (i.e., they garner desired rewards). Hence, children may begin to use observed utterances. The rapidity and creativity in the learning of language result from the fact that children learn not only from what they *do* but also from what they *see*.

The reader may feel free to ponder the relative importance of reinforcement, observational learning, and innate creativity in the learning of language. For some social psychologists (symbolic interactionists, see Chapter 4), learning language means being able to share the meanings of symbols with others. To understand that a symbol stands for some object or relationship between objects requires that one share experiences in which symbols are used in such a way. This is predicated on the ability of an individual to "take the role of the other," that is, to put oneself imaginatively in the position of the other and, hence, see the world as the other might. In this way, the individual may come to have similar and empathic experiences with others. It is these experiences that provide the basis for shared meanings. The experiences also provide the basis for a sense of self. This is another prerequisite for meaningful communication through symbols. The symbolic interactionist perspective thus provides a different view of language development. It is innate only to the extent that it assumes the existence of a central nervous system as being necessary for language development. Hence, its similarity to the Chomskyan view is limited. Although it tries to explain language development by considering experiences that people have with others, it does not regard reinforcement as the primary mechanism for language learning.

How children learn language still remains one of the most intriguing mysteries in social psychology. Interestingly, recent developments in the study of language use among higher-order primates may provide further insights into this problem.

DO OTHER ANIMALS USE LANGUAGE?

Very few social psychologists would argue with the proposition that nonhuman animals communicate. Indeed, the study of animal communication has a long and profitable history. In the past, however, social psychologists tended to draw a sharp distinction between human and animal communication. Animals, it was claimed, communicate on a stimulus-response basis that is instinctual in nature. Thus, a lateral head-down position on the part of a male chaffinch (a small bird) when approaching a female signals the initiation of courtship.[62] The female responds accordingly, and courtship proceeds in a genetically prescribed manner. The chaffinch has no conception of love. There is no room for variation; chaffinch courtship will always follow exactly the same pattern.

According to many social psychologists, human communication differs from that which takes place between animals in that humans through language—the use of symbols to represent or stand for objects and relationships between objects. Beyond this, human beings are able to be innovative and creative in the use of these symbols. As Noam Chomsky puts it, "The essential difference between man and animal is exhibited most clearly by human language, in particular, by man's ability to form new statements which express new thoughts and which are appropriate to new situations."[63]

Recently, a new twist has been added to the question of animal language use that relates to the issue of language as creative activity. Researchers have shown that chimpanzees and other great apes (e.g., gorillas and orangutangs) may possess a capacity to use language in ways that are analogous to those of human beings.

Chimpanzees are able to use symbols to represent objects and relationships in a consistent manner.One chimpanzee named Washoe was taught American Sign Language (the hand signing system used by deaf people). Washoe learned over 132 different signs in a little over four years of training. Two other chimps who started training at an earlier age than Washoe developed their repertoire of symbols at an even faster pace. Sarah, for example, was taught to place tokens on a magnetized metal board to represent objects. These chimpanzees have learned how to symbolize not only nouns but also adjective adverbs and verbs.[64]

Both Washoe and Sarah demonstrated that they understand not only the simple relationships between a symbol (i.e., a sign or token) and the object it represented, but also the category systems to which the properties of both objects and their symbols belonged. Sarah, for example, could break down both an apple and her token symbol for an apple into properties such as red and round. Washoe quickly learned how to use signs in a more generalized manner. For example, after learning how to apply the sign for "open" to door, Washoe quickly learned to transfer it to a variety of different types of containerlike objects (e.g., boxes, jars, drawers, and even the water faucet).[65] These chimpanzees demonstrated that they could think abstractly. They were capable not only of symbolizing specific objects and relationships but of understanding the general categories to which they belonged and knowing how to apply these in a more general manner. Even their mistakes suggested that they were reasoning in an abstract and categorical manner. Washoe, for example, when presented with a picture of a dog (an animal she had not been taught a sign for) incorrectly gave the sign for a "cat," suggesting that even though she had erred, she was thinking in terms of the general category "four-legged animals."[66]

Finally, both Washoe and Sara demonstrated the capacity to combine symbols in an original and creative manner. One of Washoe's word creations was enlightening even for her trainers. Unable to find a sign for bib, Washoe's trainer attempted to teach her to use the sign for napkin to represent bib. Washoe resisted. She preferred to use a sign in which she would draw the outline of a bib around her neck and on her chest. Later, after visiting an institute for the deaf, Washoe's trainers were surprised to find out that this was, in fact, the proper sign for bib. In effect, Washoe had taught her trainers a sign.[67] Another chimpanzee, Lucy, demonstrated an impressive ability in combining signs in a novel manner. The term "smell fruit" was used for lemons, "cry-hurt fruits" was used for radishes, and "candy drink" was used for watermelon.[68]

Part of Sarah's training involved a session on "creative writing." Sarah's abilities in this area are interesting from the standpoint of language as creative activity. As her trainer reports,

> About midway through the project, after Sarah had achieved a moderate degree of language competence, virtually every lesson included a period in which the words were passed to Sarah and she was allowed to use them as she chose. No longer required either to comprehend the trainer's instructions or to answer her questions, Sarah produced constructions of her own. We called this section of the lesson "Creative Writing," and in it Sarah produced constructions of basically two forms—assertions, such as "Cherry is red," and questions, such as "? is fruit" (What is fruit). [By and by large] Sarah dealt with the same topics as those dealt with by the trainer in the earlier portion of the lesson; but she also departed from the trainer both lexically and syntactically, using different words as opposed to the trainer's questions, and vice versa, in the second case.[69]

There is still considerable dispute as to whether chimpanzees use language in the same sense as human beings do. Skeptics point out that the vocabularies used by the chimpanzees are not nearly as extensive as those used by human beings, and that chimpanzees are not as accurate in their use of words. (However, Sarah had virtually a 100 percent accuracy rating in her "creative writing" exercises.)[70] The linguistic constructions produced by chimps are not as varied as those used by human beings. On the other hand, Sarah was able to use objects to symbolize items in the world, and Washoe learned a system of symbols used by deaf human beings. Beyond this, both Washoe and Sarah were able to combine these symbols in intelligible strings (evidencing some ability to produce sentences), and both were creative in producing novel words and phrases.

The cases of Washoe and Sarah are enlightening from the standpoint of language as creative activity. Initial training for both chimps was behavioral in nature. Washoe was rewarded with food or approval whenever she made the correct sign in response to some question or request from her trainers. In some cases, Washoe's trainers would shape the chimp's hands in a specific sign language formation and then reward her with the appropriate object. This process would be continued until Washoe showed that she had learned that sign. Once she demonstrated that she had learned the sign, however, the researchers devised unique ways of asking her questions to ensure that she was using the symbol in an appropriate manner and was not simply responding to some stimulus presented by the teacher. Washoe, Sarah, and Lucy as well as other chimpanzees and gorillas have learned to go beyond mere repetition and imitation. In a sense, their training illustrates both the effectiveness of reinforcement and the possibilities of creativity.

Recently, an attempt has been made to explain language development among these higher-order primates from a symbolic interactionist perspective.[71] One researcher notes that chimpanzees were able to refer to themselves as both subjects and objects, suggesting that they have at least a rudimentary sense of self. Unlike almost all other nonhuman animals, chimpanzees are able to recognize themselves in a mirror. After being placed in front of a mirror for a period of time, the chimps' behavior changed from "threatening" the "other chimpanzee" to a variety of grooming-type behaviors. To test further whether the chimps recognized the image as their own, the researchers drugged them and painted an odorless and tasteless red dot on their foreheads. When the chimps awoke, a good deal of their behavior was directed toward removing or otherwise investigating the dot.[72] Again this suggested that chimpanzees may develop an image of themselves that in some ways seems to resemble what symbolic interactionists call the *self*.[73]

For symbolic interactionists, the self develops through a process of taking the role of the other. Some chimpanzee behavior seems to reflect such a process. For example, consider this description of Washoe's behavior toward her doll:

> from her 2nd month with us, she always had dolls to play with. One day, during the 10th month of the project, she bathed one of her dolls in the way we usually bathed her. She filled her little bathtub, then took it out and dried it with a towel. She has repeated the entire performance, or parts of it, many times since, sometimes also soaping the doll.[74]

Other researchers have noted that chimpanzees in natural settings engage in complex cooperative and coordinated behaviors, suggesting that they have at least some empathy and role-taking abilities.[75]

LANGUAGE, CULTURE, AND SOCIAL CLASS

When machines transmit monologues to each other, it is generally assumed that there is a clear, unmistakable message to be communicated. If we could speak of machine "consciousness," we might insist that machines are always fully conscious of the messages they are transmitting. The problems for them are such matters as speed of transmission, the possible presence of noise, how to provide sufficient redundancy, and so on. When human beings try to communicate with each other, however, additional difficulties arise. There is a problem of what Edward T. Hall has called "the out-of-awareness" aspects of communications.[76]

The difficulties involved may be seen as arising from the specific culture or social class within which the communicator has been raised. Throughout the remainder of this volume, we shall examine the implications that culture and social class have for various kinds of human behavior. Here we wish simply to indicate their relevance for the broad problem of communication and, more specifically, their relevance for language and linguistics in general.

Although contemporary social scientists have developed literally hundreds of different definitions of the term "culture," many still find the original definition provided by E. B. Tylor in 1871 to be very useful: "Culture, or civilization, . . . is that complex whole which includes knowledge, belief, art, morals, custom, and other capabilities and habits acquired by man as a member of a society."[77]

Social scientists have long been convinced that the total content of every culture can be expressed in its own language. For Edward Sapir, this implied that individuals within a culture see things and experience things in ways that are shaped by the language available to them. The form of a language, he felt, allows people who use it to transcend experience in characteristic ways. A man who has never seen more than a single elephant in his entire life can, nevertheless, readily discuss the matter of ten or a million elephants or generations of elephants. In short, language has the power to break up experience into parts and reassemble the parts in ways that create a world of possibilities as well as a world of actualities. This

> enables human beings to transcend the immediately given in their individual experiences and to join in a larger common understanding. This common understanding constitutes culture, which cannot be adequately defined by a description of those more colorful patterns of behavior in a society which lie open to observation and interpretation.[78]

Sapir felt that as scientific experience develops, it becomes important to guard or even to fight against the implications of this influence of language over thought. Beyond this, however, those who speak the same language tend to have a sense of social solidarity with each other. Sapir observed that subforms of a language develop among groups of people who are held together by some common interest. These groups may include families, undergraduates of a college, labor unions, the underworld in a large city, members of the same club, a small number of friends who associate throughout many years despite differences in occupational or professional concerns, and untold numbers of other groups. Each of them tends to develop characteristic speech patterns that have the symbolic function of differentiating the group from the larger society in which they all exist and the standard language that they all speak. "The extraordinary importance of minute linguistic differences for the symbolization of psychologically real as contrasted with politically or sociologically official groups is intuitively felt by most people. 'He talks like us' is equivalent to saying, 'He is one of us.' "[79]

Benjamin Whorf, who for a time studied under Sapir, developed what has become known as the "principle of linguistic relativity" or, more commonly, the Sapir-Whorf hypothesis. One statement of this says, "We are thus introduced to a new principle of relativity, which holds that all observers are not led by the same physical evidence to the same picture of the universe, unless their linguistic backgrounds are similar or can in some way be calibrated."[80] In short, language shapes thought. Persons using different languages see the world differently and think differently.

For example, anthropologists have noted many variations in the classification of color in different cultures and in different languages.[81] The Torres Straits Islanders have the same word for blue and green; Brazilian Indians use a single expression for yellow and red, and blue may be included under either black or green. Whorf noted that the Hopi Indians use a single word for all flying objects such as insects, airplanes, and aviators (but not birds).

Related to this matter of color terminology is the issue of the extent to which language influences perception—ultimately, to what extent "evidence of our senses" is modified by the norms of our culture.[82]

Thus it has been reported that the Trobriand Islanders can see the resemblance between two sons and their father but apparently cannot perceive the resemblance between a mother and her children or between two brothers. Other studies indicate cultural differences with respect to auditory perception, optical illusions, and memory as well as the perception of depth in pictures. Thus, there are marked differences between children of the Nupe and Yoruba tribes when they are asked to repeat a story read to them or to describe from memory a picture they have been shown. The Nupe recall the stories and pictures in a piecemeal, enumerative fashion; the Yoruba recall them as integrated wholes.[83]

This difference is scarcely unique. It corresponds to the difference found between two major approaches to scientific investigation. One of these begins by analyzing whole phenomena into *elements*. This approach has been compared[84] with the chemical analysis of water into hydrogen and oxygen. Neither of the elements has the properties of the whole and each has properties not found in the whole. Someone trying to determine why water has certain characteristics (e.g., why it can put out a fire) may be shocked to learn that hydrogen burns and that oxygen is necessary for fire to exist. These specific discoveries are not of much help in solving the problem of water and fire.

Alternatively, if we wish to understand the properties of water, it is possible to study phenomena as units—to study molecules of water and their characteristics rather than the chemical composition of water. A unit, then, is a subject of study that retains all the basic properties of the whole. It cannot be divided without loss of these basic properties.

With respect to language, L. S. Vygotsky has suggested that the relevant unit is *word meaning*. The point is that a word does not refer to a single object but to an entire group or class of objects. Thus, each word is a generalization. Vygotsky's studies of the development of understanding and signs alone are not enough to ensure communication. It is necessary for the world of experience to be generalized and simplified before any part of it can be translated into symbols. What any given person experiences cannot be communicated directly. The experience must be included within a category that the person's society regards as a unit.

Thus, "the higher forms of human intercourse are possible only because man's thought reflects conceptualized actuality. That is why certain thoughts cannot be communicated to children even if they are familiar with the necessary words."[85]

In 1924 Vygotsky began to collaborate with A. R. Luria who conducted a series of remarkable cross-cultural studies[86] designed to investigate the developmental aspects of intellectual ability as well as the effect of differing cultural conditions on people's intellectual capacity as they grew to adulthood.

These studies were conducted in the early 1930s in two remote villages in the Central Asian regions of Uzbekistan and Kirghizia.

Uzbekistan had been a feudal society in which some outstanding scientific and poetic achievements had been made by a few persons who were part of an educated elite. Most people in its villages, however, were illiterate peasants who had been completely dependent upon wealthy landowners and powerful fuedal lords. Their economy was based mainly on the raising of cotton.

In Kirghizia, animal husbandry was the dominant economic activity. The people were strongly influenced by the conservative form of Islamic religion, which tended to keep women isolated from the daily life of the society.

After the Russian revolution, both areas underwent fundamental socioeconomic and cultural changes. The existing structure of social class relationships was destroyed, and new technology was introduced along with new forms of social and economic activity. Since both regions were undergoing transition, Luria felt that it would be possible to observe nonliterate groups in the villages of each as well as groups already involved in a more modern form of existence. All, presumably, were experiencing massive social changes.

Luria and his associates began their field work by having long conversations with their subjects. Gradually, as rapport was established, they asked specific questions and finally presented their subjects with a variety of tests. They ultimately stopped using tests that had been developed and validated in other cultures since such tests produced "experimental failures"—the subjects regarded the tests as pointless and would not participate appropriately.

A variety of specially developed tests were administered to examine cultural differences in perception, the ability to generalize and think abstractly, the ability to make deductions and inferences, reasoning and problem solving, imagination, and self-analysis and self-awareness.[87]

In one of these tests, the subjects were presented with a number of different colors and shapes. They were asked to divide these colors and shapes into a specific number of groups or to evaluate whether or not a grouping assembled by the experimenter was correct. Luria reports that subjects with a relatively "high level of cultural development (collective farm activists, young people with short-term formal education)" were able to classify colors into appropriate group clusters with relatively little difficulty.[88] Uneducated peasant women, living in remote villages, however, were completely confused by the task and gave responses such as, "It can't be done," "None of them are the same," "You can't put them together," "This is like calf's dung, and this is like a peach."[89]

In other experiments, subjects were shown drawings of four objects, three of which belonged to one category and the fourth to a different one. They were asked which objects were similar and could be placed in the same group. Object groupings included such collections as glass, saucepan, spectacles, bottle; tree, rose, ear of grain, bird; eye, finger, mouth, ear.

Among the interesting findings Luria reports is the fact that his uneducated subjects tended to respond by classifying the objects not theoretically but in terms of which went together if one wanted to accomplish a specific task.

For example, on being shown the glass, saucepan, spectacles, bottle collection, one subject reacted as follows:

"These three go together, but why you've put the spectacles here, I don't know. Then again, they also fit in. If a person doesn't see too good, he has to put them on to eat dinner."[90]

Another subject shown the same collection said

"I don't know which of the things doesn't fit here. Maybe it's the bottle? You can drink tea out of the glass—that's useful. The spectacles are also useful. But there's vodka in the bottle—that's bad."[91]

Luria's conclusion, on the basis of this experimentation, was that differences in perception, problem solving, and all the other aspects of thought he studied were due to differences in the culture within which the subjects had been raised.

This, then, is somewhat different from what Whorf was saying. Whorf was focusing upon language and suggesting that it determined or at least shaped the other aspects of culture. Vygotsky and Luria were focusing on different cultural patterns and examining their effects on thinking, perception, and related matters.

A more recent British social scientist influenced by this early work is Basil Bernstein who is best known perhaps for his work, *Class, Codes and Control*.[92] Bernstein focuses on a single, common language (i.e., English) and examines the effects of different linguistic forms or fashions of speaking have in bringing about *different* ways of relating to people and things. This, of course, raises the question of *social class* and language.

Bernstein uses the term "linguistic code" or "sociolinguistic" code to distingish variations of speech forms within a single language. Thus, for him, language is a set of rules with which all speech codes conform. The specific speech code that comes into existence and use depends upon what is essentially a subculture that has developed in connection with various social relationships (social classes). The speech pattern thus arises from the social structure but also acts to modify the social structure itself.[93]

Two codes develop what Bernstein calls "elaborated" and "restricted." They arise as a result of a particular form of social relation and may have little or nothing to do with a speaker's "innate" speech competence.

A restricted code arises where the form of social relation—the culture or subculture—makes the "we" more important than the "I." In more formal terms, it arises when the "form of the social relation is based upon closely shared identifications, upon an extensive range of shared expectations, upon a range of common assumptions."[94] The meaning communicated need not be completely explicit. Thus with couples who have been married for a long period of time, a slight shift of stress or a small gesture can communicate a highly complex meaning. People accustomed to using restricted codes exclusively may find it difficult to shift to a different set of role relations in which restricted speech codes are not appropriate (e.g., an unskilled worker accustomed to speaking with his fellow workers, their families, and friends will find it difficult to communicate effectively as a butler in an upper-class family).

An elaborated code, in a sense, is the opposite of a restricted code. It arises where the form of social relation makes the "I" more important than the "we." It arises whenever the intent of the other person involved in a communication act cannot be taken for granted. Since this is the case, speakers are forced to elaborate their meanings and make them more explicit and more specific. In principle, it "presupposes a sharp boundary or gap between self and others."[95] This requires the creation of a speech form that fits a specific other person. In this sense, the elaborated code is oriented toward a person rather than toward a social category or status. On the other hand, in restricted codes, there is a gap between persons who share the code and those who do not. In this sense the restricted code is oriented toward positions or status rather than to specific persons.[96]

One obvious effect of a social class structure is to limit access to elaborated codes.[97] (Parenthetically, we might note the extraordinary effects that varying speech patterns have traditionally had in British life—this has been the subject of innumerable stories, plays, and even musical comedies.)

Bernstein gives an interesting illustration of the differences involved by presenting two stories told by middle-class and working-class 5-year-old children in London. The children all saw four pictures showing a sequence of action. They were asked to tell the story told by the pictures. In the first picture, some boys were playing football. The second picture showed a ball going through the window of a house. In the third picture a woman looks out of the window while a man makes a threatening gesture. In the fourth picture, the children are leaving the scene.

Bernstein gives us two of the stories written by the children. The first is characteristic of the middle-class children; the second is characteristic of working-class children:

1. Three boys are playing football and one boy kicks the ball and it goes through the window and the boys are looking at it and a man comes out and shouts at them because they've broken the window so they run away and that lady looks out of her window and she tells the boys off.

2. They're playing football and he kicks it and it goes through there it breaks the window and they're looking at it and he comes out and shouts at them because they've broken it so they run away and then she looks out and she tells them off.[98]

Bernstein observes that with the first story (elaborated code), it is not necessary to see the four pictures. The second story (restricted code), however, would not make sense without the pictures. The second story is closely tied to the context from which it was generated. The first story, on the other hand, is virtually context free. Consequently, the meanings of the first story are explicit, whereas those in the second story are implicit. In short, the author of the first story using an elaborated code seems to take very little for granted, whereas the author of the second using a restricted code seems to take a great deal for granted.

Bernstein does not suggest that speakers who tend to use restricted codes will not use elaborated codes on occasion, and vice versa. He does insist, however, that the use of one or the other codes tends to become customary because of the social class position of the child and his or her family. This is associated with living within a subculture for which one or the other kind of code is more or less habitual.

CONCLUSION

We shall have more to say about the nature of human communication as it takes place in different social and cultural contexts through this book. We will pay special attention to the different forms of human communication and to the implication these have for individuals. But, first, we need to review some of the methods social psychologists employ in their study of social reality.

NOTES

[1]P. Watzlawick, J. Beavin, and D. Jackson, "Some Tentative Axioms of Communication", in C. D. Mortensen, ed., *Basic Readings in Communication Theory* (New York: Harper & Row, 1973), p. 37.

[2]C. Cherry, *World Communication: Threat or Promise* (New York: John Wiley, 1978), p. 1.

[3]W. Schramm, "How Communication Works," in Mortensen ed., *Basic Readings in Communication Theory*, p. 28.

[4]A. Schulman, "A Multi-Channel Transactional Social Model of Influence Processes," in Walter Nord, ed., *Concepts and Controversy in Organizational Behavior* (Pacific Palisades, Calif.: Goodyear, 1976), pp. 491–600. Our treatment of nonverbal communications relies in part on Mark L. Knapp, *Nonverbal Communication in Human Interaction.* (New York: Holt, Rinehart and Winston, 1978).

[5]R. Ardrey, *The Territorial Imperative* (New York: Atheneum Press, 1966).

[6]M. Knapp, *Nonverbal Communication in Human Interaction*, 2nd ed. (New York: Holt Rinehart & Winston, 1978) p. 119.

[7]J. J. Christian, and D. E. Davis, "Social and Endocrine Factors Are Integrated in the Regulation of Mammalian Populations," *Science*, Vol. 146 (1964), pp. 1550–1560.

[8]J. B. Calhoun, "Population Density and Social Pathology," *Scientific American*, Vol. 206 (1962), pp. 139–148.

[9]S. Milgram, "The Experience of Living in Cities," *Science*, Vol. 167 (1970), pp. 1461–1468.

[10]See E. T. Hall, "A System for the Notation of Proxemic Behavior," *American Anthropologist*, Vol. 65 (1963), pp. 1003–1026; and E. T. Hall, *Handbook for Proxemic Research*. Washington, D. C.: Society for the Anthropology of Visual Communication, 1974.

[11]E. T. Hall, *The Silent Language* (Garden City, N. Y.: Doubleday, 1959); see also E. T. Hall, "Proxemics," *Current Anthropology*, Vol. 9 (1968), pp. 83–100.

[12]O. M. Watson and T. D. Graves, "Quantitative Research in Proxemic Behavior." *American Anthropologist*, Vol. 68 (1966), pp. 971–985.

[13]R. Shuter, "Proxemics and Tactility in Latin America," *Journal of Communication*, Vol. 26 (1976), pp. 46–52.

[14]S. E. Scherer, "Proxemic Behavior of Primary School Children as a Function of Their Socioeconomic Class and Subculture," *Journal of Personality and Social Psychology*, Vol. 29 (1974), pp. 800–805.

[15]S. M. Lyman and M. Scott, "Territoriality: A Neglected Sociological Dimension," *Social Problems*, Vol. 15 (1967), pp. 236–249, reprinted in S. M. Lyman and M. Scott, eds., *A Sociology of the Absurd* (New York: Appleton-Century-Crofts, 1970), pp. 89–110.

[16]Ibid., p. 91.

[17]Ibid., pp. 92–93.

[18]Ibid., p. 95.

[19]See Hall, op. cit. *The Silent Language*, 1959.

[20]Knapp, *Nonverbal Communications*, p. 226.

[21]See R. Shater, "Proxemics and Tactility in Latin America," *Journal of Communication*, Vol. 26 (1976), pp. 46–52.

[22]N. M. Henley, *Body Politics: Power, Sex and Nonverbal Communication* (Englewood Cliffs, N. J.: Prentice-Hall, 1977).

[23]F. Davis, *Inside Intuition* (New York: McGraw-Hill; 1971), p. 129.

[24]J. A. Meerloo, *Unobtrusive Communication: Essays in Psycholinguistics* (Assen, Netherlands: Van Gorcum; 1964).

[25]E. T. Hall, *The Hidden Dimension* (Garden City, N. Y.: Doubleday; 1966), pp. 159–160.

[26]Meerloo, *Unobtrusive Communication*, p. 168.

[27]P. Ekman and W. V. Friesen, "Measuring Facial Movement," *Environmental Psychology and Nonverbal Behavior*, Vol. 1 (1976), pp. 56–75. Also, see P. Ekman, W. V. Frieser, and S. S. Tomkins, "Facial Affect Scoring Technique: A First Validity Study," *Semiotical*, Vol. 3 (1971), pp. 37–58.

[28]P. Ekman, E. R. Sorenson, and W. V. Friesen, "Pan-cultural Elements in Displays of Emotion," *Science*, Vol. 164 (1969), pp. 86–88.

[29]E. H. Hess, "The Role of Pupil Size in Communication," *Scientific American*, Vol. 223 (1975), pp. 110–119.

[30]E. H. Hess, *The Tell-Tale Eye* (New York: Van Nostrand Reinhold; 1975).

[31]See Knapp, *Nonverbal Communication*, p. 309–312.

[32]See A. E. Scheflin, "The Significance of Posture in Communication Systems," *Psychiatry*, Vol. 27 (1964), pp. 316–331.

[33]M. Argyle and J. Dean, "Eye-Contact, Distance and Affiliation," *Sociometry*, Vol. 28 (1965), pp. 289–304.

[34]Discussed in Knapp, *Nonverbal Communication*, p. 393.

[35]F. H. George, *The Foundations of Cybernetics* (New York: Gordon and Breach, 1977), p. 1.

[36]N. Wiener, *Cybernetics* (Cambridge, Mass.: MIT Press and John Wiley, 1948).

[37]Jagjit Singh, *Great Ideas in Information Theory, Language and Cybernetics* (New York: Dover Publications, 1966)

[38]W. R. Ashby, *An Introduction to Cybernetics* (New York: John Wiley, 1956), p. 3.

[39]N. Nyquist, "Certain Factors Affecting Telegraph Speed," *Bell System Technical Journal*, July 1928, p. 535; C. E. Shannon and Warren Weaver, *The Mathematical Theory of Communication* (Urbana: University of Illinois Press, 1949).

[40]C. E. Shannon and Warren Weaver, *The Mathematical Theory of Communication* (Chicago: University of Illinois Press, 1978), p. 7.

[41]Ibid., p. 98–113.

[42]See John Parry, *The Psychology of Human Communication* (London: University of London Press, 1967).

[43]Ibid., pp. 45–47.

[44]Ashley Montagu and Floyd Matson, *The Human Connection* (New York: McGraw-Hill, 1979), pp. 132–147.

[45]J. Henry, *Pathways to Madness* (New York: Vintage Books, 1973), p. 192.

[46]Ibid., p. 192.

[47]Ibid., p. 192.

[48]J. Ruesch and G. Bateson, *Communication: The Social Matrix of Psychiatry* (New York: W. W. Norton, 1951), p. 6.

[49]Ibid., p. 6.

[50]H. S. Sullivan, "The Illusion of Personal Individuality," *Psychiatry,* Vol. 13 (1950), p. 329.

[51]M. B. Cohen, "Introduction" to Harry Stack Sullivan, *The Interpersonal Theory of Psychiatry,* edited by Helen Swick Perry and Mary Ladd Gawell (New York: W. W. Norton, 1953), p. xii.

[52]Rollo May, "Gregory Bateson and Humanistic Psychology," in J. Brockman, ed., *About Bateson* (New York: E. P. Dutton, 1977), pp. 78–79.

[53]G. Bateson, "Foreward" in C. E. Sluzki and D. E. Ransom, eds., *Doublebind: The Foundation of the Communicational Approach to the Family* (New York: Grune and Stratton, 1976), p. xiv.

[54]A. N. Whitehead and B. Russell, *Principia Mathematica,* 2nd ed. (New York: Cambridge University Press, reprinted 1950), Vol. 1, p. 60.

[55]See H. Sacks, E. A. Schegloff, and G. Jefferson, "A Simplest Systematics for the Organization of Turn Taking for Conversation," *Language,* Vol. 50, no. 4 (1974), pp. 696–735.

[56]C. West and D. Zimmerman, "Women's Place in Everyday Talk: Reflection on Parent-Child Interactions," *Social Problems,* Vol. 24, no. 5 (1977), pp. 521–529.

[57]B. F. Skinner, *Verbal Behavior* (New York: Appleton-Century-Crofts, 1957).

[58]Ibid., p. 11.

[59]N. Chomsky, "On Skinner's Verbal Behavior," *Language,* Vol. 35 (1959), pp. 26–58.

[60]N. Chomsky, *Aspects of a Theory of Syntex* (Cambridge, Mass.: MIT Press, 1965), p. 6.

[61]A. Bandura, *Social Learning Theory* (Englewood Cliffs, N. J.: Prentice-Hall, 1977), pp. 175–179.

[62]See R. A. Hinde, *Animal Behavior* (New York: McGraw-Hill 1966), pp. 366–386.

[63]N. Chomsky, *Cartesian Linguistics* (New York: Harper & Row, 1966), p. 3.

[64]Reported in J. Meddin, "Chimpanzees, Symbols and the Reflexive Self," *Social Psychology Quarterly,* Vol. 42 (1979), pp. 99–109.

[65]Ibid., p. 102.

[66]See R. A. Gardner and B. T. Gardner, "Teaching Sign Language to a Chimpanzee," *Science,* Vol. 165 (1969), pp. 664–672.

[67]Ibid.

[68]Meddin, "Chimpanzees," p. 104.

[69]D. Premack, *Intelligence in Ape and Man* (New York: John Wiley, 1967), p. 16.

[70]Ibid., p. 17.

[71]Meddin, "Chimpanzees."

[72]See G. Gallup, "Self-recognition in Primates," *American Psychologist,* Vol. 32 (1977), pp. 329–388. See also G. Gallup, "Chimpanzees: Self-recognition," *Science,* Vol. 167 (1970), pp. 86–87.

[73]Meddin, "Chimpanzees."

[74]Gardner and Gardner, "Teaching Sign Language," p. 66.

[75]Meddin, "Chimpanzees," p. 107.

[76]E. T. Hall, *The Silent Language* (Garden City, N. Y.: Doubleday, 1959), p. 52.

[77]E. B. Tylor, *Primitive Culture* (London: Murray, 1871). Quoted in Etienne Vermeersch, "An Analysis of the Concept of Culture," in Bernardo Bernardi, ed., *The Concept and Dynamics of Culture* (The Hague: Mouton, 1977), p. 10.

[78]E. Sapir, "The Nature of Language," in D. G. Mandelbaum, ed., *Selected Writings of Edward Sapir in Language, Culture and Personality* (Berkeley and Los Angeles: University of California Press, 1958), p. 10. Originally published in *Encyclopedia of the Social Sciences* (New York: Macmillan, 1933), Vol. 9, pp. 155–169.

[79]Ibid., p. 16.

[80]J. B. Carroll, ed., *Language, Thought and Reality: Selected Writings of Benjamin Lee Whorf* (New York: John Wiley,), p. v., 1956.

[81]Otto Klineberg, "Historical Perspectives: Cross-cultural Psychology Before 1960," in H. C. Triandis and W. W. Lambert, eds., *Handbook of Cross-cultural Psychology: Perspectives* (Boston: Allyn & Bacon, 1980), Vol. 1, p. 44.

[82]Ibid., p. 45.

[83]Ibid., pp. 45–46. See also M. H. Segall, D. T. Campbell, and M. J. Herskovits, *The Influence of Culture on Visual Perception* (Indianapolis: Bobbs-Merill, 1966); H. C. Triandis, "Cultural Influences upon Cognitive Processes," in L. Berkovitz, ed., *Advances in Experimental Social Psychology* (New York: Academic Press, 1964); J. W. Berry and P. R. Dasen, eds., *Culture and Cognition: Readings in Cross-cultural Psychology* (London: Methuen, 1974).

[84]L. S. Vygotsky, *Thought and Language*, edited and translated by Eugenia Hanfmann and Gertrude Vaker (Cambridge, Mass.: MIT Press, 1962), pp. 3–8.

[85]Ibid., p. 7.

[86]A. R. Luria, *The Making of a Mind* (Cambridge, Mass.: Harvard University Press, 1979).

[87]For a detailed account of these studies, see A. R. Luria, *Cognitive Development: Its Cultural and Social Foundations,* translated by Martin Lopez-Morillas and Lynn Solotaroff, edited by Michael Cole (Cambridge, Mass.: Harvard University Press, 1976).

[88]Ibid., p. 26.

[89]Ibid., p. 27.

[90]Ibid., p. 57.

[91]Ibid.

[92]B. Bernstein, *Class, Codes and Control. Vol. 1: Theoretical Studies Toward a Sociology of Language* (London: Routledge & Kegan Paul, 1971).

[93]Ibid., pp. 173–174.

[94]Ibid., p. 146.

[95]Ibid., p. 147.

[96]Ibid., p. 148.

[97]Ibid., p. 176.

[98]Ibid., p. 178.

CHAPTER THREE
RELEVANT METHODS
IN SOCIAL PSYCHOLOGY

How do social psychologists learn about such things as social behavior and human communication processes? How do they arrive at the "scientific" basis for the statements they make? What "methods" do they use?

We feel that it is necessary and appropriate to preface our discussion of method by referring to a fascinating volume, written by the British philosopher of science Paul K. Feyerabend, *Against Method.*[1] He states:

> one of the most striking features of recent discussions in the history and philosophy of science is the realization that events and developments, such as the invention of modern atomism [kinetic theory; dispersion theory; stereochemistry; quantum theory] and the gradual emergence of the wave theory of light, occurred only because some thinkers either *decided* not to be bound by certain "obvious" methodological rules or because they *unwittingly broke* them.[2]

Furthermore, he says, this is not simply a *fact* of the history of science, it is both reasonable and *absolutely necessary* for the growth of knowledge. "More specifically, one can show the following: given any rule, however 'fundamental' or 'necessary' for science, there are always circumstances when it is advisable not only to ignore the rule, but to adopt its opposite."[3]

He goes on to say much more, but perhaps a final quote will capture the spirit of his argument:

> It is clear, then, that the idea of fixed method, or of a fixed theory of rationality, rests on too naïve a view of man and his social surroundings. To those who look at the rich material provided by history, and who are not intent on impoverishing it in order to please their lower instincts, their craving for intellectual security in the form of clarity, precision, "objectivity," "truth," it will become clear that there is only *one* principle that can be defended under *all* stages of human development. It is the principle: anything goes.[4]

It is, of course, quite possible to carry such an argument to unacceptable lengths. Feyerabend is not really calling for the elimination of all methodology; he is calling our attention to the fact that all methods have their limitations and that no single rule in methodology can lay claim to universal validity. As we proceed with our own discussion of methods used by social psychologists, we hope that the reader will remember this warning.

HYPOTHESES AND VARIABLES

Some social psychologists think that the best way in which to learn about the way people act is to apply methods borrowed from the natural sciences. By using these methods, they try to discover laws governing social action.

This characteristically leads to the use of experiments to isolate the causes and effects of particular variables. Through a tightly controlled experiment, the researcher tries to determine how a change in one variable affects other variables. In Chapter 1 we reviewed the results of a number of different social psychological experiments. We saw, for example, how Solomon Asch could reduce the rate of conformity by breaking the unanimity of the majority and how Stanley Milgram could increase the rate of obedience by creating a greater social distance between the teacher and the learner. In this way, the researchers can *test* their *hypotheses* about some state of affairs. In its most general form, an hypothesis is a statement about the world. In a more specific form, an hypothesis is a statement about the relationship between two or more variables.

Variables manipulated to produce change are called *independent variables*. In the obedience studies, the independent variables were such things as unanimity, social distance, and the credibility of the experimenter. The term *dependent variable* refers to what is expected to change as a result of some change in the independent variable. Rates of obedience and conformity are good examples of dependent variables.

The relationship between an independent or dependent variable may be positive, negative, or zero. A positive relationship refers to those situations in which a change in the independent variable (e.g., its presence/absence or increase/decrease) results in a similar change (presence/absence or increase/decrease) in the dependent variable. Higher levels of education (as measured by number of years of school), for example, appear to lead to an increase in racial tolerance. Lower education is associated with less racial tolerance. A negative relationship describes a situation in which a change in the independent variable causes an opposite reaction in the dependent variable. For example, there appears to be a negative relationship between amount of schooling and age; younger people in this country generally tend to have had more years of formal schooling than do their elders. No (or zero) relationship occurs when a change in the independent variable does not have any effect on the dependent variables. The two variables are unrelated.

Establishing casual relationships between variables is an extremely difficult process. Generally, social psychologists assume that causality is present when two variables are related to each other, when the casual (independent) variable precedes the dependent variable in time, and when other plausible explanations can be ruled out. This last criterion greatly complicates the establishment of causality because it requires the researcher to consider how a number of variables may affect each other.

Intervening variables refer to those variables that affect the relationship between dependent and independent variables. They are consequences of the independent variables and determinates of dependent variables. For example social scientists have observed a positive relationship between social status (as measured by income, education and occupation) of some fathers and the self-esteem of their sons. Sons of fathers with a high social status tended to have higher self-esteem. The researchers hypothesized that there was something about the interaction between upper-class fathers and their sons that was different from that between lower-class fathers and their sons. Upon a more detailed examination of the data, the researchers found that a higher proportion of upper-class father-son relationships could be characterized as close, whereas a greater proportion of lower-class father-son relationships were not close. Moreover, sons of lower-class fathers who had had close relationships tended to have high self-esteem. Sons of upper-class fathers who did not have a close social relationship did not have high self-esteem. Thus it was not fathers' social status per se that led to a high self-esteem but, rather, social status operating through social interaction. This relationship may be diagrammed as follows:

$$\frac{\text{Independent variable}}{\text{Fathers' social status}} \rightarrow \frac{\text{intervening variable}}{\text{social interaction}} \rightarrow \frac{\text{dependent variable[5]}}{\text{sons' self-esteem}}$$

Intervening variables illustrate why *control* is important in this kind of social psychological research. This is the attempt to account for the effects of different variables and, when appropriate, to rule out the relevance of some variables. For example, certain relationships on their face may appear to be quite significant. However, when other variables are taken into account, these relationships may be shown to be spurious (i.e., they may disappear). For example, some social psychologists have noted a positive relationship between income and tolerance toward different racial groups. However, when education is taken into consideration, the relationship between income and tolerance may no longer be as significant as it first appeared.[6] The tolerance of high-income people may largely be a result of their higher education. High-income people who are not highly educated may not appear to be so tolerant. The relationship among education, income, and tolerance may appear as shown

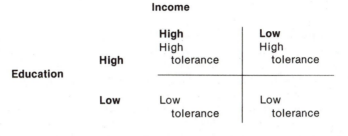

Income

		High	**Low**
	High	High tolerance	High tolerance
Education			
	Low	Low tolerance	Low tolerance

FIGURE 3-1

in Figure 3–1. In this instance, the apparent relationship between income and tolerance may actually be a function of education.

Suppressor variables also may distort the relationship between dependent and independent variables. By not taking certain variables into consideration, the researcher may fail to see a relationship when one actually exists. For example, the relationship between occupational status and earnings appears to be surprisingly low. In a national sample of men and women, earnings do not increase as one moves up the occupational hierarchy. However, when sex is taken into consideration (i.e., when the researcher looks at the relationship between occupation and earnings within each sex category), it does become significant. The relationship between occupation and earnings *is* significant when males are compared with other males and females with other females. Disparities in earnings between males and females account for the rather low surface relationship between occupation and earnings.[7]

Finally, social psychologists must be sensitive to the possibility of *interaction effects*. These occur when the combining of two independent variables produces a change in a dependent variable. If, for example, tolerance increased as a function of both a cooperative atmosphere and equal status contact (i.e., contact with other people who have approximately the same social status) with members of different groups, we would call this an interaction effect. Such an effect may be as shown in Figure 3–2. Tolerance increases only when we have both a cooperative atmosphere and equal status contact.

FIGURE 3-2

Equal status contact

		High	**Low**
	High	High tolerance	Average
Cooperative atmosphere			
	Low	Average tolerance	Low tolerance

EXPERIMENTS

Experiments are one way in which social psychologists may attempt to isolate the relationship between variables. In its basic form, the experiment may have only a simple before-after design. Let us say that we have a film depicting the harmful effects of cigarette smoking. We assemble a group of cooperative people and measure their attitudes toward cigarette smoking. We then show them the film and administer another attitude test to determine if there has been a change in their attitudes. This basic design consists of three components: the *pretest*, which establishes the preexisting state of affairs (e.g., attitudes toward cigarette smoking); the *treatment* through which we introduce the independent variable or stimulus (i.e., the film); and the posttest (i.e., attitudes toward cigarette smoking after having seen the film).

Even if we follow this design carefully, we may still draw incorrect conclusions. Errors may stem from two sources. First, factors outside the experiment itself may affect the validity of the findings. Imagine that the people we have selected as a sample for this experiment are committed antismokers. Chances are their attitudes will not change very much. This may not be the case if we had a pro-smoking audience or one that was ambivalent about smoking. For this reason, it is important that our sample be either truly random or that it accurately represent a particular group whose attitudes are relevant to the experiment. Social psychologists use the term *external validity* to refer to the extent to which the results from specific experiments are generalizeable to other contexts and events in the "real world." Having a random or representative sample is crucial to an experiment's external validity.

Bias may also stem from the administration of the experiment itself. This involves the *internal validity* of the research. In administering the pretest, for example, we may ask questions about cigarette smoking. These questions may themselves affect the attitudes of our subjects about smoking; that is, changes in attitudes may arise from the administration of the pretest rather than from the treatment. To eliminate this possibility, the researcher may use a control group that receives the pretest but *not* the treatment. If the people in both the experimental and control groups are really "equivalent," we can ascertain the extent to which attitudinal change results from the treatment as opposed to the pretest.

There are a variety of other experimental designs that help social psychologists to control internal sources of error.[8] The advantage of laboratory experiments is that they allow the researcher to manipulate dependent and independent variables and to control for internal sources of error. Some social psychologists, however, question the usefulness of laboratory experiments. They maintain that the experimental environment is artificial and that it is therefore difficult to apply the results obtained to social processes in the "real world." Indeed, there is some evidence indicating that some subjects in laboratory experiments will attempt to present themselves in ways they think will meet the approval of the experimenter.[9] Other research indicates that subjects who are aware of the hypotheses being tested will react very differently from those who do not know what the experiment is all about.[10]

Such difficulties lead some social psychologists to question the validity of the experimental approach itself. Kenneth Gergen, for example, argues that people who learn of findings from social psychological experiments undergo what he calls an "enlightenment effect." Once they become aware of the substance of the experiments, people will change their behavior and thereby contradict the previous social psychological proposition.[11] Others criticize experiments on the grounds that it is difficult to generalize from small samples of people who respond in artificial settings to a population at large. Surveys and natural field studies are seen by some social psychologists as effective alternatives to laboratory experiments.[12]

SURVEYS AND NATURAL FIELD STUDIES

Surveys may consist either of interviews or questionnaires. They may be designed to gather data on a large number of independent and dependent variables. For example, a question related to income and occupation may enable the researcher to account for important background variables such as social class. Other background variables, such as religion, race, and geographical region, may be similarly taken into consideration. As we shall shortly see, a large number of scales and measurement devices exist. These enable the researcher to take into consideration important social psychological variables such as personal attitudes and beliefs, aspects of personality, and conceptions of self.

An important difference between experiments and surveys concerns the fact that survey researchers do not always have a before-after framework with which to work, even though they typically enter the field with a specific set of hypotheses. Let us suppose that you are a survey researcher interested in whether peers influence alcohol consumption among adolescents. A "representative sample" of youths may be selected and a questionnaire designed that attempts to measure (1) how much alcohol youths consume, (2) whether their consumption is a problem (dependent variables), (3) whether or not their friends drink, and (4) if so, how much (independent variable). The survey researcher also will want to obtain information on potentially important background or intervening variables that could affect the relationship between alcohol consumption and peer influence. These may include the adolescents' exposure to mass media, social class, religion, family attitude toward alcohol consumption, familial relations, school performance, self-esteem, and so on.

Ideally, you have developed a theoretical framework in terms of which you will analyze this information once it is collected. For example, you may have hypothesized that peer influence will have a greater impact on drinking behavior when parental controls are weak.[13] In this case, we might hypothesize that alcohol use will be significantly higher among adolescents whose parents exercised minimal sanctions against drinking and whose friends are alcohol users.

Natural field studies are ways in which researchers may attempt to combine the benefits of experiments and surveys. There are two types of natural field studies: *natural experiments* and *field experiments*. Natural experiments are those in which the independent variable occurs naturally—that is, they do not result from any manipulation by the researcher. One example of this type of research is Silverman and Shaw's study of student response to racial integration.[14] After a court order required desegregation in some Florida schools, the researchers were able to measure its effects on students in integrated schools.

One difficulty with natural experiments is that the treatment is not under the control of the experimenter. For this reason, it is often difficult to obtain a baseline measure (pretest) prior to the treatment. In these cases the researcher must compare the results on the posttest with results from other settings in which no treatment has occurred. For example, if you want to measure effects of integration on students' racial attitudes, and if you are unable to measure those attitudes before integration takes place, you may have to compare the attitudes of racially integrated students with those of *other* students who have not yet been integrated. You would have to *assume* that the two groups were similar in all other important respects. Unless it can be demonstrated that the two different groups are equivalent, these *cross-sectional* studies are not as convincing as are those in which a change can be observed in the same sample.

J. Michael Ross's *longitudinal* study of parental attitudes toward school integration attempts to avoid some of the difficulties of cross-sectional studies.[15] Ross had an informed hunch that a federal court desegregation order would be announced shortly in a large eastern city. Acting on that hunch, he interviewed city residents prior to the court order. After the court order, he reinterviewed the same people to see to what extent their attitudes had changed.

Although Ross's longitudinal approach avoids some of the problems arising in connection with cross-sectional designs, it raises other difficulties. He used a "panel" study—one in which the same group of people is interviewed over time. When using this technique, the researcher must be careful to avoid confusing the effects of the independent variable with possible effects of the interview itself. Ross, for example, had to make certain his initial interviews did not sensitize the respondent and affect "posttest" responses (i.e., responses received after the "treatment," namely, the court order). One way in which to deal with this is to have a series of posttests at different points in time. The researcher may also select a portion of the sample on which an after-only design is used to compare their responses with those who are given the pretest.

Ross was both smart and lucky. Had the court found for the defendents in this case, Ross would not have had any treatment (i.e., no court order), and his efforts and energies in interviewing all those people would have been wasted. To avoid such difficulties, some social psychologists try to induce treatments in natural settings. Field experiments are different from natural experiments in that the treatment in the former is under the control of the experimenter.

One intriguing use of field experiments that did not use surveys was employed by social psychologist Murray Melbin. Melbin was interested in exploring the quality of life in what he termed "incessant communities."[16] These are settings that function for continuous 24-hour periods (e.g., all-night groceries, 24-hour cafeterias, hospital emergency rooms). Melbin hypothesized that these settings are similar or analogous to frontiers. He argued that time,

like space, has its underexplored and underexploited areas. Nighttime, he suggested, is one such underexplored temporal area. For this reason, the behavior
of people in incessant communities should share certain similarities with the
behavior of people in spatial and geographical frontiers such as the American
West.

People who are exploring new geographical frontiers are known to be
more helpful to each other than are nonfrontier people. Hence, Melbin
hypothesized that nighttime people would be more helpful than their daytime
counterparts. To test this, he employed the "lost key" experiment. A key with
instructions for how to return it by mail was left in both incessant and noninces-
sant settings. Those keys left in the incessant setting were more frequently
returned. What differentiates Melbin's field experiment from Ross's natural
field experiment was that Melbin was able to manipulate the treatment through
placing the keys in different settings. It is highly unlikely (we are pleased to
state) that judges, legislatures, and decision-making bodies will accommodate
their decisions to the research needs of social psychologists. Accordingly, those
interested in studying the effect of such decisions must be able to coordinate
their research schedules with the decisions. Needless to say, this is usually
very difficult to do.

MEASURING ATTITUDES

The concept of attitude is one of the most central as well as one of the most
elusive concepts in social psychology. For many years, it was considered to
be the cornerstone of the discipline, and it still occupies a very prominent
if not a central position. Part of the difficulty in discussing attitudes arises
because its meaning is very close to terms such as beliefs and opinions that
are used both by laypersons and social psychologists. There is no clear agreement as to where a belief or opinion ends and where an attitude begins. In
general, however, most social psychologists agree that an attitude is somehow
more complex and more central to an individual than are beliefs or opinions.
For example, you may believe that too much government spending leads to
inflation and that local control is preferable to federal control, but how many
of these beliefs must you have before you can legitimately characterize yourself
as a conservative? An attitude is deeper than any specific belief or opinion
and more comprehensive. Attitudes help us to organize our specific beliefs,
perceptions, opinions, and so on. In this sense, Gordon Allport's 1935 definition of attitudes is still an appropriate one:

> An attitude is a mental and neural state of readiness, organized through ex-
> perience, exerting a directive or dynamic influence upon the individual's response
> to all objects and situations with which it is related.[17]

Conservative attitudes, for example, underly specific opinions about government spending, the role of the federal government, foreign policy, and so on.

How does one study attitudes? Interviews and questionnaires often contain inquiries geared to measure specific attitudes. By using these devices, social

psychologists attempt to measure the *direction* of a particular attitude (e.g., whether you favor or oppose abortion) and the *intensity* of that feeling (e.g., how strongly you feel about your position). Although a simple and direct approach such as asking respondents whether they agree or disagree with specific statements is still useful in ascertaining the direction of an individual's attitude toward some particular issue, more detailed scales are used to determine both the direction and intensity of the attitude.

The *Likert scale* is an attitude scale that attempts to deal with both these attitude dimensions. Respondents are asked to indicate where they stand on a particular issue by indicating varying degrees of agreement or disagreement, approval or disapproval, and so on. With respect to abortion, for example, a person might be presented with a statement such as "It should be possible for a pregnant woman to obtain a *legal* abortion if she is not married and does not want to marry the man."[18] The respondent might then be given a 5-point scale ranging from (1) "strongly agree," (2) "agree," (3) "undecided," (4) "disagree," to (5) "strongly disagree" on which to note the intensity of his or her feelings about this issue. The respondent might also be given a number of statements related to abortion and be asked to indicate the extent of his or her agreement or disagreement. The researcher might ask, for example, whether an abortion should be possible if the woman becomes pregnant (1) as a result of rape, (2) if the family cannot afford the child, (3) if the pregnancy endangers the woman's health, or (4) if there is a strong chance of a serious defect in the baby. The respondent's attitude toward abortion is then determined by summing up the points checked on each statement (item) presented. This allows a researcher to compare the attitudes of various people on different dimensions of the abortion question. It provides the social psychologist with a more comprehensive view of how an individual respondent feels about abortion.

Likert scales are more detailed and reliable than are simple agree/disagree types of questions. They are often called *summated scales* because an individual's total score is computed by summing an individual's position on a variety of related questions.

Another type of summated scale, similar to the Likert, is known as the *semantic differential*. Here, the respondent is presented with a specific concept or idea and asked to rate that concept or idea on a 7-point scale between two contrasting word pairs. For example, the respondent might be asked to rate the president of the United States along the dimensions shown in Figure 3-3. The dimensions of evaluation (valuable/worthless, fair/unfair), potency (strong/weak), and activity (active/passive) turn out to be important explanatory variables.[19]

Cumulative scales are similar to Likert scales. Respondents are asked to indicate their agreement or disagreement with a specific statement related to a more general issue. In a cumulative scale, however, the specific items are related to each other in a hierarchical manner. Specifically, an individual who replies favorably to one statement (e.g., it should be possible for a pregnant woman to obtain an abortion if the family has a very low income and cannot afford a child) would be expected to respond favorably to another statement (e.g., it should be possible for a pregnant woman to obtain an abortion

Fair							Unfair
	1	2	3	4	5	6	7
Valuable							Worthless
	1	2	3	4	5	6	7
Strong							Weak
	1	2	3	4	5	6	7
Active							Passive
	1	2	3	4	5	6	7
Quick							Slow
	1	2	3	4	5	6	7

FIGURE 3-3

if the woman's health is seriously endangered by the pregnancy).

Perhaps the best known cumulative scale in social psychology is the *Bogardus social distance scale.* This measures people's attitudes toward other groups along the dimension of social distance. Some people will accept a given level of proximity with other specific social groups. The Bogardus scale is based on the idea that people will object to anything closer than this level of proximity. The social distance scale may be presented as done in Figure 3-4.[20] People who say they would exclude all English people from their country presumably would also say that they would refuse to admit them as visitors, grant them citizenship, have them as neighbors, and so on.

FIGURE 3-4

Directions: For each race or nationality listed below, circle each of the classifications to which you would be willing to admit the average member of that race or nationality (not the best members you have known, or the worst). Answer in terms of your first feeling reactions.

	To close kinship by marriage	To my club as personal chums	To my street as neighbors	To employment in my occupation	To citizenship in my country	As visitors only to my country	Would exclude from my country
English	1	2	3	4	5	6	7
Black	1	2	3	4	5	6	7
French	1	2	3	4	5	6	7
Chinese	1	2	3	4	5	6	7
Russian	1	2	3	4	5	6	7
And so on							

Although it is difficult to obtain 100 percent consistency using these scales, social psychologists have been able to demonstrate a fair amount of consistency with the social distance and other cumulative scales.

ATTITUDES AND BEHAVIOR

One purpose of studying attitudes is to gain a better understanding of why people behave as they do. But what if attitudes have nothing to do with behavior? At first glance, this proposition may seem ridiculous. If, for example, we say we oppose the smoking of marijuana, most people would not expect us to go home and light up a joint after work. On the other hand, this may well happen. People may smoke pot immediately after telling a social psychologist that they strongly believe pot smoking is harmful to health; that it leads to the use of harder drugs; that it ought not to be legalized.

Early studies of the relationship between attitudes and behavior produced some rather startling results. In what is now regarded as one of the classic articles in social psychology, a researcher named LaPierre[21] reported on such a study. He conducted an experiment and concluded that there was no relationship between attitudes and behavior. At a time when gasoline was much less expensive (in the early 1930s), LaPierre traveled about the United States with a young Chinese couple stopping at a total of 251 different restaurants and hotels. He and his companions were served at 250 of these places. Six months after each of these visits, LaPierre mailed a questionnaire to each of the restaurants and hotels asking them if they would "accept members of the Chinese race as guests in [their] establishment." Ironically, only one of the places gave an unqualified "yes." Ninety percent said "no," and the other 10 percent said they were "uncertain" as to what they would do. LaPierre's findings were considered to be quite dramatic in that they not only failed to demonstrate a relationship between attitudes and behavior but, in fact, showed that behavior could almost universally contradict expressed attitudes.

Although a great deal has been made of LaPierre's study, it does have some major methodological difficulties. First, there is no way of ensuring that the persons who actually served the guests were the same ones who answered the letter sent to the establishment. Second, LaPierre traveled with an extremely polite couple who spoke perfect English. There is no way of telling whether a less presentable pair would have received similar welcomes. Finally, situational constraints, such as the presence of LaPierre himself, may have caused the hotel and restaurant personnel to act differently from their attitudinal predispositions.

Since LaPierre's work in the early 1930s, a number of other researchers have investigated the attitude-behavior problem in more detail. In one study, a university professor administered to his class a questionnaire containing a number of questions related to cheating on examinations. He then gave his class five exams over a five-week period. After the exam, the papers were collected and then returned to the students who were to grade their own exams. What the students did not know, however, was that the professor had already recorded their initial answers. Over 75 percent of the class cheated at least once during the five-week period. The interesting point, however, is that there is almost no correlation between the students' reported attitudes about cheating and whether or not they actually cheated.[22]

A number of studies have investigated the attitude-behavior problem in connection with racial attitudes. Some of these studies show only a moderate relationship between attitudes and behavior. In one study, the researchers measured the racial attitudes of a number of introductory sociology students at a large midwest university. Students in the upper and lower quartiles of the scale (the most prejudiced 25 percent and the least prejudiced 25 percent) were then shown slides of interracial couples engaged in everyday conversation. The subjects were told that these pictures were being made for the purpose of improving interracial attitudes and were asked if they would themselves be willing to pose for similar photographs. The subjects were asked to sign a document authorizing the use of their photographs in a variety of settings. Surprisingly, there was only a slight relationship between the students' degree of prejudice and their willingness to authorize the use of the photographs.[23]

A second study compared the racial attitudes of 262 homeowners with their willingness to sign a petition declaring that they had no objection to black families moving into the neighborhood. Once again, attitudes were only partially correlated with the actual behavior of signing the petition.[24]

The inability to establish a strong correlation between attitudes and behavior is indeed of no small concern to social psychologists who considered attitudes to be the cornerstone of their discipline. This concern was expressed by one social psychologist who surmised that "Since attitudes . . . play no real role in behavior, an intense nothing contributes no more than a moderate nothing."[25]

It appears, however, that the problem is not so much that attitudes do not affect behavior (indeed, as we shall see, recent research demonstrates such a connection) but that the nature of the relationship between attitudes and behavior is somewhat more complex than some of the early researchers supposed. An individual may have different attitudes. There may be situational factors that interfere with a person acting according to his or her own attitudes. Beyond these factors, social norms or even laws may affect behavior. With respect to racial prejudice, for example, it would not be wise (since the passage of the civil rights amendments) for a restauranteur or hotel manager to admit that his or her establishment discriminates against any minority group, since such an admission would be certain to result in bad press at a minimum and possibly even legal action. Even the most racist restauranteur would be wiser to hold his or her tongue.

The complexity of the attitude-behavior problem may be seen if we take the general question of school desegregation as an example. Let us assume that a judge in "City X" finds the schools in that city to have been segregated and orders busing as a remedy to integrate the schools. Now let us say you have three options: (1) comply with the court order and be bused to an integrated school, (2) evade the court order by moving to another city or attending a private school, or (3) attempt to overthrow or otherwise obstruct the implementation of the court order. The decision you will make will be affected by a variety of factors. These may include your interracial attitudes, your attitudes about the law, and your feelings about busing. These different attitudes may even compete with each other. For example, some people may genuinely want to support integration but oppose certain types of busing plans. Others may be prejudiced and quite opposed to desegregation; they may feel, however, that they should "obey the law." Beyond this, perceptions of certain situational factors not necessarily directly related to desegregation may affect action decisions. For example, you may be more likely to comply if you think you will get a good education at the integrated school. Similarly, you will be less likely to attempt to obstruct the court order if you think you might be thrown in jail for such behavior. Other factors may also be important. The opinions and attitudes of your friends may affect your decision as well. Finally, certain "facts of life" may impinge upon your actions. Suppost that your attitudes lead you to want to evade the court order. This option may be blocked by the fact that you cannot afford to move to another neighborhood or by the fact that there are no private schools you can afford to attend.

Recent research on the attitude-behavior problem has attempted to account for considerations like these and has provided some hopeful results. One major study concerned the very sensitive issue of integrated housing. A total of 640 white adult homeowners were given a detailed questionnaire concerning interracial issues. One question specifically concerned racially open housing policies. It asked the respondents how they would vote for (1) a law allowing homeowners to decide to whom their houses can be sold, even if they decide not to sell it to someone because of race, and (2) a law prohibiting homeowners from refusing to sell their houses on the basis of race. Approximately three months later, different interviewers acting as volunteers supporting legislation (against water pollution) returned to the respondents and asked them to sign a petition on open housing. About 80 percent of the sample acted in a manner consistent with their previously expressed attitude on this issue. The researchers attribute the attitudinally consistent behavior to the high degree of congruence between the way in which the question eliciting the attitude was phrased (i.e., support for a law) and the behavioral criterion (i.e., signing a petition). They also cite the fact that situational interference was minimized in the second interview and that attitudes about this particular issue are very stable, forestalling difficulties resulting from competition between different attitudes.[26]

Subsequently, a number of other researchers have increased the attitude-behavior correlation by controlling or otherwise minimizing the effects of other attitudes and external interference.[27] In summary, it appears that attitudes are indeed related to behavior, but researchers must always remember that neither attitudes nor behavior exist in a vacuum.

MEASURING ASPECTS OF PERSONALITY

Personality is a salient issue in both common discourse and social psychology. How many times have you heard someone say of someone else that he or she has "no personality" or "a lot of personality"? Social psychologists do not use the term personality in this sense. Personality is not some *thing* of which individuals have varying quantities. It is not an attribute of those persons who are more lively, vivacious, or sociable than others.

For social psychologists, personality consists of a collection of traits that seem to characterize an individual. These traits apply to a variety of characteristics. In this section, we will describe the efforts of some psychologists to measure some of these aspects of personality.

Locus of Control

Who controls your destiny? Does your life depend on factors beyond your control? Or are you the architect and designer of your own destiny? If you believe that people have control over their own lives and destinies—that their outcomes in life will be determined by their actions—then you are likely to be characterized as an "internal" by some social psychologists. If you think that a person's outcome is determined by factors beyond his or her control, such as fate, luck, power, and so forth, you are likely to be classified as an "external." Some researchers have concluded that "internals" are generally more assertive and aggressive than are "externals" and generally have more "successful" undertakings.[28]

A number of different measuring devices have been developed to measure locus of control. One of these is the *Nowicki-Strickland personal reaction survey*. This consists of a series of yes-no questions such as "Do you believe that if somebody studies hard enough, he or she can pass a subject?" or "Are you the kind of person who believes that planning ahead makes things turn out better?" If you answered "yes" to both questions, then you are likely to be classified as an internal.

Locus of Causation

One concept related to the notion of locus of control (although it is analytically and empirically distinct) is the concept of locus of causation.[29] Locus of control refers to the extent to which people feel that they have some control over the contingencies of their reinforcement (i.e., the outcomes or consequences of their behavior). Locus of causation refers to the extent to which individuals feel that they are the source or the "author" of their own behavior, namely, the extent to which individuals believe that their behavior is motivated by their own personal desires and intentions rather than by the desires and intentions of others. Individuals who feel that they are the source of their own behavior are referred to as *origins*; those who believe their behavior to be determined by others are referred to as *pawns*. Locus of control is measured through the administration of a questionnaire; locus of causation is assessed in a more open-ended manner. Subjects may be asked to write a story in which some action is performed. Raters then assess the extent to which the subject of that action is an "origin" or "pawn."

Anomie and Alienation

Sociologists need continually to remind psychologists that *anomie*, as the concept was originally formulated by the French sociologist Emile Durkheim, is a characteristic of *societies* and not *individuals*. Specifically, anomie arises where the bonds holding a society together dissipate. It is manifested by a kind of normlessness. Nevertheless, the concept of anomie has been applied to individuals. An anomic individual is one who feels a sense of normlessness. This person feels disaffected from society. He or she feels a lack of power or influence. Anomie in this usage bears certain similarities to the concept of alienation.

Once again, social psychologists have developed a variety of measures of anomie. One such scale consists of statements such as "I often feel awkward and out of place" and "The trouble with the world today is that most people really don't believe in anything." If you agree with both these statements, you are leaning toward a state of anomie.[30]

One alienation scale contains three different dimensions: powerlessness, normlessness, and social isolation. Respondents are given a 5-point Likert scale ranging from strongly agree to strongly disagree for 24 different items, such as:

For powerlessness: We are just so many cogs in the machinery of life.
For normlessness: The only thing one can be sure of today is that he can be sure of nothing.
For social isolation: Sometimes I feel all alone in the world.[31]

Measures of anomie and alienation are often valuable for predicting political attitudes and voting behavior. In one very interesting study, the researchers showed that workers who do piecemeal labor in an assembly-line type of situation are much more alienated than are other workers.[32]

Authoritarianism

The California F scale was developed to measure "pro-facist" and "implicit antidemocratic" tendencies in personality. The theory of authoritarianism is based on a neo-Freudian approach to socialization (see Chapter 4). In a very simplified form, this theory asserts that children raised in an overly strict and hostile environment come to identify with the more aggressive and authoritarian roles or models. Through this process, these individuals develop an "authoritarian personality" characterized by traits such as conventionalism, authoritarian aggression, stereotyping, submissiveness to authority, destructiveness, cynicism, and a concern with power. Following is a list of some of these variables and a sample of statements with which authoritarian individuals would be likely to agree.

Variable: *Conventionalism*—rigid adherence to conventional middle-class values.

Sample statement: A person who has bad manners, habits, and breeding can hardly expect to be liked and accepted by decent people."

Variable: *Authoritarian submission*—submissive uncritical attitude toward idealized moral authorities of the ingroup.

Sample statement: "Obedience and respect for authority are the most important virtues children should learn."

Variable: *Authoritarian aggression*—tendency to be on the lookout for, and to condemn, reject, and punish people who violate conventional values.

Sample statement: "Homosexuals are hardly better than criminals and ought to be severely punished."

Variable: *Stereotyping*—the disposition to think in rigid categories.

Sample statement: "People can be divided into two distinct classes: the weak and the strong."

Variable: *Power*—preoccupation with the dominance/submission, strong/weak, leader/follower dimension of relationships.

Sample statement: "What youth needs most is strict discipline, rugged determination, and the will to work and fight for family and country."[33]

The California F scale has been revised many times. The "new F scale" includes many of the same variables, with some extras such as orderliness and liking for routine, rigidity, and intolerance of ambiguity. As we have already seen, authoritarian individuals were more obedient in the Milgram obedience studies and made better guards and prisoners in the Zimbardo prison simulation (see Chapter 1). Authoritarianism is also highly correlated with racial prejudice and intolerance.[34] Although in the past, authoritarianism was linked primarily with "right-wing" politics, recent researchers admit the possibility of "authoritarianism of the left" as well.

The preceding are just a few of many scales that social psychologists use to measure aspects of personality. No one measure pretends to "tell all" about personality. Rather, each is concerned with parts of the puzzle that is itself continuously evolving and growing. Yet such concepts help us to understand why some people with certain types of traits and characteristics are more likely to engage in some forms of behavior than are others. Who we are, who we think we are, and who we might like to be shape what we do. Even very formal and standardized activities may be affected by aspects of individual personality. One study, for example, shows that the personalities of people who analyze and predict technological development and social change have an impact on the quality of the models they develop.[35]

Self-concept and Self-esteem

The notion of self is analytically distinguishable from the notion of personality. The latter applies to some relatively enduring characteristics of an individual; the former is used to describe a process. The self is composed of how we are viewed by others. The self changes as our social milieus change. We shall have more to say about this concept throughout the book. For now, however, suffice it to note that the person you think you are (self-concept) and how much you like and value this person can be determinants of how well you fare in life. For example, children with high self-esteem have been shown to be more assertive than children with lower self-esteem. High self-esteem children also participate more frequently in extracurricular activities and may do better in their academic pursuits.[36] Social psychologists have developed a number of different scales that measure self-concept and self-esteem.

Perhaps the most extensive measuring device is the *Tennessee Self-concept Scale.* This measures self-concept along five dimensions: physical self, moral self, personal self, family self, and social self. Respondents are asked to indicate the extent to which they think a number of statements pertaining to these dimensions are true or false along a 5-point Likert scale ranging from completely false to completely true. Sample statements include

I have a healthy body. (physical)
I am satisfied with my moral behavior. (moral)
I have a lot of self-control. (personal)
I am a member of a happy family. (family)
I am as sociable as I want to be. (social)[37]

This scale enables the researcher to analyze various dimensions of self-esteem and self-concept. Results from this scale correlate fairly well with other measures of mental health and social well-being. Generally, people with high self-esteem tend to be more mentally stable and have better social relationships.[38]

Another fairly simple and direct test, used widely by social psychologists who follow a symbolic interactionist viewpoint is known as the *Twenty Statements Test (TST)*.[39] Here, respondents are required to ask themselves the question "Who am I?" 20 times. Each answer may then be coded in terms of the extent to which it reflects a derogatory or positive self image.

In some ways, the most valuable aspect of the 20 statements test is its open-endedness. The respondents themselves define the dimensions along which they will be rated. In this sense, the test may tell us more about self-concept than self-esteem. Results suggest that people are more likely to choose terms related to social roles (consenual categories) than they are to choose more idiosyncratic terms (subconsenual categories). For example, respondents were more likely to select terms such as "girl," "student," "Baptist," "from Chicago," before they selected terms like "unhappy," "bored," "thin," or "good."[40]

Another measuring device more specifically related to self-esteem is the *Self-esteem scale.* Here, the respondent indicates the extent of his or her agreement or disagreement (along a point scale) with a series of Likert items such as "I feel that I have a number of good qualities" and "I feel that I do not have much to be proud of."

Most of these scales allow the researcher to measure self-acceptance as well as self-esteem. Self-acceptance refers to the extent to which individuals are satisfied with their current selves. This concept attempts to ascertain differences between an individual's "real self" (one's present self-conception) and one's "ideal self" (who and what an individual would like to be).

Methods for Studying Communication

A variety of techniques have been used by social psychologists to study communication. These range from systematic codings systems designed to capture all or part of communicative events to more informal observational techniques. Experiments and natural field studies also have been used to analyze the effects of different aspects of the communication process. In the following pages, we will review some of these methods as they have been applied to different aspects of the communication process.

Interaction Process Analysis

Interaction process analysis provides a set of categories for coding "communicative acts." Coding requires an assessment of both the act and its socioemotional purpose. For example, the code for a remark such as "Where will the next meeting be?" would be "Asks for orientation" (number 7). Another remark, such as "You're a cruel person" might be categorized as "shows antagonism" (number 12). All communicative acts are placed in one of the following 12 categories:

1. *Shows solidarity*, raises others' status, gives help reward.
2. *Shows tension release*, jokes, laughs, shows satisfaction.
3. *Agrees*, shows passive acceptance, understands, concurs, complies.
4. *Gives suggestion*, direction implying autonomy for others.
5. *Gives suggestion*, evaluation, analysis, expressive feeling wit.
6. *Gives orientation*, information, clarification, repeats, confirms.
7. *Asks for orientation*, information, repetition, confirmation.
8. *Asks for opinions*, evaluation, analysis expression of feelings.
9. *Asks for suggestion*, direction, possible ways of action.
10. *Disagrees*, shows passive rejection, formality, withholds help.
11. *Shows tension*, asks for help, withdraws out of field.
12. *Shows antagonism*, deflates other's status, defends or asserts self.[41]

By counting the number of times communicative acts fall within specific categories, it is possible to create "profiles" of groups or individuals within groups. For example, in a supportive group geared toward making interaction comfortable for members, we would likely find a large number of communicative acts in categories 1 through 3. If we had another group, where there was a democratic-type leader, a large number of his responses would probably fall in the categories 5 and 6. The communicative acts in a group with a less democratic leader would probably fall in categories 10 through 12.

Aside from being used to develop profiles of groups or individuals, interaction process analysis has been used to study the relationships between certain types of communication and the responses they elicit. Some research, for example, indicates that stimuli expressing dependency tend to elicit responses expressing assertiveness.[42]

Methods for Studying Naturally Occurring Conversation

As discussed in Chapter 2, sociologists have had a renewed interest in the study of conversation. Research in this area is guided by the idea that the analyst, in "making sense" out of a conversation, should have available neither more nor less information (in the way of cues, etc.) than do the participants in the conversation. In this way, the researchers are required to use the same rules and procedures of interpretation as the interactants. At the same time, the researcher needs all the information available to the interactants. This means that the researcher should work in a perceptual field that is similar in as many ways as possible to the perceptual field in which the participants are working. For this reason, conversational analysts often use audio tapes of telephone conversations because these provide the researcher with essentially the same cues as the participants in the conversation.

An important advance in the study of conversation has been the development of a relatively simple notation system for transcribing these conversations into a written form. This system enables the analyst to represent subverbal as well as verbal aspects of the talk. It also allows the researcher to account for the timing and sequencing of utterances, an important focus of the conversational approach.

As discussed in Chapter 2, analysts are particularly interested in describing the processes through which turns at talk are allocated in ordinary conversation. To this end, analysts have devised certain ways of characterizing the turn-allocation process. For example, double brackets may be used to represent simultaneous starts at turns at talk.

> Person A: ⌐I used to read when I was young.
>
> Person B: └I used to read spy novels.

Single brackets represent utterances that overlap but do not begin at the same point in time.

> A: I used to read spy novels.
>
> B: └mysteries.

Through the use of such notational devices, analysts are able to discern routine ways in which turns are allocated in the course of naturally occurring conversations.[43]

Recently, attempts have been made to link visual cues with conversational units. Psychologists have long been interested in the functions of gaze and head position in the turn-allocation process. Conversational analysts through the use of video tapes have attempted to show how gaze may be correlated with different components of a turn at talk. In a recent paper, two conversational analysts have shown how topics covered in the course of a single sentence of talk shifted in part as a function of the response of the person to whom gaze was directed at the time. The completion of the sentence in this instance was shown to be a "social construction," dependent at least in part on the facial-gestural responses of the intended audience.[44]

Gaze

As discussed in the preceding chapter, gaze plays an important role as both a conveyor of information about social relationships and as a part of

the social interaction process. However, measuring gaze is an extremely problematic matter. It is difficult to estimate a person's peripheral vision or depth
of field. Gaze aversion, especially to the extent that may involve only the movement of pupils or eyelids, is equally difficult to assess.

A simple system for monitoring gaze behavior has been developed by
A. Kendon and his colleagues[45] to reflect gross vision direction.

Signifies looking at other's eyes	O
Signifies looking down	O↓
Signifies looking left	←O
Signifies looking right	O→
Signifies looking up	O↑

Numbers can be placed next to symbols to indicate the degree to which vision directed in a left, right, or upward downward direction. For example, 0 5
would indicate that a person is looking up at roughly of 15-degree angle.

Posture and Touch

Other techniques have been developed for the study of posture and
touch. Perhaps the most detailed system for representing postural positions
has been developed by Hewes, who identified over 300 different postures.[46]
As an anthropologist, Hewes was interested in the extent to which postures
varied in different cultures. Hewes's system consists of a series of drawings
representing different standing, sitting, and kneeling positions.

Edward Hall[47] has developed a notation system for representing aspects
of posture. Numerical values are assigned to gross postural positions, for example, sitting, standing, and leaning. Nonnumerical symbols are often used
to indicate body orientation. For example, the symbol P9 indicates that the
interactants are standing face to face. If this were preceded by the number
4 (for sitting), it would indicate that the interactants were sitting in a face-to-
face position.

Edward Hall and his colleagues have attempted to develop a coding
system that enables the researcher to analyze touch in an interactional contest. Numbers are assigned to various touch gestures so that sequences can
be recorded.[48] When combined with other aspects of the communicative act,
this should provide a broader view, helping the researcher to discern better
the significance of touch in social interaction.

Researchers have used a variety of structured and unstructured methods
to study communication. These methods vary in terms of their precision. One
problem that persists whether one employs a structured or unstructured technique concerns the fact that, although the study of communication may be
divided into separate channels, the significance of any specific communicative event involves all channels. In this sense, communication is made up of
different pieces organized into standardized units. These are, as one expert
puts it, "recognizable at a glance and recordable with a stroke."[49] Part of the
challenge for research in communications for the future will be the development of recording instruments that enable one to capture a global view of
the communicative event. This global view also will need to include some refer-

ence to the context of the communicative event. In this way, communication studies will come to address questions that are important for social psychology.

QUALITATIVE METHODS

A review of the methods we have examined thus far will show that the underlying model of science on which they are based is that of the natural sciences. The observation of behavior, the use of experiments, the efforts to observe regularities, and the attempts to detect relationships between "independent" and "dependent" variables will be familiar to every student of the "natural sciences."

Some social psychologists, however, have raised questions about this approach when used to understand human beings. We cannot discuss all the philosophical, theoretical, and methodological issues involved, but we will try to suggest the kind of differences involved by describing some of the methods that can properly be regarded as lying within the qualitative rubric.

Participant Observation

One of the goals of participant observation is a detailed description of the culture and social life of specific individuals and collectivities. As ethnographies, such descriptions may focus on the values and norms of different groups, their everyday round of life, rituals, socialization practices, and rules of inclusion and exclusion. Two criteria by which such ethnographies often are evaluated are the richness and completeness of the descriptions and their adequacy in addressing important theoretical and analytical issues. As we shall see later in this book, for example, a participant observation study of Little League teams was valuable not only because it provided a rich and detailed account of social life in the Little Leagues, but also because it described how interaction between Little Leaguers serves as a means for defining gender identity and learning sexual stereotypes.

Participant observation is as much an exercise in social psychology as it is a relevant methodological technique. That is, the participant observer, to maintain his or her role in the social setting, will have to understand a great deal about the culture and social structure of the collectivity under investigation. In this sense, participant observation is one of the most difficult of the methodologies used in social psychology. As one expert puts it,

> The price of doing fieldwork is extremely high, not in dollars (fieldwork is less expensive than most other kinds of research) but in physical and mental effort. It is very hard work. It is exhausting to lead two lives simultaneously. A double life is frequently required. Particularly energetic fieldworkers may risk added fatigue by trying to live a "private life" in addition to those other lives.[50]

The participant observer is by necessity a practicing social psychologist. Participant observers often classify their activities in terms of their relationship with the group or individuals they are studying. Their role in the setting can be placed somewhere along a continuum ranging from a complete participant to complete observer.

In the role of complete participant, the researcher's scientific purposes are hidden from the subjects of the research. Festinger[51] and his colleagues report that to study a group of individuals who believed the end of the world was at hand, it was necessary for them to conceal their true identities as social psychologists and pose as traveling business executives. Participation in activities with groups making doomsday prophecies often made life very uncomfortable for the researchers.

A more controversial use of the role of complete participant is found in Laud Humphreys's study *Tearoom Trade*.[52] To study homosexuals who frequented a restroom in a local park, Humphreys posed as lookout for them. He concealed his identity as a doctoral student in sociology. Although the more troublesome aspect of Humphreys's research concerned his use of individuals' license plate numbers to reinterview them at a later point in time (again, under false pretenses), his posing as a lookout raises serious questions about the obligations that the participant observer has a participant and toward his or her subjects (e.g., what does the researcher do if the subjects become lawbreakers?).

The role of complete participant is perhaps less troublesome when the researcher is already a member of the group being studied. Howard Becker's[53] insights into the world of jazz musicians were enhanced by the fact Becker is himself an accomplished musician. This enabled him to gain a more complete understanding of the musician subculture and its relationship to the society at large.

In the *participant as observer role*, the researchers will make their identities known to the individuals under study. They will attempt to use their position as sympathetic inquirer to obtain relevant information. Elliott Liebow used this role in his study of black street corner men in urban America. As a white, Jewish anthropologist, Liebow did not attempt to disguise his role. Rather, he made his purpose clear and attempted to enlist the aid of "informants" in gaining information on the culture of street corner life. This requires the establishment of trust between the researcher and his or her subjects. Liebow's success in establishing such trust was demonstrated when his chief informant admitted to lying about a particular aspect of street corner life. Liebow's notes of this event are interesting in this regard.

> All of us left Tally's room together. Tally grabbed my arm and pulled me aside near the storefront church and said, "I want to talk to you." With no further introduction, he looked me straight in the eye and started talking.
>
> "I'm a liar. I been lying to you all along now and I want to set it straight, even if it means we can't be friends no more. I only lied to you about one thing. Everything else I told you is gospel truth but I did lie about one thing and that makes me a liar. I know that some white people think that if you catch a man in a lie one time you can't never trust him after that. And even if you feel that way about it I still got to tell you. You remember when you first come around here, I told you. . . . Well, that was a lie. . . . I didn't think nothing of it at first, but then you and me started going around together and when we started getting real tight, my conscience started whomping me. I kept looking for a place to

tell you but it never seemed right. Then tonight . . . I knew this was the right time. I knew you were going to find out and I didn't want you to find out from somebody else."[54]

William Foote Whyte in his study of Italian street corner men was able to gain a similar kind of cooperation from his chief informant. At times, the informant's role *qua* informant may even interfere with normal activities as Doc, Whyte's informant, once told him.

"You've slowed me up plenty since you've been down here. Now, when I do something, I have to think what Bill Whyte would want to know about it and how I can explain it. Before, I used to do things by instinct!"[55]

In the role of *participant as observer,* the researchers must be careful not to take advantage of their subjects. They must also see that they, in turn, are not exploited by members of the group under study. Liebow, for example, reports that many of the subjects of his study recognized his middle-class position and came to him for a variety of favors. On the other hand, researchers may find that they can readily provide legitimate assistance to the subjects. Liebow, for example, assisted one of the street corner men with certain legal problems.

Even in the role of participant as observer, however, the researcher, to some extent must become a member of the group being studied. This may require changing certain aspects of one's habits and personal style and adapting to the folkways of the group under investigation. Liebow's experience is worth retelling in this regard.

Almost from the beginning, I adopted the dress and something of the speech of the people with whom I was in most frequent contact, as best I could without looking silly or feeling uncomfortable. I came close in dress (in warm weather, tee or sport shirt and khakis or other slacks) with almost no effort at all. My vocabulary and diction changed, but not radically. Cursing and using ungrammatical constructions at times—though they came easily—did not make any of my adaptations confusable with the speech of the street. Thus, while remaining conspicuous in speech and perhaps in dress, I had dulled some of the characteristics of my background. I probably made myself more accessible to others, and certainly more acceptable to myself. This last point was forcefully brought home to me one evening when, on my way to a professional meeting, I stopped off at the Carry-out in a suit and tie. My loss of ease made me clearly aware that the change in dress, speech, and general carriage was as important for its effect on me as it was for its effect on others.[56]

Success as a participant or observer may depend on one's ability to be sensitive to such subtle aspects of group life. The subtleties, themselves, are a central focus of the investigation.

The role of observer as participant entails less actual participation in group activities. The researcher, however, may become a relatively important figure in the research setting. School ethnographers, for example, rarely play an active classroom role; they are not students, teachers, or administrators. Yet it is necessary that school ethnographers spend a substantial amount of time in schools. On some occasions, school ethnographers may assume roles as aides. Most of the time, however, they are in an extremely tenuous position. Administrators may view the observer as an ally of the teachers; teachers are likely to view them as allies of the students. Students, for their part, have a tendency to view almost all adults with some suspicion. In recently integrated schools, the observer's position may be made even more tenuous as a result of racial divisions within the school. Because of these difficulties, the observer as participant in the school must be extremely cautious in how he or she gains access to the school and how he/she handles himself or herself in different social situations.

Because of these difficulties, the observer as participant may attempt to augment his or her insights and observations with other methodological techniques.

A manual recently prepared for researchers interested in desegregating schools suggests a number of auxiliary data sources that can be of use to the ethnographer.[57] These include informal interviews, sociometric tests, video tapes, content analysis of student newspapers, and school records.

The role of *complete observer* is less problematic in that the observer is unseen. Researchers coding interaction or recording nonverbal behavior through one-way mirrors or in other unobtrusive ways illustrate this kind of research role.

In addition to being sensitive to their role in the social setting under investigation, participant observers also must understand how the nature of their participation may change over time. Researchers note that there are different stages in the process of participant observation.

The first stage is gaining access. This entails obtaining formal permission (if necessary) and establishing the contact and personal bonds necessary for field work. This often means cultivating friendships with highly respected members of the group one is studying. The second stage is initial socialization into the group. The researcher learns what behavior is appropriate to the group under investigation. Third is a stage of regular participation. Here the researcher may participate as a group member in regular activities. Finally, completion of the research may require disengagement from the group.

Each of these stages contains potential learning experiences. Gaining access and disengagement may be informative about rules for inclusion and participation. Being socialized into the group may provide insights about subtle behavioral norms.

Advocates of participant observation claim that it has a number of advantages over other methodologies. In the first place, it provides direct experience. This enables the researcher to gain a more complete understanding of the meaning that social events may have for participants. Beyond this, the researcher can "check" on the validity of data gathered through other methodological techniques. Accounts of events gathered through interviews may be confirmed or disconfirmed by actual observations. It also helps to augment other methods. For example, the researcher may obtain information on matters that the group may prefer not to talk about "in public." Such information may not be at all available if one relied exclusively upon an interview approach.

Participant observation has been criticized on the grounds that it is difficult to rule out alternative hypotheses or establish clear causal relationships. Beyond this, investigation of specific cases does not provide for a high degree of generalizability. Participant observers respond that an in-depth understanding of specific social situations may be as useful as less in-depth studies that are more general. Participant observation does not allow researchers to specify the relationships between variables in as controlled a manner as experimental or survey approaches. Efforts have been made to develop strategies through which the qualitative researcher may account for alternative explanations and establish causal relationships between variables. The method of analytic induction,[58] in part, provides for this by requiring the researcher to search for "negative cases" (i.e., cases that contradict the basic hypothesis). This enables researchers to then qualify or reformulate their hypotheses.

Depth Interviews

Participant observation is often used together with *depth* or *focused interviews*. However, in some ways, each method may have advantages for different types of issues. Participant observation can provide an in-depth knowledge of *social life* within a particular group or collectivity; depth interviews can provide a great deal of knowledge about *individuals* who are members of specific groups or collectivities. Later in this book, for example, we shall see how depth interviews can provide insights into the life of young people in our society.

One very interesting study[59] of the literature on interviewing was made to document the argument that not only is very little known about the art of interviewing, but that this "lack of knowledge cannot be substantially removed through the usual variable approach that seeks the laws of interviewing by means of traditional statistical methods."[60]

The study reviews four books on interviewing and concludes that, although each of them sees the interview somewhat differently, they are in substantial agreement. They all view the interview as a measurement device. The purpose of this device is to collect valid and reliable information. Like other measurement devices, it is subject to distortions because of human fallibility. The chief task of researchers, is, therefore, to identify errors and control or eliminate them. This in turn has given rise to an enormous research literature addressed to the discovery and remedy of error in interview situations. There do not, however, appear to be any satisfactory definitions of "error." Sandra Halberstam concludes that

> the core of the problem is that the question/answer process is not a self-contained one. Thus, in different contexts, an identical question may be a loaded or extreme item or a vague or an explanatory item. Error, then, is not an intrinsic quality of a question, but a function of the investigator's purpose . . . we must not merely look at which words are used, but how the context is involved in the question/answer process as well.[61]

To deal effectively with the social context of the interview, several pieces of advice have been provided by Raymond L. Gordon.[62] He tells us:

1) Since a variety of strategies, tactics, and techniques are possible, no final choices should be made until after the problem has been clearly specified as well as the formation relevant to this problem. Thus, there is no rational way in which to decide to use black or white interviewers until we know what information the interviewer will be seeking and from whom. Some kinds of information will be provided as readily by black respondents to white interviewers as to black interviewers; other kinds of information will not. One study, for example, suggests that certain kinds of information on racial discrimination, the living conditions of blacks, and personal background was given as freely to white as to black interviewers. Information about black militant protest and the hostility of blacks to whites was given much less freely to white interviewers.[63]

2) Information that may be made freely available under one set of community circumstances may be completely unavailable under another set. Thus, when during a study in a community where a Textile Union of America (TWUA) strike was in progress, and textile workers were asked about their feelings vis-à-vis the TWUA, the respondents did not trust the interviewers to keep the information anonymous, as the consequences of leaking information to mill owners were potentially very serious. The study collapsed.[64]

3) Verbal communication problems arise between interviewer and respondent when the interviewer has not learned the special jargon used by the occupational group, social class, age level, ethnic group, political party, religious group, or geographic region of the respondent. Examples of difficulties arising in this connection are virtually endless. An interviewer approaching respondents in a hospital should be familiar with the meaning of such common abbreviations as "EST," "BM," "IV," "GP," "GI," "GU," and so on, (electroshock treatment, bowel movement, intravenous injection, general paresis, gastrointestinal, genitourinary). City-bred interviewers interviewing farmers should understand the meaning of such comments such as "we just built a new water closet." Anyone interviewing carpenters should understand the meaning of such remarks as "This ladder needs new dogs." Interviewers on skid row should understand what is meant by "Peter is a snowbird," and so on.[65]

But the possibility of misunderstanding goes far beyond this. In some cases, familiar words and phrases are used to convey different messages. In general, when wide differences exist between the unspoken assumptions made by a respondent and an interviewer, the danger of a breakdown in communications is always present.

4.) Regarding nonverbal communications problems, Gordon reminds us that the interviewer must listen to *how* the respondent says something. Auditory clues to which the interviewer should be attentive include changes in speed, pitch, intensity, and volume of what is being said. Beyond this there are visual clues that include variations in facial expression, gestures, and bodily position and movements of hands, feet, or head. Some respondents have learned to hide nonverbal clues to their feelings and attitudes. They can do this by either maintaining a noncommittal expression or pretending to have a set of attitudes or feelings directly opposite to those they really hold. Gordon feels that in the process of exercising this kind of control, most respondents will betray inconsistencies of one sort or another. Thus, a calm facial expression or casual tone of voice might hide an anxiety that is betrayed by twisting of the hands. Interviewers are urged to develop the habit of observing a *total* bodily response rather than only tone of voice or facial expression. "In ordinary conversation, most people look to facial expression more than to other bodily changes for clues to feelings and attitudes. Perhaps it is precisely for this reason that we learn to control the facial expressions more readily."[66]

SOCIOMETRY

The term "sociometry" has been the focus of many conflicting interpretations and misinterpretations since it was first formulated by J. L. Moreno in of his classic work, *Who Shall Survive?*[67]

As Gardner Murphy once expressed it, when Moreno and his collaborators first developed "the basic theory and method known as sociometry, it was an open question whether this was simply a technical device or the beginning of a new way of viewing human relationships. Time has shown that the latter is the case and that sociometric modes of thinking have profoundly influenced many aspects of social theory."[68]

Moreno[69] describes the *sociometric test* as an instrument that examines social structures through the measurement of the attractions and repulsions taking place between individual persons of a group. It requires respondents to choose their own associates for a group of which they are or might be a member. Specifically, the test characteristically asks participants to list a number of other persons in the group with whom they would like to engage in some specified activity (e.g., "With whom would you prefer to work?" "Which of the following persons would you prefer as a cottagemate?"). In Moreno's original classic study, his problem was to discover the networks of influence among 600 girls who lived in a training school for girls. Each girl was asked to list (in rank order) the other girls with whom she would like to share the same cottage. The choices were confidential, but each respondent knew that her choices would in fact constitute the basis for actual assignments insofar as this was possible.

Fundamental to Moreno's use of the sociometric test was the requirement that the choices listed be much more than simple attitudinal preferences. He felt that the responses should be used to restructure the groups involved. When this was not done or could not be done, he referred to the test as "near sociometric." To present and analyze the results of a sociometric test, a variety of techniques are available.[70]

The *sociogram* is a diagrammatic device for summarizing the choices and rejections made by members of a group. Circles may be used to represent each person, and lines are drawn to persons chosen or rejected (an unbroken line may represent choice, a dotted line may indicate rejection). The resulting diagram presents a graphic picture of the interrelationships of persons within the group. The character of the interrelationships described will vary, of course, with the sociometric criterion employed (e.g., group members may have different choices and rejections depending upon whether they were being asked to name a cottagemate or a workmate).

In addition to the use of sociograms, a number of statistical measures have been used to analyze sociometric data. Common to these measures is the effort to distinguish differences or deviations occurring by chance and those representing actual deviations from the group norms.[71]

Perhaps the central underlying concept of sociometry is from Moreno's conviction that "in the human sphere one cannot understand the social present unless he tries to change it."[72] Accordingly, sociometric tests that were *not* based on the premise that the structure of groups was subject to change— that the responses of "subjects" would in fact shape the new structure—such tests were at best "near sociometric."

Moreno was a psychiatrist who preferred to think of himself as a healer, not only for individual persons but for groups of all sizes as well. The methods he developed—psychodrama, role playing, and many others, in addition to sociometric tests of various kinds—were all subsumed under what he called "sociometry." We cannot examine all of them here, but we can summarize the "basic rules of psychodrama" that he offered as a guide to practitioners.[73]

1. The subject (i.e., patient, client, or protagonist) acts out his or her conflicts instead of simply talking about them. To help in this process, a psychodrama stage may be used (a three-level circular stage). If, however, no such stage is available, any informal room or space may be used.

2. The subject acts in the "here and now"—no matter when the event being enacted actually occurred (or even if it has never occurred).

3. Protagonists must be accepted with all their subjectivity. They must act out their own truth as they feel and perceive it no matter how distorted this may appear to be to the onlooker. "Retraining" can occur only after the protagonist has been allowed to construct his or her own private world. As part of this, all delusions, hallucinations, thoughts, fantasies, or projections are allowed to be part of the psychodramatic production.

4. Whenever possible, the protagonist is allowed to select the time, place, scene, and auxiliary egos needed to portray a scene.

5. Interpretation and insight giving in psychodrama is of a different kind than is that provided in verbal types of psychotherapy. Selection of scenes by the director constitutes a form of interpretation. Verbal interpretation is often completely redundant.

6. The psychodramatic director, at the conclusion of a session, draws from the group, in a postaction discussion, identifications with the subject. If no one else in the group feels free to make these identifications, the director tries to demonstrate not only his or her sympathy for the protagonist but the fact that he or she has been or is being similarly burdened.

7. One of the important outcomes of a psychodramatic session is the increased ability of the protagonist to see the world through the eyes of those persons with whom he or she is most meaningfully related.

Among the myriad techniques used in psychodrama are the following:

Self-presentation. The protagonist presents himself or herself as his or her own mother, father, brother, favorite teacher, and so on. All these roles are acted by the protagonist alone as seen through his or her own eyes.

Role Reversal. The protagonist, in an interpersonal situation, acts the role of the other person, and vice versa (e.g., a man may play the role of his mother while an auxiliary ego acting as the mother, or the actual mother herself, acts his role). For example, the mother of an 8-year old girl (Kay) shows how she argues with the daughter every morning about what clothing the child should wear to school. After each of the roles has become clear, Kay is asked to take the role of her mother, and vice versa. In the role of mother, Kay displays excessive authority and certainty, although in her own role she seemed anxiety ridden. Mother has to restrain herself considerably to be her rather withdrawn daughter. At the end of the scene, mother remarks: "Am I really as aggressive as Kay portrayed me? My poor Kay!"[74]

Double. While the protagonist portrays himself or herself, an auxiliary ego (another member of the audience or a trained assistant) is also asked to represent the patient to establish identity with the protagonist—to move, act, and behave as the protagonist does. For example, the protagonist prepares to get out of bed in the morning, and an auxiliary ego (as double) starts to speak:

DOUBLE:	Why get up? I have no reason for living.
PROTAGONIST:	True. I have no reason for living.
DOUBLE:	But I am a talented artist. There have been times when life has been very satisfying.
PROTAGONIST:	Yes, but that seems to be a long time ago.
DOUBLE:	Maybe I can get up and start to paint again.
PROTAGONIST:	Well, let's try and get up anyway and see what happens.

Both protagonist and double arise and go through motions of brushing teeth, shaving, washing, and moving together as if they were one. The auxiliary as double "becomes the link through which the patient may try to reach out into the real world."[75]

Moreno, in various places, has insisted that psychodrama did not have a theatrical origin. For him (and, he tells us, for Socrates and Plato), the theater is an imitation of and an alienation of life rather than a liberating and elevating agent (actually, it was an imitation of an imitation, since according to the philosophers, the reality of common life was a poor imitation of the high life of the immortal gods).

Moreno did several things, he tells us, to make psychodrama more relevant than conventional theater. To overcome the separation between actors and spectators, he completely eliminated spectators. In the psychodramatic theater, everyone is a potential actor. To overcome the separation of stage from audience, he designed the psychodramatic theater that has no space for "spectators." The entire structure is designed to meet the requirements of action. He then "liberated the actor from script by insisting that he play himself, to be his own protagonist and act out his real life episodes without a playwright, without rehearsal, with total spontaneity."[76]

Many of Moreno's ideas have been and continue to be controversial. The methods he developed under the rubric of what he called "sociometry," however, have permeated the entire field of social psychology.

CONCLUSION

In the preceding pages, we have reviewed a wide variety of approaches that are used in social psychology. There is some debate among professionals about which approaches better address different problems. We have tried to show that there may be trade-offs; where some approaches (e.g., surveys) may enable one to generalize with greater confidence, others (e.g., field work) may provide a more in depth understanding of a more limited set of circumstances. Different approaches may be more appropriate for different problems. Throughout this book, we will review a wide variety of research strategies. Evaluation of these different approaches will be considered in the context of the types of issues they are designed to address.

NOTES

[1] Paul Feyerabend, *Against Method* (New York: Schocken, 1978).

[2] Ibid., p. 23.

[3] Ibid.

[4] Ibid., pp. 23–28.

[5] M. Rosenberg, *Society and the Adolescent Self-image* (Princeton, N.J.: Princeton University Press, 1965).

[6] P.B. Sheatsley, "White Attitudes Towards the Negro," in T. Parsons and K. B. Clark, eds., *The Negro American* (Boston: Houghton Mifflin, 1966). pp. 303–324.

[7] See James A. Davis, *Elementary Survey Analysis* (Englewood Cliffs, N.J.: Prentice-Hall, 1971), pp. 95–96.

[8] See D. T. Campbell, and J. C. Stanley, *Experimental and Quasi-Experimental Designs for Research* (Chicago: Rand McNally, 1966).

[9] See M. F. Rosenberg, "The Conditions and Consequences of Evaluation Apprehension," in R. Rosenthal and R. L. Rosnow, eds., *Artifact and Behavioral Research* (New York: Academic Press, 1969). pp. 280–349.

[10] C. W. Turner and L. S. Simmons, "Effects of Subject Sophistication and Evaluation Apprehension on Aggressive Responses to Weapons," *Journal of Personality and Social Psychology* Vol. 30 (1977), pp. 341–348.

[11] K. J. Gergen, "Social Psychology as History," *Journal of Personality and Social Psychology,* Vol. 26 (1973), pp. 309–320.

[12] William J. McGuire, "Some Impending Reorientations in Social Psychology: Some Thoughts Provoked by Kenneth Ring," *Journal of Experimental Social Psychology,* Vol. 3 (1967), pp. 124–139.

[13] B. J. Biddle, B. Banks and M. M. Marlin, "Parental and Peer Influence in Adolescents, *Social Forces,* Vol. 58; no. 4 (June 1980), pp. 1057–1079.

[14] I. Silverman and M. E. Shaw, "Effects of Sudden Mass School Desegregation on Interracial Interaction and Attitudes in One Southern City," *Journal of Social Issues,* Vol. 29, no. 4 (1973), pp. 133–142.

[15] See A. L. Stinchcombe, and D. G. Taylor, "On Democracy and School Integration," in W. G. Stephen and Joe R. Feagin, eds, *School Desegregation: Past, Present and Future* (New York: Plenum Press, 1980), pp. 157–186.

[16] M. Melbin, "Night as Frontier," *American Sociological Review,* Vol. 43, no. 1 (February 1978), pp. 3–22.

[17] G. W. Allport, "Attitudes," in C. Murchison, ed., *A Handbook of Social Psychology* Worcester, Massachusetts: Clark University Press, 1935.

[18] Adapted from National Data Program for the Social Sciences, *Cumulative Code Book* for the 1972–1977 General Social Surveys National Opinion Research Center (Chicago: University of Chicago Press, 1977).

[19]C. E. Osgood, J. G. Suci, and P. H. Tannenbaum, *The Measurement of Meaning* (Urbana: University of Illinois Press, 1957).

[20]Taken from C. Seltiz, L. Writhtsman, and S. Cook, *Research Methods in Social Relations.* (New York: Holt, Rinehart & Winston, 1976), p. 422.

[21]R. T. La Pierre, "Attitudes versus Actions," *Social Forces,* Vol. 13 (1934), pp. 230–237.

[22]S. M. Corey, "Professed Attitudes and Actual Behavior," *Journal of Educational Psychology,* Vol. 21 (1937), pp. 271–280.

[23]M. L. DeFleur and F. R. Westie, "Verbal Attitudes and Overt Acts: An Experiment on the Salience of Attitudes," *American Sociological Review,* (1958), pp. 667–673.

[24]G. H. DeFrieze and W. S. Ford, "Verbal Attitudes, Overt Acts, and the Influence of Social Constraint in Interracial Behavior," *Social Problems,* Vol. 16 (1969), pp. 493–504.

[25]D. E. Tarter, "Attitude: The Mental Myth," in *American Sociologist,* Vol. 5 (1970), p. 277.

[26]R. Brannon et al., "Attitude and Action: A Field Experiment Joined to a General Population Survey," *American Sociological Review,* Vol. 38 (1973), pp. 625–636.

[27]H. Schuman and M. P. Johnson, "Attitudes and Behavior," *Annual Review of Sociology,* Vol. 2 (1976), pp. 161–208.

[28]See J. S. Coleman, et al., *Equality of Educational Opportunity* (Washington, D.C.: U.S. Department of Health, Education and Welfare, U.S. Government Printing Office, 1966).

[29]J. P. Robinson and P. R. Shaver, *Measures of Social Psychological Attitudes* (Ann Arbor, Mich.: Institute for Social Research, 1973), p. 193.

[30]Ibid., p. 193.

[31]Ibid., p. 277.

[32]R. Blauner, *Alienation and Freedom: The Factory Worker and His Industry* (Chicago: University of Chicago Press, 1964).

[33]Robinson and Shaver, *Measures of Social Psychological Attitudes,* p. 314.

[34]H. Webster, N. Sanford, and M. Freeman, "A New 'F' (Authoritarianism) Scale," *Journal of Psychology,* Vol. 40 (1955), pp. 73–85.

[35]David Joyes, "Personality and Prediction," *Technological Forecasting and Social Change,* Vol. 16 (1980), pp. 93–104.

[36]E. Dyson, " A Study of Ability Grouping and Self-concept," *The Journal of Educational Research,* Vol. 60, (1967), pp. 403–405.

[37]Robinson and Shaver, *Measures of Social Psychological Attitudes,* p. 65–69.

[38]Ibid., p. 69.

[39]M. F. Kuhn and T. S. McPartland, "An Empirical Investigation of Self-attitudes," in J. G. Manis and B. N. Meltzer, eds., *Symbolic Interaction: A Reader in Social Psychology* (Boston: Allyn & Bacon, 1978), pp. 83–92.

[40]H. A. Mulford and W. W. Salisbury II, "Self-conception in a General Population," *The Sociological Quarterly,* Vol. 5 (1964), pp. 35–46.

[41]Adapted from R. F. Bales, *Interaction Process Analysis* (Chicago: University of Chicago Press, 1950).

[42]J. Shannon and B. Guerney, Jr., "Interpersonal Effects of Interpersonal Behavior," *Journal of Personality and Social Psychology,* Vol. 26 (1973), pp. 142–150.

[43]See Appendices I and II in G. Psathas, ed., *Everyday Language: Studies in Ethnomethodology* (New York: Irvington Publishers 1979), pp. 287–292.

[44]C. Goodwin, "The Interactive Construction of a Sentence in Natural Conversation," in G. Psathas, ed., *Everyday Language: Studies in Ethnomethodology* (New York: Irvington Publishers, 1979), pp. 97–122.

[45]Discussed in M. Knapp, *Nonverbal Communication in Human Interaction,* 2nd ed. (New York: Holt, Rinehart & Winston, 1978) p. 393.

[46]G. W. Hewes, "The Anthropology of Posture," *Scientific American,* Vol. 196, (1957), pp. 123–132.

[47]See Hall, "A System for the Notation of Proxemic Behavior," and *Handbook for Proxemic Research.*

[48]Ibid., p. 1003–1026.

[49]A. E. Scheflen, "Natural History Method in Psychotherapy: Communicational Research," in L. A. Gottschalk and A. H. Auerbach, eds., *Methods of Research in Psychotherapy* (New York: Appleton-Century Crofts, 1966), p. 227

[50]I. Deutscher, "Forward" in R. Bogdan and S. J. Taylor, *Introduction to Qualitative Research Methods: A Phenomendogical Approach to the Social Sciences* (New York: John Wiley, 1975), p. vi.

[51]L. Festinger, H. Riecken, and S. Schachter, *When Prophecy Fails* (New York: Harper & Row, 1956).

[52]L. Humphreys, *Tearoom Trade* (Chicago: Aldine, 1970).

[53]H. Becker, *Outsiders: Studies in the Sociology of Deviance* (New York: The Free Press, 1963).

[54]E. Liebow, *Tally's Corner* (Boston: Little Brown, 1967), pp. 249–250.

[55]W. F. Whyte, *Street Corner Society* (Chicago: University of Chicago Press, 1955), p. 301.

[56]Liebow, *Tally's Corner*, pp. 255–256.

[57]J. Cassell, *A Fieldwork Manual for Studying Desegregated Schools* (Washington, D.C.: National Institute of Education, 1978).

[58]A. R. Lindesmith, *Addiction and Opiates* (Chicago: Aldine, 1968).

[59]See Sandra Halberstram, ed., "Interviewing in Sociology: A Brief Overview," in Lindsey Churchill, ed., *Questioning Strategies in Sociolinguistics* (Rowley, Mass.: Newbury House, 1978), pp. 5–18.

[60]Ibid., p. 5.

[61]Ibid., pp. 12–13.

[62]Raymond L. Gordon, *Interviewing: Strategy Techniques and Tactics*, rev. ed. (Homewood, Ill.: The Dorsey Press, 1975), pp. 85–103.

[63]See H. Shuman and J. M. Converse, "Effect of Black and White Interviewers on Black Responses in 1968," *Public Opinion Quarterly*, Vol. 35 (1971), pp. 44–68.

[64]See Gordon, *Interviewing*, p. 89.

[65]See ibid., pp. 92–96.

[66]Ibid., pp. 96–97.

[67]J. L. Moreno, *Who Shall Survive?* (Beacon, N.Y.: Beacon House, 1934). A completely revised edition was written by Moreno and published by Beacon House in 1953.

[68]Gardner Murphy, "New Evaluation of Sociometry," in J. L. Moreno, ed., *Sociometry and the Science of Man* (Beacon, N.Y.: Beacon House, 1956), p. 293.

[69]Moreno, *Who Shall Survive?* p. 93.

[70]For a standard social psychological discussion of sociometric and related tests, see Gardner Lindzey and Donn Byrne, "Measurement of Social Choice and Interpersonal Attractiveness," in Gardner Lindzey and Elliott Aronson, ed., *The Handbook of Social Psychology*, 2nd ed. (Reading, Mass.: Addison-Wesley, 1968), pp. 452–525.

[71]For a more detailed discussion of these measures, see ibid, pp. 456–510.

[72]J. L. Moreno, *Psychodrama* (Beacon, N.Y.: Beacon House, 1946), Vol. 1, p. 9.

[73]See J. L. Moreno in collaboration with Zenka T. Moreno *Psychodrama* (Beacon, N.Y.: Beacon House, 1975), pp. 233–246.

[74]Ibid., p. 241.

[75]Ibid., p. 240.

[76]Ibid., p. 28.

CHAPTER FOUR
RELEVANT THEORIES IN
SOCIAL PSYCHOLOGY

The word *theory* is, in many ways, a strange one. It seems to mean different things to different people. For some, it represents the highest level of scientific achievement (e.g., the theories of gravitation, evolution, thermodynamics, and probability; for others, it is roughly comparable with idle speculation or simple, impractical, wispy mush or softheaded musings ("he knows the stuff theoretically, not practically," "theoretically this machine should now operate but something seems to be wrong," "don't give me theory, give me facts," etc.).

The sad truth is that different physical and social scientists have different ideas about precisely what theory is and how useful it can be in a field like social psychology. Rather than impose our own definition prematurely upon the reader, we will say, at this time, only that theories, in general, are ways in which people explain things. For example, probability is often called a "law." Now everyone knows that Congress has had nothing whatever to do with it. In this sense it is not a law. It is an attempt to explain certain phenomena such as why, if you use an evenly balanced coin and flip it, heads may come up about half the time and tails the other half. It turns out that the law is not very precise. You may well flip a coin and get ten or more successive tails. You have not thereby refuted the theory of probability. It still helps us to explain many otherwise mysterious occurrences, and we therefore expect social scientists, physical scientists, engineers, and bookies to understand what it means.

It is in this sense that we ask the reader to learn something about the ideas and theories of some people we and others think have important and useful explanations of social psychological phenomena. We will discuss several different theories, theoretical perspectives, and theoretical topics in this chapter. These are similar in that they address fundamental concerns of social psychology: the nature of human interaction and communication and the nature of the processes through which human beings as biological organisms are transformed into persons. Each, however, has a somewhat different perspective on these questions. That they disagree with each other may mean only that future social psychologists must keep working to produce more adequate explanations. It may also mean many other things, but more of that later.

FREUD AND PSYCHOANALYTIC THEORY

Sigmund Freud (1856–1939) was not a social psychologist by profession, he was a physician. His specialty was neurology, and he had done experimental work on the nervous systems of fish as well as on the problem of cerebral paralysis in children.

In explaining how psychoanalysis was "invented" (if we may use that term), Freud himself tells us that the technique was first used as a therapeutic device by another physician, Dr. Joseph Breuer.[1]

Dr. Breuer had been treating a patient referred to as "Annie O.," a highly intelligent young woman of 21. She was suffering from paralysis of the right arm and leg and occasional paralysis of the left arm and leg. She has severe nausea when trying to eat. Her vision was impaired. She had difficulty in maintaining the position of her head. During one period of several weeks, she was unable to drink despite the fact that she was very thirsty. She suffered from speech problems and, for extended periods could not speak or understand her own mother tongue. On occasion, she was confused and delirious.

Annie O.'s difficulties first appeared while she was caring for her father who subsequently died. She had been obliged to stop caring for him because she herself had fallen ill.

Annie O. seemed to have had two distinct states of consciousness. One of these seemed to be relatively normal; during the other, she seemed to take on the personality of a naughty, troublesome child. It turned out that the "normal" phase happened to occur when Dr. Breuer visited her. She soon began to tell Breuer everything that had happened to her. On one occasion, she started to tell him about how a particular symptom started. As she did so, the symptom disappeared. She did the same with respect to other symptoms and many of these others disappeared. Annie O. herself called this new form of treatment the "talking cure" or "chimney sweeping."

One summer, when it was intensely hot, Annie O. found that she was unable to drink. She lifted a glass of water in her hand but was forced to push it away as soon as it touched her lips. To relieve her thirst, she had to eat melons and other foods with water in them; she could not drink liquids directly. While this was going on, Dr. Breuer put her under hypnosis. She started to talk about her English governess whom she disliked intensely. She recalled that on one occasion she had entered a room and saw the dog of the governess drink out of a glass. After expressing her anger to Dr. Breuer about this, Annie O. asked for a drink and took a large quantity of water without any difficulty. After she had awakened from her hypnotic state, her inability to drink water from a glass disappeared.

Years later, Freud reported that while treating his own patients, he had experiences similar to those of Breuer. He subsequently abandoned the use of hypnosis but retained the use of the couch. This, Freud found, was a useful tool, since it allowed both patient and therapist to relax and encouraged the patient to engage in what Freud called "free association." According to Freud, he instituted this technique when one of his patients complained because Freud interrupted the flow of her narrative. He felt he had to allow the patient to say what she had to say in her own way.

Although Freud did not start out as a social psychologist, as a physician concerned with physical disorders of individuals, he began by searching for biological explanations for the difficulties of his patients. When these proved to be nonexistent or at least not detectable, he tried to find other explanations for the cures he found for his patients. These explanations form the basis of his theories. They changed throughout his career, presumably as a result of his experiences with new patients.

Freudian theory has been described as essentially an interrelated set of hypotheses and ideas. To understand any specific idea, it is important to understand it in the light of his other ideas. We cannot, of course, examine all these here. We present some of the most basic ones.

The Unconscious

Fundamental to Freudian theory is a distinction between conscious mental processes and those that are unconscious. But Freud went beyond this simple distinction. He insisted that "mental processes are essentially unconscious . . . those which are conscious are merely isolated acts and parts of the whole psychic entity."[2] He recognized that this conflicted with what seemed to be ordinary common sense. This says that mental processes are those of which we are aware consciously. He insisted, nevertheless, that "the acceptance of unconscious mental processes represents a decisive step toward a new orientation in the world and in science."[3]

Understanding the unconscious motivations of an individual is critical for treatment. The requirements of living in society force all of us, according to Freud, to suppress certain drives and urges or otherwise to resolve critical life problems. Psychopathological symptoms are the result of drives and urges or problems that have not been sufficiently resolved. Annie O.'s inability to drink water was a result of her unresolved anger concerning the governess's dog. Similarly, Freud found that many problems people had stemmed from early sexual encounters that they had repressed (i.e., ceased to think about and forgotten at a conscious level) but that still troubled them at an unconscious level. These repressed thoughts would often come out in the free-floating discussions that Freud conducted with his patients. Unconscious psychological factors may thus have an important influence on behavior. The purpose of analysis is to uncover these factors.

Errors—and Why They Are Made

The unconscious elements of an individual's psychology may be seen in "normal" persons as well as in those who are "neurotic" or "sick." We all repress some life events. Indeed, it is impossible to retain all memories in a conscious state. The unconscious elements of consciousness often manifest themselves in "slips of the tongue" and in dreams.

Freud observed that all "normal" and "healthy" people commit a variety of errors. You may wish to say something and say the wrong thing (i.e., make a "slip of the tongue"). You may do the same thing when writing ("slip of the pen"). You may misread, mishear, or simply forget a name you know quite well. You may mislay an object so that you cannot find it. Related to these are some mistakes one makes—believing something for a short period of time that one knows to be untrue both before and afterward.

According to Freud, such errors almost invariably are something more than mere accidents—they have meaning. They occur when two different intentions interfere with each other. Thus, in virtually all slips of the tongue where what is said is completely opposite to what is intended, the slip is an expression of this conflict between two incompatible impulses. An example provided by Freud goes somewhat as follows.[4]

Freud met two Viennese ladies who were on a walking tour in the mountains. He accompanied them part way, and they discussed the pleasures as well as the difficulties of such tours. One of the ladies, in discussing the discomforts involved, said, "It certainly is very unpleasant to tramp all day in the sun till one's blouse . . . and things are soaked through." She hesitated at one point in this sentence and then continued, "But then, when one gets *nach Hose* and one can change . . .".

In German, the word *Hose* refers to *drawers*. The traveler meant to say *nach Hause,* which means *home.* Freud suggests that the woman had intended to give a more complete list of her clothing, including blouse, chemise, and drawers. Since she was a modest Viennese lady living early in the twentieth century, she omitted mentioning *Hose.* In the next sentence, however, in a completely separate context, the word was communicated as a distortion of *Hause.*[5]

In short, slips of tongue arise when a speaker is determined *not* to convert an idea into speech. The expression that he or she does not wish to communicate asserts itself despite this determination, either by altering the original intention or providing a slip of the tongue in place of it. "A suppression (*Underdruckung*) of a previous intention to say something is the indispensable condition for the occurrence of a slip of the tongue."[6] Similar forces operate in the other forms of error.

Dreams

Freud felt that every dream has a meaning relevant to something in the dreamer's waking life. In this sense, dreams are a little like errors, and like errors they are relatively "normal" occurrences in that they occur to people who are in good physical health and not "neurotic." Since they have meaning, they can be "interpreted." Freud tells of having come upon dream interpretation during the course of treating patients with nervous disorders. He insisted that his patients communicate to him every idea or thought occurring to them in connection with some object. While doing this, many of them started to tell him their dreams. It was in this context that he soon realized that dreams themselves had meanings similar to other psychic occurrences. He began to view dreams as symptoms and applied to them the method of interpretation he had worked out for other symptoms.[7]

All dreams represent the fulfillment of wishes. In providing examples of dream material, Freud used many of his own dreams as well as those of his patients.[8] Thus he observed that if he ate anchovies or olives or any other highly salted food in the evening, he developed a thirst during the night that awakened him. This waking, however, was preceded by a dream in which he swallows water in great gulps. He then wakes up and takes a real drink. The dream is caused by the thirst of which he becomes aware when he awakens.

Freud tells of a young lady who informs her husband of a dream in which she is having her menstrual period. For Freud, the fact that the woman dreamed of having her period meant that she had in fact missed it. The dream meant that she would have preferred not to be pregnant.

Freud realized that many objections would be raised to his assertion that all dreams represent fulfillment of wishes. It is easy to point to nightmares or other dreams that are not at all pleasant and seem to be anything *but* fulfillments of wishes.

To deal with these objections, Freud distinguished between the *manifest* and *latent* content of dreams. The manifest content may be highly unpleasant and objectionable, but Freud felt that it was nevertheless the case that the latent content would, after interpretation, prove to consist of the fulfillment of a wish.

A young physician dreams that he has received a heavy fine for understating his income on a tax return. Freud analyzes the dream as a poorly disguised wish to be known as a physician with a large income.

For a detailed discussion of dreams, the interested reader should see Freud's *Interpretation of Dreams*.

Personality Theory

For Freud, a newborn child is essentially a bundle of impulses and instincts. Its personality is governed completely by what Freud calls the *id*.[9] The id is the completely unconscious part of the personality. It is blind, impulsive, and irrational. It knows nothing of moral or ethical values; it has no organized will. It contains contradictory impulses that neither neutralize each other nor separate. It has no sense of the passage of time. It has no direction, uses no guidelines, and is completely uninhibited.

As the child begins to deal with his or her environment, a coherent organization of mental processes is developed that Freud calls the *ego*. The ego controls consciousness. It develops through the child's interaction with his or her environment. More specifically, attempts to satisfy the drives of the id are not always met with success. These experiences teach the child that certain impulses cannot be satisfied immediately while others are not to be satisfied at all. Thus, the process of ego development may be thought of as a kind of "reality testing" in which the child seeks different alternatives for reducing tensions and satisfying needs. The ego represents what seems to be reason and sanity. Where Freud compared the id with a horse, the ego was compared with its rider who both directs the horse and controls it.

One further function of the ego is to mediate between the id and the *superego*. As the child reaches the age of 2 (roughly speaking), a superego begins to form. This is solidified as the child enters adolescence and comes to identify with parents of the same sex, internalizing their norms and values. One's superego is responsible for the "sense of guilt" most of us feel when we have behaved badly—even if our bad behavior goes unnoticed or unsanctioned by others. The superego represents the conscience of personality. It contains our sense of "right and wrong." At certain times, many of us may experience rather strong contradictions between the directives of our moral conscience and the desires of the id. The ego operates to evaluate different courses of action in terms of these countervailing forces.

Libido Theory

This may well be the most widely known, the most controversial, and the most generally distorted aspect of Freudian theory. *Libido*, for Freud, referred to what has been called "the psychic energy of the sexual instincts." Beyond this, however, he meant it to refer to the energy "of those instincts which have to do with all that may be comprised under the word 'love.' "[10]

Thus, for Freud, the term "sexual" had a very wide meaning. It implied much beyond simple genital activity. It included self-love, love for parents and children, friendship for humanity in general, and a devotion to concrete objects and abstract ideas as well. The root of the word "libido" is the German word *Liebe* or love.

Libido has several important characteristics:

1. Even within the same individual, it varies in intensity. There is an ebb and flow corresponding to different phases of physiological development.
2. It is always present, even among infants, although its manifestation in infants is considerably different from manifestations in adults.
3. It is not only the sexual organs that are sensitive to the urgings of the libido. It may involve various body areas.
4. The direction of libidinal flow is always changing. When it is directed inwardly, it is called "narcissism." When it is directed outwardly, it is referred to as "object love." When arrested, it is referred to as "fixation." When it flows to levels representing earlier phases of development, it is called "regression." When blocked or dammed up, it is called "repression." When it is deflected into more socially accepted channels, it is called "sublimation."[11]

The difference between sublimation and repression is an important distinction is psychoanalytic thought. Sublimation involves the redirecting of drives and impulses into socially acceptable ways. Repression, on the other hand, would entail the blocking of the child's emotional drives. They would thus remain unresolved and could emerge as problems later in life.

The distinction between repression and sublimation may be clarified with respect to anger and aggression. Consider the following hypothetical examples. Two young boys are used to being given food whenever they desire it. As they grow older, their parents attempt to moderate their eating habits by refusing to feed them on demand. Both boys experience anger and frustration as a result of their parents' actions, resulting in a propensity for aggressive behaviors. One boy's aggressive tendencies are severely sanctioned by his parents. His father in fact threatens to beat him if he continues to act in an aggressive manner. The second boy's aggression is channeled into other directions. This boy's father may take him to a playground where pentup frustrations may be expressed in more socially acceptable ways.

According to the psychoanalytic perspective, the first boy has no channel through which to direct his anger and aggression. As a result, this anger may be repressed. At the same time, the anger that he is feeling may be projected onto the parents. The boy may thus perceive his father as having the same kind of uncontrolled rage he is experiencing. This may intensify the child's feelings of fear and anger. With no available outlet, the child may internalize these feelings even further, leading to a number of negative consequences. The child may develop a sense of guilt about the hostility he feels toward his parents. This may result in a highly ambivalent situation because at the same time that the child fears and dislikes his parents, he also loves them and needs their nurturance. In part, because of this, the child's hostility may be "turned inward." The child may direct his aggression toward himself; he will come to dislike himself. Typical outcomes of this type of situation include deep depression and an extreme lowering of self-confidence and self-esteem. In some cases, physiological symptoms such as headaches may occur. Although some repression will no doubt be necessary, one must be careful to provide some outlets for human emotions.

Oedipal Crises

The objects to which libidinous energy is attached change as a function of the maturation of the human organism. For an infant, the libido is first attached or "cathected" to the oral zone. Sucking, biting, and other oral pleasures were, in Freud's view, libidinal in origin. Subsequently (after about a year), the libido shifts to the anal area, and this becomes the main source of libidinal pleasure for the infant or child. By the time the child is 3 years old, the genitals have become the focus of the libido.

One of the central ideas associated with changes in the direction of libidinal energy is the *oedipal complex* or *crisis*. Freud felt that the attachment of all children to their parents was libidinal in nature. The initial object of attachment for infants of both sexes is the mother who in most cases is the primary care giver. As the child progresses to the genital stage, however, the parent of the opposite sex becomes a kind of love object. The libidinal feelings of the boy attach themselves to the mother, whereas those of the girl attach themselves to the father. Both boys and girls may feel that their parents of the same sex are interfering and superfluous during this period.

The oedipal complex may generate an extremely high degree of anxiety. Freud, in fact, believed that all anxiety was rooted in oedipal-related crises. The boy, for example, may project his feelings of hostility toward his father. If he feels that he would like to be rid of the father, then, it is not unreasonable, from the perspective of a young boy, to feel that his father may at the same time want to be rid of him. The anxiety generated by this state of affairs can be intense. Freud felt that it entailed the fear that the father would cut off the young boy's penis. This fear was termed "castration anxiety."

The intensity of this anxiety is one of the factors that leads to the resolution of the oedipal complex. The anxiety associated with his desires for the mother leads the young boy to renounce his sexual interest in the mother. Instead, he comes to identify with the father (i.e., he now desires to become a "man" like father). The child internalizes the father's moral directives and prohibitions, which helps to repress any desires he may have for his mother.

In the case of the young girl a similar set of events occurs. The crisis for young girls, however, concerns the fact that primary identification with the mother involves a similar desire for the father. Hence, the young girl may experience a kind of competition or rivalry with the mother with respect to father's affections. The young girl is jealous of her mother's privileged relationship with father. Like the boy, however, she comes to project a similar jealousy onto the mother. The fear associated with this leads the girl to identify with the mother and to channel her affections in different directions.

The importance of Freud's theory of personality can be appreciated best by reference to his predecessors. Prior to his work, personality tended to be viewed as a collection of traits or attributes characteristic of an individual. They appeared because of the innate physiological characteristics that formed part of what was seen as the totality of these traits. For Freud, on the other hand, personality is what emerged from the interaction between a person's inherited characteristics and his or her cultural milieu. An individual's inner needs or what Freud called "instincts" find expression through the environment that can help to fulfill, impede, or deny these needs. The culture itself emerged from the necessity to restrain the instinctual demands of people, but in turn it imposes its own sets of standards and values. The major developments in the formation of a personality occur in the early years of infancy and childhood. Freud felt that by the fifth or sixth year, the character structure of an individual was fully formed.

Freud's theories have been charged with being male centered. They seem to assume that the male and his penis is somehow of more significance than is the female and her clitoris (with which it is compared) and her vagina. The weakest elements of his theoretical structure may well be in connection with Freud's understanding or lack of understanding of the famale psyche. He was clearly biased in favor of men and very heavily influenced by his own culture, which reflected this male bias. His view of the psychological troubles of women rested on the assumption that they were ultimately traceable to "penis envy"—the desire to have a penis and the inability to have one. This narrow biological focus, many people have felt, demonstrated Freud's own failure to understand the broader social issues affecting women in various societies throughout the world.[12]

Neo-Freudian Theory

Freudian theory was modified not only by Freud himself but also by a succession of his former students and others as well. These modifications, broadly speaking, constitute a school of thought that, while basically psychoanalytic in orientation, differs with Freud on many important points. Much of the difficulty seems to have stemmed from what was seen as Freud's overemphasis upon the importance of biological and instinctual concerns and what seems to be a corresponding underemphasis on social or cultural influences in the shaping of the human personality.[13]

The first of Freud's students to break away was Alfred Adler (1870–1937) who felt that libido theory did not do justice to the basic motivations in human development. He focused on relationships people developed with other people. Children, because generally they are small and helpless, develop strong feelings of inferiority. From this emerges a need to enlarge one's ego by dominating other people or feeling superior. In a sense, then, Adler substituted the search for power for what seemed to be Freud's emphasis on sex as the focus of personality theory. Adler has been referred[13] to as "the great dissenter" who initiated a centrally important and enduring perspective in social psychology. "He was especially compassionate toward victims of social injustice, and he thought it of primary importance to help promote human dignity. Adler understood how people, out of their own inadequacies and lack of self-esteem, can bolster themselves by degrading others, and how once a group or class has been treated as inferior, these feelings intensify and can lead to compensatory maneuvers to make up for self-doubts."[14]

He was clearly well ahead of his time in perceiving the social bases for such pathologies as racism and sexism.

After Adler, perhaps the best known of the early secessionists was Carl Jung (1875–1961), who tried to broaden the concept of human being beyond that of just another animal. He focused upon the special concerns of human beings that encompassed spiritual and aesthetic needs as well as other interests.

Freud, as an innovator, had an incredibly difficult task. He wanted to understand the "emotional" behavior of human beings. His predecessors in this effort were not neurologists or psychologists but philosophers, playwrights, and novelists. At the time he did his work, little was known about the relationship between hormones and the psyche. The one area in which there seemed to be a well-established connection between physiological and psychic factors was sexuality. If sexuality were to be regarded as the root of all drives, then it could be claimed that the physiological roots of psychic factors had been discovered. It was Jung who "cut loose from this connection and in this respect made . . . a truly valuable addition to Freud's thought."[15]

Jung subsequently called his own orientation "analytical psychology" rather than psychoanalysis. He saw the libido as a much broader force than did Freud and had a view of the unconscious that differed sharply with Freud's ideas. He seemed to place more stress on conflicts in the present than in those of childhood. He discontinued the use of the psychoanalytic couch and often used short-term psychotherapeutic help rather than long-term psychoanalysis.[16]

Karen Horney (1885–1952) tried to reevaluate many of Freud's ideas in light of later findings in the social sciences as well as on the basis of her own experience with patients. She essentially discarded a biological orientation and tried to explain personality formation on the basis of interactions between parents and children, other adults and children, and adults with adults. This led to an emphasis upon the current aspects of an individual's life rather than upon the genesis of the personality in terms of its life history.

Horney was born almost 30 years after Freud and grew up in a Europe that was quite different from the one in which Freud was raised. She was influenced by what has been called the "open system thinking" of twentieth-century science and the new "humanism" that seemed to accompany it.[17] She took issue with the orthodox Freudian ideas of penis envy and the castration complex in women and argued that male and female values had been judged from a masculine orientation.[18]

As she explained it,

> Freud's postulations in regard to feminine psychology set me thinking about the role of cultural factors. Their influence on our ideas of what constitutes masculinity or femininity was obvious, and it became just as obvious to me that Freud had arrived at certain erroneous conclusions because he failed to take them into account. My interest in this subject grew over the course of fifteen years. It was furthered in part by association with Erich Fromm who, through his profound knowledge of both sociology and psychoanalysis, made me more aware of the significance of social factors over and above their circumscribed application to feminine psychology. I saw then that the attitudes and the neuroses of persons in this country differed in many ways from those I had observed in European countries, and that only the difference in civilizations could account for this.[19]

In earlier writings, Karen Horney tried to emphasize the importance of current, actually existing conflicts and the efforts of a neurotic individual to solve them. She tried to show that the relation between childhood experiences and those that occur later in life are much more complex than had been assumed by orthodox Freudian psychoanalysts, who, she felt, saw a simple cause and effect relationship between childhood experiences and difficulties in later life. For Horney, childhood experiences were important but not the only cause of later difficulties.[20]

In her later book, *Neurosis and Human Growth*, Horney formulated her definitive break with Freud's theory and explained her differences with Freud in essentially the following terms:[21]

1. Freud was not aware of the power of cultural conditions to mold human character. He shared this lack of knowledge with most European scholars of his time. Thus, for example, he saw cravings for prestige and success all about him and mistook this for a universal human propensity. He did not regard a compulsive drive for supremacy, dominance, or triumph as a problem worth examining except when it did not fit into a pattern that he regarded as "normal" (because of his own cultural bias). He did find these drives interesting when they occurred in women because then it did not conform to his cultural sterotype of "femininity."

2. Freud tried to explain neurotic drives as libidinal phenomena. He was in a sense oblivious to the pathologies in social relationships that contributed to these drives.

3. Freud's mode of thinking was essentially "evolutionistic mechanistic," that is,

"It implies that present manifestations not only are conditioned by the past, but contain nothing but the past; nothing really new is created in the process of development: what we see is only the old in a changed form."[22]

Within such a framework, Horney argues, excessive competitiveness, for example, can be explained in a satisfactory manner only if it is seen as the result of an unresolved oedipus complex or sibling rivalry. The only interpretations regarded as "deep" are those that establish a connection with libidinal experiences originating in childhood. Horney insisted that such interpretations were limited and indeed could serve to obstruct important insights.

Erich Fromm (1900–1980) emphasized the fact that human beings at birth have far fewer predetermined courses of action available to them than does any other animal. Humans adapt to their environment not by means of instinct but through learning and cultural training. The most compelling needs of human beings are not those of sex or aggression but the needs that society has created for them. In one sense, by examining such forces as economics, politics, and religion on personality, Fromm increased the number of variables that must be considered in the study of personality development.

To phrase it in these terms, however, seems to miss the enormous theoretical insights that Fromm brought to the field of social psychology. He regarded himself as a "humanist"—a person who believes in the unity of the human race and the ability of human beings to perfect themselves by their own efforts. He felt that humanism (which has a long history stretching back to the Hebrew prophets and Greek philosophers) has always emerged as a reaction to a threat to humankind. In the Renaissance, it was a reaction to the threat of religious fanaticism; in the Enlightenment, it was a reaction to the threat of extreme nationalism and the enslavement of human beings by machine and economic interests. He felt that there was a revival of Humanism in the twentieth century because these latter threats have become intensified. The contemporary fear is that human beings may become slaves of things—prisoners of circumstances that they themselves have created. All this is intensified by the wholly new threat to the physical existence of civilization posed by nuclear weapons.[23]

He felt that psychoanalytic theory and practice had undergone fundamental changes since the days of Freud. "Psychoanalysis," he said, "was originally a radical, penetrating, liberating theory. It slowly lost this character and stagnated, failing to develop its theory in response to the changed human situation after World War I; instead, it retreated into conformism and the search for respectability."[24]

He meant by this that the most creative and radical achievement of Freud's theory was the founding of a "science of the irrational"—the theory of the unconscious. Freud himself had seen his work as a continuation of the work of Copernicus and Darwin who had both attacked the illusions people had about the place of the Earth in the cosmos and the place of human beings in nature and society. Fromm felt that a third person should be added to this list: Karl Marx. Freud in a sense had attacked the last fortress that remained untouched by basic theory: the consciousness of human beings as the ultimate datum of psychic experience. "He showed that most of what we are conscious of is not real and that most of what is real is not in our consciousness."[25]

For Fromm, the theory of the unconscious is one of the most decisive steps ever taken in our knowledge of human beings and in our capacity to distinguish appearance from reality in human behavior. Before Freud, he pointed out, it was sufficient to know a person's conscious intentions to judge his or her sincerity. After Freud, this was no longer enough, and indeed, it often proved to be very little. The unconscious was the key to a person's *real* intentions.[26]

Thus, although Freud was a bold and radical thinker when making his discoveries, in applying them, he was hampered by an unquestioning belief that his society, although by no means completely satisfactory, was the ultimate form of human progress and could not be improved upon in any essential feature. Fromm saw an inherent contradiction in Freud that could be developed in two different ways by his disciples.[27] One path led to the making of discoveries on the order of those made by Copernicus, Darwin, and Marx. The other path would be restricted to the "categories of bourgeois ideology and experience."[28] Fromm felt that Freud's orthodox followers adopted the latter path.

Harry Stack Sullivan (1892–1949) referred to his own ideas as the theory of personality development. It was based on a concept of human beings as living creatures with fundamental biological needs. He did not assume the existence of instincts but focused upon the relationships of people to each other and on what can be observed in these relationships. He did assume that people have the ability to produce an effect on other persons because of the relationship existing between them. Anxiety in the mother may induce anxiety in the infant who is being mothered. In adults, anxiety may arise in connection with the actual or anticipated disapproval of other important adults. We shall be referring to some of his work in later chapters.

BEHAVIORIAL THEORIES

For some social psychologists, psychoanalytic and related theories are much too "subjective." Behaviorism is a theoretical orientation that insists that social psychology must deal only with entities that are objective. It insists that observations used as the basis for making theoretical statements be of the kind that can be observed on repeated occasions by different observers.

Currently, the most widely known behaviorist is B. F. Skinner. Skinner was interested in explaining why people behave as they do within the constraints of an objective science. He, therefore, focused on observable behavior or, more specifically, on how variations in behavior are produced. Skinner also focused on features of the environment affecting behavior. Many features of one's environment are essential if a person or other animal is to survive. Food is necessary, as is water, the ability to escape from harm, and, at least for some elements of the population, sexual relations (to prevent the disappearance of the species, if for no other reason).

Skinner's behaviorism is distinguished by the concept of operant conditioning. Previous behaviorists, relying primarily on animal studies, focused on stimulus-response (S-R) patterns (i.e., classical conditioning).[29] The presence of a bone (S), for example, would likely cause a nearby dog to salivate (R). If a bell were rung every time the dog was presented with a bone, then after a sufficient number of presentations, the simple ringing of the bell would cause the dog to salivate. Operant conditioning differs from a simple S-R perspective.

The concept of operant conditioning may best be understood through the following example. Imagine a pigeon in a box with a lever. Assume that the pigeon pecks at the lever. According to classical conditioning, the lever presented a stimulus to the bird that resulted in the specific response (the peck). Skinner, however, focuses on the consequences of the peck. Assume that the pigeon's pecking at the lever resulted in a pellet of bird food falling into a dish near the lever, which the bird then eats. The hungry bird's pecking behavior was thus *reinforced* by the pellet of food.

The logic of behaviorism is thus quite simple. Behavior having survival value is strengthened by the consequences of the behavior. The consequences are called "reinforcers." If you are hungry and do something that produces food, whatever behavior you have engaged in is reinforced by the fact that it has produced food. Accordingly, you are more likely to repeat that behavior.

If you are thirsty and go to a particular sink and fill a glass of water and drink it, you are more likely to do the same thing next time you are thirsty. The glass of water is a positive reinforcer when you are thirsty. If reinforcement no longer appears, the behavior undergoes "extinction" and may appear only infrequently or not at all. If someone cuts off the water supply to that sink, you will be less likely to return for more water. Similarly, if pecking the lever no longer produces the pellet of food, the bird gradually will stop pecking.

Many behaviorist studies have focused on types of reinforcement schedules that reduce the rate of extinction. This is critical if one wishes to reinforce certain behaviors so that they will last even if the organism moves to an environment where the reinforcement schedule is highly irregular. Regular schedules can easily be imposed in the laboratory. In a laboratory, for example, it is possible to maintain eye contact with a severely disturbed child by consistently reinforcing him or her with food each time he or she looks you in the eye. The key is to structure the reinforcements so that the child will continue to make eye contact in circumstances when reinforcement schedules may be more variable.

Types of Reinforcement

Skinner distinguished between positive and negative reinforcers. A positive reinforcer refers to any consequence of a behavior that increases the frequency of a particular response. Food in the previously discussed pigeon example constitutes positive reinforcement. Negative reinforcement refers to any behavioral consequence that, when *removed* from a situation, will also increase the frequency of a response. Assume that every time the pigeon pecked the lever it received a slight electric shock. This would decrease the times the bird would continue to peck the lever. Removal of the shock would likely increase the extent to which the bird would peck the lever. This removal of the aversive stimulus (the shock) constitutes negative reinforcement. Negative reinforcement must be distinguished from punishment. Punishment entails the *addition* of an aversive stimuli such as an electric shock to decrease the frequency of a particular behavior. If we wanted to decrease the pigeon's eating, we might arrange for it to receive a slight shock every time it pecks the lever. There has been considerable discussion of punishment as a reinforcer. Skinner himself does not view it as one of the better forms of reinforcement, although other social psychologists have expressed a renewed interest in this area.

From Skinner's perspective, many aspects of Freudian theory are not psychic processes taking place either in the conscious or unconscious mind; they are what he calls "contingencies of reinforcement": contingencies are essentially "if-then" statements. If a behavior is reinforced in a particular manner, it will probably recur or not recur, depending on the reinforcement. Thus, Skinner sees Freudian "repression" as an elaborate metaphor describing the effects of punishment. For Freud, repression would be defined essentially as "a mechanism of ego defense making unfulfillable wishes or impulses unacceptable to the conscious mind." Skinner would substitute "probability of behavior" for "wishes or impulses." He would also substitute "extinguished" or "punished" for "unfulfillable." In short, according to Skinner, "behavior which is punished becomes aversive, and by not engaging in it . . ., a person avoids conditioned aversive stimulation. There are feelings associated with this, but the facts are accounted for by the contingencies."[30]

Social Exchange Theory

Building on the general orientation of Skinner and other behaviorists, sociologist George Homans suggests that interpersonal behavior be analyzed according to a model of social interaction he calls "social exchange." This involves more complicated phenomena than was the case with Skinner's animal experiments, since for Homans, other people in one's environment rather than experimenters provide reinforcing or punishing consequences for any given bit of behavior. For Homans, interaction between persons was essentially like an exchange of goods. He adopted as his basic explanatory principles an idea that has long been familiar in European and American society: namely, people do things because it is in their own self-interest to do so. As one social psychologist has expressed it, Homans "felt that the best way to look at human interaction was to assume that each individual is concerned with getting as much as he can out of a situation. . . . People act in ways calculated to bring them some sort of benefits, and they are consciously concerned with these benefits or gains in choosing their actions."[31]

In short, exchange theory assumes that (1) individuals behave in response to benefits or rewards, on the one hand, and costs, on the other—that is, people learn through experience to know which situations are most likely to be rewarding; and (2) neoclassical economic theory provides essentially a correct description of human behavior when it asserts that people try to maximize their rewards and minimize their costs.

This leads to some interesting ideas about why people do the things they do. Thus, Peter Blau, another sociologist who uses the social exchange framework, suggests that people deriving benefits from others with whom they associate are obligated to provide them benefits in return. Blau recognizes that people often go out of their way to do favors for friends, acquaintances, and even strangers. In doing so, however, they create social obligations—people owe them favors in return. Those who fail to pay these social obligations in effect rob others of reason or incentives to continue to befriend them. They are likely to be accused of ingratitude. Even if favors are given freely, the recipients are expected to reciprocate.[32]

Since both parties profit from the rewarding experiences they supply to each other, repeated social exchanges tend to establish mutual bonds between people who are equal to each other (i.e., among people who have equal amounts of power). On occasion, however, social exchange may result in one person dominating another. This can occur when one person has something to offer that the other person needs but has nothing to offer in return. For example, I need help with my work. You can help me, but I have nothing to give you in return. Under these circumstances, I have four alternatives: I can (1) force you to help me (twisting your arm or threatening to "beat you up"), (2) go elsewhere to get help (perhaps I can do something for someone else), (3) do without help, or (4) reward you by subordinating myself to you and complying with your wishes.

If I cannot or will not adopt the first three alternatives, my only recourse is the fourth, which is subordination—a generic reward that gives you power over me and that may well induce you to help.[33]

Blau uses the term "social exchange" to refer to voluntary actions motivated by returns the actions are expected to bring from others. He excludes physical coercion from his concept of social exchange but includes giving-in to other forms of power (i.e., nonphysical forms of power). Social exchange, he tells us, differs from economic exchange in that the former entails unspecified rather than specific obligations. You may buy a car for $7,000 (you may owe your banker more than this if you have borrowed the money, but even this is quite specific if you read the fine print). On the other hand, if you do your friend a favor, the exact size or character of the obligation is never written down (not even in fine print), and neither of you may have a very clear idea of the amount involved. It remains an obligation nevertheless.[34]

Social Learning Theory

The purely Skinnerian approach has been criticized on the grounds that it is too limited. As we have seen (see Chapter 2), it has difficulty in accounting for the rapidity with which children acquire novel responses and new behavioral repertoires.

In a book published in 1963,[35] two social psychologists argued that the acquisition of novel responses can be accounted for through the concept of *observational learning.* According to this idea, a good deal of learning takes place through direct trial and error and the reinforcement that derives from that. However, children also learn by observing what others do and then imitating their behavior. Children, in a sense, "model" the behavior of others. They will tend to model that behavior that they see as positively reinforced or rewarded. The concept of *vicarious reinforcement* is used to describe how the behavior of an observer is modified as a consequence of the reinforcement administered to a model."[36] Behavior may depend both on the extent to which the responses of observers are reinforced and the extent to which they see *others* being as rewarded for producing the same or similar responses. Any individual's behavioral repertoire may be greatly expanded through the experiences that he or she comes to *observe* as well as those in which he or she actually participates.

The social learning perspective involves essentially a four-staged process (see Figure 4–1).[37] The first stage—the attention directed toward some model—includes two sets of variables: (1) characteristics of the model (modeling stimuli) and (2) characteristics of the observer that may influence what phenomena become "stimuli." Thus observers are more likely to be influenced by models with whom they have more frequent associations.

The second stage—retention processes—refers to the ways in which observed behavior is remembered. An important assumption of social learning theory is the idea that "People cannot be much influenced by modeled behavior if they cannot remember it."[38] This requires being able to "represent" the behavior to themselves. Social learning theorists cite two important representational systems: imaginal (through mental images and pictures) and verbal (through words and other symbols). "Symbolic coding" refers to the translation of images of modeled events into words or some other shorthand. This greatly enhances the rapidity with which novel behaviors are learned in that a variety of images can now be organized in accordance with certain cognitive structures (cognitive organization). For example, a child may learn that a particular response, let us say, a punch, is not unique but is part of a class of responses that may fall under the category of aggressive acts. Transforming an image into a verbal code leads to greater retention of that image. Finally, people may "rehearse" modeled behaviors either mentally (symbolic rehearsal) or physically (motor rehearsal). This also may enhance retention of new behaviors.

The third stage of the model—motor reproduction processes—concerns the individual's capacity actually to reproduce the modeled behavior. Successful reproduction may depend on a person's physical capabilities and ability to monitor his or her own productions (self-observation of reproduction). This may require a refinement of skills (breaking them down into their component parts) as well as developing means for receiving accurate information from others about one's performance. As Bandura put it,

> Skills are not perfected through observation alone, nor are they developed solely by trial-and-error fumbling. A golf instructor, for example, does not provide beginners with golf balls and clubs and wait for them to discover the golf swing. In most everyday learning, people usually achieve a close approximation of the new behavior by modeling, and they refine it through self-corrective adjustments on the basis of informative feedback from performance and from focused demonstrations of segments that have been only partially learned.[39]

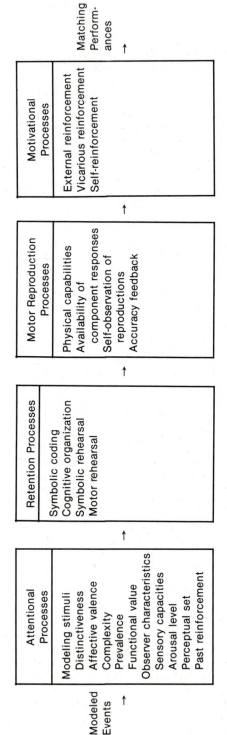

FIGURE 4-1

The fourth stage—motivational processes—refers to the extent to which reproduced behaviors will recur. Vicarious reinforcement concerns the extent to which *models* are reinforced for producing certain types of behaviors. External and self-reinforcement refer to the extent to which *observers* themselves are reinforced for producing modeled behaviors. External reinforcements refer to behaviors that receive some reward. For example a good golf swing may bring praise from one's friends or instructor. On the other hand, the successful performance may itself have intrinsic value. A good swing may make you feel fine even if no one is around and thus be a self-reinforcer.

As we shall see throughout the course of this book, social learning theory has had wide applications in different areas of social psychology. It is similar to the Skinnerian approach in that it preserves the notion of reinforcement as a central component of the motivational process. It differs from a purely Skinnerian view in that it posits the existence of complex cognitive processes for learning and motivation.

SYMBOLIC INTERACTIONISM

Certain behavioral theories have been criticized for failing to consider important differences between human and nonhuman behavior. Symbolic interactionism is a theoretical orientation focusing upon the characteristically *human* aspects of social behavior and interaction.

In this sense symbolic interactionism attempts to deal with aspects of human consciousness that are not relevant to a behaviorist or social exchange perspective. Specifically, symbolic interactionism considers human action to be reflexive. This means that the actor (i.e., a person) is able to monitor his or her actions as they are taken. In this sense, the actor can become an object to himself or herself. Inherent in this is what might be termed the dialectic of symbolic interactions. Who you consider yourself to be and how you think of yourself in relation to whatever social situations are at hand will have an important bearing on what you choose to do and how you choose to go about it. On the other hand, the nature of your social existence has an important bearing on how you think of yourself.

Symbolic interactionism traces its roots to the social philosophy of George Herbert Mead (1863–193?). The term "social interactionism" was coined by Herbert Blumer in 1937.

For Blumer, symbolic interactionism rests on three simple premises:[40]

1. Human beings behave on the basis of the *meanings* (i.e., symbolic representations of objects and relationships) that they share with other persons.
2. These meanings arise through the social interaction that a person has with other persons.
3. These meanings can be modified through an interpretative process that a person uses in dealing with the world.

The nature of meaning may be clarified if we consider some of George Herbert Mead's thoughts in a bit more detail. For Mead, all human behavior is essentially "social behavior" (i.e., it is cooperative and co-aligned). Human behavior is not, however, cooperative in the same sense that certain nonhuman animal behavior is. Ants, for example, exhibit a high degree of cooperative behavior. However, their cooperation is genetically programmed. Human behavior is cooperative in the sense that one person's action is designed in accordance with that person's understanding of some other person who may be either a recipient or an object of the action. Human cooperation is social in the sense that individuals come to imagine creatively the other's perspective and can take that perspective into consideration. Human action is co-aligned and co-oriented. It is designed with some other's orientation or alignment in mind.

When a mother hen clucks, her chicks come running to her. The hen, however, has not clucked with the *intention* of getting the chicks to her. She does not place herself (mentally) in the position of the chicks and imagine what their response will be. The hens do not see the world from the same perspective as the mother hen. When two dogs snarl at each other and then growl, bare fangs, and walk about each other with stiffened legs, they are responding to each other's gestures. Each gesture leads to an automatic, unreflected response. Neither dog is responding to the *intention* of the gesture (is he bluffing, is he trying to scare me, if I act tough will he simmer down a bit?). Moreover, neither dog engages in gesture making with the intent of eliciting a particular response from the other dog.

Human beings, however, "respond to one another on the basis of the intentions or meanings of gestures. This renders the gesture *symbolic* (i.e., the gesture becomes a symbol to be interpreted); the gesture becomes something that, in the imagination of the participants, stands for the entire act."[41]

A gesture is the initial, overt phase of an act that represents the entire act. If I shake my fist at you, I am making a gesture that represents the entire imaginative act of beating you. If I draw back my arm (thereby making a gesture), you presumably, upon perceiving my gesture, will complete it in your mind, (i.e., imaginatively). You project the gesture into the future and say, "He is going to hit me." You perceive what the gesture stands for and thereby get its meaning. You, accordingly, are responding to an *interpreted* stimulus rather than directly as is the case with the chicks and dogs.

Human beings, then, respond to each other on the basis of imaginative activity. To engage in meaningful communication, however, it is necessary for each participating person to be able to attach common meanings to the same gesture. Otherwise, it is not possible to interact with others in a coordinated manner. Each one of us can respond to our gestures and have the same meaning (or approximately the same meaning) as the other person. If I say "chair," presumably I have the same or very nearly the same image in mind as you have when you hear me say "chair." When gestures have this shared or common meaning, they contain a *linguistic* element. It is now possible to designate this as a "significant symbol." If I ask you to "Open the window," each of us must respond to the words in essentially the same way (even if you refuse to do as I ask). I must have an image of you opening the window, and you must have essentially the same image.

This imaginative completion of an act is what Mead refers to as "meaning." It is mental activity taking place through "role taking"—the process by which one person puts himself or herself imaginatively in the position of another. It is through this process that a person can see himself or herself imaginatively in the position of another. Being able to place oneself imaginatively in the position of another is a prerequisite for being able to be an object to oneself. Role taking is central to the formation of a person's self that, as Mead saw it, proceeded through three stages:

1. *The Preparatory Stage.* This is the stage in which an infant or child from about the age of 2 to 4 engages in meaningless imitation. The actions of nearby adults are mimicked, although the infant has no idea whatsoever of the meaning involved in the act. Thus, an infant might be observed "reading a newspaper," "smoking a pipe," or "writing a letter"—in imitation of parents or older brothers and sisters. Such imitation leads to the inclusions of others' behavior in the child's own behavioral repertoire.

2. *The Play Stage.* From about the age of 5 to 6, the child starts to play roles rather than engage in simple imitation. The roles are those of persons with whom the child comes in contact. In our society, they may include the roles of mother, father, older brother or sister, baby, postman, policeman, nurse, doctor, or television repairperson. The significant feature of behavior during this stage is that the child begins to act toward himself or herself while occupying one of these other roles. (See Chapter 6 for more on this.)

Since the child, in occupying these roles, may direct attention to himself or herself as a separate person, it becomes necessary to develop the concept of a separate "self." Evidence that this is occurring can be seen in the use of the third person by the child. The child now says such things as "John wants a hammer"; "Mary is hungry." At this stage, however, there is no consistent image of a self. It varies with the perspective from which it is being viewed. John may be bad when mother says he has left his room in a mess; he may be cute when a neighbor sees him swinging a club like a police officer; he may be stupid when a teacher tries to get him to memorize a word; he may be small to his older brother and a giant to the baby.

3. *Game Stage.* At about the age of 8 or 9, the child finds it necessary to respond to the expectations of several people simultaneously. The expectations of mother, father, older brother, sister, baby, letter carrier, and so on may differ from one another. The child is left in a position of finally coming to terms with the question: "Who am I?" To do this, it becomes necessary to develop a generalized role or perspective from which the child can view himself or herself. This generalized role is what Mead calls the "generalized other"—a standpoint common to the group of persons with whom the child has interacted. Having developed this, it becomes possible to view oneself from a consistent standpoint. The individual can then transcend local or present definitions to which he or she is exposed. The child has become a person with a "self."

Being a person with a self simultaneously entails membership in some larger group or collectivity. The individual has internalized an image not only of who he or she is but also of how he or she fits into some larger social collectivity. Having developed a generalized other is analogous to playing a complicated game intelligently. Being a good first baseman in baseball, for example, requires not only that the player know and understand his or her duties and entitlements on any given play but also that he or she know and understand the duties and entitlements of all other participants—teammates and opponents. This requires an understanding of one's role within a larger complex of roles.

"I" and "Me"

Society influences the behavior of individual persons through the generalized other. It is through the generalized other that the community exercises control over the conduct of its individual members. People take on the organized attitudes of the social group or community (or part of a community) to which they belong. They view social problems and social projects through these "group lenses," as it were. So, for example, people may identify with a political party and view the problems of the society through the perspective provided by that party. When people find themselves to be members of a specific social category or class such as debtor or creditor, then enter into special social relations with other persons in connection with such categories or classes. Membership in one of these more or less abstract classes or categories makes it possible for people to enter into social relations with an unlimited number of other persons.

But the self of any individual has two distinguishable aspects: the "I" and the "Me."

The "I" is the response of the organism to the attitudes of other persons in the society or community. The "me" is the set of attitudes of others that the individual assumes. It is because an individual can take on the attitudes of others that he or she can be "self-conscious." It is the taking on of these organized sets of attitudes of others that gives a person his or her own "me." You throw a ball to another member of your team because you know that is what is expected of you and you know what other members of your team expect from you. It is the "me" in your self that does the expected thing or at least is prepared to make the expected response. It is your "I" that makes either a brilliant play or an error. The "I" enables you to respond creatively to others' expectations. "The 'I' is the formulator; the 'me,' the formulated."[42] If the self did not contain both aspects, there could be neither conscious responsibility nor anything novel in experience.[43]

Forerunners of Symbolic Interactionism

It has been suggested that the ideas of symbolic interactionism have a long history. This history has been traced at least as far back as the eighteenth century to the work of the Scottish moral philosophers, including such writers as David Hume, Frances Hutcheson, Adam Smith, and Adam Ferguson.[44]

David Hume, for example, observed that because of their relative weakness, human infants are highly dependent upon their families and other human beings. Individuals and communities have interests that bring them close together. The principle of sympathy among human beings leads to the development of fellow feeling and a concern for society as well as a sense of the benefits that society can confer upon them.

Adam Smith also saw sympathy as a universal trait of human beings. It is a trait allowing human beings to place themselves in the place of other people and to see the world through their eyes. It is this ability that allows us to receive communications from other people and to change ourselves in terms of how we see ourselves on the basis of these communications. "Society becomes a vast network of interpersonal communication through which the participants are controlled by the approval and disapproval, the desires and evaluation of others."[45]

In the late nineteenth and early twentieth centuries, philosophers like William James and John Dewey developed these themes. James examined the process by which instincts become replaced by habits. Instincts, he observed, can be modified, and many of them disappear among human beings. Experience allows human beings to learn responses that become habitual.

James's concept of habit was useful in deflecting discussions of human behavior away from purely biological considerations and toward social effects on behavior and the shaping of human consciousness. It is from this consciousness, James felt, that the "self" emerged. Related to this conception of the self is the idea that human beings develop attitudes and feelings toward themselves and, in a sense, can see themselves much as they see other objects in their environment. They can use symbols to refer to these other objects in their world and react to them on various levels. They can do the same thing with respect to themselves.

John Dewey adopted and developed many of these ideas. As a pragmatic philosopher, he stressed the process by which human beings adjust to environmental conditions. He argued that a stimulus does not exist outside the activity a person is pursuing. It is not defined prior to an action and is not a cause of an action. It is defined in the context of action. In short, "The world that impinges on our senses is a world that ultimately depends on the character of the activity in which we are engaged, and changes when that activity is altered."[46]

The ideas of these philosophers entered the field of sociology and social psychology largely through the work of Charles Horton Cooley, who was born in 1864 and died in 1929. George Herbert Mead as well as later symbolic interactionists were heavily influenced by his work. Cooley developed the concept of "primary groups," which has become one of the central concepts in sociology. He defined these as groups characterized by face-to-face association and cooperation. "They are primary in several senses, but chiefly in that they are fundamental in forming the social nature of the ideals of individuals."[47]

It is through these groups that individuals are initially exposed to society. They are characterized by intimate face-to-face relationships and help develop the feeling of a "we."

It is within these groups that a specifically social human nature is formed. This human nature is characterized by ethical standards and by the development of a sense of self. It is here that we find perhaps the most widely referred to concept developed by Cooley: the *looking-glass self*.

In explaining this concept,[48] Cooley begins by raising a question about the meaning of "I" and, more generally, about the meaning of "self." He observes that "I," even in ordinary speech, refers to much more than the physical body of a person. It refers to opinions, purposes, desires, and other ideas that have no direct physical reference whatsoever. For self-feeling to occur, it is necessary for an awareness to develop of other people in one's environment. To clarify this, Cooley uses the analogy of a mirror or looking glass. If I examine myself in a looking glass, I see an image. I then develop an interest in what I see. Finally, I have a sense of being either pleased on displeased by what I see—depending upon whether or not what I see corresponds with what I would want to see reflected in the mirror. For a child, according to Cooley, another person represents a looking glass. As a child, you see your own reflection in the eyes, face, or expression of this other person. You do this by imagining what it is that the other person sees. You (1) form an image in your own mind of how it is that you appear to the other person, (2) imagine how the other person evaluates this image, and (3) develop some sort of self-feeling such as pride or mortification.

The essential difference in how you feel depends upon how important the other person is in your life and some notion about the values the other person holds. The critical point is not what that person "really" thinks but, rather, what it is you *imagine* he or she thinks. Further, if you think the person is "refined," you may feel ashamed of appearing to be "gross." If the other person in your eyes is "brave," you may feel ashamed of being seen as a "coward."

"Children," notes Cooley, "soon become very skilled in evoking desired reactions from important adults or other persons with whom they are in contact."[49] If gurgling, stretching out one's arms, or engaging in some other "cute" act will produce a desired action or attitude by an important adult, as children we soon learn to do what is necessary. This involves posing before the looking glass and may have the unanticipated effect of developing a self-concept of being "cute"—as well as having the practical effect of controlling adult behavior.

Some Contemporary Ideas in Symbolic Interactionism

Symbolic interactionism is responsible for a number of important concepts in social psychology. As we will be discussing a variety of these in some detail throughout the course of this book, we will not enter into a detailed consideration of them at this time. However, an introduction to some of the basic ideas that have proved useful in social psychological research is warranted at this point.

Situated Self

The concept of self continues to be an important idea in symbolic interactionist research. There are, however, at least two conceptions of self that guide research in this field. The first is based on the idea that self is a relatively enduring set of attitudes and beliefs that individuals have toward themselves. These attitudes and beliefs, as measured by such techniques as the Twenty Statements Test and various self-concept and self-esteem scales (see Chapter 3), are useful in explaining why people do the things they do.

There is, however, another more subtle conception of self in symbolic interactionist thought. This is the notion of a situated self, one that varies as a function of the different social milieus in which individuals find themselves. Within the course of a day, one may find oneself acting out a variety of different social roles for different sets of circumstances. At home one may be a father and husband. In another setting, one may be a lover, while in still another one may be an employer and/or employee—all within a very short period of time. This has led some symbolic interactionists to conclude that individuals may have as many different selves as there are different social situations in which they find themselves.

One conception of a situated self that has had considerable sway in social psychology is Erving Goffman's notion of self as presentation.[50] Goffman believed that when individuals appear before one another, they, for a variety of reasons, attempt to control the impressions they may project of themselves. This kind of control requires the management of two different kinds of information related to self. The first concerns information that an individual "gives off." This is information that one individual may communicate more or less directly to others about himself or herself. A teacher, for example, may tell students that he or she is a tough grader. The second kind of information concerns that which the individual may act out as being characteristic or symptomatic of different self-characteristics. Rather than tell students that he is a tough grader, the instructor may convey this by flunking half the class on the first examination. Both forms of information may be used to convey misinformation as well. Our instructor, for example, may really be a "soft touch." He may take such actions in the early part of the semester to motivate students.

Presentation of different selves may lead to a variety of discrepancies. Social life to some extent is organized so as to minimize such discrepancies and enable individuals to present themselves in a consistent manner. For example, there are techniques and procedures for dealing with what Goffman calls "communication out of character" (i.e., the revelation of information inconsistent with a preferred presentation of self). Through "team collusion," participants may work with one another to ensure that out-of-character information does not become available to others. Salespeople often use secret codes to alert others that customers may be entering the scene. When out-of-character information becomes public, realignment techniques may be used to reestablish the previous projection of self. One may change the significance of a negative comment about another by recasting it as "only a joke."

According to Goffman, the social world may be divided into "front stages," where certain performances are to be portrayed, and "back stages," where relevant props may be stored and where front-stage performances may be planned and coordinated. Resorts, for example, typically have areas marked for "staff only." Guest may be disturbed if they spend a great deal of time in such "back-stage areas." Generally, however, teams cooperate with one another in preserving different definitions. Guests rarely barge into the kitchen of a hotel to inspect the staff and facilities for cleanliness.

For Goffman, the presentation of self is analogous to a performance. It is successful when the performer portrays himself or herself successfully as a character of a certain type. This requires that individuals present themselves as truly and genuinely immersed in their roles, while at the same time being sufficiently aware of their surroundings so that they can deal with unforeseen contingencies that may threaten the presentation of self. On the other hand, there are circumstances in which we may want to establish some distance between our *selves* and the roles we may play in specific situations. For example, a doctor in dealing with a patient may use humorous anecdotes or jokes to distance himself or herself from the role of physician. Such role distance may reduce the anxiety of a medical examination.

The idea of a *situated self* raises a thorny issue in social psychology— the question of continuity and discontinuity of self and personality. As we have seen, many Freudians as well as other social psychologists employ a concept of personality or personality traits to refer to relatively enduring characteristics of individuals. Symbolic interactionists use notions of self-concept and self-esteem in a similar manner. The concept of a situated self raises questions about the validity of approaches that rely on a notion of self or personality as consisting of enduring traits. As Goffman's analysis points out, we all may have many selves, designed differently for different social situations. The answer to the question of the variability or invariability of self may go beyond the domain of social psychology. Both ideas, though, have been useful as applied to different dimensions of human behavior and interaction. For this reason, we will not limit our considerations in this book to any specific conception of self. Indeed, it may be that there are different levels of self that have different impacts on behavior and interaction.

Definition of the Situation

Symbolic interactionism is predicated on the idea that human action is self-determined and intentional in the sense that the actor proceeds with some idea of the final product. Human action takes place, as one sociologist has put it, in the "pluperfect tense" (i.e., as though it were already completed).[51] When you get dressed in the morning, for example, you are likely to have an image of the "final product" as you select each article of clothing.

Prior to engaging in any action, however, an individual must make some assessment of the circumstances at hand to help determine which action is appropriate. This is what social psychologists mean by the phrase "definition of the situation." As W. I. Thomas has put it, "Prior to any self-determined act of behavior, there is always a stage of examination and deliberation which we may call the definition of the situation."[52] One's course of action then is based on one's definition of the situation.

The concept of definition of the situation is admittedly an elusive and difficult idea. The elements of any specific situation may vary as may their definitions. Nevertheless social psychologists have been able to show that such definitions may exert an influence over their actions, even when those definitions do not represent "reality." One researcher[53] attempted to demonstrate the importance of the definition of the situation by studying how levels of anxiety among college students were affected by the amount of change they perceived in their lives. Sociologists have long maintained that abrupt changes in one's life can increase an individual's level of anxiety. Which, however, is more important: the actual amount of change that takes place or the perceived amount of change? Answering this question required information with respect to three variables: (1) how much actual change was going on in the students' lives (as measured by changes occurring in familial relations, occupation, religion, and financial affairs); (2) how much change they perceived as taking place in their lives (as measured by agreement with statements such as "The world we live in is changing so fast it leaves me breathless at times"); and (3) measures of how anxious individuals actually are. The researcher found that the relationship between high anxiety and perceived change was greater than the relationship between high anxiety and actual change, indicating that defining the situation as highly variable was an important factor in increasing anxiety.

The notion of the *definition of the situation* is of central importance to symbolic interactionism and to social psychology in general. Indeed, one important conception that underpins not only symbolic interactionism, but other forms of social psychology as well, is the idea that the objective features of any social situation do not operate independently on the organism but, rather, are mediated by some "knower" who performs transformations on that objective information in making it meaningful or relevant. The definition of the situation is one of the most important elements of such transformations.

Reference Group

In discussing the work of George Herbert Mead, we remarked on the importance of taking the role of the other for the development of self. The self develops concomitantly with the sense that the individual is a member of some social collectivity. The notion of reference group has been used to study those groups with which individuals are most likely to compare themselves when evaluating their actions or states of affairs. The concept of reference group has proven to be a powerful predictor of a number of different outcome variables. Some studies, for example, have shown that people are likely to vote in the same way that their friends and family vote. The concept of reference group is in this sense a more specific version of the concept of generalized other. The latter seems to link the individual with an abstract notion of society at large; the former links the individual to specific groups.

One of the most interesting uses of the concept of reference group was evidenced in a study of World War II draftees conducted by two sociologists.[54] They noted that better educated draftees tended to feel less deprived about being drafted than did their less educated counterparts. According to the authors, this could have been due to the fact that a higher proportion of less educated men had worked in factories, many of which were converted for wartime purposes. Many less educated or working-class people were not drafted because they were engaged in "essential" production in factories. The disgruntlement among lower-educated men resulted from the fact that many of the individuals in their reference group (e.g., their friends and relatives) had not been drafted. On the other hand, white-collar jobs were much less "essential." Most highly educated men, therefore, saw that most of their friends and relatives were being drafted and, hence, were less disgruntled by their own situation. The concept of reference group has relevance for other important substantive issues in social psychology. We shall come back to this concept later in this book.

PIAGET'S COGNITIVE DEVELOPMENTAL APPROACH

Each of the theories discussed so far focuses on different aspects of the processes by which individuals interact and are socialized, that is, how they are changed from simple biological organisms to people who can participate in the social life around them. The Freudian approach emphasizes the role of society in satisfying or frustrating basic drives and impulses of the biological human being. From this perspective, the tension between the needs of the organism and demands of living in society ultimately leads to the development of human personalities. Symbolic interactionism emphasizes the importance of meaning and communication between individuals. It centers on the importance of role taking in the formation of distinctive "selves." Behavioral theories explain behavior as a consequence of real or perceived rewards received by individuals as they do things.

Piaget's Conception of Intelligence

The focus of a Piagetian analysis is somewhat different. Since the early part of this century, the Swiss psychologist Jean Piaget (1896–1980) attempted to learn more about how human intelligence develops. He has worked primarily with children. His primary interest, however, is not limited to children; he wants to understand the nature of the underlying production of intelligent responses.

Piaget's interests in intelligence began while he was working with Alfred Binet, one of the pioneers of intelligence testing. In helping Binet to standardize some of the questions on his test, Piaget noticed that children at younger ages had a great deal of difficulty with certain specific types of questions (e.g., those concerning part-whole relationships). For example, tell children under 11 years of age that you have a bouquet of buttercups, and then ask them if the bouquet contains (1) all yellow flowers, (2) some yellow flowers, or (3) no yellow flowers. You will presumably find, as did Piaget, that they will *not* be able to provide the correct answer. Piaget surmised that young children have difficulty with questions like this because they have not yet developed the ability to subsume the part (yellow flowers) under the whole (bouquet of flowers). This general ability to understand the relationship between part and whole develops only at a particular stage of childhood.

Intelligence, for Piaget, evolves from the interaction between the maturational process of the individual, which is determined biologically or genetically, and by stimuli provided through the environment. Intelligence develops through the process by which the human organism adapts to its environment. Adaptation consists of essentially two processes: *assimilation* and *accommodation*. Assimilation refers to the extension of a behavior particularly to new objects. For example, a young child quickly learns that hunger can be relieved by sucking a milk bottle. The sucking response may, within a short period of time, be extended to a variety of foods and other objects. Accommodation, on the other hand, refers to those processes by which the organism modifies its response to meet new demands. At some point, our child will learn how to drink from a cup. For all practical purposes, the processes of accommodation and assimilation take place almost simultaneously. Each depends on the other.

By receiving different forms of food (assimilation), the child learns to change his or her approach to eating (accommodation). Eventually, the child will adopt a consistent concept of eating. Thus, by first placing rattles in their mouths, and then food, children develop and internalize ("interiorize") the categories (schemata) of edible and nonedible—they learn to tell the differences between food things and other things. They also begin to subsume different particulars under these categories and to modify the categories in accordance with their experiences in the world. ("This is *good* food"; That tastes "awful"; "Candy is sweet"; "I like candy"; "I don't like spinach.")

The preceding discussion illustrates two important aspects of Piaget's conception of intelligence. First, intelligence begins to develop in early infancy. Rudimentary thought processes, in this sense, precede the development of language—children think before they can speak. Second, intelligence is rooted in the child's practical experiences. It grows out of the interaction between the child and his or her environment. Even though intelligence is "interiorized," it is rooted in experience in the world. Intelligence grows from and is part of the child's adaptation to society. "Knowledge is derived from action," Piaget tells us. "To know an object is to act upon it and transform it."[55]

By adapting to the world, the child reaches various stages of equilibrium. Each stage represents a level at which the child's mental categories are sufficient to meet its needs. There is a point, for example, at which the child can satisfy its nutritional need through sucking. Later, it bites and chews. The process by which children move from one level of equilibrium to another is referred to as *equilibration.*

It is here that one can see how Piaget is both a maturationist (i.e., one who believes that development takes place in terms of an internal genetically determined plan) and an interactionist (i.e., one who believes that development proceeds through interaction with the environment). One of the factors that pushes the child to higher levels of cognition is maturation. Muscles mature as children walk. This allows them to run. Similarly, maturation of mental capabilities leads to possibilities for higher thought. The child may develop a category "dog," for example. Initially, this means "four-legged animals." Later the child perceives the difference between dogs and other four-legged animals. It also becomes apparent that there are different kinds or categories of dog. Thus, the category "dog" provides the basis on which the child may begin to differentiate long-haired dogs from short-haired ones or mean dogs from kind ones. The category also provides the basis for differentiating dogs from cats, cows, sheep, and other four-legged animals.

Other factors pushing the child to higher stages of cognition develop through interaction with the environment. These experiences need to be organized in the child's mind. As new experiences are encountered, preexisting categories are modified. This may be seen in connection with a group of children to be studied in more detail in Chapter Five. The early childhood of these children was spent in a Nazi concentration camp. There they had contact with only one type of animal—dogs. After their release, caretakers at a nursery in Great Britain took the children on an excursion to the country. Upon seeing a herd of cows, the frightened children exclaimed, "Dogs!" and began to cry. The caretakers had to explain the difference between cows and dogs.

In Piaget's terms this illustrates how maturation and interaction with the environment depend upon each other. The development of inetlligence requires both.

Egocentrism and Decentration

In some ways Piaget's approach bears a good deal of similarity to symbolic interactionism[56] in that the transition from a biological organism to a person consists of a consistent broadening of perspectives.

The human infant at birth cannot distinguish between itself and the outside world. The neonate does not experience a sense of self that is differentiated from nonself; it cannot tell the difference between its internal states and external stimuli. By experiencing the environment and exploring the limits of their own physical bodies (e.g., learning about feet by placing them in the mouth), children develop mental schemata that enable them to differentiate themselves from the environment. For the neonate, the experience of oneself as a separate and differentiated entity may be likened to a kind of Copernican revolution.

This revolution results in a specific form of childhood egocentrism— not unlike the pre-Copernican view of the universe. Just as the earth was considered to be the center of the universe, children begin by considering themselves to be the center of their universe.

Childhood egocentrism is not to be equated with selfishness. Rather, children have a confused and inverted sense of the relationship between their actions and the world. They may feel responsible for events unconnected to anything they have done. Often 5- or 6-year-olds will blame themselves for marital difficulties that their parents may be experiencing. In a more general sense, childhood egocentrism can be seen as the basis for magical or superstitious beliefs held by many adults. Consider, for example, the person who carries an umbrella in the belief that taking the umbrella will help ensure that it will not rain.

Egocentrism also is shown when children feel that they are the center of attention or concern and are unable to take the perspective of others. Thus, a young boy may be able to recognize that he has two brothers without understanding that he is a brother to them or that this means that there are three brothers in the family. A brother may be conceived of as "a little person who lives with us" or "a boy who lives in the same flat."[57] The child has not yet developed a mental representation or schema that provides for the reciprocity implied in the brother relationship. Indeed, until the age of 10, children are usually unable to understand fully what it means to be a brother. Thus, at the age of 7, John may understand that Bill is his brother and that, therefore, he is Bill's brother. He may also understand that he has another brother, Bob. John may have difficulty, however, in understanding that this means that Bob, Bill, and he each have two brothers and that there are a total of three brothers in the family. At this age, John has not yet developed the ability to obtain an objective view of his own relationship vis-à-vis his entire family.

John's difficulties illustrate two stages of the process of decentration. One of these is the ability to take the perspective of the other—to understand that for you to be my brother means that I am yours. A second stage is the ability to see things "objectively" (i.e., to appreciate your own position vis-à-vis a relatively complex network of relationships).

The process of decentration thus involves three stages: (1) egocentrism, (2) the ability to take the perspective of the other, and (3) the achievement of objectivity. To achieve objectivity, children must develop a "relativity of perspectives" (i.e., an ability to coordinate their perspectives with the perspectives of a wide range of other people). The reader should note the similarity between this conception of objectivity (through the relativity of perspectives) and George Herbert Mead's concept of the generalized other.

The developmental progression from egocentrism to complete relativity of perspectives is most dramatically evident with respect to the evolution of spatial conceptions and relationships. The development of the child's understanding of the relativity of spatial relationships involves essentially three stages. During the first stage, the child believes that there is only one possible viewpoint—his own. The second stage brings the realization that other viewpoints are possible. However, the child is unable to describe those viewpoints. In the third stage, the child (1) understands that other perspectives are possible and (2) imagines how things appear from these other perspectives.

To see this process more clearly, consider the following: A pasteboard display of three differently colored triangular figures representing mountains is placed on a table before a young girl. A small green mountain topped with a house is placed near the child's right hand. A somewhat higher brown mountain with a cross is placed to the left, a bit behind the smaller green mountain. In the rear toward the center is an even larger gray mountain with a cap of snow on its peak. The display also contains a small doll that is placed in various positions in the display. The child is then given a variety of tasks requiring her to reconstruct the display as viewed from the perspective of the doll.

Piaget and his colleagues observed various stages in the ability of children to represent the doll's perspective. In the first stage (after being able to understand the question), the children may consider their own view to be the only viable perspective. At this stage, the view of the child is considered to be immutable. This is the most egocentric stage. As children get a bit older, they may realize that there are different views. However, during this second stage, children still have considerable difficulty in imagining precisely how the scene would look from another perspective. Specifically, children have difficulty in understanding that the small green mountain to their right would be to the left of the doll were the doll seated facing the display from the other side of the table. Similarly, the children at this stage have trouble understanding that the distant brown mountain would be closest to the doll on the other side of the table.

An inability to perform well at these types of perspective-taking tasks persists well into middle childhood. A major step toward the decline of egocentrism is made, however, when children get the idea that the view is different from another perspective, even if they cannot describe the differences accurately. While some children at the age of 3 were able to understand that an observer might see the view differently, they could not reconstruct what that observer would see until they had reached the age of 5 or 6.

The transition from egocentrism to decentration is also evident with respect to how children use language and their ability to communicate. The development of communication skills is closely linked to the child's ability to take the perspective of the other.

Piaget characterizes this development as a movement from "egocentric speech" to "socialized speech." With egocentric speech the child "does not attempt to place himself at the point of view of the hearer."[58] There are essentially three forms of egocentric speech: echolalia (repetition), monologue, and collective monologue. In performing the first of these, children simply imitate the sounds they hear others making. During this stage of egocentric speech, children do not even attempt to make sense of the sounds. This is followed by the monologue state in which the child may string a series of sounds and words together with no apparent social purpose. In the dual monologue stage, the child may respond to another's stimulus. This is not to suggest that egocentric speech is completely nonfunctional. It may in fact help the child to orient to his or her own activities. The Russian psychologist Vygotsky describes a young boy who in the course of drawing a picture breaks the pencil he is using. The child then exclaims that the pencil is broken and continues to draw with another instrument. In this context the egocentric speech may have helped the boy to complete what he thought he was doing.[59] In any case, such speech is not designed for communication with a different person.

In contrast to these forms of speech, socialized speech represents an attempt to adapt communication to the special needs of others. Piaget's distinction between egocentric and socialized speech is, in this way, similar to Mead's distinction between the conversation of gestures and significant communication. Neither egocentric speech nor the conversation of gestures requires an attempt to relate one's response to the subjective state of another. Both socialized speech and meaningful communication specifically involve an attempt to design a response in terms of an appreciation of the other's perspective. Mead and Piaget share the assumption that the child's ability to take the perspective of the other will help to facilitate more effective communication and that a child's ability to communicate increases with age.

The second part of this assumption was investigated in some detail by a psychologist named Alvy.[60] He gave pairs of children at different ages tasks requiring them to describe the emotions of different facial expressions portrayed on a series of pictures. One child was to describe the emotion expressed by a face; the other child was to match this emotion with the correct picture selected from a variety of pictures on display. The second child (the listener) was encouraged to ask questions of the first. Not surprisingly, the listener's ability to select the correct picture increased with the age of the pairs. The ambiguity of the descriptors (defined by the number of times a child used the same word to describe two different pictures) also decreased with age. Older children did a better job of requesting additional information and better tailored their responses to such requests to the expressed needs of the listener.

The connection between role taking and the ability to communicate effectively was explored even further by Flavell.[61] He devised a task in which children of varying ages were to describe a game to a blindfolded and nonblindfolded listener. The purpose of the experiment was to examine the extent to which children would communicate in ways that were adapted to the informational needs of different listeners. Flavell found considerable differences with age. Younger children (ages 7 to 9) provided virtually identical instructions to both the sighted and nonsighted listeners displaying very little ability to tailor their descriptions to the needs of the handicapped listeners. Children at this age would be satisfied once they achieved a description appropriate to their own needs and appeared to be oblivious to the special informational needs of the nonsighted listeners. In some cases, for example, children of this age would refer to "this piece here" for both sighted and nonsighted listeners. In contrast, 12- to 14-year-olds were quite sensitive to the differential needs of their listeners. They would spend a greater amount of energy giving a name to each object to help the nonsighted listener differentiate between the pieces of the game. Flavell argues that the more effective communication of the older children was enhanced by their ability to take the perspective of the listener in formulating their response.

Flavell provides supporting evidence for this idea in other experiments. He found that while younger children would rely on a simple request, older children were more adept at designing their appeals to relate to the needs and motivations of others. These experiments had another interesting by-product. In one experimental condition, children were to assume the role of a salesperson and attempt to convince a potential buyer to purchase a new tie. Older children were more adept at assuming the role of the salesperson and in using a varied and subtle assortment of persuasion techniques. This suggests that the ability to persuade is related to "role enactment" (i.e., the ability to see things through the eyes of both salesperson and buyer). Thus, Flavell concludes that "the child's ability to persuade others appears to lie at the crossroads of numerous other developing behaviors. [These include] his social perception, his understanding of human motivation and cognition, his role-taking prowess, [and] social interactional skills."[62]

CONCLUSION

We have now completed our review of some major theoretical and methodological approaches in social psychology. Our next step is to examine the relevance of these for understanding social interaction among individuals in society. In the next four chapters, we will show how a social-psychological approach provides insights into the various stages of the life cycle. In this sense, the Freudian and Piagetian perspectives help us to understand the aspects of the individual's emotional and maturational development. The behaviorist and symbolic interactionist perspectives provide insights into the nature of communication processes and exchanges that take place among individuals in different societal contexts.

NOTES

[1]See Sigmund Freud "The Origin and Development of Psychoanalysis," in Robert Maynard Hutchins, ed., *Great Books of the Western World*, Vol. 54: *Freud* (Chicago: Encyclopedia Britannica, 1952), pp. 1–22. Also see Ernest Jones, *The Life and Work of Sigmund Freud* (New York: Basic Books, 1953), Vol. 1, pp. 221–267.

[2]Sigmund Freud, "General Introduction to Psycho-Analysis," in Hutchins ed., *Great Books of the Western World*, p. 452, Volume 54, Freud, op. cit.

[3]Ibid., p. 452.

[4]Ibid., pp. 468–469.

[5]Ibid., p. 469.

[6]Ibid., p. 470.

[7]Sigmund Freud, *The Interpretation of Dreams* (New York: Basic Books, 1955), pp. 100–101.

[8]Ibid., pp. 122–133.

[9]S. Freud, "The Ego and the Id," in Robert Hutchins, ed., *Freud*, pp. 697–717; also see Patrick Mullahy, *Oedipus: Myth and Complex: A review of Psychoanalytic Theory* (New York: Hermitage Press, 1948), pp. 37–43.

[10]Leon Salzman, *Developments in Psychoanalysis* (New York: Grune and Stratton, 1962), pp. 2–4.

[11]Clara Thompson, ed., Milton Mazer and Earl Witenberg, *An Outline of Psychoanalysis*, rev. ed. (New York: The Modern Library, 1955), p. 617.

[12]William Healy, Augusta F. Bronner, and Anna Mae Bowers, *The Structure and Meaning of Psychoanalysis* (New York: Alfred A. Knopf, 1930), p. 2.

[13]Paul Roazen, *Freud and His Followers* (New York: Alfred A. Knopf, 1975), pp. 202–211.

[14]Ibid., p. 211.

[15]Erich Fromm, *Greatness and Limitations of Freud's Thought* (New York: Harper & Row, 1980), pp. 5–6.

[16]See Roazen, *Freud and His Followers*, pp. 224–296, for a more extended discussion of the relationship between Freud and Jung.

[17]Harold Kelman, "Introduction" to *New Perspectives in Psychoanalysis: Contributions to Karen Horney's Holistic Approach* (New York: W. W. Norton, 1965), p. 9.

[18]Ibid., p. 9.

[19]Karen Horney, *Our Inner Conflicts* (New York: W. W. Norton, 1945), pp. 11–12.

[20]Karen Horney *The Neurotic Personality of Our Time* (New York: W. W. Norton, 1937,) especially "Introduction," pp. vii–xii and Chap. 1, "Cultural and Psychological Implications of Neurosis," pp. 13–29.

[21] Karen Horney *Neurosis and Human Growth* (New York: W. W. Norton, 1950), pp. 370–371.

[22]Ibid., p. 371.

[23]Erich Fromm "Introduction" to Erich Fromm, ed., *Socialist Humanism: An International Symposium.* (Garden City, N.Y.: Doubleday, 1965), pp. viii–ix.

[24]Erich Fromm, *The Crisis of Psychoanalysis* (New York: Holt, Rinehart & Winston, 1970), pp. 4–5.

[25]Ibid., p. 5.

[26]Ibid., p. 6.

[27]Ibid., p. 6.

[28]Ibid., pp. 6–7.

[29]See S. Berger and W. Lambert, "Stimulus Response Theory in Contemporary Social Psychology," in G. Lindsey and E. Aronson, eds., *Handbook of Social Psychology* (Reading, Mass.: Addison-Wesley, 1978).

[30]B. F. Skinner, *The Behavior of Organisms* (New York: Appleton-Century-Crofts, 1966), p. 47.

[31]Webster J. Murray, *Actions and Actors* (Cambridge, Mass: Winthrop, 1975), p. 223.

[32]Peter M. Blau, *On the Nature of Organizations* (New York: John Wiley, 1974), p. 205. Also see his *Exchange and Power in Social Life* (New York: John Wiley, 1964).

[33]Peter M. Blau, *Inequality and Heterogeneity* (New York: The Free Press, 1977), p. 141.

[34]Blau, *Exchange and Power in Social Life*, pp. 88–114.

[35]A. Bandura and R. J. Walters, *Social Learning Theory and Personality Development* (New York: Holt, Rinehart and Winston; 1963).

[36]Albert Bandura and Richard Walters, "Principles of Social Learning," in E. P. Hollander and R. G. Hunt, eds., *Classic Contributions to Social Psychology* (New York: Oxford University Press, 1972), p. 58.

[37]Albert Bandura, *Social Learning Theory* (Englewood Cliffs, N.J.: Prentice-Hall, 1977), p. 23.

[38]Ibid., p. 25.

[39]Ibid., p. 28.

[40]Herbert Blumer, *Symbolic Interactionism: Perspective and Method* (Englewood Cliffs, N.J.: Prentice-Hall, 1969), p.1.

[41]Bernard N. Meltzer, "Mead's Social Psychology," in Jerome G. Manis and Bernard N. Meltzer, eds., *Symbolic Interaction*, 3rd ed. (Boston: Allyn & Bacon, 1978), p. 16.

[42]C. P. Stone and H. A. Farberman, *Social Psychology Through Symbolic Interaction* (New York: John Wiley, 1981), p. 88.

[43]George H. Mead, *Mind, Self and Society* (Chicago: University of Chicago Press, 1934), pp. 135-178. Also see Meltzer, "Mead's Social Psychology," pp. 18-20.

[44]Sheldon Stryker, *Symbolic Interactionism: A Social Structural Version* (Menlo Park, Calif.: Benjamin Cummings, 1980), pp. 16-50. Also see Bernard M. Meltzer, John W. Petras, and Larry T. Reynolds, *Symbolic Interactionism: Genesis, Varieties and Criticism* (London and Boston: Routledge & Kegan Paul, 1975). For a discussion of symbolic interaction and its relation to the phenomenology, see Robert Boguslaw and George Vickers, *Prologue to Sociology* (Santa Monica, Calif.: Goodyear, 1977), pp. 149-173.

[45]Ibid., p. 19.

[46]Ibid., pp. 21-23.

[47]Ibid., p. 26.

[48]Charles Horton Cooley, *Social Organization* (New York: Scribners, 1909), p. 23.

[49]Charles Horton Cooley, *Human Nature and the Social Order* (New York: Scribners, 1902), pp. 150-168.

[50]Erving Goffman, *The Presentation of Self in Everyday Life* (Garden City, N.Y.: Doubleday, 1959).

[51]Alfred Schutz, *The Phenomenology of the Social World*, translated by George Wash and Frederick Wash (Evanston, Ill.: Northwestern University Press, 1967), pp. 45-97.

[52]W. I. Thomas, *The Unadjusted Girl* (Boston: Little Brown, 1937), p. 42.

[53]R. H. Lauer, "Rate of Change and Stress: A Test of the 'Future Shock' Thesis," *Social Forces*, Vol. 52 (1974), pp. 510-516.

[54]R. K. Merton and A. Kitt, "Contributions to the Theory of Reference Group Behavior," in R. K. Merton and P. F. Lazarsfeld, eds., *Studies in the Scope and Method of the American Soldier* (Glencoe, Ill.: The Free Press, 1954), pp. 42-53.

[55]Quoted in Hugh Rosen, *Pathway to Piaget* (Cherry Hill, N.J.: Post Graduate International, 1977), pp. 11-12.

[56]J. H. Flavell et al., *The Development of Role-Taking and Communication Skills in Children* (New York: John Wiley, 1968).

[57]Rosen, op. cit. p. 43.

[58]Jean Piaget, *The Language and Thought of the Child*, translated by M. Gabin (Cleveland: Meridan Books, 1955), p. 32.

[59]See Rosen, *Pathway to Piaget*, pp. 195-197.

[60]K. T. Alvy, "Relation of Age to Children's Egocentric and Co-operative Communications," *Journal of Genetic Psychology*, Vol. 112 (1968), pp. 275-286.

[61]See Rosen, p. 39.

[62]Ibid., *Pathway to Piaget*, p. 146.

CHAPTER FIVE
COMMUNICATION WITH INFANTS AND YOUNG CHILDREN

Man cannot live by milk alone.

Love is an emotion that does not need to be bottle or spoon-fed, and we may be sure that there is nothing to be gained by giving lip service to love.

Harry Harlow

John, Ruth, Leah, Paul, Miriam, and Peter had a very special relationship. They were not siblings. In the conventional sense, they were not related at all. In some ways, however, they were closer than most brothers and sisters ever become. These six children were survivors of a Nazi concentration camp. What makes their case interesting with respect to our understanding of communication and socialization of infants and young children is that all of them were separated from their parents at a very early age (within 12 months of birth). Because of this separation, their adaptation to the social world differed from that of most children in our culture. For example, upon their arrival at a nursery in Great Britain after the war, they were extremely protective of each other:

> The children's feelings were centered exclusively in their own group. It was evident that they cared greatly for each other and not at all for anybody or anything else. They had no other wish than to be together and became upset when they were separated from each other, even for short moments. No child would consent to remain upstairs while the other was downstairs, and no child would be taken for a walk or on an errand without the other.[1]

The children were reported to be extremely suspicious and easily frightened by strangers.

Why this strange behavior? Why the suspicion and fear of outsiders? Why the strong attachment to each other? The answers to these questions require a more complete understanding of how children, at very early ages, communicate and interact with parents and significant others. This, in turn, involves an understanding of how communication fosters the growth of "attachment bonds" between infants and significant others.

EARLY SOCIAL INTERACTION: SOCIAL AND EMOTIONAL DEVELOPMENT IN NONHUMAN ANIMALS

Concern with interaction among young children and infants has been an important theme both in social psychology and the study of childhood development. Researchers have studied the effects of early contact on the development of both nonhuman and human babies. Early parent-child interaction, they have concluded, can have an important impact on the emotional and cognitive development of the child.

Originally, many thought that the attachment of the child to the mother was a result of the feeding process. According to this view, a child's attachment to the mother is a secondary response resulting from food as the primary reinforcement. This theory is referred to as the "secondary drive theory."[2]

Recently child psychologists have come to recognize that infants have certain attachment needs operating independently of their need for food. These may be thought of as "generalized," that is, not contingent on any one particular environmental stimulus or biological characteristics.[3]

The idea that parents and infants become strongly attached to one another should not seem strange to anyone who has observed a young child separated from mother and father for the first time. The baby will often cry as it searches for mother with its eyes. Many animals (especially mammals) have similar responses. The physiological response of pig-tailed monkeys to separation from their mothers was measured over a four-day period. The researchers found fluctuations in both heart rate and body temperature, leading to the speculation that premature separation may result in "an instability of thermoregulatory mechanisms . . . [in which] coping mechanisms [go] awry or out of control."[4]

Similar observations have been made on other mammals as well. Placing dogs between 3 to 12 weeks of age[5] and young lambs[6] in strange environments produces a variety of behavioral disturbances, including crying and heightened activity. These disturbances can be reduced if the mother or some other object of attachment is present in the strange environment.

Observers of nonhuman primates have noted considerable evidence of strong attachment bonds between mother and infant monkeys in natural settings. Some young chimpanzees, for example, may remain dependent on their mothers long after they have developed the necessary motor skills to make them independent. One rather exceptional example concerned an 8-year-old male chimpanzee who remained dependent on his mother until she died. After her death, the chimp stayed near her body and interacted only briefly with other members of the troupe. The son displayed increasingly severe signs of anorexia and depression until he himself died 26 days later. Although the chimp developed an infection which became the primary cause of the son's death, observers believe that the death of the mother was an important contributing factor in the son's death. Other observers have reported similar findings. In one case, two chimps orphaned at the age of 4 developed signs of depression. One of them ultimately died of malnutrition.[7]

The depression exhibited by these monkeys is not unlike what psychologists term "anaclitic depression" shown by human infants when separated from their mothers.[8] The symptoms of this depression often include fear, apprehension, withdrawal, crying, sadness, and dietary malfunctions, including anorexia. In cases of normal children, these symptoms are relieved upon the mother's return.

Some researchers believe that the more secure an infant is prior to separation, the less distress there will be during separation and the more easily this state will be relieved after the mother's return.[9] Of course, the mother's response to the child upon return is a critical factor for both human beings and nonhuman primates. This is not to suggest that all infants will have the same reaction. One must be sensitive to the existence of important individual and social differences. In studying human beings, as we will see, it is important to pay attention to how reactions may vary in different groups and cultures. Even with monkeys, however, the structure of social life will affect the ability of baby monkeys to cope with separation. For example, among those species of monkeys where multiple mothering takes place (i.e., where the role of the care of the infant is shared among different female monkeys), response to separation is less severe than it is among species where only the mother cares for the infant. This "allomothering" prepares the infant for a specific kind of social life. Among species where only one mother cares for the baby, the infant's future life and social relationships will revolve to a large extent around the mother. This is different in allomothering species. According to one expert in this field,

> the infant transfer pattern undoubtedly prepares the infant for a social life characteristically not based upon exclusive and long-lasting special ties with members of one's lineage but, instead, based on forming adult relationships that develop rather independently from those of the mother.[10]

Such research indicates that among other animals as well as human beings, there is a complex and important relationship between the structure of society and the forms of individual development. In the case of the allomothering Indian langur monkeys, multiple mothering serves a related function in giving younger females the chance to "play mother" and thereby to learn appropriate mothering behavior. The idea that mothering, even in primates, is a learned rather than purely instinctive response gains credence from studies showing that isolated female monkeys make poorer mothers than do those who have had the opportunity to observe others care for their infants. These so-called "motherless mothers" are often indifferent and in many cases brutal in their treatment of their offspring.[11]

ATTACHMENT

This importance of attachment was first apparent in Conrad Lorenz's classic "imprinting" studies of goslings and ducklings.[12] Lorenz observed that during a period of time shortly after birth, goslings and ducklings follow moving objects. After a "sensitive" period, they would then become "attached" to one specific object. Such objects ranged from match boxes to human beings and, of course, to mother duck and goose. In any case, the baby birds would quickly develop a pattern in which they selected only *one* object and continued to follow *only* that object. After some time, they tried to escape from other objects to which they were not attached. These studies indicated that the roots of attachment behavior in young goslings and ducklings develop without food as a reinforcer, apparently without any reinforcement whatsoever.

The importance of social contact for the emotional development of the infants was demonstrated experimentally in the Harlow studies of rhesus monkeys. During a period of over 20 years, Harry and Margaret Harlow and their colleagues raised rhesus monkeys under a variety of different conditions. In their early research, the infant monkeys were raised with two "make-believe" mothers. Some were fabricated from terrycloth, others from wire. Half the terrycloth surrogates could provide milk through bottles placed in the general area of the breast. Half the wire mothers could also provide milk while the others were dry. In this way, the researchers could determine the relative importance of both "contact-comfort" and "feeding-comfort" for the new born monkeys. Harlow was surprised to find that "contact-comfort" was even more important than "feeding." Infant monkeys would spend considerably more time clinging to the cloth surrogate even if it did not produce milk. When given access to a cloth surrogate that produced milk, the infant monkeys, if they had a choice, spent almost no time with the wire surrogate. They spent between 15 and 20 hours a day clinging to the cloth mother surrogate. If allowed to choose between a wire surrogate with milk and a dry terrycloth mother, the infant monkeys spent more of their time clinging to the terrycloth object. The time spent with the cloth mother increased with the age of the monkey. Between the age of 1 to 5 days, infant monkeys in the wire-fed condition would spend 6 to 7 hours a day clinging to the cloth surrogate (as compared with less than 1 hour on the wire surrogate). When they reached the age of 16 days, these monkeys would spend about 16 hours a day with the cloth mother and almost no time with the wire surrogate. These early experiments led Harlow to conclude that contact comfort was of "overwhelming importance," whereas the importance of lactation was negligible.[13] This is not to suggest that other factors, including food, are unimportant. As later research indicates, mother surrogates who are warm, provide milk, and cuddle are preferred to those that cannot.[14]

On the basis of these experiments, Harlow surmised that the mother's function in providing a comfortable environment was critical for the infant's sense of safety and security. To test this, Harlow and his colleagues devised another experiment in which infant monkeys were placed in a strange room for a period of time. When a cloth surrogate was also placed in the room, the infant monkeys rushed to the mother surrogate and clung to it. After a period of time, the infants used the surrogate mother as a base of operations. They ventured off to explore other parts of the room, returning periodically before taking off for further explorations. Among primates, the mother plays a critical role in directing the young child's explorations. These explorations are important for developing motor skills and for fostering a sense of security in the infant. This sense of security is important for the development of curiosity that enhances the infant's cognitive development. Socially restricted infants are less able to deal with novel objects.[15] The mother apparently acts as a base from which the infant may explore new things in the environment. The mother may keep the infant in view during its exploitations and, after a period of exploring, the infant will return to the mother before going off again. This pattern of "refueling"[16] that has been noted among human infants as well will be dealt with later in this chapter.

The baby monkeys reacted much differently when no mother or mother surrogate was present in the room. They often crouched in a frozen position. When the surrogate was removed from the room, the monkey often ran to the spot where the surrogate was usually placed and then ran from object to object in the room screaming and crying.

Prolonged separation from mother and other members of the species can have important short-term and in some cases lasting consequences for the development of monkey and human infants. Monkeys raised in total isolation (i.e., isolated from their mother and prevented from viewing either other monkeys or humans) almost immediately developed bizarre behavioral patterns, including nonnutritional orality, self-clutching, a vacant stare resembling a kind of social apathy, and stereotyped repetitive movements such as pacing back and forth in their cages. Monkeys isolated as infants were considerably more aggressive than were nonisolated monkeys. When an experimenter ran his hand (protected by a heavy black glove) over the cage, isolated monkeys attacked the glove more frequently and with greater vigor than did their nonisolated counterparts. Isolated monkeys would also attack their own bodies, biting their own hands and feet.

Isolates had considerably more difficulty in adjusting to social life. Monkeys isolated for 6 months to a year failed to develop appropriate forms of play. They exhibited either signs of fear at the sight of other monkeys or an inability to stem any antisocial aggression. Beyond this, monkeys isolated for more than 6 months failed to develop normal sexual behavior. Although those isolated for less than 3 months generally would develop an appropriate behavioral repertoire after contact with other monkeys, total isolation for 6 months or a year had devastating effects. Isolated monkeys would become more aggressive. Because of their lack of play experience, however, they had not developed adequate fighting skills. For this reason, their assaults on nonisolated monkeys would often be counterproductive. In one case, the mixing of 12-month isolates with nonisolates had to be stopped because the "control animals were mauling and abusing the helpless isolates to the point that the isolates could not have survived continued interaction." These isolated monkey youths even suicidally attacked much larger adult males.[17]

Monkeys are not alone among mammals with respect to social adjustment problems following early childhood isolation. Other animal studies indicate that isolated infants are reluctant to approach members of their own species or inanimate objects. Isolated colts have a difficult time developing "normal" relationships with other horses. There is some evidence that non-isolated animals will reject, at least temporarily, isolated members of their own species. A lamb removed from its maternal ewe, for example, will tend to be rejected by other members of the flock when returned.[18]

Harlow's experiments reflect the devastating effect prolonged total isolation has on the social development of young monkeys. But total isolation has a rather extreme state of affairs. In everyday life, there is a greater chance that infants may be deprived of some particular type of social contact. Children may be orphaned or placed in a situation where they cannot make friends their own age. Field studies of primate life indicate that, through play with peers, young monkeys develop the motor skills necessary for adult life. In some cases, primate play may become quite complex, resembling human games such as "King of the castle" and "Follow the leader."

To examine the relative importance of maternal and peer isolation in monkeys, experiments were devised in which some baby monkeys received maternal care but were deprived of peer contact while others received the opposite treatment. These experiments indicate that both mother and peer interaction have positive values. Deprivation of only one of these two forms of contact, however, is much less serious than is total isolation. Monkeys given no maternal affection, but allowed to interact with peers, developed adequate social behavior. Those who had early contact with different peers developed less aggressive tendencies and subsequently were able to form closer ties with other monkeys. Monkeys raised with only one partner showed considerable loyalty to their partner but were less able to develop close ties with others and were much more aggressive. Those raised with several peers developed a larger repertoire of play activities.

In some cases where maternal care was provided but no peers, the baby monkey attempted to play with the mother. This often resulted in a negative response from the mother. Mothers were not completely adequate as peer substitutes. Mothered infants denied peer associations tended to be more hostile than othes and also failed to develop as varied a repertoire of play style.[19] It should be noted that there is a considerable variation both within and across species in the extent to which mothers playfully interact with their offspring. For example, chimpanzee mothers tend to play with their infants a great deal more than do rhesus monkeys. Human mothers, of course, play extensively with their infants—some more than others.

Although it is dangerous to draw too many conclusions about human behavior from research on animals, it is interesting to note that play also has an important role in human development. As we shall discuss shortly, such theorists as Mead and Piaget compare play with social development. Mead views play as a mechanism through which children learn to "take the role of the other." Piaget suggests that play is critical for the development of moral judgment in that through play, children gain a sense of how to legislate their own activities. Being deprived of this type of social contact may hamper the development of these capabilities.

A number of additional factors modify the effects of separation and isolation. These may include the physiological capabilities of the mother and infant, the length of separation, the age at which separation takes place, and the response of the mother during reunion. The nature and quality of care provided prior to separation is especially important for human infants. Throughout all this, it is necessary to keep in mind that mother-infant attachment is fostered through a communicative and interactive system. It is, therefore, important to consider not only whether mother-infant interaction takes place but also the quality of such interaction. Suomi and Harlow show that mother-infant interaction among monkeys after separation may be adversely affected by the separation. Thus, after having been separated, mother and infant may engage in close clinging behavior rather than exploratory play. This may lead to delayed or arrested maturation and may in fact be more important than the separation itself.[20]

With respect to the study of human behavior, two important issues emerge from the seminal research carried out by the Harlows and their colleagues in comparative psychology and anthropology. The first is the importance of socialization for normal social and emotional development. "In primates—monkeys, apes and men—socialization is essential to survival and the hazards of normal socialization are multiple and diverse."[21] Remember (from Chapter 2) that chimpanzees are unique among nonhuman animals in that chimpanzees appear to have the rudimentary elements of a self-concept. Isolated chimps, however, do not appear to develop any sense of self. They do not treat their mirror image as a reflection of themselves, but rather as a strange animal or something to be ignored.[22]

The remainder of this chapter and part of the next focuses more specifically on the importance of socialization for the cognitive, social, and emotional development of human beings as well as other animals.

The second, and more specific, point illustrated by these investigations is the importance of the role of the mother or primary parent in the early stages of socialization. A good deal of discussion in this area has concerned the necessity of "mother." With respect to animals, a number of points are now obvious:

1. There is considerable species variation. While for some types of monkeys, one mother assumes virtually all the responsibilities of caring for the infant, in other species a variety of females may share these responsibilities.
2. Even within a specific species, there may be considerable individual variation. Among chimpanzees in which one mother assumes virtually all care responsibility, other females may attempt to provide care for orphaned infants and young chimps.
3. The mother is important, but she is neither absolutely necessary nor sufficient as a socializing agency. Peers may be especially important for the development of a varied play repertoire. In some cases, the lack of peer associations may lead to a deterioration in the mother-child relationship. The mother does, however, play a role in providing a base of support for the infant. She may regulate the infant's explorations of the larger world and provide emotional support for these sojourns.

Finally, maternally deprived monkeys and other animals may attempt to develop attachments to substitute mothers. It is in this context that animal studies provide a glimpse at part of the underlying dynamics of the situation faced by John, Ruth, Leah, Paul, Miriam, and Peter mentioned at the beginning of this chapter. Like some of Harlow's monkeys, these six children were abruptly separated from their natural families, and like some of Harlow's monkeys, they showed unusually intense signs of fear and hostility. The six human children also developed very strong and close attachments to each other. Maternally deprived monkey infants may develop similar contacts with each other. Unmothered infants raised in pairs often cuddle close to one another in a ventral-ventral clinging position. Groups of unmothered infant monkeys often huddle together in what is called a choo-choo pattern—each monkey cuddling to the back of the other in a line consisting of up to six animals. To some extent, the close attachment of the six previously mentioned human children may be seen as a similar response to the emotional privation suffered as a result of their separation from their natural families and the deprivation they surely suffered in the concentration camp. To understand the more specific consequences of such privation and deprivation, however, it is necessary to have a closer look at the nature of communication and interaction with infants and young children.

ARE BIOLOGICAL FACTORS SUBJECT TO CHANGE?

In the previous section, we indicated the importance of the social environment for the "normal" development of primates and other nonhuman animals. All species develop within the limits of certain genetic and physiological constraints. These constraints may, however, be quite broad, and the successful maturation of an organism depends on the nature of its interaction with its environment. There is growing evidence that even some aspects of the biology and physiology of organisms can be modified by environmental circumstances. Indeed, some environmental effects may seem to be quite obvious. Children not properly nourished ordinarily are not as healthy as are those who are properly nourished. Accordingly, it is not surprising to learn that dwarfism and even mental retardation may be related to such privation. It is not surprising to learn that such deprived children have more difficulty in school and in other activities than do their better nourished counterparts.

The idea that physiological aspects of development could be influenced by environmental factors was suggested in a rather crude way in the late nineteenth century by the French physician and anthropologist Paul Broca (1824–1880). Broca observed that medical students had larger heads than did male nurses. Since he believed that the two groups were actually equal in ability, he concluded that larger craniums of medical students were due to their extended training and education.[23] Obviously, there are many problems with Broca's research. His measures were extremely unreliable. For example, there is no demonstrated relationship between skull size and brain size (let alone between brain size and intelligence). However, Broca's hypothesis is interesting in that it indicated that experience might affect the physiological development of the brain. In 1892 a post mortem performed on a blind deaf mute showed that those parts of her cortex related to vision and hearing were considerably underdeveloped. Although this research is quite primitive, it does suggest that different forms of sensory stimulation can differentially affect the physiological development of the brain. Thus kittens deprived of visual stimulation failed to develop adequate visual functioning.[24] This suggests that other aspects of physiological development may be differentially affected by sensory stimulation. In this sense, different forms of deprivation may result in different kinds of cognitive impairment.

Interestingly, an Italian anatomist by the name of Michelle Gaetano Malacorne demonstrated a similar hypothesis among animals some 100 years before Broca. Malacorne took two puppies from the same litter and two sets of birds from the same clutch of eggs. He then isolated one of the puppies and one set of birds, while he spent considerable time training their siblings. Later Malacorne dissected all the animals and found that the cerebellums of the trained animals had more folds than did those of the untrained animals.[25]

The implications of this early research have been more thoroughly studied in the past two to three decades. In one set of experiments, rats from the same litter were separated. Some were placed in an "enriched environment." These rats lived in large cages containing a variety of play objects that were changed every day. Their siblings were placed alone in a cage. The researchers found considerable differences not only in the chemical activity of the brains of the two different groups of rats, but also in their anatomical structure and development. Rats raised in the environmentally enriched cages had a heavier cortex with respect to the rest of the brain.[26] From these results, one could speculate that the slower development of isolated monkeys may have been in part a result of physiological causes that were themselves the result of social isolation.

Other research indicates how human beings may be affected by environmental factors. Privation of early visual stimulation among children may result in later visual disorders.[27] In a broader sense, early sensory deprivation appears to hinder the child's development of models and strategies with which to deal with the environment. Although there is considerable debate about the value of I.Q. tests as a reliable measure of intelligence,[28] some research indicates that environmental as well as hereditary factors may affect I.Q. scores. Genetically identical twins raised in different environments score differently in I.Q. tests. Generally, those raised in more stimulating environments achieve higher test scores.[29] Stimulus privation appears to be a major factor in mental retardation. In fact, retardation in some young infants can be reversed by increasing the amount of stimulation these infants receive.[30] The nature of the infant's social environment may thus have important short-term and long-term implications for the emotional and cognitive development of the child.

Finally, evidence suggests that even though the general pattern of brain function and structure is genetically determined, experience may play a role in its continued growth and development. Specifically, recent studies have shown that after birth a period of massive brain cell death is then followed by a period of secondary growth and development among both human beings and non-human animals. During such "critical periods" the organism may be particularly sensitive to certain kinds of stimuli. Initial attachments in ducklings and goslings may be formed during such sensitive phases. Studies of other bird species indicate that these critical periods may overlap with the formation of preferences for mate selection. According to Steven Suomi, the sensitive phase for sexual attachments among a bird species known as the Zebra finch "coincides almost perfectly with a major transformation in the architecture of specific regions of the brain."[31] The patterns of attachment and sexual preference among human beings certainly do not evolve in an identical fashion to those among ducks, geese, or Zebra finch. However, cranial and neurological development in human beings continues after birth and such development may be sensitive to environmental stimuli. In fact, human neonates have only 23 per cent of their cranial capacity developed at birth. This is substantially less than other primates. The human brain continues to develop for the first decade of life. Among other animals, brain development is completed long before then.[32]

THE HUMAN INFANT'S CAPACITY
FOR COMMUNICATION

Human infants are more dependent, for longer periods of time, than are most other species. Their survival as well as their emotional well-being and cognitive development hinges on the care they receive from others.

Infancy, as we shall use the term, includes roughly the first 36 months of life. During this time, profound physiological changes occur. Because of this, many social psychologists believe that the infant's interaction with its early environment is of critical importance. This is not to suggest that infancy is the only period in which a child's personality can be affected in significant ways. Individuals are continuously socialized. Infancy is one period in which significant developments take place.

At birth, the average neonate (an infant during the first two to three weeks of life) weighs between 6 and 12 pounds. The lack of fatty tissue often makes babies look like "little old men." While the head is very large, the rest of the newborn's body is disproportionately small. The brain is not yet fully developed. By the end of infancy, the baby may weigh as much as 25 pounds. Although the head is still large, the rest of the body has begun to fill out, so that the differential is not nearly so striking. Neurological development has also occurred. The infant, at the age of 18 months, has the capacity to stand and maybe even to walk.

The neonate is completely dependent on its caretakers. The "grasping" and "sucking" reflexes are its two primary reactions. Crying is almost the only way in which an infant can get attention. However, parents may quickly come to distinguish between different types of cries; those indicating pain, for example, may be differentiated from those expressing hunger.

Despite his or her dependency, the human infant is capable of sensory discrimination at a very early age. Neonates as young as 2 or 3 days old can visually fixate on light and even follow its movement for short periods of time.[33] Blind babies will often tilt their heads in the direction from which a sound emanates.[34] Although neonates may respond to a variety of visual, auditory, and tactile stimuli at early ages, it is not until later infancy that they begin to integrate these stimuli—to realize that a particular sound may be associated with a specific visual object. Although some researchers suggest that visual and auditory coordination may develop as early as 1 month,[35] other researchers believe that the visual sensory mode is more important at this age.[36]

Infants as young as 4 days show a definite preference for certain visual forms. This was first demonstrated through a series of experiments conducted by Robert L. Fantz,[37] who used a device called a "looking chamber." Young infants were placed in this chamber lying flat on their backs. The researcher then placed a series of drawings in the baby's visual field. By looking through a lens at the top of the chamber, the researcher followed the infant's pupils and thereby noted exactly those patterns on which the baby's eyes focused. Infants between the ages of 4 days and 6 months were shown a variety of different pairs of visual patterns: bulls eyes versus stripes and triangles versus circles. Interestingly, young infants preferred round as opposed to vertical or angular objects.

In one of the more intriguing experiments, the infants were presented with a variety of facial drawings. In some cases, the faces were drawn in a scrambled fashion; in others, they were drawn normally. Neonates as young as 4 days showed a preference for the unscrambled faces.

Scrambled   **Unscrambled**

As infants grow older, they tend to favor more complex designs.[38] Human babies, as compared with infant chimpanzees, are more easily bored by simple patterns. Young infants also appear to have a capacity to differentiate among a variety of different facial expressions. In one experiment, the researcher found that 3-month-old infants reacted differently to pictures of sad, happy, and surprised faces.[39]

These research findings have been interpreted in a variety of ways. The sensitivity of infants to visual patterns and cues has led some researchers to emphasize the importance of early visual and nonverbal communication between parents and infants. In discussing the results of their study of infant discrimination of different facial expressions, the authors conclude that

> The fact that such subtle stimulus changes are even noticed by young infants has implications for the role of facial expressions during parent-infant interactions and for the later association of appropriate emotional responses with dif-

ferent facial expressions. It is now conceivable that facial expressions displayed by parents could come to function as discriminative stimuli for appropriate emotional responses at a very early age.[40]

A more recent study demonstrated that 3-month-old boys and girls distinguished between smiles and frowns on strangers as well as on parents.[41]

Some researchers also believe that the early age at which infants show a preference for round as opposed to angular objects is evidence for the idea that they have some primitive knowledge of the environment that assists their interaction with the world. This view is consistent with Piaget's idea that infants develop mental schemata at very young ages.

PIAGET'S SENSORIMOTOR PERIOD

The physiological developments during infancy are accompanied by certain cognitive developments as well; most important is the development of object constancy and a rudimentary sense of causality. These capacities develop during what Piaget refers to as the "sensorimotor period," which lasts from the time of birth until the infant is roughly 18 to 24 months of age. It consists of six stages.

The first stage lasts until the chlid is roughly 1 month old. It is characterized by a complete state of egocentrism. The child has not yet distinguished between itself and external reality. It has only neonatal reflexes, such as sucking and grasping.

The child first develops cognitive structures (schemata) based on the assimilation of new experiences. In the young infant, the early schemata are related to "sucking," the primary method of food intake. The development of these schemata are accidental at first. Through random movement, the neonate may find his hand in his mouth. This constitutes perhaps the first schema. Based on this, the child may intentionally place his fist in his mouth. This represents what Piaget terms the "circular reactions" of the sensorimotor period. The child first develops schemata or cognitive structures accidentally and then repeats the activity based on those structures. Later, the child may begin to innovate on the basis of internalized structures. He or she may begin to explore items other than his or her fist with the mouth. Exploration marks the second stage of the sensorimotor period, namely, a transition from simple reflexes to learned behaviors.

In the third stage (4 to 8 months), more complex activity is initiated. Here the infant may attempt to sustain an accidental change in the environment. Piaget tells about a young child who became interested in the movement of a doll she had kicked accidentally. She then tried repeatedly to kick the doll again.[42] The child then moved on to execute a similar action with other objects.

The fourth stage (8 to 12 months) marks a significant development in the sensorimotor period. During this stage, children may begin to manipulate the environment to achieve a desired end. For example, they may push away a screen to get a toy located behind it. This activity shows the rudiments of "object constancy"—the ability to realize that an object may be available in the environment even if it is not within their immediate perceptual field. At this stage, children may begin to be delighted by such games as peek-a-boo. This may lead to a more directed searching in which they begin not only to repeat a particular action, but also to execute new actions to obtain a desired goal. These abilities continue to develop during the fifth and sixth stages of the sensorimotor period.

During the latter stages of the sensorimotor period, children have developed certain primitive competencies that are essential to later development. First is the *object constancy*. This refers to the capacity to understand that ojbects have an existence independent of one's perception of them. This realization helps children to form a conception of themselves as separate entities in the world. At this point, they also begin to retain an image of items in the world that extend beyond their immediate perceptual environment. Second, the child has developed a basic notion of *causality* by having developed schemata in which certain actions affect certain outcomes. The combination of these two factors (object constancy and causality) help to form the basis for hypothetical-deductive thinking so important in later periods of development. As will be discussed later in this chapter, object permanence is related to the child's emotional development.

The developmental progress of the sensorimotor period entails both maturational and interactional components. In developing physiologically, the infant is capable of more extended explorations. These explorations facilitate the development of cognitive structures and become the basis for more extended interaction with the world. One study, for example, demonstrated that the infants' visual-motor coordination could be advanced by providing the baby with increased opportunities for touching and looking.[43] In this sense, the interaction and communication beteen the infant and others may be an important part of the growth process.

WHEN DOES COMMUNICATION BEGIN?

Exactly when parents and children begin to communicate is, to some extent, a mystery. In some ways, the foundation for care begins even before the child is born. This is evident in nonhuman as well as human behavior. Anyone who has watched the behavior of a pregnant cat will have noticed how the mother cat seeks out a warm, dark place for the birth. After birth, the cat will continuously groom and clean the kittens. As one researcher puts it,

> The observations of species-specific maternal behavior patterns (such as nesting, exploring, grooming and retrieving) which have been noted in animal mothers before and immediately after birth have been very useful. They have demonstrated that nature has not left the survival of the species to chance, but has provided intricate mechanisms that trigger maternal behavior in females during and after delivery.[44]

Certainly these practices are more complex among human beings and are equally as important. With us, the period before birth is a critical time in which important attitudes may be formed about the coming baby. One researcher characterizes the nervousness and anxiety that may occur during pregnancy as a kind of "rechanneling [of] the circuits for new attachments."[45]

Pregnancy stimulates changes among family members and in the family structure as a whole. It requires the mother to make two specific psychological adjustments: (1) recognizing the fetus as an integral part of herself and (2) becoming aware that the fetus will become a separate individual.

The role of the father during pregnancy—assisting and being an emotional support to the mother—may also be important for future relationship among family members. The birth of a new child may be something of a shock for other children in the family. The mother's feelings about the fetus, and the relationship of the mother to the fetus (and other family members), can affect how the infant will be treated after birth.[46]

The quality of birth itself may have an important bearing on the future relationships between parents and child. A difficult pregnancy or a traumatic birth experience may result in bad feelings toward the child, which may become manifest in later stages of childhood. Characteristics of the infant also may influence the interaction between parents and child in ways to affect the formation of attachment bonds. The birth of a premature or sick infant also may have significant consequences. This may cause a feeling of shock, followed by disbelief, sadness, anger, and anxiety. During this time, the role of the father and other family members in adjusting to new and unexpected demands and in providing emotional support to the mother is of great importance. Gender typing, in our society, begins almost directly after birth. Parents of male infants, for example, are more likely to characterize their babies in terms such as big, strong, and firm, whereas female infants tend to be described as little, cuddly, and soft. This leads the researchers to believe that little girls and boys are treated differently as early as infancy.[47]

Birth is a complex process. It may induce extreme joy and exuberance at the same time it produces anxiety and apprehension. These emotions are managed through the communication that takes place among family members and other significant others. This communication is important in setting the stage for the child's entrance into the world and integration into the preexisting interpersonal network.

The early communication between mother and child is interactive. The mother learns to distinguish the different sounds the child makes and responds to these accordingly. Similarly, the child quickly learns to recognize his or her mother's voice and face and begins to respond to her. Infants as young as 30 days become noticeably distressed when a tape recording of the mother's voice emanates from one part of a room while the mother is in another part of the room.[48]

Some researchers believe that actual communication between infants and adults may begin as early as the first days of life. In one study, researchers used film to record the relationship between adult vocalization and the movement of newborn infants. The findings suggested that kinesthetic movements of newborns are synchronized with adult speech patterns.[49] In a more recent study, newborns were divided into two experimental groups. One group was held (cuddled) while hearing "mother talk" while the other group was not. The research demonstrated that the children who were held were generally more responsive than were the children in the control group.[50]

ATTACHMENT AND
THE SEPARATION-INDIVIDUATION PROCESS

The early communication between parents and infants is important in the formation of attachment bonds between the child and family members. Visual, verbal, and tactile communication in the form of holding and cuddling may be quite important in this process. This early interaction between the infant and others is important for the development of a sense of trust in infants. This sense of trust may itself be important in the infant's mastery of his or her own functioning.[51] In this sense, cognitive and emotional development may be tied both to the early interaction between the child and significant others and to the formation of attachment bonds with these others.

Mary Ainsworth[52] in her classic study of infancy in Uganda has identified three different patterns of attachment. Infants who have a stable relationship with *one* care giver are described as "attached" by Ainsworth. She noted that some Uganda infants were raised in polygamous families. These received care from multiple care givers. They did not tend to establish a specific bond with any particular care giver. Ainsworth termed these infants the "unattached." Finally, there were those infants whose bonding process had been disrupted in some substantial manner. Although, these children had developed bonds with others, they appeared to be quite anxious with respect to these attachments. These children were the "insecurely attached." Ainsworth noted that the insecurely attached infants tended to be less healthy and less socially adept than either their securely or nonattached counterparts.

Subsequent studies have tended to confirm many of Ainsworth's insights. Recent work[53] has shown that as toddlers, securely attached children are more interested in peers, behave more positively towards peers and are more effective in peer interactions than are insecurely attached children. Other studies have shown that parental acceptance or rejection may affect a child's intelligence. The provision of a warm and positive family atmosphere leads to accelerated verbal development. One study which examined mothers at home with their children over a period from nine to eighteen months showed that a child's social, linguistic, and cognitive competence was enhanced by the quality of the play and interaction the child had with the mother.[54]

Bonds thus are formed through the interaction and communication between the child and mother and other significant persons in his or her life. In fact, the process may be reciprocal. As a care giver responds often and frequently to an infant, so may the infant's responses to the care giver increase. Securely attached infants who were confident of mothers' availability and responsiveness) were less anxious than were their insecurely attached counterparts. These infants had mothers who were more responsive to their cues during the first few months: they tended to respond more frequently to their babies' cries, held their infants more tenderly, and exhibited greater sensitivity in initiating and terminating feeding. Significantly, mothers who provided the more responsive care tended themselves to have more secure social support networks.[55]

According to Ainsworth, the formation of attachment bonds is facilitated through two processes which she calls the "attachment-exploration balance" and the "secure-base phenomenon." Attachment-exploration balance refers to the proximity between the infant and the care giver. According to this idea, sufficient closeness needs to be maintained in order to provide the child with a sense of security. Too much proximity may hinder the child's exploration of the surrounding environment. Securely attached infants are typically able to show signs of attachment to a nearby care giver at the same time that they can venture forth to examine new and interesting occurrences.

The secure base phenomenon refers to the process in which an infant may leave its care giver for such explorations while periodically returning for the emotional refueling necessary for continued exploration. The care giver acts as home-base for such explorations. One should note with respect to these two ideas, that the success of attachment for Ainsworth is not simple proximity between the infant and the care giver, but rather a feeling of security that contributes to a developing sense of independence in the young child.[56] This independence evolves through a process of attachment, separation, and individuation which may continue throughout childhood—if not longer.

In his two-volume work *Attachment* and *Separation,*[57] John Bowlby attempts to set forth the major characteristics of mother-child interaction during the first three years of life. Bowlby argues that, although genetic factors play a role in setting the general outline of personality, the specific characteristics of an individual are dependent on the relationships that grow between the child and family members. Crucial to this, according to Bowlby, is the relationship that grows between mother and child.

The child's relationship with mother entails a strong attachment followed by separation and individuation—the process by which the child comes to distinguish himself or herself from mother and the establishment of a sense of himself or herself as a separate and individual being in the world.

Bowlby divides the attachment process into four stages. The first stage is the "preattachment period." This lasts for the first few weeks of life. During this stage the infant's basic reflexes (e.g., crying, rooting, sucking, and grasping) promote closeness between the infant and the care giver. However, the infant's responses are biologically driven and are not directed to a specific person.

The second phase, which Bowlby calls "attachment in the making," is characterized by the infant's initial orientation to the care giver. The infant may smile at the mother or attempt to reach for her.

It is not until about six or seven months of age that the infant develops a "clear-cut" attachment to the mother. During this stage, the infant may become wary or anxious at the presence of others. As Piaget has noted, it is at about this age that the child is able to conceive of an absent object and it is at this point that the bond between the mother and child may continue to persist even in mother's absence. At this point, the relationship between mother and child is not dependent on mother's continued presence.

The fourth stage is termed "goal-directed partnership." This stage is predicated on the child's having developed sufficient verbal and cognitive capabilities to orient toward mother as an individual with her own goals and motives. The child may begin to modify his or her behavior in order to accord with mother's goals and motives. At the same time, he or she may begin to try to manipulate mother. Teasing is often characteristic of this stage as is a child's daring to do activities previously prohibited by the parents.

The dynamics of the separation-individuation process have been studied most intensively by Margaret Mahler[58] and her students. Mahler established a nursery to which mothers brought their children and in which the researchers were able to observe and categorize the various processes and phases of separation and individuation over time.

Initially, mother and child exist in a "symbiotic" relationship. Directly after birth, mother and child adapt to each other to meet basic nutritional and other needs. This period is dominated more by physiological than by psychological functioning. The child has not yet developed a "concept" (or what Piaget would call a schema) of self and other.

After the second month of life, the child begins to become aware of his or her relationship with mother. The child first thinks of mother as a "needs-satisfying object." In this stage, the infant behaves and functions as though the relationship between infant and mother were "an omnipotent system." During this period, the child comes to learn that its needs will be met regularly and systematically. Many mothers breast-feed their children. However, as the authors note, this alone is not enough to provide a secure environment for the child. It is important that the child be held in a secure manner during feeding, regardless of the method used. The authors report that the discomfort that one mother felt in breast-feeding her child was itself transmitted to the child through the awkward and tenuous way in which the child was held.

At about 4 or 5 months, the child has reached the peak of symbiosis. At this point, the child will often greet the mother with what different writers have termed a "special smile." This smile, according to Mahler and her colleagues, signals the establishment of a specific bond between mother and child.

The first subphase of the separation-individuation process is called "differentiation and the development of body image." This stage begins at about the age of 5 or 6 months. The infant becomes more alert and goal directed. At about 7 months, infants develop a visual pattern of "checking back to mother." The baby often appears "interested" in mother as another entity and will spend a great deal of time in the tactile and visual exploration of mother's face and body. In this way, the child begins to differentiate himself or herself from mother. The researchers believe that the seeking of distance during this subphase is "accompanied by a greater awareness of the mother as a special person."[59]

It is at this point that the child also becomes interested in persons other than mother. The researchers report that there is considerable variation among children in how they respond to others. However, once s/he is able to recognize the mother's face, the infant may turn with some wonderment to the faces of others. The infant's emotional development is tied to increasing perceptual and motor skills. Toward the end of the differentiation subphase, three developments occur that facilitate the differentiation process: (1) the child distinguishes the boundaries of his or her own physical body from mother's, (2) a specific bond is established with mother, and (3) autonomous cognitive functioning grows while the child is in close proximity to mother.

The second subphase is the "practicing period." It lasts from about 6 to 15 months. This period contains two stages. During the first stage, the infant attempts to move away from the mother while still holding on. Later, the child will move freely about in an upright position. The child "practices" and "masters" his or her newly developed and quickly improving ability to move about in an independent manner. Young toddlers use mother as a "home base" to which they return for "emotional refueling" after their adventures in somewhat stranger territory. In this way, children learn to maintain a conception of mother even when she is not directly there. This object permanence is an important part of development. Interestingly, the development of the ability to walk has important emotional as well as practical implications to both mother and child. It appears to be an important step in the child's differentiation from mother and the formation of his or her own identity.

The third subphase of the separation-individuation process is "rapprochement." It lasts from the age of 15 months to 2 years. This phase marks a change in the relationship between the child and mother. At about the age of 15 months, the toddler no longer views mother as a "home base" for emotional refueling, but sees her as an individual with whom to share his or her increasingly varied experience in the world. At this age, the child may begin to bring toys or food to share with mother. Also at this age, the child's interest in the world shifts from his or her own explorations to the enjoyment of social interaction through imitation games. The child's greatest enjoyment shifts from locomotion and exploration to play with others and social interaction.

During this subphase, the child begins to form relationships with persons other than the mother. The child develops closer ties to the father. Mahler observed that children at this age developed relationships with other adults in the nursery. At about 16 or 17 months, children would spend increasingly longer periods of time in a room without the mother. In general, the first stage of the rapprochement subphase is characterized by an increasing awareness of their own separateness and a greater enjoyment of their individual autonomy.

The second stage of the rapprochement subphase, however, is marked by conflicts. Just before they reach the age of 2 years, children may begin to experience ambivalence resulting from their increasing independence on one side, and continued dependence on the other. Toddlers at this age demand mother's constant attention. At the same time, they are gaining a greater awareness of their own separateness. Children at this stage use mother as an extension of themselves. A boy, for example, may pull at his mother's hand, using it to obtain a desired object. In some instances, children expect their desires to be filled by some unintelligible gesture, which mother is somehow (perhaps magically) supposed to understand.

This subphase is also marked by a phenomenon called "losing mother" (i.e., children begin to show signs of anxiety as though the mother had left, when in fact she had not moved at all from the room). At this age, children may experience a resurgence of stranger anxiety and shyness.

The resolution of these conflicts are important for the child's subsequent development. In some ways, this stage requires that new skills be developed. The child learns, for example, that his or her magical gesture will not suffice to secure the desired end. The child, therefore, begins to learn to express his or her desire in a language that both he or she and mother share. The rapprochement stage evidences a more highly developed use of language to express specific desires.

The fourth subphase of the separation-individuation process is "consolidation of individuality and the beginnings of emotional object constancy." As we have seen, Piaget and his students established that object constancy occurs at roughly 18 to 20 months, parallel to what Mahler and her colleagues term the rapprochement subphase. For Piaget, object constancy pertains primarily to physical entities. During what Mahler calls the rapprochement stage, the child acquires an inner representation of mother or other significant individuals in his or her life that facilitates the separation process. This inner representation may be seen as a more specific form of object constancy. It enables the child to understand that a temporary absence does not mean that mother is gone for good.

During the fourth subphase (20 to 22 months through 30 to 36 months), the child develops a concept of himself or herself as a distinct and separate being in the world. This is accompanied by increased communication skills and more developed cognitive functioning. At this stage, the child is en route to developing what symbolic interactionists call the "self."

A mother can do subtle things during the separation-individuation process that may affect the child's development. For example, Mahler reports that one "ambitious" and "success"-oriented mother held her baby in an upright position on her lap before the child was ready to stand. At a subsequent stage, the child began to stand at a time when most children propelled themselves forward by crawling. Standing had, in effect, interfered with the development and coordination of arm and leg movement necessary for crawling. This baby may not have suffered irreversible damage as a result of this early interaction, but the example illustrates how certain parental needs (in this case, ambition and success) can be communicated to children at very early ages and can affect aspects of their child's development.

According to Mahler and her colleagues, disruptions in the separation-individuation process may be at the root of some psychological problems experienced by adults. These difficulties are themselves rooted in the ability of mother and child to achieve an "optimal distance" at each of the various subphases. The rapprochement stage, however, is particularly crucial. Mother is required to satisfy certain needs in a consistent and regular fashion. Too much attention, however, may limit the child's reliance upon his or her own developing abilities. The mother-child relationship is thus in a delicate state of balance. Too much contact (smothering) may result in too much dependency; too little contact may result in the child's failure to develop object constancy with respect to mother. This may, in turn, affect other emotional and cognitive developments as shown in Figure 5–1.

Mahler's research provides many interesting and important insights into the nature of early parent-child communication and how this relates to the subsequent development of the child in our culture. There is still some question, however, about the extent to which observed patterns of mother-child interaction are culturally invariant. Mary Ainsworth,[60] as we have seen, suggests that a special bond develops between mother and child in a variety of

Subphase 1   Differentiation (1 to 6 months): initial development of body image

Subphase 2   Practicing (6 to 15 months): initial development of object constancy with respect to the mother

Subphase 3   Rapprochement (15 to 24 months): resolution of conflicts resulting from continued tension between increased motor and cognitive capabilities and continued dependence

Subphase 4   Individuation (24 to 36 months): consolidation of individual identity

FIGURE 5-1   Subphases of the separation-individuation process

cultures. This bond is solidified through culturally invariant patterns of tactile and visual communication (i.e., holding the infant in a cradlelike manner, the fostering of eye contact between mother and child, and the development of the "special smile" between mother and child). Other research, however, shows that some of these patterns may be quite varied. For example, in some cultures, men and women share equally in child-rearing activities. Among the Arapesh of New Guinea, mother and father share jointly in the early care of the child. The verb "to bear" a child is applied indiscriminately to both mother and father.[61] In some cultures, children are weaned after only 6 months of life; in other cultures, children may be breast-fed for as long as 3 to 6 years. In some cultures, weaning entails a gradual transition from breast milk to other forms of food; in other cultures, it may entail a rather abrupt change. These patterns may be tied to the specific conditions of life in different societies.

Finally, recent studies question the necessity of the biological mother for the development of human infants. As we shall discuss later in this chapter, social and sensory deprivation can have significant consequences for the development of young children. If children receive adequate care and sufficient stimulation, communication, and interaction from persons other than their biological mothers, they are likely to develop into healthy and socially competent individuals. As demonstrated in an early but important study, institutionalized children who were picked up and held tended to be both more responsive and more emotionally stable than were those who did not receive such attention.[62] One recent study suggests that fathers as well as mothers may be important for the formation of attachments and social bonds as early as the first year of life.[63]

TWO ASPECTS
OF THE HUMAN ENDOWMENT

In studying human beings as opposed to nonhuman species, it is important to keep in mind two human characteristics: As do other animals, we have more or less specific physiological requirements. We share certain biological needs including such basic tissue needs as the need for food, drink, and warmth. Beyond these are sexual drives. As do other animals, human beings have a need for activity and stimulation. Some would say that we share certain emotional needs. These drives and needs constitute the biological heritage of the human animal, and they serve to chart our development according to a particular maturational course. Beyond these needs human infants are endowed with specific biological capacities. Basic physiological responses such as crying, coughing, and sneezing are crucial for survival. Spontaneous motor acts such as kicking may help develop and maintain muscle tone. Head turning and the basic rooting reflex is important for feeding.

Beyond these basic biological similarities we, as human beings, also share a cultural heritage. It is in accordance with this endowment that our biological needs will be satisfied. Culture influences physiological functioning in important ways. Although all human beings will get hungry, culture tells us how, when, and with what we will be fed. While some cultures may classify bird's nest soup and quail eggs as delicacies, they may be regarded as junk food to members of a culture raised on McDonald's hamburgers. Similarly, patterns of child rearing may vary extensively from one culture to another. These patterns may be particularly suited to the specific needs of different cultures.

The way in which a society cares for its young is related to the development of certain personality traits among its people. These traits are, in turn, closely associated with the dominant work in a culture as well as its other aspects.

Erik Erikson,[63] for example, examined two different native American cultures: the Sioux and the Yurok. The Sioux lived and hunted in the plains of the Dakotas and were quite liberal in their care of the young. Sioux mothers would nurse their children whenever they so much as whimpered, and nursing would continue in some cases for as long as the first 5 years of life. There was no definitive weaning time for Sioux children. This early generosity of the mother, according to Erikson, is related to a more general kind of generosity characterizing Sioux culture.

Because of this extended nursing period, however, young Sioux children had to learn not to bite their mother's breast. Erikson suggests that the necessity for suppressing early biting wishes may have contributed to developing the ferocity necessary for the tribe's hunters. Thus the dominant virtues of Sioux society seem to have been generosity on the one hand and ferocity on the other. Erikson observes that people who live by hunting depend on the generosity of the most successful hunters. Hunting itself, however, requires a degree of ferocity if it is to be successful.

The Sioux roamed wide-open plains. The Yurok, however, lived in a narrow river valley. The Yurok were primarily fishermen. They would build small dams along the Klamath river in what is now Washington State from which they would extract salmon, the most important component of their livelihood.

With respect to child rearing, the Yurok stopped breast feeding at the age of 6 months and began to wean their children quite early and regularly. This, according to Erikson, is consistent with the emphasis on the acquisition and retention of possessions in Yurok culture.

Erikson notes that early conditioning of Yurok children teaches them to subordinate all instinctual drives to economic considerations. Children are weaned gradually, reflecting the Yurok's overall concern with conservation. Toilet training begins early and is strict, leading to what some might term an anal compulsive personality type.

This is not to suggest that patterns of child rearing determine the subsequent personality development of individuals in any automatic fashion. It is to suggest that child rearing is linked to other experiences forming a complex pattern that constitutes the human endowment. It is through this endowment that the human animal adjusts to the exigencies of daily life.

SOME CONSEQUENCES OF SOCIAL DEPRIVATION

As we have seen, social deprivation can have an important impact on the development of both nonhuman and human infants. However, the specific effects of different types of deprivation have only recently been studied in great detail. Moreover, the impact of specific forms of deprivation on human infants is very difficult to ascertain. Obviously, it is extremely unethical to subject human infants to the same kind of experiments to which nonhuman infants have been subjected. Therefore, our knowledge of the effects of social deprivation on human infants must be derived from studies of children who have been in some way adventitiously deprived. These children, however, may have undergone various forms of deprivation simultaneously. At the same time that they were deprived socially, they may have also been deprived nutritionally or placed in conditions where they received less than optimal levels of sensory stimulation. For this reason, it is difficult to determine the exact cause of an individual's suffering (i.e., Was it a disruption of the bonding process, a general lack of care, or a failure to be provided with adequate sensory stimulation?). All these factors may affect the child's development. In this section, we will examine some of the effects of social and sensory deprivation on the cognitive and emotional development of human infants.

Evidence suggests that children prematurely separated from their families may suffer emotionally. Premature separation may even affect physiological aspects of the child's development. Separated infants often do not gain weight as fast or as regularly as do infants who remain with their families. Being reared in a cold and hostile emotional environment may lead to a growth failure.[64]

Orphans often experience a deep sense of loss. Children given up for adoption may carry feelings of rejection into later life, which can affect their ability to form relationships with others. Some orphans carry a deep-seated interest about mysteries concerning their biological parents well into later life.[65]

Childhood depression and a variety of social and emotional difficulties also are associated with family disruption.[66] Children who become juvenile delinquents often are products of broken homes. Delinquency seems to be more strongly associated with disruptions resulting from divorce or separation than with those resulting from the death of a parent, suggesting that the quality of interaction and communication rather than the separation per se is a more important variable.[67]

Institutionalized children suffer cognitive impairments and emotional difficulties more frequently than do children who grow up in noninstitutionalized settings. Children reared in institutions that provide only minimal custodial care often do poorly on various intelligence tests. Even as infants, these children appear to be less responsive than do children reared in more stimulating settings.[68] Also, the longer children remain in institutions, the more serious their problems may become. Retarded children, or even those who have Down's syndrome, removed from an institution and placed in a private home, generally make more progress than do similar children who remain in the institution. In some cases, their condition has even been reversed.[69]

It is not clear, however, whether the problems of these children result from the emotional difficulties associated with separation or from other factors related to the institutions in which they are raised. Some evidence suggests that children raised in institutions that provide a more stimulating environment and greater emotional support do not suffer the same cognitive and emotional difficulties as do children who are placed in institutions that do not. Also, children raised in families where the emotional environment is cold and hostile and the relationships between the various members are strained or distorted may themselves experience emotional problems in later life.[70]

A variety of problems may occur as a result of disruptions of the bonding process and separation-individuation process. The failure to form bonds may result in a different type of psychological harm than does a disruption of bonds that have already been formed. Initially, children who have been deprived of early life attachments become excessively dependent on others. Later in life, they may develop difficulties in forming lasting relationships. These children also have more trouble in following rules. Failure to form bonds may result in what is called the "affectionless character"; a general apathy toward others, marked by the inability to place an emotional investment in other individuals. Such traits are not generally characteristic of children who are able to form parental bonds that are disrupted later on.[71]

Due in part to the rather dramatic results of Harlow's research, a good deal of the thinking about bond disruption has focused particularly on maternal deprivation: the separation of child and mother. As we have seen, initial separation from mother usually engenders despair on the part of the child. The extent of despair and the long-term implications of the separation for the child are contingent on a variety of factors. First, individual children with different temperaments and dispositions may respond differently to separation. Short-term distress may be less severe if the child has enjoyed a warm and positive relationship prior to separation.[72] Anxiety is less intense if others are available to comfort the child during the separation. Also, previous separation experiences may desensitize the child, making subsequent experiences less traumatic. Children who had previous separation experiences (such as staying overnight with relatives), for example, showed less distress when admitted to a hospital than did children who did not have such previous separation experiences.[73]

Once children are separated from their parents, a variety of things can be done to lessen the distress. Some suggest that distress is related to boredom and that playing with a child will alleviate the tension. Institutionalized infants become more responsive when they receive more attention and communication from caretakers. Such communication has been observed to be beneficial for the child's cognitive development as well. In one study, the comforting of crying infants increased their alertness and reduced their distress.[74]

There is some evidence suggesting that the effects of long-term maternal deprivation can be modified if a child is able to develop bonds with other adults or perhaps even other children. Siblings are often good candidates for such attachments. Institutionalized children who are able to maintain a long-term relationship with one adult generally have fewer social and emotional problems than do children who do not have such relationships. In general, it appears that while mother is an important primary caregiver, others may also assume this role. If the child is able to establish attachment bonds with these others, the foundation for trust in the world necessary for cognitive development and emotional stability can be maintained.

Social deprivation may take forms other than bond disruption. Separated or isolated children often suffer sensory deprivation. Earlier in this chapter we saw how sensory deprivation could impair physiological and neurological development among nonhuman animals. The lack of sensory stimulation may affect cognitive functioning among human beings as well. Stimulation may enhance cognitive functioning. Visual functioning and motor coordination, for example, are enhanced by increased opportunities to see, touch, and move. One study demonstrated that 10- to 14-week-old infants raised in a setting in which they recieved considerable social stimulation suffered less cognitive impairment than did children of the same age raised in an institution where there was a low degree of stimulation.[75]

Social stimulation may be especially important with respect to the development of language skills. A variety of studies have shown that children who grow up in a stimulating and meaningful linguistic environment tend to develop language skills more quickly than do children who grow up in settings where there is limited communication or where that communication is either truncated or distorted.[76]

The rather strange reactions of our six concentration camp survivors can now perhaps be better understood. Faced with a situation in which normal communication was prevented in infancy, these children formed special relationships with one another. One can only wonder about how similar circumstances may affect other children in the world today. While millions of infants and young children all over the world (including Western society) suffer various forms of privation and deprivation, others as a result of political upheaval or natural disaster undergo a variety of forms of disruption and disaster. Like our concentration camp victims, many of these children will, by and large, cope with their adversity, and, if they are lucky, adjust to a better life. Human beings are malleable, and many of the effects of early deprivation can be reversed. To gain a better understanding of these processes, it is necessary to consider the ongoing maturation and socialization of human beings.

NOTES

[1]Anna Freud and S. Dann, "An Experiment in Group Upbringing," *Psychoanalytic Study of the Child,* Vol. 6 (1951), pp. 127–128.

[2]J. Dollard and N. E. Miller, *Personality and Psychotherapy* (New York: McGraw-Hill, 1950).

[3]Robert B. Cairns, "Attachment Behavior of Mammals," *Psychological Review,* Vol. 73, no. 5 (1966), p. 410.

[4]M. Reite, R. Short, I. C. Hautman, A. J. Stynes, and J. D. Pauley, "Heart Rate and Body Temperature in Separated Monkey Infants," *Biological Psychology*, Vol. 13 (1978), p. 91.

[5]P. J. Scott and F. H. Bronson, "Experimental Exploration of the Etepimelectric or Care Soliciting Behavioral System," in P. H. Leiderman and D. Shapiro, eds., *Psychobiological Approaches to Social Behavior* (Stanford, Calif.: Stanford University Press, 1964), pp. 174–193.

[6]R. B. Cairns and D. L. Johnson, "The Development of Interspecies Social Preferences," *Psychonomic Science*, Vol. 2 (1965), pp. 337–338.

[7]Robert A. Hinde, *Biological Bases of Human Social Behavior* (New York: McGraw-Hill, 1974), pp. 213–214.

[8]R. A. Spitz, "Anaclitic Depression," *Psychoanalytic Study of the Child*, Vol. 2 (1964), pp. 313–342.

[9]Hinde, *Biological Bases of Human Social Behavior*, p. 210.

[10]J. J. McKenna, "The Evolution of Allomothering Behavior Among Colobrine Monkeys: Function and Opportunism in Evolution," *American Anthropologist*, Vol. 81 (1979), pp. 832–833.

[11]H. F. Harlow, M. D. Harlow, R. O. Dodsworth, and G. L. Arling, "Maternal Behavior in Rhesus Monkeys Deprived of Mothering and Peer Associations in Infancy," *Proceedings of the American Philosophical Association*, Vol. 110 (1966), pp. 58–66.

[12]See Hinde, *Biological Bases of Human Social Behavior*, pp. 149–161.

[13]H. Harlowe, "The Nature of Love," *American Psychologist*, Vol. 13 (1958), pp. 673–685.

[14]H. Harlowe and S. J. Suomi, "The Nature of Love-Simplified," *American Psychologist*, Vol. 25 (1970), pp. 161–168.

[15]Hinde, *Biological Bases of Human Social Behavior*, p. 237.

[16]Margaret S. Mahler, F. Pine, and A. Bergman, *The Psychological Birth of the Human Infant* (New York: Basic Books, 1975).

[17]H. Harlow and M. Harlow, "Effects of Various Mother-Infant Relations in Rhesus Monkeys," in B. Foss ed., *Determinants of Infant Behavior* (New York: Wiley, 1961), p. 18.

[18]Cairns, "Attachment Behavior of Mammals."

[19]Harlow and Harlow, "Effects of Various Mother-Infant Relations," pp. 20–34.

[20]S. Suomi, and H. Harlow, "Early Separation and Behavioral Maturation," in A. Oliverio, ed., *Genetics, Environment and Intelligence* (Elsevier: North Holland Biomedical Press, 1977), pp. 197–214.

[21]Harlowe and Harlowe, "Effects of Various Mother-Infant Relations," p. 36.

[22]Jay Meddin, "Chimpanzees, Symbols and the Reflective Self," *Social Psychology Quarterly*, Vol. 42 (1979), pp. 99–109.

[23]See Mark Rosenzweig, et al., "Brain Changes in Response to Experience," *Scientific American*, Vol. 226 (February 1972), pp. 22–29.

[24]Michael Rutter, *Maternal Deprivation Reassessed* (Baltimore: Penguin Books, 1972), p. 55.

[25]Rosenzweig et al., "Brain Changes in Response to Experience," p. 22.

[26]Ibid., p. 23.

[27]See Rutter, *Maternal Deprivation Reassessed*.

[28]David Layzer, "Heritability Analyses of I.Q. Scores: Science or Numerology?" *Science*, Vol. 183 (March 29, 1974), pp. 1259–1256.

[29]Ronald Wilson, "Twins' Early Mental Development," *Science*, Vol. 175 (February 25, 1972), pp. 914–917.

[30]Rutter, *Maternal Deprivation Reassessed*, p. 75.

[31]Stephen J. Suomi "Biological Foundations and Developmental Psychobiology," in C. B. Kopp and J. B. Krakow (Eds.) *The Child: Development in a Social Context*. Reading, Mass.: Addison-Wesley, 1982, p. 67.

[32]C. B. Kopp, B. Vaughn and D. Cichetti, "Getting Organized: An Agenda for the First Two Years of Life," in Kopp and Krakow (Eds.) *The Child*, p. 98.

[33]John Bowlby, *Attachment and Loss*. Vol. I: *Attachment* (New York: Basic Books, 1969), p. 269.

[34]D. G. Freedman, *Human Infancy: An Evolutionary Perspective* (Hillsdale, N. J.: Erlbaum Associates, 1974).

[35]Eric Aronson et al., "Space Perception in Early Infancy: Perception Within a Common Auditory Visual Space," *Science*, Vol. 172 (June 11, 1971), pp. 1161–1163.

[36]J. Fidd, "Coordination of Vision and Prehension in Young Infants," *Child Development*, Vol. 48 (1977), pp. 97–103.

[37]Robert L. Fantz, "The Origin of Form Perception," *Scientific American* (May 1961), pp. 66–72.

[38]Robert L. Fantz and Joseph F. Fagan III, "Visual Attention to Size and Number of Pattern Details by Term and Pre-Term Infants During the First Six Months," *Child Development*, Vol. 46 (1975), pp. 3–18.

[39]Gail Young-Brow et al., "Infant Discrimination of Facial Expressions," *Child Development*, Vol. 48 (1977), pp. 555–562.

[40]Ibid., p. 562.

[41]M. Barrera and M. Dophne, "The Perception of Facial Expressions by the Three-Month Old," *Child Development*, Vol. 52 (1981), pp. 203, 206.

[42]Jean Piaget, *The Origins of Intelligence in the Child*, translated by M. Cook (New York: W. W. Norton, 1963), p. 159.

[43]B. L. White, *Human Infants: Experience and Psychological Development* (Englewood Cliffs, N. J.: Prentice-Hall, 1971).

[44]John Kennel et al., "Parent-Infant Bonding," in Ray Helfer and Henry Kempe, ed., *Child Abuse and Neglect* (Cambridge, Mass: Ballinger, 1976), p. 26.

[45]Ibid., p. 26.

[46]Ibid., p. 42.

[47]Jeffrey Rubin et al, "The Eye of the Beholder: Parents' Views on Sex of New Borns," in J. Williams, ed., *Psychology of Women* (New York: W. W. Norton, 1979), pp. 134–141.

[48]Eric Arons et al., "Space Perception in Early Infancy: Perception Within a Common Auditory Visual Space," *Science*, Vol. 172 (June 11, 1971), pp. 1161–1163.

[49]William Condon and Louis Sander, "Neonate Movement Is Synchronized with Adult Speech: Interactional Participation and Language Acquisition," *Science*, Vol. 183 (January 11, 1974), pp. 99–101.

[50]Evelyn B. Thoman et al., "Modification of Responsiveness to Maternal Vocalization in the Neonate," *Child Development*, Vol. 48 (1977), pp. 563–569.

[51]Dorothea McCarthy, "Affective Aspects of Language Learning," in Aline Kidd and Jeanne Rivoire, eds., *Perceptual Development in Children* (London: London University Press, 1966).

[52]M. D. Ainsworth, *Infancy in Uganda: Infant Care and the Growth of Attachment* (Baltimore: John Hopkins University Press, 1967).

[53]See C. B. Kopp et al. "Getting Organized" pp. 128–135.

[54]Ibid., p. 129. See also R. Erlardo et al., "The Relation of Infants' Home Environment to Mental Test Performance from Six to Thirty-Six Months: A Longitudinal Analysis," *Child Development*, (1975), Vol. 46 (1975), pp. 71–76.

Elizabeth Bing, "Effect of Childbearing Practices on Development of Differential Cognitive Abilities," *Child Development*, Vol. 34 (1963), pp. 631–648.

R. Erlardo, et al., "A Longitudinal Study of the Relation of Infants' Home Environment to Language Development," *Child Development*, Vol. 48 (1977), pp. 595–603.

[55]S. B. Crockenberg, "Infant Irritability, Mother Responsiveness and Social Support in Sciences on the Security of Infant-Mother Attachment," *Child Development*, Vol. 52 (1981), pp. 857–865.

[56]For a contemporary review of Ainsworth's work see Kopp et al., "Getting Organized," pp. 128–135.

For a review of the evidence on bonding, see H. M. Sluckin and A. Sluckin, "Mother-to-Infant 'Bonding,' " *Journal of Child Psychology and Psychiatry*, Vol. 23 (1982), pp. 2095–2121.

[57]John Bowlby, *Attachment and Loss*. Vol I: *Attachment* (New York: Basic Books, 1969), and *Attachment and Loss*, Vol. II: *Separation* (New York: Basic Books, 1973).

[58]Margaret Mahler et al., *The Psychological Birth of the Human Infant* (New York: Basic Books, 1975).

[59]Ibid., p. 61.

[60]Ainsworth, *Infancy in Uganda*.

[61]Margaret Mead, *Sex and Temperament in Three Primitive Societies* (New York: William Morrow, 1963).

[62]R. A. Spitz, "Hospitalism," *The Psychoanalytic Study of the Child*, Vol. 2 (1964), pp. 313–342.

[63]Michael E. Lamb, "Father-Infant and Mother-Infant in the First Year of Life," *Child Development*, Vol. 48 (1977), pp. 167–181.

[64]Erik H. Erikson, *Childhood and Society* (New York: W. W. Norton, 1963), pp. 114–186.

[65]See Rutter, *Maternal Deprivation Reassessed*, p. 53.

[66]Fernando Colon, "In Search of One's Past: An Identity Trip," *Family Process*, Vol. 12, no. 4 (December, 1973), pp. 429–438.

[67]See Rutter, *Maternal Deprivation Reassessed*, p. 53.

[68]See J. W. B. Douglas, J. M. Ross, and H. R. Simpson, *All Our Future: A Longitudinal Study of Secondary Education* London: Peter Davies, 1968.

[69]See Rutter, *Maternal Deprivation Reassessed*, p. 23.

[70]See ibid., p. 75.

[71]See ibid., p. 23.

[72]See Michael Rutter, "Parent-Child Separation: Psychological Effects on the Child," *Journal of Child Psychology and Psychiatry*, Vol. 12 (1971), pp. 233–270.

[73]See Rutter, *Maternal Deprivation Reassessed*, pp. 31–32.

[74]See B. L. White, "An Experimental Approach to the Effects of Experience on Early Human Behavior," in J. P. Hill, ed., *Minnesota Symposia on Child Psychology* (minneapolis: University of Minnesota Press, 1967), Vol. 1.

[75]See Rutter, *Maternal Deprivation Reassessed*, p. 41.

[76]Ibid., p. 75.

[77]Ibid., p. 43.

CHAPTER SIX
GROWING UP:
Late Childhood

By the open French window of the dining room Jenny Blair Archibald was reading *Little Women* for the assured reward of a penny a page. Now and then she would stop to shake her head, toss her smooth honey-coloured plaits over her shoulders, and screw her face into a caricature of Aunt Etta's expression. "It isn't safe to skip," she thought. "Grandfather would be sure to find out. Well, even if Mamma did form her character on Meg and Joe, I think they're just poky old things." Poky old things, and yet spreading themselves over five hundred and thirty-two pages! "Mamma may call the Marches lots of fun," she added firmly, "but I'm different. I'm different."

The book dropped from her hands, while her startled gaze flew to the top-most branch of the old sycamore in the garden. Deep pulsations of light were flooding the world. Very thin and clear through the May afternoon, there was the chime of distant bells striking the hour. Somewhere, without or within, a miracle had occurred. At the age of nine years and seven months, she had encountered the second important event in human experience. She was discovering her hidden self as once before, in some long forgotten past, she had discovered her body. "I don't care. I'm different," she repeated exultantly.

From the warm mother-of-pearl vagueness within, a fragment of personality detached itself, wove a faint pattern of thought, and would gradually harden into a shell over her mind. But all she knew was, "I am this and not that." All she felt was the sudden glory, the singing rhythm of life. Softly, without knowing why, she began crooning, "I'm alive, alive, alive, and I'm Jenny Blair Archibald." Ages before, in the time far back beyond the vanishing rim of memory, she had composed this refrain, and she still chanted it to herself when happiness overflowed. For it was all her own. No one, not even her mother, not even her grandfather, knew how she loved it. Jealously, she kept it hidden away with her chief treasure. . .

"Jenny Blair, are you getting on with your book?" With her hand poised above the coat of blue pique she was braiding in white, Mrs. Archibald turned her animated glance toward the French window "Jenny Blair," she called again in an imperative tone, "do you hear me?"

"Yes, Mamma, but I'm thinking."

"Thinking?" repeated Aunt Etta, who was frail and plain and sickly. "What on earth do you have to think about, Jenny Blair?"

"Nothing, Aunt Etta."

"How, my dear, can you think about nothing?"

"Aren't you getting on with your book?" Mrs. Archibald asked, removing a pin from her mouth and running it into the sleeve of the pique coat. "I hope it isn't too old for you. Are you sure you understand what you're reading?"

"Oh, Mamma, it is so dreadfully poky."

"Poky? Why, I could never have too much of *Little Women* when I was a girl. I remember I tried to form my character on Meg—or it may have been Joe. But I can't understand children to-day. I don't know what they're coming to."

"How soon may I stop, Mamma?"

"Finish that chapter, and then we'll see what time it is."

"Bit I've just begun a new chapter."

"Well, finish it anyhow. Your grandfather will be sure to ask how much you've read."

"Do you think he will pay me when I'm half through. I need a new pair of roller-skates more than anything in the world. There is a very nice pair in Mrs. Doe's window for a dollar and a half."[1]

The preceding reflections concern Jennifer Blair Archibald, a 9-year-old girl growing up in a Southern community in the United States at the beginning of the twentieth century. Growing up in the year 1900 was in many ways quite different from growing up in the 1980s. Children had no television: no Saturday morning cartoons, "Captain Kangaroo," or "Sesame Street." There were no space-age superheroes: no Superman, Wonder Woman, or even Incredible Hulk. Toys were different: bicycles were not made to look and sound like motorcycles because motorcycles had not yet been invented. Children perhaps may not have played "war," but if they did, they used sticks as "play guns" rather than carefully designed replicas. They did not play "Asteroids," "Space Invaders," or "Pac-Man." Dolls were simpler; they didn't talk, cry, or wet their pants, and they certainly were not battery operated.

Nevertheless, there are many similarities between Jennifer Blair Archibald and children of the 1980s. Although today's children may not read *Little Women* (many, of course, will read it), at about Jenny's age, they begin to look to other sources *outside* of the immediate family for "role models." Parents and children may well differ with respect to which role models are appropriate. Growing up in either 1900 or 1980 involves exposure to and involvement in a larger world.

Characteristically, 1980s children will begin to experience the feeling of exhilaration associated with increased independence from the family. This may be manifested in activities such as skating, cycling, sledding, and skiing that test the developing perceptual and motor capabilities of children and their capacity to integrate different skills in the performance of one activity. Given the current fascination with roller skating, it is not unlikely that many contemporary children will share at least one specific activity with Jenny Blair.

Like Jenny Blair, many children today will learn to disassociate rewards from simple reinforcement and may learn to manipulate rewards to maximize their outcomes. Jenny may finish *Little Women* to buy that new pair of skates. Modern children may finish their math homework to get an "A" in the course, praise or other rewards from parents, admission to college, and ultimately a good job. Beyond this, children may begin to develop a sense of fairness, equity, or appropriateness—the idea that outcomes for others, as well as for themselves, should be a function of the effort and time put into achieving a specific goal. This may involve a growing sense that "ill-begotten gains" are not as valuable as those that are truly "earned." Growing up for Jenny Blair as well as for children of the 1980s can involve the replacement of childhood egocentrism with a more general and inclusive sense of "justice."

Finally, like Jenny Blair, children of the 1980s will have fantasies and flights of imagination of all sorts. Some of these may involve a newfound sense of separateness and independence: a new autonomy and a feeling of differentness from parents or initial caretakers. Other fantasies may pertain to the new social worlds to which they are exposed; new friends at school, teachers, and others. Early adolescents in particular are likely to develop "crushes" and spend more than a few hours a day in romantic musings which though trivial from the standpoint of parents and other adults, may be quite serious for the child. Many childhood fantasies may reflect newly developed cognitive capabilities—in particular, the ability to reason hypothetically. Some of these flights of imagination may reflect strange combinations of both reason and unreality which may give adults reason to reflect as well. If peace is possible in one part of the world, a child may reason, then why not the world over? If one large hamburger company can sell over 2 billion burgers in one country, then why are people in other countries starving? In one sense such flights of imagination may seem to be unrealistic dreaming. In another sense, however, they may reflect concerns that motivate innovative and imaginative approaches to critical moral and ethical problems in later life.

STAGES OF GROWING UP

This chapter and the next one fall under the general heading of "Growing Up." We use this term to refer to an extended period of time between early childhood and adulthood. It is difficult if not impossible to define this period in terms of specific years. Indeed, childhood, as a specific phase of development may have widely different meanings in different cultural and historical circumstances. Some contemporary western observers have concluded that childhood as a specific phase of development is essentially an artifact of twentieth century industrial societies.[2] The life cycle in many preindustrial societies consists of only two phases: immaturity and adulthood. Children in Medieval Europe, for example, dressed and were expected to act precisely as adults did. Childhood was hardly the idyllic time of "fun" and "make-believe" it often appears to be in popular literature or in the media. Lloyd De Mause has commented on the plight of children in European history:

Virtually every child-rearing tract from antiquity to the 18th century recommended the beating of children. We found no examples from this period in which a child wasn't beaten, and hundreds of instances of not only beating, but battering, beginning in infancy.

One 19th-century German Schoolmaster who kept score reported administering 911,527 strokes with a stick, 124,000 lashes with a whip, 136,715 slaps with his hand and 1,115,800 boxes on the ear. The beatings described in most historical sources began at an early age, continued regularly throughout childhood, and were severe enough to cause bruising and bloodying.

Children were always felt to be on the verge of turning into actual demons, or at least to be easily susceptible to "the power of the Devil." To keep their small devils cowed, adults regularly terrorized them with a vast army of ghostlike figures, from the Lamia and Striga of the ancients, who ate children raw, to the witches of Medieval times, who would steal bad children away and suck their blood. One 19th-century tract described in simplified language the tortures God had in store for children in Hell. "The little child is in this red-hot oven. Hear how it screams to come out . . . ."

Another method that parents used to terrorize their children employed corpses. A common moral lesson involved taking children to visit the gibbet. . . . They were forced to inspect rotting corpses hanging there as an example of what happens to bad children when they grow up. Whole classes were taken out of school to witness hangings, and parents would often whip their children afterwards to make them remember what they had seen.[3] [*Reprinted from* Psychology Today Magazine. *Copyright* © 1975 (APA)]

According to one scholar, such harsh child-rearing practices are not found among nonhuman primates, suggesting that in this respect at least, we are only beginning to "catch up with our more civilized relatives."[4]

Childhood, as a specific stage of development, did not emerge in North America until the early twentieth century. In nineteenth-century rural American life, children worked in the fields as soon as they were physically capable of doing so. Similarly, prior to the passage of child labor laws, children in urban centers began working in factories. Their childhood was severely truncated when compared with many middle-class children of the 1980s for whom "growing up" may be extended into the midtwenties or even later. This has led some to suggest that our society has institutionalized a new phase of the life cycle that they call "youth."[5] During this phase, the assumption of adult duties and responsibilities may be delayed as the adolescent acquires advanced skills and techniques required for work in a highly technological society. However, there is evidence that even among preliterate cultures, as well as in earlier periods of American history, growing up may have been extended to enable children to obtain necessary skills. Among Stone Age people still living in New Guinea, children do not emerge into adulthood until they have mastered necessary skills and rituals.[6] The apprenticeships of nineteenth-century American youth postponed adulthood until the early twenties. Interestingly, the "licentious ways" of these apprentices were often bemoaned by their elders.[7]

Even for today's children, childhood can be a period of anxiety. Many of the "nursery tales" handed down through the ages may engender the same kinds of fears as did the child-rearing practices recorded by De Mause, and indeed, there is some controversy in mental health circles about the advisability of reading frightening and violent stories to children. Some claim that such stories affect the child adversely, creating unnecessary fears; others argue that a totally nonfrightening repertoire of stories may hinder the child's adjustment to a world that for the child may have frightening aspects. Specifically, it is argued, horror stories help children to deal with fears they may have toward adults whom they perceive as threatening. "Jack in the Bean Stalk," for example, reflects the fear that young male children may have toward other older and larger males. By repeating the story, children may learn to express those fears and see adults as less frightening. The issue remains a matter of debate.[8]

Childhood abounds in problems and conflicts as well as in opportunities for realizing the potentials of individuals. The relevance of social psychology for helping us to understand some of the problems and opportunities of late childhood is the prime focus of this chapter.

LATE CHILDHOOD

For the purposes of discussion, let us consider "growing up" in two separate phases, while remembering that these may vary with time and culture. The first phase, late childhood or preadolescence, refers to the period in which children emerge from the conditions in which they were raised as infants and young children. In our culture (i.e., contemporary America), this includes the ages of roughly 3 to 12 years. The second phase, adolescence, will be considered in the next chapter.

During late childhood, the child begins to develop an integrated concept of self. Psychoanalytically oriented social psychologists have termed this the *ego ideal*,[9] a child's conception of what he or she should be and do. One's ego ideal is a moral guide that serves to direct the child's behavior as he or she enters the wider world of peers and school. From a psychoanalytic perspective, the ego ideal results from the successful resolution of conflicts related to the oedipal complex (see Chapter 4) and the child's identification with the parent of the same sex. A child does what he or she thinks is right as he or she enters new social realms, in part because that is what he or she believes mother or father would do in similar circumstances. The child has internalized an image of mother or father, and this image serves to guide his or her behavior in new social situations. The child of this age has internalized his or her own sense of "guilt." When he or she does wrong, the child will feel badly, whether or not he or she fears parental sanctions.

As the child moves from the home into new social situations, his or her self-concept may be expanded. Children may be influenced by other role models that may reflect different values. Although still influenced by parents, children do not require parental approval for every action, nor do parental sanctions necessarily mean that certain disapproved actions will not be taken.

COGNITIVE DEVELOPMENTS IN LATE CHILDHOOD

Late childhood marks a transition in most children's cognitive capabilities. Piaget[10] termed this the transition from *preoperational* thought to *concrete operations*. During late childhood, children develop the capacities for what

Piaget termed *conservation* and *reversibility*. Conservation is the ability to understand that some aspects of an object may remain stable and constant even though other aspects change. Assume that a child is shown two round balls of clay that are equal in mass. If one of the balls is formed into a longer sausage-shaped object, the preoperational child is likely to believe that the longer object also is larger (i.e., contains greater mass). Similarly, if the same amount of water is poured from a short, fat beaker into a long, thin beaker, the preoperational child is likely to say that there is more water in the second beaker because the water level is higher. The ability to understand that the amount of water and clay remains essentially the same, regardless of the shape of the ball or the beaker, is known as conservation.

Reversibility is the capacity to understand that reversing a transformation will result in the previous state of affairs. For example, the preoperational child would not understand that if the sausage-shaped ball of clay were rolled back into a ball, it would be essentially identical to the original round-shaped ball of clay and that the water, if poured back into the first beaker, would still reach only the lower water line. These "competencies" are important for other cognitive developments in late childhood (e.g., multiplication, seriation, and classification) as well as for more advanced hypothetical-deductive thinking that typically develops in early adolescence. Finally, in late childhood, there occurs a further development of a child's ability to reason causally (i.e., to understand that an event that precedes another may or may not be the cause of the latter event and an understanding of how to determine when causality is present by examining the circumstances in which different events may be present or absent).

SEXUAL IDENTITY AND GENDER

One of the most important aspects of any individual's identity concerns who they are in terms of sex and gender. Such identities continue to form during late childhood.

Recently, social psychologists have come to draw a distinction between sexual identity and gender identity. Sexual identity is commonly thought of as a biological category. Conventionality leads us to divide people into two basic categories—males and females. We presume that these categories are exhaustive and mutually exclusive, i.e., that all people will be either a male or female and that no one person will be part male and part female. More specifically, this means that men will tend to have chromosomes, hormones, and reproductive organs that are different than those of females. There are, however, some instances where matters are not quite so simple. Androgen insensitive syndrome, for example, refers to a condition where an individual is genetically male, but has the reproductive organs of a female. Such individuals are biologically insensitive to the effect of male hormones.

Social psychologists are interested in sexual identity primarily insofar as it bears upon the development of gender identity. Gender identity refers to an individual's psychological acceptance of his or her biological sexuality. Social psychologists are also interested in gender role—i.e., the behaviors and attitudes that are socially prescribed as appropriate for each sex. Gender roles are like stereotypes which may vary in different historical and cultural contexts. For example, the idea that boys should be aggressive, active, and domineering whereas girls should be passive and submissive is almost exactly reversed among the Arapesh, a primitive tribe studied by Margaret Mead.[11] Some current observers would claim that contemporary sex-role stereotypes are even now undergoing a considerable change.

Each of the theoretical perspectives discussed in Chapter 4 offers a different view of the development of gender identity and gender role. According to the Freudian view, gender identity results from the resolution of the Oedipal complex. At about the age of four, young children have a preference for the parent of the opposite sex. Such desires generate considerable anxiety within young children. These anxieties are resolved as the child comes to "identify" with the parent of the same sex.

For a young boy the sequence is as follows: The boy feels he is in competition with his father for the mother. He resents his father but he also fears that his father will castrate him for these feelings. Simultaneously, the boy represses his desires for his mother and his resentment towards the father. At the same time he tries to be like his father.

According to Freud this process varies for girls. At about the age of four the young girl notices that boys have a penis while she and her mother do not. According to Freud, she resents her mother for failing to give her a penis ("penis envy"), and assumes that her mother similarly resents her. As with her male counterpart, this resentment generates considerable anxiety which is resolved as the young girl comes to identify with her mother.

Freud's views of sexual development have been criticized from a variety of perspectives. Perhaps the most controversial point concerns the assumption of penis envy. As Karen Horney and others (See Chapter IV) have argued, this assumption is a reflection of the male-centered views that predominated during the time in which Freud had been working. Although girls may envy the superior position that men enjoyed at that time, they do not envy boys for biological reasons. Anthropologists have not demonstrated the universality of either penis envy or the Oedipal complex. However, Freud's views provide us with insights into family dynamics and the role of identification with parents in the development of gender identity. As we shall discuss shortly, Freud's ideas have relevance for understanding aspects of childhood play.

Behavioral theories posit that gender identity is a function of reinforcement, imitation, and modelling. Boys and girls tend to be gender-typed by their parents at birth. Parents also have different expectations for their sons and daughters. Hence young boys tend to be rewarded for acting in a manner consistent with our stereotypes of what it means to be a "man," while little girls tend to be rewarded for acting in a manner that is consistent with our stereotypes of what it means to be a "woman."

According to this view, both boys and girls will begin by modelling the parent with whom they have the most initial contact—in most cases, the mother. However, as children grow older they tend to prefer and hence to imitate same-sex models. Girls will continue to behave like their mothers whereas boys will begin to imitate their fathers. This results primarily because of differential reward structures for males and females.

Behavioral approaches to the formation of gender identity have been criticized for a variety of reasons. It is not clear why or even if children imitate same-sex parents more than they do opposite sex parents. In this regard, there is no apparent explanation for the shift of boy models from mother to father if in fact there is such a shift.[12] Despite these problems, the behavioral perspective highlights how our society differentially rewards males and females and the implications of this for the development of gender identity.

From a symbolic interactionist perspective the formation of gender identity is essentially a matter of role taking. Like the behavioral view, symbolic interactionism posits that young children begin by imitating significant others. Imitation, however, evolves into role playing. Here boys come to adopt those roles that are socially defined as male appropriate—e.g., father, fireman, doctor, policeman, etc., while girls come to adopt those roles that are socially defined as female-appropriate—e.g., mother, librarian, nurse, teacher, etc. Interestingly, while children at play may shift roles rather frequently within sex categories (e.g., boys may shift from playing father, to policeman, to doctor), they are less likely to adopt roles from the opposite sex category (e.g., boys are not likely to adopt the role of nurse).

Aside from role-taking, symbolic interactionists also focus on how children learn the meaning of what it is to be a man or a woman in any society. This entails an interpretation of the attitudes and behaviors associated with each. Young boys learn what it means to act as a "man" with respect to both women and other men. Young girls learn the same thing. This learning takes place primarily amongst peers. Young boys may in a sense practice at being "men" with other boys. Shortly we shall discuss how such practicing and interpretation may reinforce existing sex-role stereotypes.

The cognitive approach provides a still different view of the formation of gender identity. According to this view, the child first needs to understand that boys and girls are biologically and anatomically different. The child then realizes the sex to which he or she may belong and proceeds to try to act in a manner that is consistent with socially defined role attributes for each gender. Central to the cognitive approach is the idea that the adoption of gender-appropriate behavior is motivated by the desire to behave as a competent male or female.

The cognitive approach is helpful in sensitizing us to the importance of cognitive development for the establishment of gender identity and role. Clearly, understanding that one is a male or female is based at least on rudimentary categorical thinking. The development of gender constancy (i.e., the idea that one remains either male or female across time and different situations) is predicated on having developed object constancy and appears to be related to the development of conservation and reversibility.[13]

Like the other perspectives we have discussed, the cognitive approach is not without some difficulties. Most importantly, the development of some aspects of gender role appear to precede the development of gender identity. Boys and girls begin to behave in accordance with the socially defined attributes of being male or female *before* they understand the biological differences and they know the category to which they belong. Sex-typed play, for example, appears before the age of two. It is not until children reach at least that age that they understand that boys and girls are different biologically, and it is not until the age of three that gender identities begin to evidence some stability and constancy.[14]

In sum, it is probably the case that no one theoretical perspective can totally account for the formation of gender identity and role. Each highlights different parts of a complicated process relevant to "growing up." Each needs to be considered in terms of the different contexts in which children develop.

PLAY AND SOCIAL DEVELOPMENTS IN LATE CHILDHOOD

One of the most important social developments in late childhood is the entrance of the child into a society of peers. Peer interactions help to foster a sense of "industry" and "responsibility."[15] This, in turn, helps to develop a feeling of adequacy and personal efficacy (i.e., personal causation—the belief that one is the source or author of one's actions). This feeling may well be related to successful performance of various kinds of activities in adolescence and adulthood. Beyond this, peer associations provide an opportunity for children to acquire social skills and attitudes useful in later life. These skills and attitudes may be developed through play with other children.

PLAY AND SOCIALIZATION

Childhood play may take a variety of different forms that contribute in different ways to the socialization and maturation of the individual. Drama is one form of childhood play. Through drama, children are provided an opportunity to enact different roles. This serves a variety of socialization and developmental functions. First, it facilitates the development of a conception of self and identity. Gregory Stone, a social psychologist who has examined childhood play in great detail, offers the following observation:

> To establish a separate identity, the child must literally get outside himself and apprehend himself from some other perspective. Drama provides a prime vehicle for this. By taking the role of another, the child gains a reflected view of himself as different from but related to that other. Thus, we find little children playing house, store or school in which they perform the roles of parent, merchant, or teacher, gaining a reflected view of identities whose roles they perform. Indeed, in playing house, it is difficult to recruit a child to play the role of child or baby. Such a role has no implication for the building of his own identity. A doll, therefore, is better suited to this role.[16]

Through play, the child experiences role contrasts (e.g., mother-father, teacher-student). These experiences help the child to expand his or her understanding not only of specific roles, but of a number of roles and how they are both different and independent.

Play as drama has a number of other functions as well. Role play may help to prepare the child for the actual enactment of adult roles. Play in this sense may be seen as a form of *anticipatory socialization*; by acting out adult roles, the child may come to be familiar with some of the rudimentary skills and attitudes characteristic of those roles. Sex roles in particular are learned at a very early age. By the age of 3, most children know the sex to which they belong and will shortly learn some of the basic traits associated with being male or female in their own society.[17] In traditional Western society, sex role stereotypes appear to be the most constraining of all the roles children may enact in their play. Although children of either sex may switch rather rapidly from the role of doctor to patient, boys would not likely switch to the role of "nurse" or girls to the role of "doctor."[18]

Childhood drama is, of course, not always so "realistic." Such drama may serve to revitalize a culture's past—its myths, legends, heroes, and villains. "Cowboys and Indians" may perform such a function in our society. In addition, childhood drama may project into a society's future. Consider children in the 1950s whose play may have involved space travel long before space travel actually occurred.

Drama, of course, is only one form that childhood play may take. As we discussed in connection with the theories of George Herbert Mead (see Chapter 4), childhood games provide an arena in which children learn about social organization and their relationships to larger social collectivities. As we shall see shortly, games also provide an opportunity for children to learn how to regulate and, in a sense, govern their own activities in an autonomous and independent manner.

Beyond this, play serves as a means for children to explore "tabooed" areas of life. Children's concerns, ideas, and often misconceptions about sex may become apparent in their play. Childhood play is also a way of testing the limits of social acceptability. Pranks in particular may provide children with their first experiences of handling their own embarrassment as well as embarrassment in others. The development of such "social skills" may be important for the management of social interaction in later life. Pranks help to "prepare the child for the maintenance of self-control in later life."[19]

PSYCHOANALYTIC INTERPRETATIONS
OF CHILDHOOD PLAY

Psychoanalytically oriented researchers view play as serving a number of important functions. These include simple pleasure and enjoyment, the execution of newly developed cognitive and physiological capabilities, and the management of fear and other anxieties that may occur during preadolescence. Most important, however, play is viewed as an expression of specific underlying psychosocial developments and processes. For example, the preadolescent boys' rejection of dolls and other "girls' games" reflects, according to this view, the transfer of identity from the mother to the father.

Girls' jump rope rhymes have been analyzed in terms of their articulation of underlying psychological processes.[20] Some rhymes, for example, have been analyzed in terms of the notion of sibling rivalry—the sense of jealousy and dislike older siblings may have toward younger brothers and sisters who are perceived as usurping once privileged parental attentions. The following jump rope rhyme may be interpreted in terms of this idea:

> I had a little Brother
> His name was Tiny Tim
> I put him in the washtub
> To teach him how to swim
> He drank up all the water
> Ate up all the soap.
> He died last night
> With a bubble in his throat.[21]

A number of rhymes depict similar fates for "little brother."

Other jump rope rhymes reflect a disdain that preadolescent girls may have toward boys. This disdain may result in part from the necessity of breaking off affections for the father (see Chapter 4) and learning to identify herself as a girl. The following lines, for example, have been interpreted in terms of this idea:

> Boys are rotten
> Made of dirty cotton
> Girls are dandy
> Made of sugar candy.[22]

As girls grow older, however, boys come to be more accepted in girls' rhymes.

Finally, jump rope rhymes reflect the resolution of oedipal-related conflicts. The oedipal symbolism of one such rhyme is not difficult to discern:

> I love Papa, that I do,
> And Mama says she loves him too,
> But Papa says he fears someday
> With some bad man I'll run away,
> Who will I marry?[23]

Other rhymes reflect not only romance but more general concerns with home, clothes, fortunes, and the preadolescent girls' more long-term concerns with marriage and romance. As such, they are significant not only as a reflection of underlying psychological processes, but also as a form of anticipatory socialization.

MORAL DEVELOPMENT AND PLAY

How do children develop a sense of fair play? What role does play have for a child's moral and social development? How do children learn about rules? These questions were addressed by Jean Piaget in his studies of how children play the game of marbles. In this research, Piaget combined his general skills as a social psychologist with some very sensitive participant observation. He and his colleagues asked children of different ages to teach them how to play the game of marbles. During the period of instruction, the researchers probed the children about their attitudes toward the rules of the game.

Like Mead, Piaget thought that play is of critical importance in the development of the person. It is through play that children first begin to symbolize their activity. Play is, therefore, critical in developing the ability to think in terms of abstract symbols. Even more important, however, play has a significant role in the development of morality and the child's sense of justice. This is illustrated in marbles.

Piaget and his colleagues analyzed children's play in terms of two major categories. The first is the actual *practice of rules* (i.e., "the way in which children of different ages effectively apply rules").[24] Under this category, Piaget identified four stages of the application of rules. The first two are highly individualistic. During the *motor period* (ages 1 and 2), the child will play pretty much "at the dictation of his desires and motor habits."[25] Play is characterized by repeated executions of the same motor activity. Play at this stage appears random and geared toward no particular end. Collective rules do not apply at this stage.

The *egocentric stage* covers the ages of roughly 2 to 5. At this stage, children may imitate rules learned from others. They do not, however, play with others. This stage of the practice of rules is still highly individualistic.

The third stage, *incipient cooperation*, occurs when children are about 7 or 8 years old. Here they begin to play to win. When questioned about the rules of the game of marbles, however, they often give conflicting and contradictory accounts.

It is not until the fourth stage (ages 9 to 12), the stage of the *codification of rules*, that rules are standardized for all children. "Not only is every detail of procedure in the game fixed, but the actual code of rules to be observed is known to the whole society."[26] Piaget reports a "remarkable concordance" in the knowledge that children of different European cultures have of the rules of the game.

The second category used by Piaget is *consciousness of rules*. Unlike the practice of rules, this refers to how children understand the nature of rules as they grow older and develop. Initially, rules are not obligatory. Subsequently, in stage 3, children consider rules to be sacred and immutable. Every rule violation is considered to be a transgression. Rules become highly authoritative and sovereign. This is mirrored in the attitudes children of this age have toward parental authority. In the final stage, "mutual consent," rules are viewed as agreements among the players and can be altered if the players agree. This marks an important moment in the child's moral and social development.

PIAGET'S CATEGORIES

PRACTICE OF RULES	CONSCIOUSNESS OF RULES
Stage 1. Motor period	Not obligatory
Stage 2. Egocentric period	Sacred and immutable
Stage 3. Incipient cooperation	Mutual consent
Stage 4. Codification of Rules	

The relationship between play and moral development can be illustrated by the game of baseball. During the early stages of learning how to play the game, children will begin by simply imitating basic motor movements. This involves learning how to run, throw, and perhaps swing a bat. Later, the rules may become clearer, but children still will not have the organizational ability to play competitively. They may understand that to throw the ball to first base is to obey a rule. They may not, however, understand the consequences of such action in terms of the game as a whole. Later, by playing at school and in other settings, children begin to play the game to win. During this stage, they may feel that they must abide strictly by the rules. Children at this stage may insist on having teams of equal numbers of players and having a player for each position specified in the rules.

It is at this point that the most important development in the child's consciousness of rules takes place. At this stage, children acting as a group may go so far as to change the rules to improve the game or to accommodate players of varying abilities. In baseball, for example, when enough players are not available, a game may be arranged where players may simply rotate from fielding positions to batting, thus alleviating the need to have nine players on a side. In softball, the rules are often manipulated so that batting teams supply their own pitchers and catchers.

Important lessons about social development can be learned from the play in which children engage and from the improvisations they make in their play. As the child's attitudes toward rules become more legislative, a concern with equality and the idea of justice replaces the previous emphasis on the sovereignty and immutable authoritativeness of rules. Piaget argues that the child's sense of justice can develop only through interaction with peers in which all feel equal. In this context, the child comes to accord to others a similar degree of respect and concern.

It is in this sense that one can see the importance of decentering (see Chapter 4) for moral and social development. It is through this process that the child learns to assume the perspective of the other. The ability to do this is a crucial prerequisite for the kind of discussion required to codify rules. As they move from following rules to negotiating and, in some senses, creating the rules for the games they play, children learn to view a situation from a variety of perspectives. Ultimately, they must learn to take the role of the other in a wide variety of real-world contexts.

PEER ASSOCIATIONS AND CHUMS

Preadolescent peer associations can be a source of considerable enjoyment for children. At the same time, they may create problems and conflicts. On the one hand, peer associations provide a base of support for the preadolescent child, supplying a context in which the child's identity and self-concept as an individual separate from his or her family may begin to take form. On the other hand, peer groups may espouse values that conflict with those that the child has learned in the family. Through peer associations, children may come to view their parents from another perspective and reevaluate their parents' basic values and ideas. Where previously parental authority may have appeared infallible, children may now learn that there are different ways of doing things. As the child matures, the authority of the rules decreases. They come to be viewed as a matter of mutual consent. "Decentration" (see Chapter 4) in the Piagetian sense may be facilitated through participation in a widening variety of play activities and through association with peers.

Such associations may have other important consequences. Late childhood peer associations may serve to bolster values that are taught in the home and to stress accepted societal norms. Some societies may attempt to structure peer groups to reinforce dominant societal values. In our culture, for example, consider the values that are stressed in organizations such as the 4-H Clubs or the Boy Scouts. Late childhood peer associations may be fraught with conflicts and contradictions at the same time that they provide for new discoveries, new social relationships, and more complete sense of independence.

Some social psychologists believe that one of the most important activities of late childhood is the development of a relationship with a special friend or "chum." According to Harry Stack Sullivan;

> One of the most important experiences a child can have during this period revolves around membership "inclusion" and "exclusion" which may grow out of such membership. It is at this time that the child may begin to understand some of the positive feelings of group membership as well as the entitlements and obligations of such membership. At the same, s/he may come to understand some of the feelings associated with being excluded from a group. Through this, the child may begin to develop a sensitivity to others with whom s/he has friendly as well as unfriendly interactions.[27]

The establishment of a relationship with a "special friend" or "chum" may play an important role in the development of these sensitivities. Sullivan continues:

> your child at pre-adolescence when he finds a chum begins to develop a real sensitivity to what matters to another person. And this is not in the sense of "what should I do to get what I want," but instead, "what should I do to contribute to the happiness or to support the prestige and feeling of worthwhileness of my chum."[28]

One's chum may provide a base of support as the child comes to form new peer associations and face new and challenging life experiences. Special friendships also provide a confidential and private area for sharing of information about "tabooed" topics and for testing the limits of social acceptability. Most pranks, it has been noted, tend to be played on "best friends."[29]

PEERS AND SEX SEGREGATION

During early childhood little boys and girls play freely with one another. As they enter the preadolescent period, peer groups in some cultures tend to become sex segregated, and strict prohibitions may be enforced regarding sexual as well as other forms of contact between young people. It should be noted that this is not a culturally invariant pattern. Some cultures, the Trobriand Islanders, for example, encourage sexual activity at what may seem to us to be a very early age. Boys as young as 10 and girls as young as 6 are given instructions on how to perform sexual intercourse and are provided with opportunities for sexual activity. Among some cultures, it is believed that young girls will not mature properly unless they have early sexual contact. Other cultures are even more strict than contemporary American society in forbidding contact between preadolescent boys and girls. The Arapoho Indians of North America prohibit all contact between preadolescent boys and girls.[30]

Some psychoanalytically oriented theorists maintain that sex-segregated peer groups serve a function with respect to the resolution of oedipal-related conflicts. Boys, in particular, may come to feel more independent of their mothers. In U.S. society, for example, it is interesting to note that one of the most shattering insults that can be directed to a preadolescent boy is to call him a "sissy." By rejecting feminine-type role characteristics, the boy's identification with the male role may be facilitated. For girls, interaction with peers may help to diffuse any sense of "competition" existing between mother and daughter. Given the diversity of peer relationships in different cultures, one may question this interpretation of the significance of sex segregation. In many contemporary Western societies, however, sex segregation has tended to reinforce predominant cultural conceptions of masculinity and femininity. The very fact of sex segregation itself reflects the idea that certain activities are more appropriate for members of one sex than they are for members of the other.

In sex-segregated peer groups, children may begin to test what it means to be a male or female in this culture. Symbolic interactionist Gary Alan Fine[31] has analyzed the interactions between boys on Little League baseball teams with respect to this idea. One boy's advice on how to approach a "sexy girl" is worth quoting in this regard.

According to Tom,

> First you walk in, you see a sexy girl in the telephone booth. You don't know who she is, just see the back of her. Gotta make sure she doesn't have a big butt, you know. . . . You just walk into the telephone booth, put your arm around her and say "Hi." And she goes "unhh! Ohh, Hi" (tone sounds surprised at first, then "feminine" and "willing").[32]

Such talk is hardly geared toward providing "objective information" about sexual activities. Rather, it provides a forum in which boys may experiment in enacting what they consider to be appropriate male behavior. As Fine puts it, young boys "learn how to present themselves to male peers as 'males.' "[33]

The quotation illustrates how peer interactions reinforce prevalent sexual stereotypes. Tom appears to believe that males are supposed to be sexually aggressive and demanding, whereas girls are supposed to be passive and receptive. More generally, Tom's remarks reflect the prevalent cultural stereotype of male dominance and female submission.

Girls' peer associations are somewhat different. First, boys appear to be more susceptible to peer influences at an earlier age. This may result from the fact that parents tend to be more protective of and exert more control over their daughters than their sons. Girls may spend more time "in the house" with mother.[34]

As girls grow older, however, peer association may become more important. According to Theodore Lidz,

> As the girl passes ten and is almost prepubertal, desires for intimacy with other girls increase. Cliques that are formalized into clubs or secret societies afford opportunities to exchange knowledge or fantasies about menstruation, sex, and crushes. The approaching changes in physique and physiological functioning can be faced more securely when fears and hopes are shared.[35]

Just as sex-segregated groups provide boys with an opportunity to test what it means to be a "man," similar groups provide girls with an opportunity to test what it means to be a "woman." In this regard, one sociologist has referred to "girls' culture" as a "bedroom culture." According to S. Firth;

> girl culture becomes a culture of the bedroom, the place where girls meet, listen to music and teach other make-up skills, practice their dancing, compare sexual notes, criticize each others' clothes and gossip.[36]

Interestingly, this "culture" is both distinct from and in some ways contradictory to the subcultures of boys. One researcher has noted a distinct antipathy on the part of boys toward girls' rock and role idols who may be viewed as "poofs." Girls may rather fiercely defend their idols against attack by young boys. One ethnographer has described the response of young girls whose idolization of pop stars Donnie and Marie Osmond became the brunt of some teasing by older male brothers.

> Osmond baiting was, in fact, one of the most familiar weapons used by older brothers in their continuous bickering with their younger sisters. A fourteen year old boy told how "we went by the Rainbow [Theatre] once and we started screaming out of the window 'Osmonds are bent, all queers' and they were lobbing everything that come in sight. You should see one of the girls, she's in a state crying over the railing, going 'You bastards' and the next minute she picked up a bottle and threw it at the bus."

From a psychoanalytic perspective, sex segregation and animosity between prepubscent boys and girls is a normal part of the development process. The young boy's identity as a male is being solidified as is the young girl's as a female. This entails some rejection of traits characteristic of the opposite sex. Many of the jump rope rhymes sung by young girls contain negative images of boys, and some theorists view the antipathies expressed toward "little brother" as symptomatic of this rejection.

Recently, however, writers have linked sex segregation with a kind of differential socialization that effectively discriminates against girls. Specifically, it is argued that girls are taught to be receptive, passive, and submissive and to play a role as spectator whereas boys are socialized to be more aggressive and active. Simon de Beauvoir sees a certain tragedy in the fact that little girls may come to repress and thus sacrifice their more active inclinations and desires to conform to socially accepted stereotypes. As she puts it, "The less [a young girl] exercises her freedom to understand, to grasp and discover the world about her, the less resources will she find within herself, the less will she dare to affirm herself as subject."[38] Indeed, recent empirical studies show that young boys generally experience increases in self-esteem as they approach adolescence, whereas the self-esteem of most girls remains essentially the same during that time period.[39] The popular media may provide stereotypes that reinforce differential socialization as well. Sociologist Lenore Weitzman examined the content of award-winning picture books for children. She found that male characters outnumbered female characters by a ratio of 11 to 1. While boys were typically engaged in a varied array of very active types of play, girls were more likely to be portrayed as passive. The author noted a number of pictures that showed girls in the kitchen helping their mothers. Boys were rarely portrayed in such a manner.[40] Differential socialization may be further reinforced as the child progresses through school.

SCHOOL AND FAMILY

Perhaps one of the most significant events for children in our culture is their first day of school. Indeed, education is generally regarded in our society as a critical part of the democratic process, providing all children with an equal opportunity for success. Despite this, a number of important studies of performance levels at different schools have suggested that school characteristics such as the number of books in the library, the kinds of special programs, the conditions of the facilities, and even per capita expenditures do not significantly affect academic achievement.[41] Rather, certain background variables appear to have a more significant impact. For example, certain characteristics of the family in which children are raised can have an impact on their subsequent academic performance. Persons raised in less authoritarian families in which they play some role in decision-making activities appear to have less difficulty learning than do those raised in a highly authoritarian manner. Such families use less authoritarian child-rearing practices and provide a context in which children may develop their own sense of independence, curiosity, and responsibility, which in turn, enhances academic performance.[42]

Researchers have found strong relationships between parents' aspirations for their children and children's educational aspirations.[43] Some research suggests that these differences are class based; in the middle and upper classes, parents tend to place a greater value on education than do their working-class counterparts. As a result, their children tend to value education more than do working-class children.[44] It is not clear, however, that this correlation results from the fact that education per se is more highly valued. It may well be the case that education is perceived by the middle class simply as a more viable means of social mobility. One recent multivariate study strongly suggests that there is no significant direct relationship between social class and student aspiration but rather that social class affects parental aspirations that then have an important effect on student educational expectations.[45] Given the importance attributed to parental influence on the child's educational performance, it is interesting to note that both mothers and fathers tend to place a greater emphasis on the importance of college for their sons than they do for their daughters. This correlation appears to hold across social class boundaries and applies to parents of different educational backgrounds.[46]

Other research suggests that children arrive at school with certain personality characteristics that also enhance their educational potential. Positive relationships have been found between children's self-images and academic success, especially in reading.[47] More recent research, however, suggests that positive valuation of academic-related self-characteristics is more important than is general self-image.[48] Also, children who believe that they have control over their own reinforcements (internals rather than externals)[49] and those who believe that they are the sources or authors for their own behavior (i.e., origins rather than pawns)[50] tend to have higher levels of academic success as measured by performance on achievement tests. Although such personality characteristics may be modified by the child's school experience, it does appear that the child with high self-esteem and the sense that he or she can control his or her destiny may enjoy an initial advantage over other children.

SCHOOL AND SEX ROLE SOCIALIZATION

School, as a socialization process, may reinforce important cultural stereotypes. This may be seen with respect to sex roles, as evidenced in one study of boys and girls in a nursery school classroom. The researchers noted that teachers were more likely to encourage and reward independent problem solving by boys than by girls. Boys, for example, would be granted more time to try and solve a problem on their own. Help would be offered to girls at earlier stages of the process. One instance of such differential socialization is worth noting:

> In one classroom, the children were making party baskets. When the time came to staple the paper handles in place, the leader worked with each child individually. She showed the boys how to use the stapler by holding the handle in place while the child stapled it. On the girls' turn, however, if the child didn't spontaneously staple the handle herself, the leader took the basket, stapled the handle herself, and handed it back.[51]

According to the authors, such training can account for the fact that boys tend to show greater aptitude for problem solving, spatial reasoning, and mathematics.[52] The authors note that the types of instruction and directions a child receives can have an important effect on the development of such capabilities. They attribute the differential performance of boys and girls in these areas more to early training and socialization than to innate differences between the sexes. Beyond this, the greater independence granted to boys may lead to stronger feelings of fate control and personal causation, which in turn may enhance academic performance. Whereas boys are trained to succeed in tasks for their intrinsic value (e.g., to do a good job), girls are socialized to perform for extrinsic reasons (e.g., to satisfy the teacher).[53]

Differential socialization for boys and girls does not end with nursery school. Sociologist Sue Sharpe argues that while in school, girls are exposed to a hidden curriculum that perpetuates sex role stereotypes.[54] This is evidenced in some characteristics of textbooks. For example, a study of elementary school readers used in the United States revealed that boy-centered stories outnumbered girl-centered stories by a ratio of 5 to 2. There were three times as many stories featuring boys as there were featuring girls.[55] Beyond this, where boy characters are portrayed as creative, brave, persevering, achieving, autonomous, and athletic, girl characters tend more often to be dependent, passive, incompetent, fearful, docile, and aimless.[56] While girls are often portrayed as benefiting from positive consequences that did not result from their own actions, boys are more often presented as benefiting from consequences that resulted from their own actions.[57] From a social learning perspective, girls through their textbooks have been provided with a very different set of models than have boys.

Teachers tend to act differently toward boys than toward girls. Teachers tend to spend more time with boys and to direct their attention toward more academic pursuits. Boys' tendencies toward misbehaving have the ironic consequence of garnering for them a larger share of teacher attentions, which under some conditions contributes to the likelihood that they may misbehave in the future, gaining still more teacher attention. Moreover, teachers tend to reprimand girls differently from boys. Where boys' failures are treated as evidence that they are not performing up to their capabilities, girls' failures are treated as evidence of a lack of ability.[58] Given such factors, it is not surprising that girls' self-esteem appears not to increase throughout the school years in the same manner as boys'. Moreover, as girls grow older, they come to view domestic activities and marriage as more important than preparing for a vocation or career. Essays written by grammar school girls reflected a preoccupation with marriage over career concerns.[59]

Although school may help reinforce prevalent cultural stereotypes, the classroom may under some conditions serve to facilitate changes in social roles and expectations. In the United States, federal regulations requiring equal treatment of girls and boys may begin to reduce the impact of differential socialization. For example, one study found that when girls are given leadership roles in the classroom, they and the boys in the class were both less likely to view leadership as a male prerogative.[60]

TEACHERS AND STUDENTS: EXPECTANCIES AND SELF-FULFILLING PROPHECIES

Can teachers' attitudes toward students affect students' performance? This question was investigated experimentally by two social psychologists, Robert Rosenthal and Lenore Jacobsen.[61] The two researchers told a group of teachers that they had developed a "test" that would identify those pupils who were likely to be "intellectual bloomers" during the upcoming school year. The "test" was administered to students in grades 1 through 6. Their teachers were then given lists that purportedly identified the fast learners or "spurters." The test did not actually predict "intellectual bloomers," and the "spurters" were in fact students selected randomly.

After the school year was over, Rosenthal returned to the school. He administered a test that measured improvements in reasoning and vocabulary. In certain grades, those students identified as spurters had made greater strides than had their counterparts. Rosenthal and Jacobsen hypothesized that the initial identification of certain students as "spurters" changed the attitudes of the teachers, creating an "expectancy" that the spurters would perform better than their counterparts. This expectancy was then communicated to the students in a way that improved their performance. Rosenthal and Jacobsen hypothesized that the teacher, "by what she said, by how she said it, by her facial expression, postures and perhaps by her touch . . . may have communicated to the children of the experimental group that she expected improved intellectual performance.[62]

These findings suggest that a kind of self-fulfilling prophecy may be said to operate with respect to education. According to this notion, people may be offered a false definition of the situation that eventually becomes accepted. Because it is accepted, it evokes behavior that helps to make it true.[63]

Generalizing from Rosenthal and Jacobsen's findings, one could hypothesize that just as the "false definition" of a student as a fast learner could improve that student's performance, a false definition of a student as a slow learner might impede his or her academic progress. In this regard, Burton Clark,[64] for example, has described what he calls the "cooling-out" process in American education. Unwanted students are slowly given signals that they are not likely to succeed educationally. This increases their disaffection with school and learning, leading them to drop out. Clark maintains that "cooling-out" is more prevalent among lower-class students.

Other studies have found that white teachers tend to have more negative perceptions and lower expectations of minority group children.[65] One study had teachers rate students in desegregated schools. White students were consistently rated as being more intelligent, more perservering, more organized, and, over all, more intellectually suited for school. White students also were rated as being more social than their black and Hispanic counterparts.[66] Ray Rist has described the subtle ways in which teachers in an inner-city, predominantly black, elementary school communicated their expectations to students and the effect that this had on students' subsequent performances.[67]

Attempts to replicate Rosenthal and Jacobsen's findings have produced varying results.[68] While some studies show that teachers may develop expectations based on stereotypes related to race and social class, other research does not show that these expectations are directly translated into student performance.[69] However, one recent study suggested that ability grouping of students did in fact affect the behavior of teachers toward students placed in different groups and student performance. Teachers tended to be more responsive and more attentive to students placed in "higher-ability" groups.[70]

When minority students are involved, expectancy has been observed to have a complicated effect. To examine this, Rubovits and Maehr[71] established a series of discussion groups. Each contained one teacher and four students: two blacks and two whites. Students were selected from the same ability groupings. Teachers, however, were told that two students in each group, one black and one white, were especially gifted. As one would predict from the Rosenthal study, Rubovits and Maehr noted a significant difference in the teachers' treatment of the white and black students who were identified as gifted. Black students, however, received less praise and more criticism despite the fact that their responses did not differ essentially from those of their white counterparts. This led the researchers to conclude that the expectancy effect on performance could be mediated by other factors:

> the expectation of giftedness is associated with a generally positive response of teachers—if the student is white. For the black students, if anything, a reverse tendency is evident, in which the expectation of deviance is associated with less positive treatment.[72]

Rubovits and Maehr's work does not necessarily negate Rosenthal's general findings with respect to expectancy. Rather, it shows how the impact of expectancies may be conditioned by other variables—in this case, race.

COMPETITION AND LEARNING

School officials often attempt to encourage a sense of achievement orientation and independence among students. Succeeding in school allows children to demonstrate that they can obtain certain goals independently. This may increase their sense of personal efficacy. Succeeding in public, by answering a question correctly, for example, may increase the esteem in which others hold the child. As a result, the child's opinion of himself or herself may be enhanced. In this sense, competition—one of the most important values stressed in contemporary Western education—may contribute to the child's developing sense of himself or herself as a competent adult in the competitive games or struggles in which adults engage.

There is, however, another side to competition—failure—and this too can affect a child's development. Anthropologist Jules Henry describes the following occurrence in an American high school. Unquestionably, it is not one with which you are totally unfamiliar.

> Boris had trouble reducing $^{12}/_{16}$ to the lowest terms, and could only get as far as $^{6}/_{8}$. The teacher asked him quietly if that was as far as he could reduce it. She suggested he "think." Much heaving up and down and waving of hands by the other children, all frantic to correct him. Boris pretty unhappy probably mentally paralyzed. The teacher, quiet, patient, ignores the others and concentrates with looks and voice on Boris . . . After a minute or two, she becomes more urgent, but there is no response from Boris. She then turns to the class and says, "Well, who can tell Boris what the number is?" A forest of hands appears, and the teacher calls Peggy. Peggy says that four may be divided into the numerator. Thus Boris's failure has made it possible for Peggy to succeed; his depression is the price of her exhilaration; his misery the occasion of her rejoicing. This is the standard condition of the American elementary school.[73]

Just as success in a competitive event can enhance one's self-esteem, failure can harm it. School provides a series of opportunities for both and is in this sense an appropriate latent training ground for life in a competitive society, although it may not always be effective for helping children to learn the manifest content of school curricula.

CHOICE, CONTROL, AND SCHOOLING

Social psychologists have for some time been interested in social and psychological factors that affect the learning process. As research on expectancies and self-fulfilling prophecies shows, school performance is not simply a reflection of an individual's intellectual capabilities, but reflects the social context in which learning takes place as well.

For a number of years, certain social psychologists have been investigating learning as a function of choice and control. Earlier in this chapter, we discussed how the extent to which individuals believed that they were in control of their reinforcers (internals) and the degree to which they felt that they were the authors or originators of their own actions (origins) tended to enable them to do better in school than those who believed that they could not control their reinforcers (externals) or who did not feel that they were the originators of their behavior (pawns). Findings such as these have led some social psychologists to hypothesize that providing individuals with a choice in making decisions about their education increases their sense of control and will enhance the learning experience. Research in a wide variety of areas has shown that having a choice and being in control can have certain positive effects on the decision maker. Laboratory experiments have found a positive correlation among choice, control, and learning. In one study, for example, two groups of students were given a test measuring their recall of paired words. Students given the initial opportunity to choose the response word did significantly better on the test than did those for whom the response word was initially assigned by the experimenter.[74] Choice appears to improve classroom performance as well. One study demonstrated an improvement in reading comprehension when children were given the opportunity of choosing the stories to be read.[75] Math performance improved when children selected their own goals.[76] Improvements also may occur when students are allowed to choose their rewards. Math performances among preschoolers improved when successful attempts were rewarded; they improved even more dramatically when children were allowed to choose their rewards.[77] Similar improvements have been noted among fifth graders who were allowed to choose how much material would be covered within a specified period of time.[78]

On a more generalized level, some research has shown that teachers who themselves are origins tend to produce greater academic achievement among their students. Researchers believe that such teachers provide an "origin climate" and less control in the classroom. Such a climate presumably leads to greater feelings of personal causation among students, which in turn, increases their motivation to learn.[79]

LEARNING IN DIFFERENT CULTURAL CONTEXTS

It is easy to forget that schooling is an interactive process. Studies such as those just described highlight the importance of communication between students and teachers in the learning process. When this communication is impaired, learning may be hampered. When extensive cultural differences exist between students and teachers, communication often is severely impaired. White teachers in schools serving large minority and multicultural populations may still operate in terms of a dominant Anglo culture. Often, these teachers may fail to consider that for children of other cultures some expressions may have different meanings. In this regard, the linguist William Labov[80] has identified a number of characteristics that differentiate the speech of lower-class black youths growing up in America's central cities from the speech of their more middle-class counterparts. According to Labov, these differences are quite distinctive. He sees black speech as having a recognizable pattern, which he has termed "black English vernacular" (BEV).

There are a number of phonological differences between black and standard English. These differences in the sounds of words may affect a child's ability to understand the teacher and, perhaps more important, the teacher's ability to understand the child. For example, Labov and his colleagues point out that there is a tendency in black English speech to drop the "r" when it appears in certain positions in a word. Labov terms this characteristic "r-lessness." As a result, the following English words would be pronounced differently in BEV:

ENGLISH SPELLING	BEV PRONUNCIATION
nor	gnaw
sore	saw
fort	fought
Carol	cal
trial	child
trolley	Charley
true	chew[81]

Other BEV patterns include the tendency to drop "l's"—for example, fault = fought, toll = toe, all = awe—and the leaving off of consonants at the end of a word—for example, past = pass, mend = men, hold = hole, guest = guess. These differences, along with other differences between black and standard English, can create problems of communication between teachers and students. Thus, a student could be corrected by a teacher if she or he reads "fort" as fort but pronounces it as "fought." The tendency to drop the final consonant may create special problems for learning the past tense. The verb "passed" may be pronounced as "pass" even if the student reads it as passed. Teachers in inner-city schools according to Labov need to be able to distinguish between mistakes in reading and differences in pronunciation between children of different subcultures.

This research should sensitize us to the fact that children from different cultural and class backgrounds may develop skills that although different are not necessarily superior or inferior to those of children from other class or cultural backgrounds. Recently, some researchers have analyzed the "street play" of lower-class youths and have noted that such play exhibits at least three different types of cognitive skills. The first of these is *action skill* demonstrated through activities involved in the exploration and development of physical capabilities (e.g., climbing rooftops, jumping from high places, exploring abandoned buildings). Action skills also include decision-making and planning activities such as setting up games. The researchers note that these activities often are pursued with a very high degree of concentration and that children engaged in street play tend to experiment with that environment in a creative manner. Other forms of cognitive activities—*symbolic play* (through imagining and role playing) and *language development* (through experimentation with word meanings)—are pursued with a similar degree of concentration. According to this view, children of poverty should not be labeled as inferior simply because the areas in which they have learned to demonstrate their competencies are not valued as highly as those in which middle-class children play.[82]

GETTING ALONG WITH OTHERS: FACILITATING RACIAL INTEGRATION

As we have seen, growing up entails becoming part of a wider social world. The child emerges from the family and forms new associations with peers. Such associations play an important role in social development.

School provides an area in which children from different cultural and social backgrounds may come together. Since 1954, school systems throughout the United States have been under a legal mandate to integrate their classrooms racially. Social psychologists have examined some of the factors that tend to facilitate racial integration in schools. Simply "mixing" children of different groups does not guarantee a quality learning experience. Rather, a number of factors related to the community, the school, and the classroom are important if integration is to take place. Sociologist Ray Rist has vividly described the difficulties that small numbers of blacks face when isolated in predominantly white schools. Such students may come to feel alienated and isolated from the main student body. Their sense of being left out may be exacerbated when there are large social class differences between the two groups.[83] Murray Wax has argued that blacks in predominantly white schools may be forced to give up a part of their culture and heritage to comply with white norms and values.[84]

Findings such as these have led some policymakers to recommend that each classroom should contain relatively equal proportions of minority and majority students.[85] Even this, however, may not guarantee a harmonious integrated experience. Aspects of the social psychology of prejudice and the dynamics of classroom interaction must be considered.

Much of the early research on prejudice and social integration suggested that integration is likely to be more successful and prejudice reduced when there is equal status contact between the groups and when the groups do not perceive themselves to be in competition for scarce resources.[86] Some recent studies indicate that equal status interaction appears to facilitate school integration. Status may be understood as one's position as defined by others in a particular set of social circumstances. Any classroom contains a number of different statuses, the most important being the distinction between teacher and student. In any classroom, students may act as teachers for other students. A common assumption is that "good" students act as teachers for the "poorer" students. For a variety of reasons, minority students are often thought to be poorer students than their majority counterparts. As a result, majority students often tend to dominate classroom activities. This may hinder the participation of minority students in the learning experience and, hence, hamper their academic development.

To counter this condition and provide minority students with a more meaningful learning experience, experiments were designed to facilitate racial integration between children of different groups. A number of groups of children were exposed to what the researchers termed "expectation training." Minority children were provided with an opportunity to explain a difficult task to their majority counterparts. The class was then given a common task. Minority participation and equal status contact increased considerably among the groups who had participated in expectation training.[87] This has proven successful for not only black and white but also for Chicano-white relations and for relationships between Western and Eastern European Jews in Israel and for Indian-Anglo relations in Canada.[88]

Other approaches have been used to reduce the competition among students. One technique currently being investigated by both educators and social psychologists is the notion of "multiple ability curriculum." According to this idea, classrooms that focus on only one ability will have more rigid status hierarchies, making the possibility of equal status contact more difficult. To demonstrate the viability of multiability curricula, the following experiment was designed. Students were allowed to demonstrate competence with respect to three different types of cognitive skills: visual thinking, intuitive thinking, and analytic reasoning. The children were first introduced to each skill through a short film depicting adults and children solving a "real-life" problem using each of the skills. The students were then put in racially mixed groups. Each group contained a number of children who were behind in reading. However, these children developed higher expectations because of capabilities they demonstrated in the other cognitive areas. This occurs, in part, because the children who may have had problems reading were able to show that they were competent with other skills, and because the group interaction was structured to prevent the formation of negative self-fulfilling prophecies. Similar types of experiments have been conducted in different classrooms at a variety of different schools. Although some preliminary findings are hopeful, further research is required.[89]

One final technique to deemphasize competition and create equal status contact is the notion of a jigsaw approach.[90] Rather than having students attempt to complete the same task, they are each given a separate part of that task. As a result, they have to rely upon each others' efforts for completing the task. This generates a more cooperative approach to problems; it increases the extent to which students help one another, and it appears to enhance the learning of less advanced students without hindering the more advanced students. More important, perhaps, the technique increased the self-esteem of all students and their overall appreciation of school.[91]

Viewed from a social psychological perspective, classrooms and schools are very complex institutions. Although cross-sectional surveys have not found that school characteristics are an important predictor of academic success, experimental studies show that the social organization of classrooms may have an impact on student performance. Beyond this, it is clear that schools are important as an agency of socialization not only for preadolescents but also for adolescents and young adults. In fact some social psychologists have noted that the school's role in the socialization process has increased considerably in recent years and that it has begun to assume many of the socialization functions previously assumed by the family.[92] For this reason, more attention needs to be paid to the role of education in adolescent socialization.

CONCLUSIONS

The emergence of children from the homes of their families of origin marks the beginning of their participation in a larger social world. There is an increase in the number of others in terms of whom children may define themselves. Although individuals may enter this world with partly formed personality characteristics, their self-concepts and self-esteem will continue to be shaped through their experiences with peers, teachers, and others. It is in this sense that the evolution and development of self is a social process. As a person's social experiences broaden, so does his or her sense of participation and membership in larger social collectivities. My "self" is a product not only of my biological heritage or of early training provided by my family but, in a crucial sense, of all these memberships and participations.

NOTES

[1]Adapted from E. Glascgow, *The Sheltered Life* (Garden City, N.Y.: Doubleday, 1932) pp. 1–10.

[2]Phillipe Aries, *Centuries of Childhood*, translated by Robert Baldick (New York: Alfred A. Knopf, 1962).

[3]Lloyd De Mause, "Our Forebearers Made Childhood a Nightmare," *Psychology Today* (April 1975), p. 85. See also Loyd De Mause, ed., *The History of Childhood* (New York: The Psycho-History Press, 1974).

[4]J. D. Fleming, "Infant T.L.C.: Simian Style," *Psychology Today* (April 1975), p. 88.

[5]Theodore Lidz, *The Person: His and Her Development Throughout the Life Cycle* (New York: Basic Books, 1976), pp. 377–379.

[6]Ibid., p. 379.

[7]Ibid., p. 379.

[8]B. Bettleheim, *The Uses of Enchantment: The Meaning and Importance of Fairy-Tales* (New York: Alfred A. Knopf, 1976).

[9]Lidz, *The Person*, p. 253.

[10]J. Piaget, *The Language and Thought of the Child* (Cleveland: Meridian Books, 1955).

[11]M. Mead, *Sex and Temperment in Three Primitive Societies*, New York: Dell, 1935.

[12]N. Eisenberg, "Social Development" in C.B. Kopp and J.B. Kralvow (eds.) *The Child: Development in a Social Context*. Reading, Mass.: Addison-Wesley; 1982, p. 228.

[13]Ibid., p. 232–3.

[14]Ibid., p. 234.

[15]E. Erikson, *Childhood and Society* (New York: W. W. Norton, 1950).

[16]Gregory P. Stone, "The Play of Little Children," in G. Stone and H. Farberman, eds., *Social Psychology Through Symbolic Interaction* (New York: John Wiley, 1981), p. 253.

[17]Spencer K. Thompson, "Gender Labels and Early Sex-Role Development," *Child Development*, Vol. 46 (1975), pp. 339–347.

[18]Stone, "The Play of Little Children," p. 253.

[19]Ibid., p. 255.

[20]H. Goldings, "Jump Rope Rhymes and the Rhythm of Latency Development on Girls," *Psychoanalytic Study of the Child*, Vol. 29 (1974), pp. 431–451.

[21]Ibid., p. 438.

[22]Ibid., p. 440.

[23]Ibid., p. 447.

[24]Jean Piaget, "Moral Judgment: Children Invent the Social Contract," in H. Graber and J. Voneche, eds., *The Essential Piaget* (New York: Basic Books, 1977), p. 160.

[25]Ibid., p. 161.

[26]Ibid., p. 163.

[27]H. S. Sullivan, *The Interpersonal Theory of Psychiatry* (New York: W. W. Norton, 1953), p. 245.

[28]Ibid., p. 55.

[29]Stone, "The Play of Little Children," p. 255.

[30]Clellan Ford and Frank A. Beach, *Patterns of Sexual Behavior* (New York: Harper & Row, 1951); see also Vern L. Bullough, *Sexual Variance in Society and History* (New York: John Wiley, 1976).

[31]Gary Alan Fine, "Friends, Impression Management and Preadolescent Behavior," in Stone and Farkerman, eds., *Social Psychology Through Symbolic Interaction*, pp. 257–272.

[32]Ibid., p. 267.

[33]Ibid., p. 268.

[34]Lidz, *The Person*, p. 278.

[35]Ibid., p. 280.

[36]S. Frith, *The Sociology of Rock* (London: Constable, 1978).

[37]D. Robins and S. Cohen, *Knuckle Sandwich* (Hammodsworth: Penguin, 1978), p. 52.

[38]Simon de Beauvoir, *The Second Sex* (New York: Alfred A. Knopf, 1953), p. 280.

[39]Deborah Fein, Sylvia Oneil, Frank Constance, and Kathryn McCall Velit, "Sex Difference in Preadolescent Self-esteem," *The Journal of Psychology*, Vol. 90 (1975), pp. 179–183; see also Letty C. Pogrebin, *Growing Up Free* (New York: McGraw-Hill, 1980), and Peter J. Watson and Martha Mechrick, "Race, Social Class and the Motive to Avoid Success in Women," *Journal of Cross-Cultural Society* (1970), pp. 284–291.

[40]Lenore J. Weitzman et al., "Sex Role Socialization in Picture Books for Pre-School Children," *American Journal of Sociology*, Vol. 77 (1972), 1124–1149.

[41]See James S. Coleman et al. *Equality of Educational Opportunity* (Washington, D.C.: U.S. Government Printing Office, 1966); Christopher Jencks et al., *Inequality: A Reassessment of the Effects of Family and Schooling in America* (New York: Basic Books, 1972); also see C. Jencks and S. Bartlett, *Who Gets Ahead: The Determinants of Economic Success in America* (New York: Basic Books, 1979).

[42]See, for example, E. E. Levitt and S. L. Zelen, "The Validity of the Einstelang Test as a Measure of Rigidity," *Journal of Abnormal and Social Psychology* (October 1953), pp. 573–580; and Nora C. Foster, W. E. Vinacke, and J. M. Digman, "Flexibility and Rigidity in a Variety of Problem Situations," *Journal of Abnormal and Social Psychology* (March 1955), pp. 211–216.

[43]William H. Sewell and Vimal P. Shah, "Parents' Education and Children's Educational Aspirations and Achievements," *American Sociological Review*, Vol. 12 (April 1968), pp. 191–208.

[44]William H. Sewell, "Inequality of Opportunity for Higher Education," *American Sociological Review*, Vol. 36 (1971), pp. 793–808.

[45]Mark Davis and Denise B. Kandell, "Parental and Peer Influences on Adolescents' Educational Plans: Some Further Evidence," *American Journal of Sociology*, Vol. 87 (September 1981), pp. 363–383.

⁴⁶Sewell and Shah, "Parents' Education," pp. 206–207.

⁴⁷William W. Wattenberg and Clifford Clare, "Relation of Self-concepts to Beginning Achievement in Reading," *Child Development*, Vol. 35 (1964), p. 461.

⁴⁸Morris D. Caplin, "The Relationship Between Self-concept and Academic Achievement," *The Journal of Experimental Education*, Vol. 37, no. 3 (1969), pp. 13–16.

⁴⁹H. M. Lefcourt, *Locus of Control: Current Trends in Theory and Research* (Hillsdale, N.J.: Erlbaum Associates, 1976), pp. 69–72.

⁵⁰Richard de Charms, "Personal Causation and Perceived Control," in L. C. Perlmuter and R. Monty, eds., *Choice and Perceived Control* (Hillsdale, N.J.: Erlbaum Associates, 1979), pp. 29–40.

⁵¹L. A. Serbin and D. O'Leary, "How Nursery Schools Teach Girls to Shut Up," in J. Williams, ed., *Psychology of Women* (New York: W. W. Norton, 1979), pp. 185–186.

⁵²Ibid., p. 187.

⁵³Ibid., p. 187.

⁵⁴S. Sharpe, *Just Like a Girl* (Hammondsworth: Penguin, 1976).

⁵⁵"Without Bias: A Guidebook for Non-discriminatory Communication" (Pamphlet), Washington, D.C.: Study Group on Sexual Discrimination, 1978.

⁵⁶Myra Sadker, *Sex Equity Handbook for Schools* (New York: Longman, 1982), p. 65.

⁵⁷Terry Saario et al., "Sex Role Stereotyping in the Public Schools," *Harvard Educational Review*, Vol. 3 (1973), pp. 386–416.

⁵⁸See Sadker, *Sex Equity Handbook*. See also Joan Abramson, *The Invisible Woman* (San Francisco: Jossey-Bass, 1975); and Judith Stacey, ed., *And Jill Came Tumbling Down* (New York: Dell, 1974).

⁵⁹M. Brake, *The Sociology of Youth Culture and Youth Subcultures* (Boston: Routledge & Paul Kegan, 1980), p. 142.

⁶⁰M. Lock, "Fifth Grade Study Finds Boys View Girls as Smart but Not as Leaders: Girls Agree," *Educational Testing Service Developments*, Vol. 25, no. 2 (1978), discussed by E. Cohen, "Design and Redesign of the Desegregated School," in W. Stephan and J. Feagin, eds., *School, Desegregation: Past, Present and Future* (New York: Plenum Press, 1980), p. 275.

⁶¹R. Rosenthal and L. Jacobson, *Pygmalion in the Classroom: Teacher Expectation and Pupils' Intellectual Development* (New York: Holt, Rinehart and Winston, 1968).

⁶²Ibid., p. 429.

⁶³Ibid., p. 430.

⁶⁴Burton Clark, "The 'Cooling-Out' Function in Higher Education," *American Journal of Sociology*, Vol. 66 (1960), pp. 569–576.

⁶⁵Jane R. Mercer, Peter Iadicola, and Helen Moore, "Building Effective Multi-Ethnic Schools," in Stephan and Feagin, eds., pp. 281–307.

⁶⁶J. R. Mercer, M. Coleman, and J. Harloe, "Racial Ethnic Segregation and Desegregation in American Public Education," in W. Gordon, ed., *Uses of the Sociology of Education: The 73rd Year Book of the National Society for the Study of Education* (Chicago: University of Chicago Press, 1974), Vol. 2.

⁶⁷Ray C. Rist, "Student, Social Class, and Teacher Expectations: The Self-fulfilling Prophecy in Ghetto Education," *Harvard Educational Review*, Vol. 40 (1970), pp. 411–451. See also Ray C. Rist, *The Urban School: A Factory for Failure* (Garden City, N.Y.: Doubleday, 1973).

⁶⁸Sarah Spence Boocock, "The Social Organization of the Classroom," *Annual Review of Sociology* (Palo Alto, Calif.: Annual Reviews, 1978).

⁶⁹Mercer, Iadicola, and Moore, "Building Effective Multi-Ethnic Schools," p. 290.

⁷⁰Donna Eder, "Ability Grouping as a Self-fulfilling Prophecy: A Micro-Analysis of Teacher-Student Interaction," *Sociology of Education*, Vol. 54 (July 1981), pp. 151–162.

⁷¹P. C. Rubovits and M. L. Maehr, "Pygmalion Black and White," *Journal of Personality and Social Psychology*, Vol. 25 (1973), pp. 210–218.

⁷²Ibid., p. 217.

⁷³J. Henry, *Culture Against Man* (New York: Vintage Books, 1963), pp. 295–296.

⁷⁴R. E. Savage, L. C. Perlmuter, and R. A. Monty, "Effect of Reduction in the Amount of Choice and Perception of Control on Learning," in Perlmuter and Monty, *Choice and Perceived Control* (New York: Halstead Press, 1979), p. 91.

⁷⁵Ibid., p. 105.

⁷⁶T. A. Brigham, "Some Effects of Choice on Academic Performance," in Perlmuter and Monty, *Choice and Perceived Control*, p. 139.

[77]Ibid., p. 140.

[78]Ibid., p. 135.

[79]C. deCharms, "Personal Causation and Perceived Control," in Perlmuter and Monty, pp. 29–40.

[80]William Labov, *Language in the Inner City: Studies in the Black English Vernacular* (Philadelphia: University of Pennsylvania Press, 1972).

[81]Adapted from ibid., p. 12.

[82]Mathew Foley and Donald McGuire, "Cognitive Skill and Street Activity," *Urban Education* (April 16, 1981), pp. 13–36.

[83]Ray C. Rist, *The Invisible Children: School Integration in American Society* (Cambridge, Mass.: Harvard University Press, 1978).

[84]M. L. Wax, *When Schools are Desegregated: Problems and Possibilities for Students, Educators, Parents and the Community* (Washington, D.C.: National Institute of Education, 1979).

[85]See E. Cohen, *Design and Redesign of the Desegregated School: Problems of Status, Power and Conflict*, in J. Feagin and W. Stephan, *School Desegregation*, pp. 259–260.

[86]See Gordon W. Allport, *The Nature of Prejudice* (New York: Addison-Wesley, 1952), pp. 262–263.

[87]See Cohen, *Design and Redesign of the Desegregated School*, p. 265.

[88]Ibid., p. 265.

[89]Ibid., p. 268.

[90]Elliott Aronson, *The Jig-Saw Classroom* (Beverly Hills, Calif.: Sage, 1978).

[91]Ibid., pp. 30–31.

[92]U. Brofenbrenner, *Two Worlds of Childhood: U.S. and U.S.S.R.* (New York: Russell Sage, 1970).

CHAPTER SEVEN
GROWING UP:
Adolescence

Adolescence typically refers to that period of life between the onset of puberty and physical maturity. It is marked by a number of significant changes and important social and psychological developments. In contemporary American and European societies, adolescence may include the ages of 11 or 12 to 19 or 20. Colloquially, children in this age cohort have been termed "teenagers," and this period is often referred to as the "teens."

As with all stages of development, it is difficult to discern where one period ends and another begins. A 9- or 10-year-old may begin to appropriate some of the behaviors and attitudes of adolescence. This may take the form of a preference for certain types of clothes, music, peer associations, and so on. Such anticipatory socialization may help to set the stage for similar behaviors and attitudes in later life.

Physiologically, the child's emergence into adolescence is identified with the onset of puberty. For boys, there is an increase in the size of the genitalia. Pubic hair appears. Later, a beard and other body hair may appear, and the young man's voice may begin to deepen. For girls, the onset of puberty is marked by the enlargement of the ovaries. However, one of the first signs of puberty in adolescent girls is the enlargement of the breasts and a rounding of the hips. Later, the labia and clitoris develop and pubic hair appears. Adolescence also is characterized by a general growth spurt. Girls typically gain 11 to 12 pounds and may grow 3 to 4 inches per year. The young person's overall strength may double during this time period. These physiological changes have an important effect on an individual's self-image as they signal the beginning of the transition from childhood to adulthood.

Adolescence in contemporary Western societies can be divided into three subphases. The first subphase encompasses the period immediately prior to and including the onset of puberty. During this period, many of the patterns established during late childhood may persist. One to two years after the onset of puberty, the midadolescent subphase begins. This is often characterized by a simultaneous process of "revolt and conformity." The child may begin to *reject* parental standards and values in favor of those of peers. *Conformity* to peer values may become quite strong. Early adolescence may be a time for initial sexual explorations. During the third subphase—late adolescence—the young person may begin to take stock of the future. Both young women and men may begin to face important career choices. Long-term relationships with the opposite sex may develop, leading to marital decisions and other choices. As we shall see, however, the process of growing up in contemporary American and European cultures may be quite tumultuous, and the passage through the phases of adolescence is not always smooth.

From a social psychological standpoint, the physiological changes that occur during adolescence are less important than are the profound sociological and psychological transformations. In late childhood, children develop what some social psychologists call an "ego ideal" (i.e., a moral conception of what they should be and how they should behave). This is formed initially through the internalization of parental expectations. During adolescence the child's "ego ideal" is transformed into an "ego identity" (i.e., a sense of himself or herself as a more autonomous and independent individual). As Theodore Lidz puts it,

> the young person . . . gains . . . an identity in her or his own right and not simply as someone's son or daughter, an identity in the sense of a unique consistency of behavior that permits others to have expectations of how the person will behave and react.[1]

The establishment of an ego identity is an active and synthetic process. It is not accomplished by simply passing through the subphase of adolescence. The achievement of new cognitive capabilities and the formation of social relationships are critical to its development. The young person may reflect on different childhood identities, accepting some and rejecting others and fusing the accepted conceptions into an image that will serve to guide future behavior. At the same time, one's identity will be further modified as the person comes to have new experiences and to engage in new social relationships. The establishment of an ego identity in this sense is not the endpoint of the developmental process. Rather, it represents a basis on which further developments may proceed. The self-concept that develops during adolescence then is part of a continuous process; at the same time that one's ego identity is solidified, new challenges and experiences occur that may threaten and/or lead to the modification of that self-concept.

EGO DIFFUSION AND COMMITMENT IN ADOLESCENCE

Problems of ego development are often intensified in adolescence, especially when the young person may be faced with difficult choices or when aspired-to goals become unattainable. Adolescents who are unable to consolidate a sense of self may experience a kind of "ego diffusion"[2] in which they come to feel helpless, defeated, and alienated. They may "give up" trying to direct their own lives. Kenneth Kenniston, in a sensitive discussion of uncommitted youth, describes some of the characteristics of ego diffusion as they were manifested in a young man whom Kenniston calls Inburn:

> Inburn's generally distrustful view of his fellow man was amplified when he was asked what harms and benefits he chiefly anticipated from his fellowmen. He listed "hostility, injustice, hypocrisy, slander, abuse." Asked whom he admired, he said "I never thought about it. Alexander maybe. Hemingway in Paris. Chopin," but asked whom he disliked, he responded with a long catalogue which begins "nearly everything and everyone that's complacently middle-class . . . . I hate officious, supercilious, imperious, pompous, stupid, contented or bigoted persons. I especially dislike opportunists." And asked what his chief satisfactions and ambitions were, he said, "I don't think I'll ever have a main source of satisfaction. Only to live so that I may have the truest picture of the world possible when I die . . . ." And asked how he would reform the world if he could, he said, "This is an unfair question. I guess I'd like to have us all go back to the womb."[3]

Inburn's uncommittedness reflects some of the key characteristics of ego diffusion: a deep sense of pessimism, resentment, and distrust of others; the feeling of being an outsider and having only distant and impersonal relationships with others; and the rejection of conventional goals and values without replacing them with other goals and values. Late adolescence for such uncommitted youth may be characterized as a "meaningless interlude" between childhood and adulthood.

Ego diffusion has both psychological and sociological roots. It results in part from one's family life. Uncommitted youth typically have negative or unstable parental images.

However, ego diffusion cannot be explained solely in terms of family dynamics. Some of the difficulties result from the interconnection of processes of identification, family life, and the world of work. For example, many mothers of uncommitted girls had abandoned careers to have families. Their self-reproaches were conveyed more or less subtly to their daughters who came to devalue both work and family life. Fathers who treat work as a necessary unpleasantness devoid of all value save monetary reward and who treat family life as an escape or refuge from the world of work may convey negative feelings about both work and family life.[4]

Many social psychologists believe that an important achievement of late adolescence is the development of an occupational identity. Here, young people may be faced with an important contradiction: while they may be socialized to perform important, useful, and rewarding tasks, many of their actual employment opportunities may be trivial and unrewarding. As Paul Goodman notes,

The majority of young people are faced with the following alternative: either society is a benevolent racket in which they'll manage to boondoggle . . . or society is serious . . . , but they are useless . . . . Such thoughts do not encourage productive life.[5]

Kenniston and Goodman's work was completed in the 1960s and is in that sense dated. However, a more recent study conducted in an upper-class suburban high school in the 1970s indicates that many students suffer a similar malaise. According to W. Larkin,

in the struggle to maintain physical security and social status, the other needs have been ignored. Thus, the struggle of the students is around the need for belonging, love, esteem, and self-actualization. The world around them is not so much hostile as it is veiled, "unreal," and impenetrable. They are isolated by hidden curtains. They feel that adults are holding out on them, both emotionally and intellectually. Adults, for the most part, maintain their distance and have a tendency to mystify social relationships.

Students' relations with their peers are not much better. A few trusted friends are the most one could possibly ask for. They are competing with each other for certain scarce resources, which, on the one hand, the level of scarcity or future scarcity is unknown. On the other, no one is sure that even if a scarce position could be obtained, whether it would really be what was wanted in the first place.[6]

These youth face problems that result in part from a lack of integration between maturational and developmental processes, on the one hand, and the structure of social life and the world of work, on the other.

Youths from different social classes may have different problems in adjusting to the world of work and developing an occupational identity. Ego diffusion and the overall sense of not being able to find a place for oneself in life may be more of a problem for middle-class and upper-class youth who are faced with a "choice." Many working-class young people may face a different set of problems—they may be "locked" into a job at a relatively young age. Most of them leave school earlier than do their middle-class counterparts and "settle into" occupations that have little advancement potential. Although some research in the 1960s indicated that working-class youths were on the whole more content in their jobs,[7] recent studies indicate that they are more often dissatisfied and unhappy in "dead-end" jobs.[8]

Ego diffusion is only one potential outcome of the identity formation process. Some youths, rather than experiencing a dissipation of social goals and ties, may experience a renewed sense of commitment similar to that found among some of the "young radicals" of the 1960s. One of these has described his developing sense of self in the following terms:

I started off being very insecure in terms of what I was thinking and what I was saying. I usually felt I was wrong, and that I should follow other people's directions. But then, over the last years, I have realized that I am usually right . . . . It's not a matter of whether my predictions are right, whether Bobby Kennedy will run or not.

. . . But I feel much more secure in myself, and I am much more willing at this point to project my alternatives into people, and to push them very hard.

I am more willing now to have people follow my direction and to take responsibility for it. That means the possibility of failure and getting people angry at
you and all kinds of things. That was a very big struggle within myself.[9]

Another "young radical" has described the positive values of
participation:

You get these periodic shots in the arm that are very essential. Just like the parties around here. You'd think that in this place you wouldn't feel isolated. But
after you get back to your apartment or to wherever you live, you see how few
you are, and it gets to be very discouraging. There are billions of *them* out there,
and we can't even move the students, we can't even get ten per cent of the
students. But then, you have a party after the meeting on Thursday night and
you get sixty guys who you really like that are radical, and you say, "All right,
sixty is enough." You feel reinspired and reinvigorated. It's the same with national meetings. You get people together and they give you a shot in the arm.
You figure there are some other people around, and you're ready to go back to
your own turf and do something yourself.[10]

These statements reflect some of the more important characteristics of
committed youth: the importance of acting on the basis of one's principles,
engaging in socially meaningful actions, and being involved with others. What
makes the "young radicals" different from the "uncommitted"? Family
dynamics appear to be a factor: the young radicals had generally positive parental images and tended to view their parents as highly principled individuals.
Once again, however, family factors do not tell the entire story. Larger social
processes are required for a more complete explanation. With respect to the
young radicals, being raised with high moral standards combined with perceptions of social inequality and an unjust war contributed to a sense of mission
and commitment and a desire to make changes in the world.

Thus important social psychological developments occur during
adolescence. These developments, however, are not simply a function of
maturation alone. Rather, they represent a confluence of maturational, psychological, and sociological factors. Let us examine some of these developments more closely and try to understand how they arise.

COGNITIVE DEVELOPMENTS IN ADOLESCENCE

Important developments in thinking take place during adolescence. According to Piaget, the child at about the age of 11 or 12 enters a new stage of
cognitive development called the period of formal operations. This stage is
distinguished by an increased capacity for analytical thinking. As one authority
puts it,

The young adolescent . . . can assess a situation, isolate single variables while holding all other variables constant, and proceed to draw logical conclusions based
upon accurate observations of what takes place. Further, he has acquired the
ability to successfully solve some problems through the use of combinatorial
analysis. Given a range of elements and a task of discovering which particular

combinations produce a specifically desired effect, he can arrange the elements in a way as to systematically and exhaustively test all possible combinations.[11]

Adolescents begin to develop the ability to operate with ideas and abstractions in and of themselves—without having to refer to concrete objects. Indeed, ideas often take on great importance for young people. They may become deeply absorbed with literary concepts such as romanticism or realism, political concepts like democracy or totalitarianism; and economic concepts such as socialism or capitalism. Where the preadolescent child's concern with such concepts is limited to tying them to specific sets of circumstances (e.g., the United States is a "democracy"; England has a "socialist" economy; and John Percy Bysshe Shelly was a "romantic" poet), the adolescent begins to understand that democracy is a set of principles, rules, and practices of governance apart from the government of any specific country; that romanticism was more than the poetry of one person or of a literary movement—that it is an attitude toward life; that socialism is not merely how the economy is run in the United Kingdom or France or some other country, but rather a set of general ideas about values and the production and distribution of goods that may be applied differently in different settings. In short, the adolescent begins to be able to connect ideas with other ideas—to understand concepts.

One aspect of dealing with ideas is the ability to reason hypothetically (i.e., to begin to draw consequences and implications of imagined or purely conceptual states of affairs and to speculate about their consequences and implications). Adolescents may begin to speculate about the "possible" as well as the actual and, more important, to treat possible states of affairs in a logical manner. They may begin to deduce consequences from imagined or unforeseen social conditions; a young person may begin to wonder about what it would be like to live in a world where everyone had enough to eat or about the implications of atomic warfare and global conflict even though these conditions are not currently a reality. Through such reasoning, the young person may begin to transcend his or her immediate social circumstances and gain a broader understanding of his or her place in a larger world system.

In some cases, this newly found ability to reason hypothetically may lead to an overevaluation of one's imagined or hypothetical scenarios. The young person may lose sight of the fact that others may have developed hypothetical scenarios that differ from his or her conceptualizations. "Why doesn't everyone see the world as I do?" young adolescents may wonder. Their parents may have similar concerns. Piaget has termed this the "egocentricity of formal operations."[12] Adolescents reduce this egocentricity through the engaging in debate and discussion with peers—an important aspect of adolescent social life.

MORAL DEVELOPMENT

What does it mean to act in a moral or ethical manner? This is a question that has baffled philosophers for thousands of years, and it would be presumptuous to dictate a "textbook" answer here. There have been, however, many studies of how adolescent children deal with moral and ethical issues. Successive changes seem to occur as a child matures.

Lawrence Kohlberg,[13] a psychologist strongly influenced by Jean Piaget, has investigated moral development by presenting children of different age groups with hypothetical situations that reflect moral dilemmas. Suppose, for example, that your wife is ill and that you cannot afford the medicine needed to treat her. The pharmacist will not allow you to buy the medicine on credit either. What do you do? If you had the opportunity, would you steal the medicine? What would be the reason for your decision? Kohlberg found that as children grow older, their justifications for specific decisions become less tied to the immediate consequences of those decisions in terms of their own well-being and tied more to a concern with the well-being of others and general moral principles. Kohlberg distinguished the following stages of moral development:

LEVEL I: PRECONVENTIONAL MORALITY

Stage 1. *Punishment and obedience orientation.* Child is most concerned with sanctions attached to prohibited behaviors (e.g., "I should not steal because the money will help my wife and I might be put in prison").

Stage 2. *Hedonistic orientation.* Child is most concerned with the possible loss of reward attached to prohibited behavior. (e.g., "I should steal because I will be happier with my wife than without her").

LEVEL II: CONVENTIONAL MORALITY

Stage 3. *Social approval orientation.* Child is most concerned about whether others think of him as good or bad (e.g., "Dad says it is bad to steal. I shouldn't steal").

Stage 4. *Law and order orientation.* Child is most concerned with whether or not behavior is in accord with established rules or laws (e.g., "I should not steal because it's against the law").

LEVEL III: PRINCIPLED MORALITY

Stage 5. *Social contract orientation.* Individual is concerned with mutual obligations, responsibilities, and entitlements (e.g., "The druggist was not fair in refusing to extend credit to me for the medicine. Therefore, it's okay if I steal it").

Stage 6. *Orientation of universal ethical principles.* Individual is concerned with overarching moral principle in terms of which socially defined laws and rules can be evaluated (e.g., "Life and health are more important than property. It's okay to steal the medicine").

Some studies suggest that moral development is a continuum. Stage 3 children, for example, have less difficulty in understanding justifications based on reasoning characteristic of stage 4 than they do justifications based on stage 5 reasoning.[14] Moreover, people at different stages of moral development tend to behave differently. Stage 3 adolescents tend to be more susceptible to social pressure than do adolescents at stage 5 or 6.[15] Another study found that stage 5 and 6 adolescents were more likely to reward group members who attempted to help in completing a task but were unable to.[16] One study of adults demonstrated that the persons at stages 5 or 6 were less likely to administer shocks on orders from an experimenter in a social psychology experiment.[17]

Although it is difficult to assign specific ages to each stage of moral development, it does appear that it is not until the individual enters adolescence that he or she is prepared for principled morality. As we have seen, the network of childhood-peer associations provides a context for developing the social sensitivities required for the later stages of moral development. At the same time, the development of hypothetical thinking and the capacity for dealing with abstractions is required for the application of moral principles in the "real world." It is in this sense that moral development represents a confluence of social and maturational factors.

Moral Reasoning: Males and Females

According to Kohlberg's formulation, moral development is evidenced by an increased ability to generalize. This involves the capacity to recognize a dilemma, apply a super-ordinate principle and resolve the dilemma. Thus a young boy may view the question of whether or not to steal the medicine as a conflict between the value of property on the one hand and the value of life on the other. He may use the supremacy of the latter value to justify a decision to steal the medicine. Morality is a combination of valuation and logical deduction. Because life is more important than property, stealing the drug is justified. In the past, research indicated that boys appeared to be more facile with such logic than did girls.

In a recent book, Carol Gilligan argues that girls reason differently with respect to such matters. Rather than construing the matter as a problem of principles and generalization, girls, she argues, tend to view the issue as a problem of social relationships. Where boys are concerned with the "logic of justice," girls reason from the standpoint of an "ethics of care." Where boys see the problem as a "conflict between life and property that can be resolved by logical deduction," girls tend to see the dilemma as a "fracture of human relationships that must be mended with its own thread."[18]

Gilligan uses the response of a young girl she calls Amy to illustrate such an approach to the dilemma. Asked if stealing the drug is justified, Amy responds:

> Well, I don't think so. I think there might be other ways besides stealing it, like if he could borrow the money or make a loan or something, but he really shouldn't steal the drug-but his wife shouldn't die either.[19]

Upon further probing, Amy says:

> If he stole the drug, he might save his wife then, but if he did, he might have to go to jail, and then his wife might get sicker again, and he couldn't get more of the drug, and it might not be good. So, they should really just talk it out and find some other way to make the money.[20]

From a purely logical standpoint, Amy's response appears vague and evasive. According to Gilligan though, Amy's answer reflects other qualities, which, when viewed from the standpoint of social relationships, are a valid basis for a moral decision. For Amy, the problem is not one of conflicting rights; it is the druggist's failure of response. Amy argues that the husband should attempt to persuade the druggist that he should just "give it to the wife and then have the husband pay back the money later." Amy appears confident that the druggist can be convinced to allow the husband to pay for the medicine on credit. The druggist should be made aware of the importance of the relationship between the husband and his wife. Amy's apparent indecision is really an implicit belief in the power of social relationships and potency of communication and social influence. In this regard, as Gilligan puts it, "the possibilities of imagination outstrips the capacity of generalization." Amy's morality has not somehow been stagnated at a social approval stage. Rather, she is using the capacities of mind and imagination to try to preserve life and social relationships.

SPORTS AND ADOLESCENCE

Adolescence is a time when many youths explore values and lifestyles that may differ from those of their parents and the society at large. As we shall discuss in the next chapter, the subject of juvenile delinquency or adolescent deviance is one in which social psychologists have made a substantial contribution. At the same time, other social institutions serve to inculcate dominant societal norms. Two such institutions are sports and education, and from the standpoint of the adolescent, sports may be the more highly valued activity.[22]

In the previous chapter, we saw how play served to facilitate important psychological, cognitive, and social developments. Sports may assist social development in other ways. Through participation in sports, adolescents may learn how to control aggression and how to live with rules in the context of some larger social organization.[23] Sport as a social institution also plays a role in socializing the adolescent to societal values; it provides an opportunity for the youth to engage in quasi-adult behaviors and may begin to ease the transition from childhood to adulthood.[24]

To understand sports as a socializing agency, it is important to note some important differences between sport and play. Play is primarily spontaneous and unorganized; its sole purpose is enjoyment. Sport, on the other hand, is highly organized and planned. It is pursued for some purpose—to win or to obtain some objective. Thus, where the enjoyment that stems from play is contained within the activity itself, the enjoyment that results from sports is often tied to some objective outside of that activity.[25]

In our culture, sports provide an opportunity for young people to experience winning and losing and to learn the appropriate ways to behave as both a winner or loser. The positive value of winning may be emphasized as early as Little League and reinforced in junior high school and high school athletics. Although conventional logic posits that youths develop "character" through sports, it may be that those who excel in sports have *already* internalized the importance of competition and that failure in sports can have negative social and psychological consequences for youths who live in a "competitive" society and who, at an early age, may come to identify themselves as "losers."[26]

Can sports be noncompetitive? On the surface, this appears to be an unrealistic possibility. Both amateur and professional sports are quite competitive. This is true of countries with radically different political ideologies and economic systems. Nevertheless, sports have been devised to deemphasize competition. Some Israelis, for example, have developed a paddleball–type game where the object is to maximize the number of times each player returns the other's volley rather than to try to make the other player miss as in tennis or racquetball. Competitive sport also has been deemphasized in modern China, where the perfection of skill and the development of teamwork are more highly valued than is winning.

Sports in many preliterate societies often are oriented toward cooperation rather than competition. Members of one such culture in New Guinea play a game where two teams attempt to land a spinning top on wooden stakes driven into the ground. The idea, however, is not for one team to hit the most stakes but, rather, for each team to hit an equal number. Some native American cultures consider it to be unfair to allow superior athletes to participate in athletic events. Intense rivalry was viewed as detrimental for both the sport and the society. In other cultures, violence and aggression in sports may be the norm. Among African Zulus, for example, being a "man" means being a "warrior."[27]

It appears that aggressive and competitive sports are highly valued in cultures where those traits themselves are highly valued. One anthropologist has noted a correlation between the extent to which a culture's sports are highly competitive and aggressive and the extent to which those cultures engage in war. Richard Sipes argues that aggressive sports and war are part of a cultural pattern that is learned. Sipes provided evidence for both a "synchronic" and "diachronic" relationship between war and aggressive sports; that is, a cross-cultural ("synchronic") analysis showed that highly aggressive sports were more popular in warlike societies and that a longitudinal (diachronic) analysis of the relationship between sports and war within the United States showed that aggressive sports were more prevalent during times of war.[28]

Sports in highly competitive and aggressive societies tend to be quite militaristic. For adolescents, then, sports may function as a kind of anticipatory socialization for military life. This may occur in a number of different ways. First, through participation in sports, young people are exposed to and become facile with a militaristic vocabulary and the rudiments of military thinking. Aphorisms such as "the best defense is a good offense" may become commonplace. One need only listen to a football game for a few minutes to hear a proliferation of phrases that emerged from modern warfare to describe events on the field (e.g., "the long bomb" and "the blitz"). The adumbration of football with parades and marching bands highlights some of its militaristic aspects. One may wonder about the extent to which the current fascination with video games may relate to future wars that may be carried out via cathode-ray tubes connected with highly sophisticated computers. Second, there is a congruence between some of the major values of both sports and war; most specifically, the emphasis on winning and the necessity of sacrificing one's personal ends for the collective effort. Through participation in sports, youths may learn the importance of the "division of labor" and the specification of tasks. In this sense, sports function not only as a kind of quasi-military activity, but also as a kind of anticipatory socialization for work in contemporary society. Young people learn what it means to be a "team player," an important concept in much of organizational life.[29]

More generally, sport, through the mass media, provides important role models for children and young adults. Except for actors and actresses, sports personalities are the most highly visible of any other occupational group. (When was the last time you saw a social psychologist advertising shaving cream?) Sports personalities are important as role models in two senses. First, the values and attitudes of these figures are likely to be adopted by many youths. Second, certain youths may select a career in sports, hoping to follow in the footsteps of their hero. In recent years, the proliferation of black superstars has led to the idea that athletics is an important and significant channel of upward mobility for black youth. In reality, however, the number of actual places for black and white athletes on professional teams (let alone the number of superstars) is minuscule relative to the population at large. The availability of coaching and other auxiliary positions is quite limited, and black and other minorities are systematically underrepresented in those positions. Beyond this, an athletic career is often quite short. (The average length of a professional football player's career is slightly over three years.) Hence, sports provides an interesting example of how societies may socialize individuals toward ends that are not always consistent with societal needs. From a social psychological standpoint, adolescent participation in sports evidences both continuities and discontinuities in the structure of roles and the socialization process. Such discontinuities will be discussed in more detail later in this chapter. Now let us turn to a more detailed consideration of the relationship among sports, violence, and aggression and their relevance for adolescents.

Sports and Aggression: A Contrast of Social Psychological Perspectives

Recently, considerable concern has been expressed about violence in sports. Critics of sports such as hockey and football charge that such sports can have a negative effect on viewers, particularly children and adolescents. Defenders of such games claim that sports such as these provide a necessary outlet for aggression.

Can social psychology resolve this debate? Probably not. However, there are a number of perspectives in social psychology and a body of empirical findings that bear rather directly on the issue.

One important social psychological theory that relates to this concern is known as the *catharsis hypothesis*. According to this view, all persons have innate aggressive tendencies. Unless these are channeled in socially acceptable and constructive ways, they are likely to "boil over," resulting in harmful consequences. Sports, according to this view, is one way of channeling aggressive energies in a positive direction. As one expert has commented, "Competitive games provide an unusually satisfactory outlet for the instinctive aggressive drive."[30]

The catharsis hypothesis derives in part from research on the relationship between frustration and aggression. This states that frustration, produced through goal blockage or through the presentation of some noxious or aversive stimulus (such as an insult), produces aggression. Initial support for the frustration-aggression theory can be found in a classic experiment conducted in the 1940s.[31] Psychologists provided two groups of children with a roomful of toys. One group was allowed to play with the toys immediately; the other group's members were forced to wait outside the room for a period of time before they were allowed to play with the toys. The first group played rather happily with the toys; the second group was much more destructive. Other studies have provided support for the idea that blocking a goal can increase one's propensity for aggression. One study for example has shown that angered subjects will aggress against their victims to a greater extent than will nonangered subjects.[32] Another study showed that angered aggressors were less responsive to signs of pain from the victim than were nonangered aggressors. Signs of pain served to inhibit the aggression of unangered subjects. They did not appear to have any effect on the angered subjects.[33] However, the extent of such aggression also is dependent on the extent to which the victim is perceived as being associated with aggression in the past[34] and the amount of aggressive cues (e.g., weapons) in the environment.[35]

Although research has supported a relationship between frustration and aggression, catharsis is a much more dubious phenomenon. Will the expression of aggression necessarily lead to a reduction of aroused aggressive drives? The answer to this question appears to be "no." Indeed, evidence suggests that under most circumstances, direct participation in some aggressive activity as well as vicarious participation such as watching others engage in aggressive activities tends to heighten aggressive potential.

Does direct participation in an aggressive act increase the likelihood of further aggression? This question was explored experimentally by a social psychologist in the following manner.[36] Two groups of college students were given a battery of physiological tests. During the testing, the person administering the test "inadvertently" insulted members of one of the two groups. Members of the insulted group were then given the opportunity to report the tester's behavior to the administrator of the experiment with the assumption that this report would result in some sanction of the tester. The second group was given no such opportunity. The researchers were surprised to find that the group given the opportunity to report the tester's behavior generally disliked the tester more than the group that was not provided with such an opportunity. In this case, at least, having the opportunity to aggress increased the individual's aggressive potential.

How far will individuals go in aggressing toward others? Some research suggests that an equity principle may operate with respect to aggression.[37] According to this idea, people will attempt to "get even" with those they think have harmed them. Once they have "gotten even," they will cease their aggression. Subjects insulted by an experimental confederate and then given the opportunity to administer shocks to the confederate tended to administer the same number of shocks even if their "vengeance" was delayed. This suggests that principles of equity may limit or control the expression of aggression. However, when subjects who were not insulted voluntarily aggressed, they tended to continue to derogate their victim. Social psychologists argue that the actions of these subjects resulted from the fact that their actions could not be justified in terms of some equitable principles (i.e., they had no reason to "get even"). Their behavior, however, may seem less reprehensible to themselves if the victim is thought of in a negative manner. The danger is that thinking of someone in a negative manner may serve as a stimulus for further aggression.

Research from a social learning perspective suggests that vicarious participation in aggressive activities may heighten aggressive states. According to this view, people will tend to engage in aggressive behavior if they perceive others as being rewarded for engaging in such behavior. However, among children, at least, simple exposure to aggression appears to increase aggressive states. In one experiment,[38] children observed adults repeatedly strike a plastic air-filled doll. The doll would bounce back in an upright position after each punch. The researchers found that children who had observed adults hit the doll tended themselves to beat the doll more furiously than did those who had not been exposed to the aggressive adult behavior.

In another series of experiments,[39] subjects were shown a film in which Kirk Douglas, playing the role of a boxer, received a rather brutal beating. One group of subjects was told that the boxer was receiving his "just deserts." Another group was told that the violence was not justified. Following the film, subjects who were angered *and* told that the boxer deserved this beating tended to engage in more verbal hostility than did members of the control groups. Experiments such as these suggest that engaging in "justified" aggression tends to lead to a heightening rather than a reduction of aggressive potential.

What are the implications of these findings for our concerns about sports and aggression? First, even though there appears to be evidence for the frustration aggression hypothesis, there is little support for the catharsis hypothesis. As Leonard Berkowitz has put it, "a rapidly growing body of carefully controlled research raises serious questions about this . . . formulation and . . . casts doubt on its validity."[40] Second, we cannot assume that either participation in, or viewing of aggressive sports, is likely to reduce levels of aggression. In some cases, vicarious participation in aggressive sports may even increase aggressive potential. Interviews of football fans before and after a game showed that the fans were more aggressive after the game than they were before it. This was true of fans of the winning as well as the losing team.[41] One psychologist who has worked in depth with athletes claims that there is no necessary relationship between participation in aggressive sports and reductions in tendencies toward aggression.[42]

The expression of aggression may be influenced by a variety of factors. If an atmosphere of fairness and equity is maintained, participation in aggressive sports may serve to control the amount and direction of aggression. Under other circumstances, especially where the reasons for aggression are unclear, or where victims have been derogated in some sense, the potential for aggression may be increased.

Here then is the dilemma of sports and aggression for adolescents in the American context. On the one hand, sports may provide adolescents with a way of channeling aggression in socially acceptable ways. Participation in aggressive sports may teach adolescents how to control their aggression, how to use aggression in appropriate circumstances, and how to direct it toward legitimate aims. On the other hand, the social context of sports may increase rather than decrease levels of aggression.[43] While football fans tended to become more aggressive during a game, fans at a wrestling match (accompanied by less militaristic fanfare) showed no increase (nor did they show a decrease) in their aggressive potential.[44] The frustration associated with losing, the tendency to denigrate one's opponent, and the association of sports with other forms of violence may have an effect that is in fact opposite to that predicted to the catharsis hypothesis.

EDUCATING ADOLESCENTS

According to many experts, one of the most important accomplishments of late adolescence and young adulthood is settling into a career trajectory. The career decision has important social and psychological ramifications as well as obvious economic consequences. From a social standpoint, making a career decision signals an end to childhood and adolescence. The young adult formally adopts a role embedded in adult society, even though for many youths training may persist into their late twenties or early thirties. From a psychological standpoint, reaching a decision to be a lawyer, doctor, or teacher helps to solidify one's identity in a more concrete manner. Rather than being "just a student," one can now claim to be "pre-law" or "pre-med."

Education is typically one of the most important means through which the individual makes career choices. Not only does the educational system teach skills and screen and select students, it also serves to socialize students for future occupations. In the following pages, we will examine the place of education in the socialization of adolescents and young adults.

HIGH SCHOOL

High school has been a popular topic for movie producers, television script writers, composers of popular songs, and sociologists and social psychologists. One of the first major studies of high schools was carried out by James Coleman in the 1950s.[45] Coleman investigated the culture and social structure of adolescent life through an analysis of ten schools located in cities and towns of varying size. Students were interviewed concerning their activities, attitudes, values, opinions, and so on. Apart from the formal organization of the school, Coleman was concerned with the informal social structure—the pattern of associations that existed between students and their implications for students.

Some of Coleman's findings are interesting, even today. First, Coleman noted that the informal organization of student life was stratified. There were different crowds and various types of elites. Being "popular," a goal that was highly valued by many adolescents at the time, was contingent on being in the right crowd. Being in the right crowd, in turn, was contingent on a combination of other factors. For girls, wearing the proper clothes, being involved in school activities, and coming from the "right family" were important attributes. These attributes were important for boys as well, with the additional attribute of being an athlete. Significantly, neither girls nor boys placed a high value on academic achievement.

Coleman investigated the effect that being or not being a member of a leading crowd or elite had on students. In this regard, he noted that in the small schools, boys and girls who were not chosen as friends by others on sociometric tests (see Chapter 3) tended to have weaker self-concepts. Many of these students responded positively when asked, "If you could trade, would you be someone different from yourself?" Significantly, the extent of these feelings appeared to be stronger for girls than for boys. The effect of being popular on a youth's academic activities was a bit more complex. In small schools, where there was little "specialization," boys who were accepted in the leading crowds tended to want to be remembered as both athletes and scholars. In larger schools, where scholars and athletes tended to be differentiated, the boys wanted to be remembered in terms of their dominant role in the school; those who played sports wanted to be remembered as athletes, and the scholars wanted to be remembered as intellectuals. Girls tended not to want to be remembered for their academic pursuits.

Coleman was not pleased with what he found in American high schools. He argued that the reward structures and values in terms of which adolescents were being socialized were not necessarily consistent with dominant societal needs. Moreover, Coleman noted a trend with which a number of sociologists have been concerned: the assumption by other institutions of socialization functions previously handled by the family. The school is one such institution. In the school, however, the youth is not socialized by the adult culture and value system, but rather by an adolescent culture and value system. To articulate better the needs of society and the socialization of youth, Coleman advocated that greater control be returned to the family and that the social structure of the school be reorganized so that adult values would predominate. More recently, this view has been expressed by Daniel Bell, who is concerned about the limited extent to which schools prepare young persons for participation in what he perceives to be a highly "meritocratic" society.[46]

From another standpoint, however, schools and classrooms are settings in which adolescents do assimilate important societal norms and values. School is organized to reinforce personal habits that will later make for "good workers." Teachers tend to reward students who are punctual, consistent, and dependable. The school experience also fosters a high degree of deference to authority, loyalty, and conformity, and there is some evidence that teachers are more responsive to these qualities than they are to grades.[47]

In a more subtle sense, the school constitutes the child's first experience with a large-scale bureaucratic organization and is thus representative of the kind of organization in which many of us are likely to spend a good portion of our lives.[48] Rules, regulations, and hierarchies provide an initiation into bureaucracy. According to two researchers:

> the relationships of authority and control between administrators and teachers, teachers and students, students and students, and students and their work replicate the hierarchical division of labor which dominates the workplace. . . . Students have a degree of control over the curriculum comparable to that of the worker over the content of his job.[49]

Some social psychologists insist that these relationships lead to an emphasis on extrinsic rewards, which hampers learning.

In school, children come to understand that in the classroom they are not "special" in the same way that they may be in their families or peer associations. The teacher-student relationship is formal and circumspect, dependent on specific role-related characteristics (e.g., academic performance and classroom deportment). Students are supposed to be judged according to universalistic standards, and fairness is espoused as an important educational value.

As we have seen, however, the extent to which schooling is truly meritocratic is a matter of some debate. Teachers and other administrators tend to have expectancies based on stereotypical views of students, and these expectancies can affect a student's performance. A social class bias was evident in a study conducted by two sociologists of a counseling system in an urban high school. Lower-class students received a lower quality of counseling than did middle-class students. Middle-class students were more likely to be given the "benefit of the doubt." Given ambiguous, if not unreliable, tests, social class operated as a criterion by which children were evaluated by their guidance counselors.[50] A recently published study showed that highly anomic students tended to have lower grade-point averages. The study also found a negative correlation between anomie and social class, suggesting that anomie and a lower social class position may combine to hinder academic development among specific groups of students.[51]

PROFESSIONS AND SOCIALIZATION

As discussed at the beginning of this chapter, in our culture, adolescence may extend through a period known as "youth." An important aspect of this period involves the preparation of the adolescent for a role in adult society. Part of this preparation concerns socialization for a profession in the world of work. Although professional socialization occurs throughout adulthood, we shall pay particular attention to how "youths" learn the requisite attitudes for specific professions.

One of the most interesting areas of professional socialization concerns medical students. Along with the skills associated with being a doctor, medical students learn to adopt a particular attitude toward their work. Sociologists Howard Becker and Blanch Geer[52] conducted what is now regarded as a classic study of the socialization of medical students. Based on in-depth interviews with medical students at a major university, Becker and Geer noted that a decline in idealism accompanied progress in medical school. According to the authors, most freshman medical students enter the professional school greatly impressed by the wonders of medicine and anxious to use those wonders to make the world a better place in which to live. The first two years of medical school are spent attempting to learn a massive amount of facts. The students learn shortcuts in order to pass exams and become more concerned with "playing the game" than with the idealism that led them to medical school in the first place. The only actual medical experience a student has during the first two years is some experience with autopsies at the end of the second year. During the third and fourth years, the students have a good deal of actual contact with patients. The students' primary concern, however, is not to help the patient but to understand the "case" as an instance of a general medical problem. They become "preoccupied with the technical aspects of the case."[53]

Other researchers have found increasing cynicism among other medical professionals and semiprofessionals. Two researchers found that dentists become less concerned with ethics and more cynical as they progress through dental school.[54] Sociologist George Psathas compared freshman and senior nursing students. He found that the seniors were generally less idealistic and less optimistic than were the freshmen. Although seniors were more confident when faced with difficult situations, they did not have as high expectations as to their overall importance for the patient's case as did the entering freshmen. According to Psathas, entering students had a more idealized view of hospital personnel and of their own role in patient care. The seniors by contrast had a clearer perception of the hospital hierarchy. For freshmen, patients were their primary "significant others." Seniors considered professionals on the hospital staff as their "significant others."[55]

Preprofessional socialization can provide the student with informal experiences that may be relevant to professional activities. Reneé Fox has described how the medical student is faced with considerable ambiguity: one's place in the class is not clearly defined, and large amounts of material are covered with little specification as to which is most important. For the first time, the student may learn that there are great gaps in medical knowledge. Learning to handle such ambiguities may aid the student in dealing with the uncertainties of diagnosis and treatment that he or she will no doubt face as a physician.[56]

Medical school thus socializes prospective doctors for some of the more subtle aspects of working as a professional physician as well as providing necessary knowledge and skills. Not all preprofessionals undergo such extensive socialization. Law schools, for example, provide almost no such socialization for prospective lawyers. The law student is not provided with practical knowledge about how to deal with clients, other attorneys, judges, and so on. Even practical knowledge such as how to bill clients is not part of either the formal or informal law school curricula. For this reason, the neophyte lawyer starting out on his or her own may be somewhat lost in the "real world." One researcher characterizes the transition from law school to actual practice as a kind of "reality shock."[57] As we shall discuss shortly, such "shocks" may be a more or less general component of the transition from adolescence to adulthood.

SOCIALIZATION IN TOTAL INSTITUTIONS

Socialization into any occupation entails some redefinition of an individual's goals and values. Redefinition of self and identity also occurs. The nurse or prospective doctor may not only come to redefine values in a more "professional" manner; they may also come to see themselves not as "helper to others" but as a "professional." In some cases, resocialization and the development of a new identity is extreme, necessitating resocialization in "total institutions."

One such institution is the U.S. military academy at West Point. As in other "total institutions," all aspects of life take place at one location; there is a definitive hierarchy, and the entire day (24 hours) is governed by a strict and inflexible schedule; rules, especially for freshmen, may govern even the smallest detail of life (e.g., how to eat, walk, or address upper classmen). The academy itself is secluded from the civilian environment.

One occupational sociologist suggests that a kind of "stripping" of self occurs at West Point not unlike that which takes place in prisons or mental institutions.[58] This stripping process involves a breakdown of one's previous self-concept and its replacement with one appropriate to the governing institution. One researcher describes some of the characteristics of such a process for new military cadets in the following terms:

> The raw recruits are labeled "beasts." On the day of arrival, they are given regulation haircuts, issued regulation service clothing, deprived of all civilian apparel and most possessions. The academy as a total institution is at its peak at this stage. All recruits are dressed and treated alike. They are separated from parents and friends. They are subject to constant discipline, which is based far more on negative than positive sanctions.[59]

Such socialization performs two functions that are most interesting from a social psychological perspective. First, the initiation process and the subsequent deference to authority provides for what sociologists term "self-mortification" (i.e., the dissipation, devaluation, and abandonment of one's prior self-concept and self-esteem). Once an individual's prior self has lost its importance, a new self-image consistent with the goals and needs of the institution in which the individual is to participate is more easily developed. This, in turn, accelerates the adoption of new values and hastens the pace at which an individual accommodates himself or herself to a new way of life—in the case of West Point, to the "Army way."

Second, the adversities of academy life (particularly the first two years) may foster strong social ties among the cadets, increasing the social cohesion of the group as a whole and thereby strengthening the ties between the individuals and the institution.[60]

It is interesting to note, though, that while this may hold for men at the academy, it does not appear to hold for women. Rather, preliminary research suggests that women occupy a marginal role while they are at the academy. Greatly outnumbered by the men, they occupy a subordinate position. Moreover, female cadets are faced with the difficult task of managing the often contradictory expectations of being a woman and acting like a soldier and officer—a role that generally implies a good deal of masculine if not even "macho" characteristics.[61]

The socialization of women differs from the socialization of men at the academy in other ways as well. While men in military establishments often had "mentors" (i.e., officers or upperclassmen who provide personal assistance with respect to socialization and professional development), female cadets were unable to form such relationships. Male cadets did not want to act as mentors for fear of being accused of "fraternizing" with newly arrived female cadets. Upperclasswomen, who in many cases were the first female cadets at the academy, had different reasons. They had not been mentored themselves and, therefore, did not know how to act as mentors. Others resented the new cadets whom they viewed as having an easier time than the original pioneers. One quote from an upperclasswoman may serve to illustrate this point: "I think we probably feel ourselves to be somewhat superior. They've just had it easier because of us."[62] It is not surprising then to learn that first classes of graduating women generally did not feel as committed and attached to the institution as did the male cohort.[63]

EMERGING INTO ADULTHOOD: ROLE TRANSITIONS AND DISCONTINUITIES

In one sense, growing up can be seen as a series of successive transitions; from infant to young child, to adolescent, and to young adult. Within each of these categories, the person is expected to fulfill certain expectations and to play specific roles. As we have seen in the past two chapters, as children grow older, the diversity in expectations and the roles they are to play increases considerably. Young children are typically "good" and "bad." Such a characterization of adolescents becomes too simplistic since "good" and "bad" may depend on an individual's particular reference group. From a social, as well as a psychological, cognitive, and moral standpoint, growing up entails transitions from a simpler to a more complex world.

Transitions in the life cycle are often referred to as "status passages."[64] Status passages are important from the standpoint of both the individual and society. From the standpoint of the individual, status passages mark significant life accomplishments often signified by new obligations and entitlements. From the societal standpoint, status passages serve to weld individuals to new roles containing new duties and responsibilities.

The passage from childhood to adulthood in our culture is a particularly jarring one. There are substantial discontinuities between expectations of childhood and those of adulthood. Children are expected to be submissive, sexless, and playful; adults are expected to be aggressive, sexually active, and serious. Anthropologist Ruth Benedict has contrasted this pattern to certain native American cultures where sexual play between children is encouraged and where children and young people as well as adults are expected to act in a more assertive and aggressive manner.[65]

In contemporary societies, there are a number of ways in which transitions in the life cycle can create stress and other problems for individuals.[66] Role transitions may require a reduction in status. The valedictorian from a small high school in Missouri may have more than intellectual difficulties when he or she attends Harvard and discovers that he or she is only one among a number of valedictorians in the class. Not meeting expectations can also create stress. The boy who has been groomed to be a doctor throughout high school and who fails to be accepted in medical school may experience both social and psychological stress—the former resulting from his having disappointed others, the latter resulting from disappointing himself.

Status passages can be stressful whether the new status represents a gain or a loss. In both cases, the individual's reference groups and support networks change. For a period of time, the individual may feel that he or she is alone in a new and unfamiliar world. This "anomic" condition may be exacerbated when the expectations of new roles and statuses are ambiguous or contradictory. "Learning the ropes" in a new job, for example, involves more than job-related skills; it means learning about informal networks and hierarchies relevant to job activities. Transitions in one area of life may disrupt other areas. A new job may contain greater responsibilities that may limit an individual's opportunity to spend time with family and friends.

One particularly important problem that often characterizes life transitions concerns discrepancies in one's expectations of what a new role or status entails and the reality of the new position. For example, many of the ideas of "romance" promulgated in the public media convey an unrealistic view of marital and family life. These ideas create expectations that are difficult and often impossible to realize. The discrepancy between one's expectations of marital and family life and the reality may be in part responsible for marital unhappiness and the rising divorce rate.

All societies contain certain practices geared toward easing life transitions. Certain "rites of passage" (e.g., puberty rights, confirmations, bar mitzvahs, graduations) serve to honor the individual and to highlight the societal significance of the status passage itself. Anticipatory socialization may also serve to ease transitions by preparing individuals for some of the more subtle components of roles they are expected to play. However, when the anticipatory socialization is not accurate, the problem of role transitions may be aggravated rather than alleviated. The practice of granting young people of high school and college age a period of "off time" during which they may make up their minds about career, marriage, and so on may help youths in a complex society to deal with the multiple problems and decisions that characterize the transition to adulthood.[67]

Role discontinuities characteristic of particular stages of the life cycle may be exacerbated as a result of role transitions. We have seen how adolescents may be exposed to a variety of different roles that may at times contain conflicting expectations. Role conflict may create a number of different problems for youths. Choices may have to be made about which roles an individual is to adopt. Often, such choices can be quite difficult to make, especially if old friends do not share the interests or have the proper attitudes and behaviors relevant to an individual's new role. Such persons may have to learn how to manage multiple reference groups. A new graduate student may feel embarrassed by the behavior of a "buddy" from the old neighborhood at a party attended by fellow graduate students and professors. At the same time, the "old buddy" may find the student's new friends to be pretentious and snobby.

The transition from adolescence to adulthood may be one of the most important and most difficult in the life cycle. However, is not to suggest that passing through adolescence and entering adulthood means that one has found one's place and solidified one's identity. As one researcher has put it:

> A myth supported by most theories of pre-adult development is that at the end
> of adolescence you get yourself together and, as a normal, mature adult, you
> enter into a relatively stable, integrated life pattern that can continue more or
> less indefinitely. This is a rather cruel illusion since it leads people in early adult-
> hood to believe that they are, or should be, fully adult and settled, and that there
> are no major crises or developmental changes ahead.[68]

Finally, given the complexity of adult life in contemporary industrial and post-industrial societies, undergoing multiple crises of status passage and role transitions en route to adulthood may itself serve as a kind of anticipatory socialization. Life in a complex society requires the ability to manage complex social situations adeptly. There are no formal school curricula to provide the necessary skills, yet it is perhaps the most important set of lessons that adolescents must learn.

CONCLUSION

We began our discussion of growing up as though it were a biological and maturational process. We have discussed some of the physiological and cognitive processes and developments that virtually all "competent" human beings undergo from early childhood through adulthood. We have seen that these developments can be impeded or facilitated by a wide variety of sociological factors. Cognitive and social developments will not occur unless the young person is exposed to sensory and social stimulation. As we proceeded through the life cycle, we saw that the course of development, even in the early years of life, varied considerably from one culture to another. We saw that different conceptions of the life cycle predominate in different cultures and in different historical periods. We noted the important influence that one's position in society vis-à-vis others can have on the course of development.

All this suggests that the developmental process needs to be understood as a social psychological as well as a biological and maturational process. Social-psychological factors include the structure of roles and the mechanisms through which individuals may move from one to another while fulfilling specific responsibilities and expectations. The significance of these factors becomes accentuated as we move ahead to our discussion of adulthood, the next phase of the life cycle.

NOTES

[1]Theodore Lidz, *The Person: His and Her Development Throughout the Life Cycle* (New York: Alfred A. Knopf, 1976), p. 308.

[2]Ibid., pp. 361–362.

[3]Kenneth Keniston, *The Uncommitted: Alienated Youth in American Society* (New York: Harcourt, Brace and World, 1965), p. 27.

[4]Ibid., p. 60.

[5]Paul Goodman, *Growing Up Absurd: Problems of Youth in the Organized System* (New York: Random House, 1960), pp. 33-34.

[6]Ralph W. Larkin, *Suburban Youth in Cultural Crisis (New York: Oxford University Press, 1979), pp. 207-208.

[7]Peter Willmott, *Adolescent Boys of East London* (London: Penguin, 1966).

[8]See M. Brake, *The Sociology of Youth Culture and Youth Sub-Culture* (Boston: Routledge & Kegan Paul, 1980), pp. 161-178.

[9]Kenneth Kenniston, *The Young Radicals: Notes on Committed Youth* (New York: Harcourt, Brace and World, 1968), p. 31.

[10]Ibid., p. 33.

[11]Hugh Rosen, *Pathway to Piaget* (Cherry Hill, N.J.: Postgraduate International, 1977), p. 22.

[12]B. Inhelder and J. Piaget, *The Growth of Logical Thinking from Childhood to Adolescence*, translated by A. Pearsons and S. Milgram (New York: Basic Books, 1958).

[13]Lawrence Kohlberg and R. Kramer, "Continuities and Discontinuities in Childhood and Adult Moral Development," *Human Development*, Vol. 12 (1969), pp. 93-120.

[14]E. Turiel, "An Experimental Test of Sequentiality of Developmental Stages in the Child's Moral Development," *Journal of Personality and Social Psychology*, Vol. 3 (1966), pp. 611-618.

[15]H. D. Saltzstein, R. M. Deamond, and M. Belenky, "Moral Judgment Level and Conformity Behavior," *Developmental Psychology*, Vol. 7 (1972), pp. 327-336.

[16]D. W. Gunzberger, D. M. Wegner, and J. Anooshian, "Moral Judgment and Distributive Justice," *Human Development*, Vol. 20 (1977) pp. 160-170.

[17]Kohlberg and Kramer, "Continuities and Discontinuities," p. 118.

[18]Carol Gilligan, *In a Different Voice: Psychological Theory and Women's Development* (Cambridge, Mass.: Harvard University Press, 1982), p. 31.

[19]Ibid., p. 28.

[20]Ibid., p. 28.

[21]Ibid., p. 59.

[22]J. Coleman, *The Adolescent Society: The Search for Life of the Teenager and Its Impact on Education* (Glencoe, Ill.: The Free Press, 1961). See also S. D. Eitzen, "Sport and Social Status in American Public Secondary Education," *Review of Sport and Leisure*, Vol. 1 (Fall 1976), pp. 139-155.

[23]See, for example, D. Ball and J. Loy, *Sport and Social Order* (Reading, Mass.: Addison-Wesley, 1975).

[24]See, for example, J. Brun, A. Jolly, and K. Sylva, *Play—Its Role in Development and Evolution* (New York: Basic Books, 1975).

[25]For a discussion on the finer points of play, see J. Huizinga, *Homo Ludens: A Study of the Play Element in Culture* (Boston: Beacon Press, 1950). For a discussion of the differences between playing games and sport, see Roger Callois, *Man, Play and Games*, translated by M. Brash (New York: The Free Press, 1961); and J. Loy and G. Kenyon, *Sport Culture and Society* (New York: Macmillan, 1969).

[26]W. Johnson, "Guilt-Free Aggression for the Troubled Jock," *Psychology Today* (October 1970), pp. 70-73; p. 303.

[27]K. Read, *The High Valley* (New York: Scribners, 1965).

[28]R. C. Sipes, "War, Sports and Aggression: An Empirical Test of Two Rival Theories," *American Anthropologist*, Vol. 75 (1973), pp. 64-85.

[29]William H. Whyte, *The Organization Man* (New York: Simon & Schuster, 1956).

[30]W. Menninger, "Recreation and Mental Health," *Recreation*, Vol. 42 (1948), pp. 340-346.

[31]R. Barker, T. Dembo, and K. Lewin, "Frustration and Aggression: An Experiment with Young Children," *University of Iowa Studies in Child Welfare*, Vol. 18 (1941), pp. 1-314.

[32]J. Dollard, L. Doob, N. Miller, O. Mowrer, and R. Sears, *Frustration and Aggression* (New Haven, Conn.: Yale University Press, 1939). See also A. H. Buss, "Instrumentality of Aggression, Feedback and Frustration as Determinants of Physical Aggression," *Journal of Personality and Social Psychology*, Vol. 3 (1966), pp. 153-162, and P. C. Ellsworth and J. M. Carlsmith, "Eye Contact and Gaze Aversion in an Aggressive Encounter," *Journal of Personality and Social Psychology*, Vol. 28 (1973), pp. 280-292.

[33]R. A. Baron, "Magnitude of Victim's Pain Cues and Level of Prior Anger Arousal as Determinants of Adult Aggressive Behavior," *Journal of Personality and Social Psychology*, Vol. 17 (1971), p. 236.

[34]L. Berkowitz and R. Geen, "Film Violence and the Cue Properties of Available Targets," *Journal of Personality and Social Psychology*, Vol. 3 (1966), pp. 525–530.

[35]L. Berkowitz and A. LePage, "Weapons as Aggression—Eliciting Stimuli," *Journal of Personality and Social Psychology*, Vol. 7 (1967), pp. 202–207. See also A. H., Buss, A. Booker, and A. Buss, "Firing a Weapon and Aggression," *Journal of Personality and Social Psychology*, Vol. 22 (1972), pp. 296–302.

[36]M. Kahn, "The Physiology of Catharsis," *Journal of Personality and Social Psychology*, Vol. 3 (1966), pp. 278–298.

[37]A. Doob and L. Wood, "Catharsis and Aggression: The Effects of Annoyance and Retaliation on Aggressive Behavior, *Journal of Personality and Social Psychology*, Vol. 22 (1972), pp. 156–162. See also E. Walster, E. Berscheid, and G. Walster, "New Directions in Equity Research," *Journal of Personality and Social Psychology*, Vol. 25 (1973), pp. 151–176.

[38]A. Bandura, D. Ross, and S. Ross, "Transmission of Aggression Through Imitation of Aggressive Models," *Journal of Abnormal and Social Psychology*, Vol. 63 (1961), pp. 575–582.

[39]L. Berkowitz, "Some Aspects of Observed Aggression," *Journal of Personality and Social Psychology*, Vol. 2 (1965), pp. 359–369. See also Berkowitz and Geen, "Film Violence."

[40]L. Berkowitz, "Experimental Investigations of Hostility Catharsis," in C. Fisher, ed., *Psychology of Sport* (Palo Alto, Calif.: Mayfield, 1976), p. 255.

[41]J. Goldstein and R. Arms, "Effects of Observing Athletic Contests on Hostility," in Fisher, ed., *Psychology of Sport*, pp. 288–294.

[42]Johnson, "Guilt-Free Aggression," p. 70.

[43]J.P. Scott, "Sport and Aggression," in Fisher, ed., *Psychology of Sport*, pp. 296–311.

[44]Goldstein and Arms, "Effects of Observing Athletic Contests," p. 293.

[45]J. Coleman, *The Adolescent Society*.

[46]D. Bell, *The Coming of Post-Industrial Society* (New York: Basic Books, 1973).

[47]J. Roberts, *Scene of the Battle: Group Behavior in Urban Classrooms* (Garden City, N.Y.: Doubleday, 1970).

[48]W. H. Whyte, *The Organization Man* (New York: Simon & Schuster, 1966).

[49]S. Bowles and H. Gintis, *Schooling in Capitalist America* (New York: Basic Books, 1976), p. 12.

[50]A. Cicourel and J. Kitsuse, *The Educational Decision-Makers* (Indianapolis: Bobbs-Merrill, 1963).

[51]S. Fisher, "Race, Class, Anomie and Academic Achievement," *Urban Education*, Vol. 16 (July 1981), pp. 149–173.

[52]H. S. Becker and B. Geer, "The Fate of Idealism in Medical School," *American Sociological Review*, Vol. 23 (1958), pp. 50–56. See also H. S. Becker et al., *Boys in White: Student Culture in Medical School* (Chicago: University of Chicago Press, 1961).

[53]Becker and Geer, "The Fate of Idealism in Medical School," p. 54.

[54]R. Morris and B. Sherlock, "Decline of Ethics and the Rise of Cynicism in Dental School," *Journal of Health and Social Behavior*, Vol. 12 (1971), pp. 290–299. See also B. Sherlock and R. Morris *Becoming a Dentist* (Springfield, Ill.: Charles C Thomas, 1972).

[55]G. Psathas, "The Fate of Idealism in Nursing School," *Journal of Health and Social Behavior*, Vol. 9 (1968), pp. 52–65.

[56]R. G. Fox, "Training for Uncertainty," in R. Merton et al., eds., *Introductory Studies in the Sociology of Medical Education* (Cambridge Mass.: Harvard University Press, 1957).

[57]D. C. Lortie, "Layman to Lawman: Law School, Careers and Professional Socialization," *Harvard Educational Review*, Vol. 29 (1959), pp. 352–369.

[58]See E. Goffman, *Asylums* (Chicago: Aldine, 1961).

[59]G. Ritzer, *Working: Conflict and Change* (Englewood Cliffs, N.J.: Prentice Hall, 1977), p. 85.

[60]R. C. U'Ren, "West Point: Cadets, Codes and Careers," *Society*, Vol. 12 (1975), pp. 23–29.

[61]J. D. Yoder, J. Adams and H. T. Prince, "The Price of a Token," *Journal of Political and Military Sociology*, 11 (1983), pp. 325–333.

[62]J. D. Yoder, J. Adams, S. Grove and R. Priest, "To Teach is to Learn: Reducing Tokenism with Mentors," *Psychology of Women Quarterly* (in press).

[63]Ibid., pp. 1–2.

[64]D. M. Bush and R. G. Simmons, "Socialization Processes over the Life Course," in M. Rosenberg and R. Turner, eds., *Social Psychology: Sociological Perspectives* (New York: Basic Books, 1981), pp. 133–164.

[65]Ruth Benedict, *Patterns of Culture* (Boston: Houghton Mifflin, 1961).

[66]See M. F. Lowenthal, M. Thurber, and D. Chiriboga, *Four Stages of Life: A Comparative Study of Women and Men Facing Transitions.* (San Francisco: Jossey-Bass, 1975).

[67]Bush and Simmons, "Socialization Processes over the Life Course," p. 148.

[68]D. J. Levinson, C. M. Darro, E. B. Klein, M. H. Levinson, and B. McKee, "The Psychosocial Development in Early Adulthood and the Midlife Transition," in D. F. Richs, A. Thomas, and M. Roth, eds., *Life History Research in Psychotherapy* (Minneapolis: University of Minnesota Press, 1977), p. 250.

CHAPTER EIGHT
ADOLESCENT TROUBLES
AND DEVIANCE

The young people today love luxury. They have bad manners, they scoff at authority and lack respect for their elders. Children nowadays are real tyrants, they no longer stand up when their elders come into the room where they are sitting, they contradict their parents, chat together in the presence of adults, eat gluttonously and tyrannize their teachers.[1]

Deviance is by no means peculiar to adolescents. It is interesting to note, however, that this excerpt was not directed to the "greasers" of the 1950s. Neither was it aimed at the "hippies" of the 1960s or the "punkers" of the 1980s. These were words spoken by Socrates about 400 years before the birth of Christ, and they refer to the children of ancient Greece. Socrates' words reflect common concerns that adults have had about young people throughout history. Social psychologists working from a variety of perspectives have provided useful insights for understanding deviance in general and deviance among adolescents in particular. In this chapter, we shall discuss specific social psychological perspectives that relate to deviance and consider how they have been applied to the subject of adolescent deviance.

Before discussing different social psychological perspectives on deviance, it is necessary to consider one further perplexing question concerning adolescent deviance. This question concerns the extent to which adolescent troubles result from characteristics of adolescence as a special phase of the life cycle or the extent to which they typify more unusual youths, who may have been affected differently by extreme social or psychological factors. Put simply, are the problems of adolescence a normal, natural part of growing up or are they created by relatively distinct sets of circumstances?

Psychoanalytic and Piagetian perspectives suggest that there are characteristics of adolescence as a phase of the life cycle that explain some of the troubles that occur during this period. From a psychoanalytic perspective, adolescence, like other stages of development, contains critical crisis points that, if left unresolved, can lead to problems in later life. An adolescent boy, for example, who has not resolved oedipal-related conflicts and who continues to resent his father may act out a kind of competition with him by engaging in "macho"-type behaviors such as fighting. A young girl with unresolved conflicts may express desire for her father's affections by seeking to please other men through promiscuous behavior. However, as recent psychoanalytic theorists point out, these processes are not mechanical in any sense, and specific outcomes may depend on a wide variety of intervening factors.[2]

From a Piagetian perspective, many adolescent troubles can be understood as the young person's newly developed cognitive capabilities are translated into an obsession with "deviant" types of activities. These may then interfere with the pursuit of socially approved activities. The passion of some youths for games such as "Dungeons and Dragons" or "Rubic's Cube" to the exclusion of other activities exemplifies such troubles. The "egocentricity of formal operations" may lead to what some adults may consider to be a rather strident questioning of established views and an unwarranted impatience with respect to change.[3]

A PSYCHOSOCIAL APPROACH TO ADOLESCENT TROUBLES

Perhaps the most exhaustive empirical attempt to assess the extent to which troubled or problem behavior is a life-cycle phenomenon was a study conducted by Richard and Shirley Jessor[4] in the 1970s. The Jessors interviewed a random sample of high school and college students at four-year intervals between 1969 and 1973. This enabled them to conduct both a cross-sectional analysis (i.e., comparing different types of students at the same point in time) and a longitudinal analysis (i.e., comparing the same students at different points in time).

Three categories of variables were under investigation. "Antecedent" or background variables included a number of demographic measures (i.e., parents' education, occupation, and religion and their attitudes toward different forms of problem behavior). The home climate (i.e., the extent of mother-child interaction and the degree of control and regulation of the child's behavior) also was included as a background variable.

The second category of variables were termed "social-psychological variables." These included questions about how students valued academic achievement and independence and to what extent they engaged in social criticism, felt alienated, and tolerated deviancy, or were religious, and the level of their self-esteem. Also included among the social-psychological variables were questions about the extent to which they received parental and peer approval or disapproval for "problem behavior."

The third category of variables was termed "social behavior variables," that is, the extent to which individuals engaged in problem behaviors (e.g., marijuana use, sexual intercourse, activist protests, and drinking and problem drinking) as well as conventional behaviors (e.g., church attendance and academic performance).

It would be impossible to review all the findings from this very large and important study. Three general patterns deserve some attention, however.

First, certain background and social psychological variables (e.g., lower value of academic achievement, higher independence, greater tolerance of deviance, less religiosity, greater approval of problem behavior from parents and friends, and less participation in conventional activities) predicted problem behavior. Second, as children progressed through adolescence, there was both an increase in "problem behavior" and an intensification of related social attitudes. For example, eleventh graders generally devalued academic achievement, had a greater value of independence and more friends who approved of, and/or engaged in, problem behavior than did ninth graders. Third, the same variables that distinguished adolescents with problem behaviors from those who did not have problem behaviors in the cross-sectional analysis also served to predict the onset of problem behavior in the longitudinal analysis. For example, ninth graders who engaged in problem behavior devalued academic pursuits, placed a greater emphasis on independence, and had a higher tolerance for deviance than did ninth graders who did not engage in problem behavior. However, as students in general advanced from the ninth to the eleventh grades, they also tended to devalue academics, valued independence, and expressed a higher tolerance for deviance.

The patterns led the authors to conclude that many of the "troubles" of adolescence are in some senses not very abnormal. Rather, adolescence is a period of status transition from childhood to adulthood, and many of the changes taking place, especially an increasing valuation of independence, are characteristic of adulthood. According to the authors,

> Although our focus has been upon problem behavior and problem proneness, it is possible to view the observed developmental changes from a different perspective, namely, a perspective on the move toward maturity. Many of the examined changes are in the direction that is socially defined as more mature or more "grown up." This is even true of the increase in problem behavior itself, since these behaviors for the most part are culturally age graded and, while proscribed for young persons, are permitted for those who are older and serve to characterize the occupancy of an older status. Thus what we have been describing as problem proneness has many attributes that may well be seen as "maturity proneness," and the changes we have been describing may perhaps be taken as part of coming of age in America.[5]

Many of the troubles of adolescence in this sense are to a large extent a normal, natural part of "coming of age" in this society.

SOCIAL DEVIANCE PERSPECTIVES

In sum, there does appear to be something about adolescence as a phase of the life cycle that contributes to the kind of "bad manners" of which Socrates complained. However, the forms of adolescent deviance may vary considerably. Not all adolescents become punkers or join motorcycle gangs. Why some young people engage in certain forms of deviance while others do not may depend less on features of adolescence as a specific phase of the life cycle than it does on social factors. For this reason, sociological perspectives in social psychology provide for a more complete understanding of adolescent troubles.

Anomie and Social Control Perspectives

The concept of anomie (see Chapter 3) was originally developed by the French sociologist Emile Durkheim to describe a state of affairs in which societal norms and values are weak, absent, or confused. When this occurs, according to Durkheim, it becomes difficult to regulate human aspirations; people lack direction and guidelines for their behavior, and the potential for deviancy and other social ills increases considerably.

This idea has had a powerful influence on the area of deviance in general and the problem of adolescent deviance in particular. Some early studies as well as more recent research found that a disproportionate number of adolescents who engage in problem behavior were products of divorced or broken homes. One classic study[6] carried out in the 1960s used a variety of self-esteem and self-image measures to compare adolescents who had engaged in problem behavior with a comparable group of those who had not. The study noted that broken homes, low self-esteem, and negative self-images were antecedents of problem behavior. However, the authors note that, in general, children who had close and stable relationships with their parents were less likely to engage in problem behavior, suggesting that it is not simply whether or not parents are separated or divorced, but rather the quality of interaction among family members that has a greater impact on whether a child becomes a juvenile delinquent. Juvenile delinquents and drug abusers tend to come from families characterized by inner turmoil and emotional distance as well as marital discord.[7]

The American sociologist Robert Merton[8] has refined Durkheim's concept of anomie with respect to deviance. According to Merton, social deviance can be explained in terms of discontinuities between socially approved goals and means. Deviance may be seen as a way in which individuals adapt to the availability or unavailability of socially accepted goals and means for achieving these goals. Merton has distinguished four different forms of deviance according to an individual's acceptance or rejection of social goals and means:

MODE OF ADAPTATION	ACCEPTS SOCIETAL GOALS	ACCEPTS SOCIETAL MEANS
Conformity	Yes	Yes
Innovation	Yes	No
Ritualism	No	Yes
Retreatism	No	No
Rebellion	No (creates new goals and means)	No

Conformity is not a form of deviance. This term refers to those "respectable youths" (e.g., "scholar-athletes") who accept societally approved goals and attempt to achieve these goals through socially approved means. Innovation applies to individuals who strive for socially approved goals but do so through nonapproved means. The student who cheats on a test shares the socially approved goal of doing well in school but has chosen a socially disapproved means for achieving that goal.

Ritualism, like conformity, entails the acceptance of socially approved means. The youth, however, loses sight of the goals those means were supposed to serve. Youths who have done well in school may continue to study and to try to do well on tests, even though they have lost sight of why they are doing all this. Studying can become a mechanical routine leading to the kind of alienation and uncommittedness discussed by Kenniston. Eventually, these youths may reject both the goals and the means. Merton referred to this form of social deviance as retreatism. Retreatists are best exemplified by the "glue sniffer" or "drug addict." Their behavior implies a rejection of both socially approved goals and means.

Rebellion also entails a rejection of both socially approved goals and means. Unlike retreatists, however, rebels create new goals and means. Attempts to establish communal living arrangements, for example, reflect both a rejection of "establishment" views and the establishment of a new goal. Kenniston's "young radicals" fit in this category.

A number of sociologists have applied anomie theory to the study of gangs of delinquents. According to one view, juvenile gangs result from the fact that lower-class youths lack the means and resources to achieve societally approved goals.[9] As a result, they turn to gang life. In gangs, youths are able to secure self-esteem and respect from peers based on "gang culture" rather than on middle-class values. According to this theory, youths may be said to "fail" into juvenile delinquency.

Two other sociologists, Richard Cloward and Lloyd Olin,[10] have carried this work one step further. They suggest that different types of juvenile gangs reflect different modes of adaptation to discontinuities between social goals and means. The *criminal gang* resembles Merton's innovators, seeking material improvements through theft and other crimes against property. In some cases, criminal gangs serve as a kind of apprenticeship into adult crime, with adult criminals acting as role models for adolescents.

Conflict gangs are oriented toward fighting and "gang warfare" rather than specific criminal activities. Their primary concern is territorial defense. The toughest gang members or battle heroes are more likely to be selected as role models than are adult criminals. Qualities such as bravery, daring, and "street smarts" are highly valued by youths in this type of gang.

A third type of gang discussed by Cloward and Olin are *retreatist gangs*. Members of these gangs engage in activities such as alcohol and drug use. Members of retreatist gangs have been characterized by sociologists as "double failures" in that they have not succeeded in either legitimate or illegitimate cultures.

Social control theory[11] is similar to the anomie approach in that it looks for the cause of social deviance, not in individuals, but in their social relationships. According to social control theory, deviance occurs when an individual's ties to conventional social life are disrupted. Social control theorists have investigated four different types of social bonds: attachment to others such as family and peers; commitment to social goals; involvement in major social institutions such as school; and belief in approved social values. Youths who lack such ties to "normal" society according to social control theory are more likely to engage in deviant activities.

The anomie approach to adolescent deviance and juvenile delinquency has been criticized from a number of different perspectives. Some sociologists have challenged the assumption that working-class gang members "fail" into delinquency. John Kitsuse, for example, has pointed out that there is little evidence to suggest that working-class youths had ever accepted middle-class values. Hence, it is not correct to think of working-class youths as "failing" into delinquency.[12] Walter Miller has argued that the culture of working-class gangs is in fact an extension of working-class culture, highlighting values such as "toughness," "smartness," "excitement," and "autonomy."[13] These criticisms suggest that one problem with research on working-class gangs is that the researchers tend to view such gangs from the standpoint of the middle class. One implication of this criticism is that more attention should be paid to the troubles of youth within different social classes. In this connection, it is interesting to note that deviancy in the middle class does reflect a sense of disassociation with middle-class goals and values. In his study of middle-class "hippie" types in the 1960s, Brake claimed a high level of "disenchantment with higher education . . . , boring curricula, decreased graduate employment, lower financial reward than expected contributed to the dropout culture of the student hippie period."[14] Wieder and Zimmerman found a similar pattern in their 1970 study of hippie communities. The authors described a sense of hostility toward conventional American society and a rejection of conventional values. These youths rejected Protestant ethic–related values such as hard work and future orientation, favoring instead hedonism and immediacy.[15]

One further limitation of the anomie approach should be noted. The characterizations of different forms of deviance and different types of gangs are "ideal types." No one individual need necessarily fit into a specific category. In fact, individuals may "drift" from "normalcy" to delinquency as well as among the different categories of delinquency. In this sense, any youth who takes a drink before he is legally eligible to do so, or who smokes pot, or gets into a fight need not be considered an incurable "conflict gang" member or retreatist. As the Jessors' research suggests, many youths may be engaging in a kind of anticipatory socialization.

Social Ecology and Adolescent Deviance

A related approach to adolescent problems links deviance and delinquency to modern urban living. Social bonds, according to this theory, are weakened when individuals move to cities. The bonds that held people together in rural areas are dissipated, and other forms of social organization emerge. The urban youth gang is one such form of social organization. As such, the "gang" needs to be understood as a response to changing social and economic conditions—especially poverty. One early sociologist described the formation of urban gangs in the following terms:

> the gang occupies what is often called the "Poverty Belt" . . . characterized by deteriorating neighborhoods, shifting populations and the mobility and disorganization of the slum . . . . As better residential districts recede before encroachments of business and industry, the gang develops as one manifestation of the emerging economic, moral and cultural frontier.[16]

In the slum, "street life" becomes a mode of association. Preadolescent peer groups evolve into adolescent gangs in an almost natural progression. As different gangs and peer associations are located in different neighborhoods, their internal cohesion is strengthened through opposition to other gangs from other neighborhoods. The youth's identity and self-esteem are established with reference to the gang.

Conflict gangs are not new to urban settings. Cities in seventeenth- and eighteenth-century Europe contained areas that were controlled by youth gangs. These gangs often formed a quasi government. Sections of medieval Damascus, for example, were "governed" by organized and uniformed street gangs known as Zu'ar. According to one expert, these gangs resembled a "melange of Hell's Angels, mafiosi, soldiers of fortune, and Robin Hoods, all rolled into one."[17]

The social ecology approach to adolescent deviance also has been criticized from a variety of perspectives. Some critics claim that it is the composition of specific groups that move into cities and not cities per se that leads to gang formation. Other researchers have pointed out that city politics and intentional actions by city officials may have a bearing on adolescent deviance. One study of youth in Glasgow, Scotland, showed that official policies toward youth exacerbated relationships between youth and city officials. Sections of the city designated as "problem areas" were policed in a more impersonal and formal manner ("policing from the outside"), which further aggravated the relationships between youth and the police. Further research shows that more complaints about police were lodged in poorer neighborhoods than in middle-class areas.[18]

Social Learning Approaches to Deviance

A third approach to adolescent deviance is based upon social learning theory (see Chapter 4). Social learning theory posits that adolescents will tend to engage in deviant behavior if they are rewarded for doing so or if they perceive others as being so rewarded. According to this view, delinquency results from an individual's imitation and/or modeling of a deviant actor or role model. If youths are exposed to other youths or to adults who are perceived as engaging successfully in deviant behavior (e.g., the pimp or dope dealer who drives an expensive car), the youths are likely to model that behavior themselves.

Differential association theory is based on a social learning approach. The basic assumption of differential association theory is that youths who tend to become deviant do so because they tend to associate with others who are deviant. Hence, they are exposed to a disproportionate number of deviant role models, values, and goals. "A person becomes delinquent because of an excess of definitions favorable to violation of the law."[19]

One of the most ambitious tests of a social learning approach to adolescent troubles was constructed by sociologist Ronald Akers and his colleagues in their study of drug and alcohol use among adolescents.[20]

Akers hypothesized that differential association, differential reinforcement, exposure to a disproportionate number of positive definitions of alcohol and drug use, and imitation of models who are favorable toward and/or use drugs themselves would explain a substantial amount of drug use among high school students. To test the differential association hypothesis, Akers administered a questionnaire to over 3,000 junior and senior high school students. He asked a number of questions concerning their use of drugs and alcohol and their perception of parental and peer attitudes toward drug and alcohol use. The questionnaire also contained questions on their own reactions to having tried drugs and alcohol.

Analysis of the data confirmed the general hypothesis. Beyond this, Akers was able to begin to specify the temporal order of the onset of problem behavior. Differential association occurs first. Through this, individuals are exposed to deviant role models. Next is imitation. The young person begins to model the behaviors of his or her new friends. Through modeling, appropriate definitions are learned. The young person is then reinforced for participating in deviant acts. Reinforcement occurs in two ways: (1) through the actual consequences of using drugs and/or alcohol (i.e., "getting high") and (2) through positive responses from one's friends. As another sociologist, Howard Becker, has pointed out, one of the functions of friends in learning to be a marijuana smoker is to teach the novice how to appreciate the effects of the drug.[21] The user learns the appropriate definitions that then serve as guides for future behavior. As a result, imitation becomes less important as the learned definitions suffice to guide behavior in future situations.

According to the social learning approach, then, an adolescent boy may come to be a marijuana user in the following way. First, he meets and befriends a number of young people who "smoke pot." After a few associations with them, he begins to imitate and model their behavior. They praise him for this, and he learns to enjoy the effect of the drug. Gradually, smoking "pot" comes to be defined as a highly valued activity that has enjoyable consequences. As a result, the youth is likely to engage in it on a more frequent basis.

The reader should note an interesting contradiction at this point between the social learning and the social control perspective in its initial formulation. Where social control theory posits that the inability to form bonds with peers is connected with delinquent behavior, social learning theory implies that attachment to deviant peers may increase the likelihood of deviant behavior. Recent approaches in social control theory have attempted to take this into consideration. One study, for example, suggests that peer attachments are not an important bond with respect to deviant behavior.[22]

Another of Akers's more interesting findings concerned the role that parents may play in this process. Akers found a negative relationship between drug and alcohol *use* (moderate use of these substances) and the severity of parental sanctions for such use (i.e., children of parents who had strong sanctions against use of drugs and alcohol tended to use less drugs and alcohol). This is consistent with the social learning perspective in that parental sanctions constitute potential punishments and, therefore, should act to deter drug and alcohol use. However, Akers found a curvilinear relationship between drug and alcohol *abuse* (heavy use) and parental sanctions; that is, drug *abuse* was higher among children whose parents had few sanctions and those whose parents maintained *extremely harsh* sanctions (see Figur 8–1). Drug and alcohol abuse was lower among children whose parents exerted moderate sanctions. According to the authors, this relationship does not necessarily contradict the social learning approach. Rather, it indicates that, as a child becomes an abuser, parental reactions become less important even though sanctions may become more severe. High-abuse youths are more strongly influenced by peers than by parents.

The relationship between peer and parental influence and adolescent problems was the subject of a study conducted by Charles Biddell and his colleagues.[23] They contrasted students who were alcohol users with those who did well in school (i.e., high academic achievers). Interestingly, Biddell found that parental influence was more important for academic achievers, whereas peer influence was of greater importance for alcohol users. More important, Biddell examined the nature of parental and peer influence, noting that each tended to operate in a different way. Where parental influence occurs primarily through the internalization of norms and values, peer influence occurs more through modeling and imitation.

Social learning approaches have been criticized for having too mechanical a conception of the relationships among exposure to different role models, rewards, and likelihood of engaging in deviant activities. This relationship need not be a linear one. Indeed, the popular literature is replete with examples of youths who emerged from deviant subcultures into "normal" ways of life, and vice versa.

Differential identification theory has been offered as an alternative to differential association. According to this approach, deviant behaviors are not learned in a mechanical sense. Rather, they are acquired as a result of identification with persons, real or imagined, for whom deviant behavior appears to be a reasonable and acceptable way of acting. Differential identification maintains that deviance needs to be explained through an "integrative" approach, that is, one that takes into consideration the different variables that may lead one into deviance as well as the mechanisms by which one learns deviant behavior. According to this view,

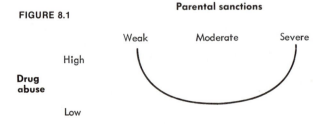

FIGURE 8.1

Parental sanctions

Weak   Moderate   Severe

High

Drug abuse

Low

Most persons in our society are believed to identify themselves with both criminal and non-criminal persons in the course of their lives. Criminal identification
may occur, for example, during direct experience in delinquent membership
groups, through positive influence of criminals portrayed in the mass media or
as a negative reaction to forces opposed to crime.[24]

Differential identification theory notes that any youth may be exposed to a
variety of different and even countervailing influences. Whether an individual
engages in deviant behavior is a function of a variety of social control, social
learning, and situational factors.

Drift

Drift theory is based on the assumption that there is no hard and fast
distinction between "delinquents" and "normals." Rather,

> the delinquent transiently exists in a limbo between convention and crime, re-
> sponding in turn to the demands of each, flirting now with one, now with the
> other, but postponing commitment, evading decision.[25]

All youths live in both nondeviant and deviant subcultures. Drift into one world
or another may hinge on a variety of subtle factors: losing friends, joining a
gang, engaging in deviant activities, getting caught.

Drift theory is useful in sensitizing us to the fact that deviant and delinquent adolescents are not radically different from "normals," but may, in fact,
be different only for certain circumstances at certain points in time. Some
aspects of deviant subcultures may in fact reflect or even support dominant
values. Consider, for example, the familiar association of "sex and drugs and
rock and roll." Interestingly, delinquents often attempt to justify their behavior
in terms of dominant moral values. Such justifications have been termed "techniques of neutralization." These techniques include

> Denial of responsibility—denying that the harm was intentional
> Denial of injury—denying that any harm was perpetrated
> Condemnation of the condemners—condemning those who disapprove of the
> deviant action
> Denial of the victim—denying that anyone was harmed or claiming that the
> victim deserved the punishment
> Appeal to higher loyalties—claiming that friendship loyalty or some other over-
> arching principles warranted the deviant act[26]

Through such rationalizations, youths may attempt to neutralize the suggestion
that their behavior is either immoral or abnormal. In this sense, although deviant adolescents may violate dominant cultural norms, they do not necessarily disregard them.

Labeling and Adolescent Deviance

One further approach that has proved useful for understanding social
processes related to adolescent deviance is *labeling theory* or the labeling per-

spective. Although this has generated considerable controversy, it does help to sensitize one to some of the subtler ramifications of being defined as "abnormal" in this society.

Labeling theory begins with the proposition that social deviance is basically ubiquitous. Virtually everyone engages in some form of deviant behavior at some point in time. Most of this "primary deviance" remains undetected. Situational factors and not qualities of the person or the deviant act itself determine whether an individual is apprehended and "processed" as a deviant. Some research indicates that virtually all adolescents engage in some form of deviant activity. According to the labeling perspective, the most important questions are whether they are apprehended, labeled as a deviant, separated from the mainstream of society, and placed in a situation where they interact with more experienced deviants. Such events according to labeling theory lead the youth to develop an image of himself or herself as impaired. This, in turn, leads to the formation of a deviant identity. According to the labeling perspective, the most important reason for embarking on a deviant career is the detection of a deviant act and the subsequent labeling and identification of an individual as "delinquent" by some official person or agency.

The process of being labeled a deviant involves a number of different steps or stages through which the adolescent's self-image may be gradually changed. One part of this process entails what sociologists term "status degradation ceremonies."[27] Through such ceremonies, an individual's identity in the eyes of others is transformed into a lower social type. The central idea is that the person is not viewed as simply having done something wrong but is now viewed as flawed in some fundamental sense. For example, once it is learned that an individual is homosexual or has been mentally ill, many other aspects of his or her life tend to be reinterpreted in terms of this new knowledge. In this sense, being defined as deviant involves what one sociologist calls the attribution of a "negative essence."[28] For example, a relatively large number of youths may abduct private cars for "joy rides," later abandoning them in different parts of town. The youth who is caught, however, and convicted of "larceny" may be viewed differently by peers, parents, police, teachers, and other adult authorities. The youths who were not apprehended or convicted may be seen as "mischievous"; the one who was caught is now a "thief."

The labeling perspective alerts us to the fact that a wide variety of circumstances not specified either in law or official regulations may affect how individuals are defined and processed. How a young boy, for example, "handles" himself when interacting with officials may have an effect on whether he is arrested or released with a warning. Acting too deferential or too disrespectful may increase the youth's chances of being arrested.[29] Another sociologist notes that judges may make character assessments based on a juvenile's courtroom demeanor and that these may have a bearing on the disposition of the case.[30] Informal assumptions held by police, case workers, judges, and others who deal with juveniles may have an important bearing on how youths are treated. Juvenile officials may consider the status and demeanor not only of the youth, but his family, their resources, and their perceived willingness to cooperate with official agencies before making treatment recommendations.[31]

Social class may be an important factor in how youths are labeled and processed. Differential treatment as a function of social class was noted by sociologist William Chambliss[32] in his study of two juvenile gangs in the same small community. The "Saints" was a middle-class gang engaged in a variety of delinquent activities. One of the favorite escapades of its members involved getting drunk and driving around town in their cars performing various pranks on unwitting motorists. One such adventure was described in the following terms:

> Construction sites and road repair areas were the special province of the Saints' mischief. A soon-to-be-repaired hole in the road inevitably invited the Saints to remove lanterns and wooden barricades and put them in the car, leaving the hole unprotected. The boys would find a safe vantage point and wait for an unsuspecting motorist to drive into the hole. Often, though not always, the boys would go up to the motorist and commiserate with him about the dreadful way the city protected its citizenry.
>
> Leaving the scene of the open hole and the motorist, the boys would then go searching for an appropriate place to erect the stolen barricade. An "appropriate place" was often a spot on a highway near a curve in the road where the barricade would not be seen by an oncoming motorist. The boys would wait to watch an unsuspecting motorist attempt to stop and (usually) crash into the wooden barricade. With saintly bearing, the boys might offer help.[33]

The Saints, however, were from upper-middle-class families; they did fairly well in school and were not perceived as problems by either the community or the police.

The "Roughnecks" was a gang of young boys the same age as the Saints. These youths were from lower-class backgrounds and did not generally do as well in school as did the Saints. The Roughnecks drank a great deal. Some of their more frequent activities included fighting and theft. Because Roughneck gang members did not own cars, much of their drinking took place on street corners or in other places where their activities were highly visible. In part because of the visibility of their activities, their social class backgrounds, and their school performances, the Roughnecks were perceived as being a much greater problem by both the community and the police, the consensus being that they would never "make anything of themselves." As a result, Roughneck activities were treated more seriously by the police and other adult authorities.

Why did adult authorities choose to focus their enforcement activities on the Roughnecks rather than the Saints? Part of the answer according to Chambliss has to be understood in terms of the general class structure of American Society:

> The answer lies in the class structure of American society and the control of legal institutions by those at the top of the class structure. Obviously, no representative of the upper class drew up the operational chart for the police which led them to look in the ghettos and on street corners—which led them to see the demeanor of lower-class youth as troublesome and that of upper-middle-class youth as tolerable. Rather, the procedures simply developed from experience— experience with irate and influential upper-middle-class parents insisting that their son's vandalism was simply a prank and his drunkenness only a momentary

"sowing of wild oats"—experience with cooperative or indifferent, powerless, lower-class parents who acquiesced to the law's definition of their son's behavior.

The community responded to the Roughnecks as boys in trouble, and the boys agreed with that perception. Their pattern of deviancy was reinforced, and breaking away from it became increasingly unlikely. Once the boys acquired an image of themselves as deviants, they selected new friends who affirmed that self-image. As that self-conception became more firmly entrenched, they also became willing to try new and more extreme deviances. With their growing alienation came freer expression of disrespect and hostility for representatives of the legitimate society. This disrespect increased the community's negativism, perpetuating the entire process of commitment to deviance. Lack of a commitment to deviance works the same way.[34]

Chambliss's account reflects some of the social psychological consequences of the troubles often encountered by adolescents. The lower-class gang members came to be treated as the subordinate group. The gang members then adopted an image of themselves as propagated by the adult authorities. As was discussed with respect to education, such negative definitions may act as self-fulfilling prophecies, helping to facilitate a "deviant career."[35]

Institutionalization may further serve to weaken the bonds between the labeled youth and "nondeviant" friends at the same time that it may strengthen ties to deviant subcultures. The youth may come to be socialized into the values of the deviant subculture. He or she may also come to learn necessary skills and techniques for performing deviant acts. Professional thieves, for example, undergo a period of apprenticeship. Younger thieves may work with more experienced or accomplished "journeymen" before striking out on their own.[36] Individuals may learn about other persons with whom they can work as contacts for further criminal activities. In a detention center or other juvenile institution, our "joy rider" may learn about "fences" willing to pay for stolen automobiles. Prostitutes may undergo a period of apprenticeship in which they learn the social skills appropriate for different clients. It is in this sense that one may speak of a deviant life-style as a "career." It requires not only skills but also "contacts" and gaining an understanding of where, how, and when skills can be used.

Being institutionalized may facilitate assimilation into a deviant life-style and the development of a deviant identity. In the previous chapter, we discussed how total institutions, as agencies of resocialization, are designed to provide a setting in which individuals may develop new identities. Such a process is most evident in prisons and many juvenile detention centers. Upon arrival at the institution, the individual may be stripped, deloused, and showered in a standardized manner along with other recent arrivals. Following that, the youngster is given a uniform. Personal items such as watches and rings may be retained by the staff. The daily round is scheduled in an inflexible manner. Wake-up, meal, and lights-out times are established by the staff, and in most cases little or no deviation is permitted. Moreover, there is a rigid hierarchy; superior and subordinate positions are fixed and unalterable. At the same time, the individual's ties to the outside world are broken. His or her goings and comings are severely restricted.

Personal space within the institution also is severely limited. The inmate may be forced to share a room or cell with other inmates. Unavailability of drawers and other means of storing clothes and personal possessions may add to the sense in which one's total being is available for scrutiny by the staff. All these factors represent a kind of "stripping" of an individual's previous identity and sense of self. With respect to adolescents, assimilation into the prison subculture may reinforce the young person's sense of himself as a delinquent and an "outsider."

Critics of labeling theory have raised a number of important issues. Some critics claim that, although labeling may provide a fairly adequate explanation of "secondary deviance" (i.e., why after having been apprehended and processed for one deviant act, an individual is likely to engage in more deviance), it is inadequate as an explanation of "primary deviance" (i.e., why individuals engage in deviant behavior in the first place). Other critics argue that deviance is not uniformly distributed throughout the population and that the processes of detection and apprehension are not totally random. These critics argue that, even though almost all youths engage in some deviant act at some point in time, those who are apprehended and arrested are the ones who have committed the more serious offenses. Beyond this, there certainly are youths who have committed serious offenses who are never apprehended or arrested. What accounts for their deviance?[37]

The Subcultural Approach

A final explanation of adolescent deviance may be termed the "subculture" approach. According to this view, "deviant behavior . . . is a meaningful attempt to solve problems faced by a group or isolated individual."[38] Deviant subcultures result from tensions and contradictions in the dominant culture. The antiwork and antiestablishment values of many of Britain's black and brown youths result from complex interconnections between their subculture and British society. Recent black and brown immigrants came with the hope of finding "meaningful work." Economic crisis and social discrimination have made finding such work almost impossible. For some youths, only menial jobs are available, while for others there are no jobs at all. In this case, "rebellion" may become a "meaningful response" to real economic and social exigencies.

Interestingly, the nature and character of these rebellions often include many of the characteristics of the original cultures of these black and brown youth. Thus, many Jamaican immigrant youth are attempting to continue to speak Creole; Reggae music has come to have political as well as artistic meaning; and a renewed interest in Rastufarianism (a Caribbean-based religion) may "make sense" in terms of the difficult relations between Jamaican youths and British authorities.[39]

Deviance and the Adolescent Girl

Commenting on studies of girls and adolescent deviance, one sociologist notes the following:

The history of the sociology of deviance, as far as women and girls are concerned, is a history of the uncritical adoption of conventional wisdom about the nature of women, namely, that anatomy is destiny.[40]

A good deal of early thinking on female criminality implied that it was physiologically based. Lombroso has argued that because women are less physiologically mobile than men, they also are psychologically passive, easily compromised, adaptive, amoral, cold, and calculating.[41] W. I. Thomas also related female delinquency to fundamental physiological differences between men and women. According to Thomas, delinquency among adolescent girls results from their attempts to obtain certain ends by manipulating the male's sexual desires.[42] Freud similarly presumed that female deviancies resulted from their different anatomical features. The deviant woman, according to Freud, is one who has not adjusted to her biologically determined role of being passive and submissive. Commenting on Freud's view, one sociologist notes that the deviant woman "is aggressively rebellious, and her drive to accomplishment is the expression of her longing for a penis. . . . The deviant woman should be treated and helped to adjust to her sex role."[43] Much thinking about adolescent deviance among girls has followed the Freudian line. One researcher, for example, has conceptualized female delinquency as a maladjustment to the feminine role. According to other researchers, however, female adolescent deviants do not reject the feminine role, but rather use it as an imitation of "male machismo competitiveness."[44]

More recent empirical research on adolescent delinquency among girls reflects an interesting pattern. According to official statistics, girls are more likely than boys to be referred to juvenile court for "status offenses" (e.g., incorrigibility, truancy, running away from home) and moral and sexual offenses. Boys are more likely than girls to be arrested for serious offenses (e.g., burglary, auto theft, robbery, assault, and larceny). However, according to studies based upon self-reports, males are almost as likely to commit "status offenses" as are females, and the differences between boys and girls with respect to serious offenses is not nearly as great as is that reflected in official statistics. What is the basis for this discrepancy? Some researchers cite "chivalry" and a belief that women should be "protected" as a reason for their differential treatment. In some instances, however, protection takes the form of indeterminate sentences that may actually provide longer and more indeterminate periods of internment.[45]

A social-psychological explanation of female deviance and delinquency need not be rooted in physiological differences between the sexes. Girls' gangs may be as varied as boys' and provide similar psychological functions. The same kinds of strains, stresses, and contradictions between expectations and opportunities that lead boys to deviance may affect girls as well.[46] In some ways, however, deviance may be even more complicated for girls. A girl charged with a status offense undergoes a kind of double-labeling; she is both a delinquent and immoral. Where delinquency for boys need not necessarily involve a violation of norms related to masculinity (e.g., aggressiveness, adventurousness, danger), delinquency for girls more often than not involves *both* a violation of law and norms regarding gender-appropriate behavior.[47]

Finally, it is important to remember that much of our society in general is male-dominated and that these attitudes and practices may pervade adolescent subcultures as well. Delinquent subcultures often are quite machismo. The girl's role is to be a partner to the "macho man." Consider, for example, the image of the female motorcycle gang member riding on the back of a boy's bike. One authority characterizes the girl's role in such gangs as the "invisible girl."[48] Similar attitudes are evident in "rock 'n roll" music. Most of the cults have surrounded male musicians (e.g., The Beatles, the Rolling Stones, etc.). "Groupies" are predominantly young girls who follow these rock 'n roll idols. In the past, women vocalists have tended toward the blues (e.g., Janis Joplin) or "sweet" sounds (e.g., Judy Collins) rather than a "hard" or more aggressive sound. Vocalists like Pat Benatar and Debra Harry (Blondie) may be changing that image. However, the overall position of girls in delinquent subcultures as well as in rock and roll may be symbolized in the lyrics to one female star's recent hit: "Hit me with your best shot."[49]

Is There a Youth Culture?

One question that emerged during the 1960s and has continued since then concerns the extent to which there exists a youth culture, that is, some set of tastes, shared beliefs, and values to which most youths subscribe and that differ from those of their parents and other adults.

Popular music often is cited as one element of youth culture. Indeed, one researcher estimates that 12- to 20-year-olds buy over 75 percent of all the popular music produced on records and tapes.[50] What role does popular music play in the lives of adolescent youth?

Through music, adolescents may identify with symbols and ideas that are independent of their parents and other adults and yet common to other youths. In this sense, identification with a particular musical style enables an individual to locate himself or herself as a member of a specific age cohort and generation. Identification with a particular generation serves to place a person in an historical as well as a social frame of reference and may be an important, though often overlooked, part of the socialization process.

Sociologist Karl Mannheim has noted how belonging to a specific generation or age group limits one's range of potential experience and also establishes directions in which an individual's experience may be expanded. Being contemporaries in time is not sufficient; being a member of a generation "involves participation in the same historical and social circumstances.[51]" Music may signify such participation. As such, the different musical styles that comprise what generally is termed "rock 'n roll" may reflect participation in different sectors of history and society. Sociologists,[52] in this regard, have noted how different social classes tend to have different tastes in rock 'n roll. The themes as well as the rhythm of rock music has changed over the years, reflecting different historical conditions and circumstance. One may contrast, for example, the seemingly frivolous themes of much 1950s rock (e.g., Elvis Presley's "You Ain't Nothing but a Hound Dog") to the more serious and political orientation of many 1960s songs.

The existence of a youth culture raises the further question of a "generation gap" (i.e., the existence of a radical and substantial disjuncture among the tastes, attitudes, and values of adolescents and young adults and those of their parents and other adults). A major study of high school students conducted in the 1950s revealed that youths were much more influenced by peers than they were by parents. This led the author to conclude that an adolescent society existed with a culture that was not in accord with the dominant culture of adult society.[53] Recent surveys, [54] however, suggest that the gap between generations is not nearly as large as some have assumed. As we have discussed, a number of studies reveal a correlation between parental expectations and children's educational aspirations. Similarities also exist between adolescents' political views and those of their parents.[55] As Kenniston's study of 1960s radicals showed, many of these youths were not rebelling against their parents, but were in fact following through on what they perceived to be their parents' ideals.[56] Despite considerable public discussion concerned with changing sexual mores and behavior, certain trends of continuity still are evident. According to one study, premarital sex does not necessarily mean promiscuity; most premarital relations involve some degree of commitment and are monogamous in nature.[57] Other studies indicate that most youths do not welcome increased sexuality[58] and that the differences between adolescents on this issue are as great or greater than the differences between adolescents and adults.[59] In this regard, important "gaps" may exist within as well as between generations.

NOTES

[1]Quoted in Mike Brake, *The Sociology of Youth Culture and Youth Subcultures* (Boston: Routledge and Kegun-Paul, 1980) p. 1.

[2]Theodore Lidz, *The Person: His or Her Development Throughout the Life-Cycle* (New York: Alfred A. Knopf, 1976), pp. 241–243.

[3]Ibid., p. 8.

[4]R. Jessor and S. Jessor, *Problem Behavior and Psychosocial Development* (New York: Academic Press, 1977).

[5]Ibid., pp. 162–163.

[6]Morris Rosenberg, *Society and the Adolescent Self-image* (Princeton, N.J.: Princeton University Press, 1965).

[7]E. J. Smith, "Adolescent Drug Abuse and Alcoholism: Directions for the School and the Family," *Urban Education*, Vol. 16 (October 1981), pp. 311–332.

[8]Robert Merton, "Social Structure and Anomie," in R. Merton, ed., *Social Theory and Social Structure* (Glencoe, Ill.: The Free Press, 1949), pp. 125–150.

[9]A. K. Cohen, *Delinquent Boys: The Subculture of the Gang* (London: Collier-Macmillan, 1955).

[10]R. Cloward and J. Olin, *Delinquency and Opportunity* (Glencoe, Ill.: The Free Press, 1960).

[11]T. Hirschi, *The Causes of Delinquency* (Berkeley: University of California Press, 1969).

[12]J. I. Kitsuse and D. C. Dietrich, "Delinquent Boys: A Critique," *American Sociological Review* (April 1959), pp. 208–215.

[13]W. Miller, "Lower Social Class as a Generating Milieu of Gang Delinquency," *Journal of Sociological Issues*, Vol. 14 (1958), pp. 5–19.

[14]Mike Brake, *The Sociology of Youth Culture and Youth Subcultures*, p. 60.

[15]D. L. Wieder and D. H. Zimmerman, "Generational Experience and the Development of Freak Culture," *Journal of Social Issues*, Vol. 30, no. 2 (1974), pp. 137–163.

[16]F. M. Thraser, *The Gang* (Chicago: University of Chicago Press, 1927), p. 27.

[17]Claude S. Fischer, *The Urban Experience* (Chicago: Harcourt Brace Jovanovich, 1976), p. 89.

[18]See M. Brake, *The Sociology of Youth Culture and Youth Subcultures*, pp. 37–40.

[19]E. H. Sutherland and D. R. Cressey, "The Theory of Differential Association," in S. H. Traub and Craig B. Little, eds., *Theories of Deviance* (Itasca, Ill.: F. E. Peacock, 1975), p. 114.

[20]R. L. Akers, M. Krohn, L. Lonn and M. Raclosevich, "Social Learning and Deviant Behavior: A Specific Test of a General Theory," *American Sociological Review*, Vol. 44 (1979), pp. 636–655.

[21]H. S. Becker, "Becoming a Marijuana User," *American Sociological Review*, Vol. 59 (November 1953), pp. 235–242.

[22]M. D. Wiatrowski et al., "Social Control Theory and Delinquency," *American Journal of Sociology*, Vol. 46 (November 1981), pp. 525–541.

[23]B. J. Biddle, B. J. Bank, and M. M. Martin, "Parental and Peer Influence on Adolescents," *Social Forces*, Vol. 58, no. 4 (June 1980), pp. 1057–1079.

[24]D. Glaser, "Criminality Theory and Behavioral Images," in Traub and Little, eds., *Theories of Deviance*, p. 124.

[25]D. Matza, "Delinquency and Drift," in Traub and Little, eds., *Theories of Deviance*, p. 152.

[26]See G. M. Sykes and D. Matza, "Techniques of Neutralization: A Theory of Delinquency," in Traub and Little, eds., *Theories of Deviance*, pp. 141–151.

[27]H. Garfinkel, "Conditions of Successful Degradation Ceremonies," *American Journal of Sociology*, Vol. 66 (1956), pp. 420–424.

[28]Jack Katz, "Deviance, Charisma and Rule-Defined Behavior," *Social Problems*, Vol. 20 (1972), p. 192.

[29]Donald Black and A. Reiss, "Police Control of Juveniles," in R. Scott and J. Douglas, eds., *Theoretical Perspectives on Deviance* (New York: Basic Books, 1972).

[30]R. Emerson, *Judging Delinquents* (Chicago: Aldine, 1972).

[31]A. V. Cicourel, *The Social Organization of Juvenile Justice* (New York: John Wiley, 1968).

[32]W. J. Chambliss, "The Saints and Roughnecks," *Society*, Vol. 11 (1973), pp. 24–31.

[33]Ibid., pp. 27–28.

[34]Ibid., pp. 30–31.

[35]E. Goffman, "The Moral Career of the Mental Patient," in G. Manis and B. Meltzer, eds., *Symbolic Interaction: A Reader in Social Psychology* (Boston: Allyn & Bacon, 1978), pp. 362–379.

[36]D. Maurer, *Whiz Mob* (New Haven, Conn.: Yale University Press, 1964).

[37]For a critique of the labeling perspective, see T. Hirschi, "Labelling Theory and Juvenile Delinquency," in W. Gove, ed., *The Labelling of Deviance* (New York: John Wiley, 1980), pp. 217–381.

[38]Quoted in Brake, *The Sociology of Youth Culture and Youth Subculture*, p. 21.

[39]Ibid., pp. 122–128.

[40]D. Wilson, "Sexual Codes and Conduct: A Study of Teenage Girls," in C. Smart and B. Smart, eds., *Women Sexuality and Social Control* (London: Routledge & Kegun-Paul, 1978), p. 66. See also R. Giallombardo, "Female Delinquency," in R. Giallombardo, ed., *Juvenile Delinquency: A Book of Readings* (New York: John Wiley, 1972).

[41]See D. Klein, "The Etiology of Female Crime: A Review of the Literature," *Issues in Criminology*, Vol. 8 (1973), p. 9.

[42]Ibid., p. 11.

[43]Ibid., p. 17.

[44]Ibid., p. 21.

[45]See, for example, G. Armstrong, "Females Under the Law: 'Protected but Unequal,'" *Crime and Delinquency*, Vol. 23 (1977), pp. 109–121; M. Chesney-Lind, "Judicial Paternalism and the Female Status Offender: Training Women to Know Their Place," *Crime and Delinquency*, Vol. 23 (1977), pp. 121–131; and A. Conway and C. Bogdan, "Sexual Delinquency: The Persistence of a Double Standard," *Crime and Delinquency*, Vol. 23 (1977), pp. 131–135.

[46]J. Figueira-McDonough and E. Selo, "A Reformulation of the Equal Opportunity Explanation of Female Delinquency," *Crime and Delinquency*/(1980), pp. 333–343.

[47]Brake, *The Sociology of Youth Culture and Youth Subculture*, pp. 140–144.

[48]Ibid., pp. 137–154.

[49]For a discussion of social psychological aspects of popular music, see S. Frith, *The Sociology of Rock* (London: Constable, 1968).

[50]Brake, *The Sociology of Youth Culture and Youth Subculture*, p. 155.

[51]Karl Mannheim, "The Problem of Generations," in P. Keckskemeti, ed., *Essays on the Sociology of Knowledge* (New York: Oxford University Press, 1952), p. 298.

[52]See Frith *The Sociology of Rock*. Also see G. Murdock, "Mass Communication and the Construction of Meaning," in N. Armistead, ed., *Reconstructing Social Psychology* (Hammondsworth: Penguin, 1974).

[53]J. Coleman, *The Adolescent Society: The Search for Life of the Teenager and Its Impact on Education* (Glencoe, Ill.: The Free Press, 1961).

[54]R. C. Williamson, "Variables in Adjustment and Life Goals Among High School Students," *Adolescence*, Vol. 12 (1977), pp. 213–225.

[55]J. C. Woelful, "Political Attitudes: Sources for White American Youth," *Youth and Society*, Vol. 9 (1978), pp. 433–452.

[56](New York: Harcourt, Brace and World, 1968).

[57]John Conger, *Adolescence and Youth: Psychological Developments in a Changing World* (New York: Harper & Row, 1973).

[58]D. Yankelovich, *The New Morality: A Profile of American Youth in the Seventies* (New York: McGraw-Hill, 1974).

[59]Conger, *Adolescence and Youth*, p. 119.

CHAPTER NINE
THE ADULT YEARS

Moving from one phase of the life cycle to the next often involves role discontinuities and internal conflicts. We have seen how such discontinuities and conflicts can present problems for adolescents who are emerging into adulthood. Although conventional wisdom holds that such problems disappear during adulthood, more detailed examination of reality suggests that the problems of life may become even more profound. Social psychologists have developed a number of concepts useful for understanding some of the problems of adulthood. This chapter considers the relevance of some of these ideas. But, first, consider what it means to be an adult.

THE THING CALLED "ADULTHOOD"

"Adulthood" is another one of those mysterious and powerful words. Throughout the United States of America, for example, you may buy an alcoholic drink (legally) if you are an "adult." How do you establish the "fact" that you are an adult? By presenting a "card" that certifies that you are 18 years of age or 21 years of age or conceivably some other age. If you engage in sexual relations with a person of the opposite sex who is not an "adult," you may be charged with statutory rape. Here, again, the definition may be 18 (or some other age). If you wish to drive an automobile, you must be an adult to obtain a driver's license. Age? In some places 16; in others 18 or 17.

If you wish to vote, you must be 18 years of age (not many years ago, it was 21). And so it goes.

"Adulthood" seems to provide many benefits and privileges as well as responsibilities, but the meaning of the term seems to vary even within contemporary society, and, of course throughout history there have been enormous changes in the concept. It is clearly a social rather than a well-defined physical or physiological concept.

To obtain some perspective on the changes that have occurred even within Anglo-American society, we have only to turn to Blackstone, the influential expert on English common law who, in the eighteenth century, issued the following pronouncement:

> The ages of male and female are different for different purposes. A male at *twelve* years may take the oath of allegiance; at *fourteen* is at years of discretion, and may therefore consent or disagree to marriage, may choose his guardian, and, if his discretion be actually proved, may make his testament of his personal estate; at *seventeen* may be an executor and at *twenty-one* is at his own disposal, and alien his lands, goods, and chattels. A female also at *seven* years of age may be betrothed or given in marriage; at *nine* is entitled to a dower; at *twelve* is at years of maturity, and therefore may consent or disagree to marriage, and if proved to have sufficient discretion, may bequeath her personal estate; at *fourteen* is at years of legal discretion, and may choose a guardian; at *seventeen* may be executrix; and at *twenty-one* may dispose of herself and her lands.[1]

With respect to criminal responsibility, Blackstone notes that at the age of 14, a person could be executed for committing a capital crime. Under the age of 7, this could not be done. Between the ages of 7 and 14, however, it depended upon the circumstances of the case. Thus, he cites the example of a girl, aged 13, who was burned for killing her mistress. In another case, a boy, younger than 13, was hanged because after killing his companion, he had gone into hiding. This, according to the court, proved that he could distinguish between good and evil. He knew he had done wrong.[2]

As the twentieth century draws to a close, the term "adult" is still undefined in the Anglo-American legal system. A general determination is made of who is to be recognized by the state as an "adult" as opposed to a "child" person. But the state sets only minimum standards for acquiring and maintaining the status of adult. It presumably does not, for example, establish rules for raising children in accordance with some specific religious or scientific ideal. The authority of parents to raise children in accordance with their own beliefs and values is presumably very wide. Parents need meet only "minimum" standards of child care. (They must not abandon children, neglect them, or abuse them—and they must send them to school, keep them out of the labor market, and have them vaccinated against smallpox, etc.) The criminal law in contemporary society "does not hold a person to the highest ethical or moral standards, nor does it compel them to be generous, kind, completely honest, or, as some might say, 'adult' in their relationships with others."[3]

In short, in the eyes of the law, at least, to be "an adult" is not equivalent to "acting as an adult" in one's own eyes or in the eyes of one's family, teachers, friends, or neighbors. From a legal perspective, a person need only reach a given statutory age to be declared "adult."[4] This leads to a series of contradictions, since the law varies from state to state and often from community to community. To be an adult with respect to voting does not make one adult with respect to the right to buy alcoholic beverages or the right to engage in sexual relations. Being an adult with respect to qualifying for an automobile driving license does not necessarily qualify one for adulthood in other roles.

In short, "adulthood" clearly is not a fixed "thing" or "condition" that can be studied as if it were composed of an invariant combination of chemical components. It means different things to different groups, societies, and people, and its meaning seems to change even within the same society with the passage of time and changing circumstances. Nevertheless, it seems to retain a more or less discernible core of meaning. To obtain more insight into this meaning, we can begin by examining its connotations in different societies, among different groups, and under varying social conditions.

At what appears to be the opposite pole from the American or British legal view is what has been referred to as the "Confucian perception"[5] of adulthood. From this perspective, reaching any specific age is in many ways quite irrelevant. The core meaning of adulthood is "to become a person."[6] The Confucian term for adulthood is *ch'eng-jen*—one who has *become* a person. The interesting linguistic feature of the term *ch'eng* is that, like many other expressions in the Chinese language, it carries the meaning of both a noun and a verb. The noun indicates that something has been completed; the verb connotes a process of development. Thus, the *ch'eng-jen* denotes not simply a stage of life but "a many-sided manifestation of man's creative adaptation to the inevitable process of aging, a proven ability to mature further, as well as an obvious sign of maturity itself."[7]

Thus, the idea of adolescence as a separate stage of existence is alien to this Confucian view of life. "Adulthood" cannot mean simply an endpoint of adolescence. Maturity cannot be achieved suddenly and given to someone with a single *rite de passage*. The process of aging begins with birth, and there is no specific stage of life that cannot be characterized as the time of "growing up."[8]

But there is no necessity to go to ancient China to find variations on the theme of adulthood. Within the boundaries of the contemporary United States, there are, of course innumerable cultural traditions each of which seems to deal with adulthood in distinctive terms. To avoid the complexities involved in coming to terms with this diversity, at least one author has decided to discuss only "prevailing ideas in America—most evident and predominant in the non-ethnic middle class."[9] The alternative would require dealing with such phenomena as "ten-year old black youths calling each other 'man' as well as with their fathers who are called—or at least used to be called—'boys.' We would have to deal, too, with Irish Catholic families in which sons become 'Fathers' to their parents. There are myriad similar problems."[10]

What, for example, does it mean to "become a person" for someone brought up in a contemporary "Chinese-American" family? According to one distinguished Chinese-American scholar, Francis Hsu, traditional Chinese culture stresses that the bonds individuals develop with members of their immediate family and other close relatives ought to be close and continuous.

Thus, within this framework, an individual's self-esteem and future are linked to his or her family or kin. The family continues to be of great significance throughout a person's lifetime, even if that person becomes physically separated from the others by great distances. On the other hand, however, so-called "Western culture" emphasizes "rugged individualism," which has the effect of pushing people to find their own roots away from the affectionate and intimate bonds first learned in the family. Thus, those socialized in Western culture tend to lose these bonds and find meaning elsewhere.[11]

Interestingly, this observation about Chinese and American socialization orientations coincides very closely with another set of observations made about Japanese and Americans:

> In Japan, the infant is seen more as a separate biological organism who, from the beginning, in order to develop, needs to be drawn into increasingly interdependent relations with others. In America, the infant is seen as a dependent biological organism who, in order to develop, needs to be made increasingly independent of others.[12]

In short, we have been examining at least three relatively distinct perspectives with respect to adulthood. The first of these—the legal perspective—in essence seems to define the status of adult for a person when he or she has reached a stated chronological age. With respect to both the Chinese-Japanese or "Asian" perspective and the middle-class nonethnic or "American" perspectives, adulthood seems to be viewed as more amorphous in character and to depend, in large measure, upon circumstances in the social environment of the individual involved. This environment for what we may call the Asian perspective seems to focus more strongly on the nuclear and extended family. Adulthood seems to be more or less equivalent to assuming certain family roles (father, mother, breadwinner, etc.). The precise nature of what is thought of as adulthood, however, may change according to the presence or absence of significant others in the immediate setting. A married son who lives with his wife or near his own parents or his wife's parents may feel that he is somewhat less than a full-fledged adult. A younger couple, who find themselves more or less isolated (with respect to family influences), may feel that they have completed adulthood at a much earlier age than have their age peers.

If we are to accept the model presented of "American" adulthood, then it would appear that family influences are of much less significance. The reference points for middle-class Americans presumably are the values of independence and economic self-sufficiency stressed in their early training. Adulthood is presumably achieved when the job market certifies the status by providing a "living" wage, salary, or profit in return for services provided. In this sense, it would appear that the "world of work" has replaced the family as the mirror reflecting an image of adulthood.

When we turn to the subculture of blacks or Afro-Americans in U.S. society, we find yet another perspective. Several decades have now gone by since publication of the notorious "Moynihan report."[13] The impression left by this report created an enormous amount of controversy. It stated or at least implied that the black family was "pathological" and was in the process of disintegrating at an alarming rate. It was characterized by a high rate of illegitimacy, divorce, desertion, separation, and family instability. All this was presumably heightened by the absence of an adult husband-father figure. The black family was increasingly becoming more of a matriarchy in form—a structure in which black adult women were becoming the dominant authority figures. Black women became decision makers becaue of their capacity to earn a disproportionately high share of the family income. The Moynihan report seemed to suggest that a matriarchy itself was pathological and that the survival of the black family depended upon the ability of the family to produce more two-parent structures and to decrease the number of black families on public welfare.[14]

James E. Blackwell has summarized most of the objections to this report as follows:

1. Even at the time the Moynihan study of 1965 was written, three-fifths of black families were two-parent families. Other studies indicate that the equalitarian family type (i.e., a family in which authority is shared equally by father and mother) is far more pervasive in the black community than is either the matriarchy or patriarchy.

2. The matriarchal family is not necessarily pathological. A two-parent family in which the father is marginal to the family structure may be far less healthy and supportive than one headed by a capable and emotionally strong female.

3. There is no firm evidence to support the claim that the absence of a father contributes directly to pathological conditions or that it has such adverse effects on family members as increasing delinquency, causing poor school achievement or confused sexual identity.

4. Moynihan failed to explain adequately all the facts relating to instability and may have unintentionally implied that the victims of the situation were somehow to be blamed for their own condition.[15]

The roots of this controversy seem to extend far beyond the report that set it off. Perhaps the underlying issues involved can be seen more clearly if we focus on the elitist connotations of the word "adult" and how it is used not only to assert levels of competence based on age but to assert superiorities with respect to ethnic and even sexual identifications. Black slaves and "pretty" white women have often been viewed and treated as "children." For a more realistic view of slavery in America, one should read George P. Rawick's fascinating volume, *The American Slave: A Composite Autobiography,* and his edited collection of thousands of interviews with ex-slaves.[16] Rawick rejects the notion that American slaves were "infantilized" and totally dominated by their masters. "They found ways of alleviating the worst of the system and at times of dominating the masters. They built their own community out of materials taken from the African past and the American present with the values and memories of Africa giving meaning and direction to the new creation."[17]

Rawick points out that the major adaptive process for blacks in America during the period of slavery was the establishment of a slave community that ultimately seemed to become even more important to the slaves than did the nuclear family. The family could be and regularly was broken. Individual slaves could be taken to another plantation hundreds of miles away and become part of another community where they knew how to behave and where they would be accepted. The patterns of communication for this community were set up by the daily and nightly exchanges of conversations, social activities, and fellowship that became the most significant events in the lives of the slaves. Nevertheless, they were not totally isolated. They constantly communicated not only with their masters and the families of their masters, but with overseers, poor whites, artisans, professionals, merchants, and laborers as well. If they were influenced by white society because of the conditions of their subjugation, they heavily influenced it as well.[18]

They could influence it sufficiently to "get a piece of the pie," however, only by exerting massive efforts to change existing patterns of discrimination and prejudice. The development of "Black Pride" and a forthright insistence upon the positive values of a black identity have done much to erode the image, even in the minds of whites, of blacks as helpless children who must be cared for by the dominant race. The civil rights movement and the subsequent efforts of blacks to assert the positive features of their own distinctive culture have, in the final analysis, been tantamount to asserting their own adulthood. For whites who suffer from strongly ingrained patterns of prejudice, this evokes hostility not unlike that experienced by some parents when their children begin to assert their own distinctive adult personalities.

Women of all colors have encountered difficulties similar in many ways to those experienced by blacks of both sexes. As Betty Friedan noted many years ago and as many others have observed subsequently, women's magazines and advertisers have traditionally reinforced the notion of being "feminine," meaning "not only pretty and submissive but also childlike and basically incompetent at anything other than housework."[19]

Despite many efforts to change the sexist nature of advertising, television commercials still seem to recognize only two types of women. One is the housewife-mother "usually blandly pretty, always interested exclusively in trivia, the whitest laundry and the shiniest floors, and often stupid. Some man has to tell her what products to use even in her supposed area of expertise, and she will listen to any man no matter how strange his form—tornado, knight, or disembodied voice from the ceiling."[20]

The other type of woman is the "sex kitten" who "is also not very bright, but then she clearly is good for only one thing and that presumably doesn't require brains. Very infrequently a deviant like Josephine the Plumber is thrown in, obviously for comic relief. She, of course, is neither young nor pretty."[21]

But these stereotypes of women did not originate with American advertising executives. A survey of male "intellectuals" throughout history reveals the deeply ingrained prejudices of Western thought that have persisted in viewing women as subadults and, in a sense, subhuman beings who in many ways are like lower-order animals. Thus, according to Aristotle, "it is a general law that there should be naturally ruling elements and elements naturally ruled . . . the rule of the freeman over the slave is one kind of rule, that of the male over the female is another . . . the slave is entirely without the faculty of deliberation; the female indeed possesses it, but in a form which remains inconclusive."[22]

And Lord Chesterfield: "Women, then, are only children of larger growth; they have an entertaining tattle, and sometimes wit, but for solid, reasoning good sense, I never knew in my life one that had it, or who reasoned or acted consequentially for four and twenty hours together."[23]

And Schopenhauer: "[Woman is] in every respect backward, lacking in reason and true morality . . . a kind of middle step between the child and the man, who is the true human being."[24]

And Darwin: "The chief distinction in the intellectual powers of the two sexes is shown by man attaining to a higher eminence, in whatever he takes up than woman can attain—whether requiring deep thought, reason or imagination or merely the use of the senses and hands."[25]

And finally, Napoleon Bonaparte: "Nature intended women to be our slaves . . . they are our property, we are not theirs. They belong to us, just as a tree that bears fruit belongs to a gardener. What a mad idea to demand equality for women! . . . Women are nothing but machines for producing children."[26]

A contemporary British sociologist, Sara Delamont, has observed that, "calling women 'adults' raises certain important problems, because there are many senses in which British women are *never* accorded the same adult status as men."[27] This is illustrated vividly by the popular cry of "women and children first," which classifies women with nonadults. Beyond this, however, was the denial of suffrage to women prior to the third decade of this century when women were classified with children and convicts as nonpersons. Although women in Britain (and the United States) have now been given the right to vote, the traditional attitudes are very slow in fading away. Thus, Delamont recalls a fascinating experiment reported in the literature in which the researcher asked psychotherapists to rate the qualities of the ideal healthy man, woman, and child. Adult women were rated very much like the healthy child and quite unlike the adult male.[28]

SEASONS OF LIFE

As we have seen, the concept of adulthood can mean different things in different cultures and in different historical periods. Moreover, as we have seen with respect to other phases of development, it would be a mistake to consider adulthood as a "thing" in any determinate sense. The demarcation points between adulthood and the other phases of the developmental process are not drawn in any hard and fast manner. In this sense, it is better to think of adulthood as a process rather than as a thing, and as a process adulthood may be said to consist of activities and events that may be more or less salient for people who are considered to be adults. Adulthood, like the different stages of childhood, may be thought of as a form of *becoming* as well as *being*, with the possible exception that as an adult it is expected that the phrase *Je suis arrivé* is perhaps most appropriate. We shall have more to say about what this may mean shortly in this chapter. At this point, we shall take a look at how one sociologist has attempted to characterize the processes of being and becoming an adult in contemporary society.

Perhaps the most ambitious attempt to capture the meaning of adulthood in modern America is represented by Daniel Levinson's study, *The Seasons of a Man's Life*.[29] Unfortunately, there is no comparable study of adult women. Nevertheless, Levinson's study highlights some interesting aspects of adulthood.

Levinson and his colleagues interviewed 40 adult men (between the ages of 35 and 45). The sample was selected from a variety of occupations ranging from wage laborers to business executives. The interview length ranged from 10 to 20 hours. The men were interviewed at two points in time; first in the late 1960s and then two years later. The researchers then constructed individual biographies for each subject. At the same time, they searched for patterns of sequences that characterized all the subjects.

Levinson identified three major periods of middle life. The first of these might be termed early adulthood or the novice period. This period overlaps to a large extent with what we have discussed as "youth" at the end of Chapter 7. Levinson focused on four specific activities that may be said to comprise the novice period: (1) forming a dream or some image of who and what one would like to become, (2) forming a mentor relationship with an older adult who may act as a general role model or guide through the early years of an individual's career, (3) selecting a career and beginning to take the first steps on a specific occupational "ladder", and (4) finally, beginning to form love relationships with a "special woman."

These processes of becoming an adult do not occur in the same way for all individuals, nor need they always take place in a smooth and untroublesome manner. Where forming a dream may be quite elaborate for many professional men (one scientist in Levinson's sample imagined himself as a Nobel Prize winner), many of the wage laborers had not formed any dreams at all. As we have seen (see Chapter 7), difficulties faced by some individuals in forming mentor relationships may have long-term career consequences.

Many of the men in Levinson's sample experienced difficulties in establishing an occupational direction. Where some men had difficulty "getting started," others made decisions that "locked" them into careers with which they became dissatisfied. Love relationships were rife with problems. Some of these resulted from the fact that some men were "in love" with women other than those to whom they were married. Other conflicts arose between a man's love and his dream or choice of an occupation. Such problems are, of course, not limited to men.

During the novice period, individuals build what Levinson terms life structures, "the basic pattern or design of a person's life at a given time."[30] These may pertain to multidimensional aspects of any individual's life (e.g., their dreams, careers, and loves). These life structures may change as a result of internal motivational factors (e.g., unhappiness) as well as external factors (e.g., being laid off from a job).

Levinson terms the second phase of adulthood (age 32 to 40) as "settling down." In settling down, individuals establish a niche in society and begin to advance toward their dreams. Completion of settling down involves what Levinson terms becoming "one's own man," that is, being "more independent and self-sufficient and less subject to the control of others."[31] Settling down entails the building of a second life structure. This requires going beyond many of the problems of early adulthood. Individuals may emerge from early failures or disappointments to pursue new and different careers or occupations. This may, in turn, affect other aspects of a person's life.

Settling down is hardly a smooth process. As with other developmental processes, there may be troubles and setbacks. Levinson has identified five general sequences that may characterize settling down. The first of these involves advancement within a stable life structure. In this case, an individual's early decisions establish a relatively unproblematic course of life marked by the achievement of desired goals. A second sequence is in some ways the obverse. Here an individual may begin on a relatively established course. Rather than advancing, however, he fails in moving from one stage to another. In one instance, an individual's lack of success at business was linked to his mentor's leaving the firm at which they were working. The individual unhappily remained with the firm for some period of time.

A third sequence entails "breaking out" (i.e., establishing a new life structure). This may involve finding a new career, new loves, and new dreams. Breaking out may result from the realization that one's life course has become intolerable. The fourth sequence of settling down also requires the establishment of new life structures—in this case, however, it is not the intolerability of one's current life course, but advancement along that life course that requires the change. Being promoted from a professor to a college dean or provost, for example, may require one to engage in new activities and form new associations. The university board of directors that may have been comprised of faceless names in the past may now become significant others. One's professor colleagues, who were once one's "buddies," may now be defined in more formal terms. Such "promotions" can adversely affect other aspects of an individual's life.

Finally, in an ironic sense, settling down may not entail much settling down at all. One's early decisions may have resulted in one being placed on a course that was itself in a constant state of flux. Levinson describes the life of one Hugh McCloud. After joining the army and being wounded in combat, McCloud spent three years in a veteran's hospital. According to Levinson, this was the high point of McCloud's settling down period. Here, he established a hospital radio station on which he was one of the disc jockeys. After gaining some radio training, McCloud traveled about the country taking various jobs. However, he was unable to establish a clear occupational direction and found himself in a variety of different positions: salesman, purchasing agent, counselor, and office clerk. As he approached 40, McCloud was unable to cite a major occupational accomplishment.

McCloud's occupational flux had implications for his family life. If he was unable to secure a firm financial basis, it was likely that his wife, a former nurse, would have to go back to work. His in-laws, who had never really liked him, would end up caring for the children, resulting in McCloud's being continuously reminded that their early predictions of his chances for success had unhappily come true. McCloud had not become his own man.

Finally, the individual may enter middle adulthood. En route, however, most individuals go through what Levinson terms a midlife transition. According to Levinson, this is a time for reevaluation of the past and a more realistic appraisal of the future:

> It is time in the Mid-life Transition for a man to modulate the powerful imagery of the ladder. Without losing all desire for accomplishment, power and excellence, he comes to be less driven by ambition and more aware of the magical qualities he formerly attributed to reaching the top of the ladder. It is no longer *essential* to succeed, no longer *catastrophic to* fail. He evaluates his success and failure in more complex terms, giving more emphasis to the quality of experience, to the intrinsic value of his work and products, and their meaning to himself and others.[32]

For 80 percent of Levinson's sample, the midlife transition entailed a deep personal crisis. These may arise from diverse sources. One source may be an individual's inability to fulfill his dreams or to reevaluate his life accordingly. Unfulfilled dreams may engender deep personal disappointment for individuals themselves. Beyond this, though, they may have consequences for other aspects of a person's life. Levinson states,

> If he feels he has lost or betrayed his own early Dream, he may find it hard to give his wholehearted support and blessing to the Dreams of young adults. When his offspring show signs of failure or confusion in pursuing their adult goals, he is afraid that their lives will turn out as badly as his own. Yet, when they do well, he may resent their success. Anxiety and guilt may undermine his efforts to be helpful and lead him instead to be nagging and vindictive.[33]

Levinson's work is not without faults. Some have questioned whether adulthood is properly treated as a developmental phase. Much change may take place during this period, though it need not necessarily be viewed as growth. Others have questioned whether the midlife transition need necessarily result in personal crises. Other studies with larger samples, but with less in-depth probing, have not shown that midlife necessarily entails crises. One study of average professional athletes indicated that they were quite resourceful in adjusting to the fact that they had not become "stars."[34] However, other studies have shown that life changes can be quite stressful, especially if they are ill-timed, if they result in a loss of status, if they are unanticipated, if individuals lack the resources with which to deal with them, or if they lack attachments to other persons or institutions to help compensate for losses.[35]

Most importantly, Levinson's study design failed to consider patterns of development and maturation among women. As Carol Gilligan's recent work suggests, women may hear a "different voice" enroute to the fulfillment of their dreams.

In Levinson's account of the "Seasons of a Man's Life," development is marked by increased independence and continued achievement. The man's most important objective is the "fulfillment of his dream." Although it is important for the novice adult to form social relationships with others (especially with a "mentor" and "special woman") these relationships are not seen as ends in themselves, but rather as facilitators of the dream. For men, according to Levinson, becoming an adult is a process of continued individuation. The fulfillment is "becoming one's own man."

According to Carol Gilligan, Levinson's formulation does not provide an adequate account of female development and maturity. For women, maturity entails what she terms a "fusion of identity and intimacy." A woman's identity is not based solely upon her sense of being separate from others. Rather her identity is informed by her present, past, and future relationships to others and by her membership in a larger social collectivity.

In this regard, many highly successful and motivated women may experience a conflict between the independence required for their professional lives and sense of caring, nurturance, and responsibility that makes up an important part of their identity. Such a conflict is evidenced in an account rendered by a woman Gilligan calls Nan. This account concerns Nan's medical school experiences.

> When I first applied to medical school, my feeling was that I was a person who was concerned with other people and being able to care for them in some way or another, and I was running into problems the last few years as far as my being able to give of myself, my time, and what I am doing to other people. And medicine, even though it seems that profession is set up to do exactly that, seems to more or less interfere with your doing it. To me it felt like I wasn't really growing, that I was just treading water, trying to cope with what I was doing that made me very angry in some ways because it wasn't the way that I wanted things to go.[36]

For this aspiring physician, becoming a doctor is not valid as an end in itself. Becoming a doctor, in fact, makes sense only in the context of other social relationships. As Nan later elaborated:

> By yourself, there is little sense to things. It is like the sound of one hand clapping, the sound of one man or one woman, there is something lacking. It is the collective that is important to me, and that collective is based on certain guiding principles, one of which is that everybody belongs to it and that you all come from it. You have to love someone else, because while you may not like them, you are inseparable from them. In a way, it is like loving your right hand. They are part of you; that other person is part of that giant collection of people that you are connected to.[37]

From a woman's perspective, development is as much a matter of connection, as it is one of individuation. Interconnection is as important as separation.

Whether men and women are truly different in these respects awaits further study and research. However, Gilligan's work causes one to question conventional, male-dominated conceptions of maturity and the place of attachment and individuation in adult life.

On the positive side, Levinson has at least shown that crises may persist throughout life and are not solely a characteristic of childhood. Such crises are not only applicable to men. Indeed, they may be more intense for women. Consider, if you will, the former "housewife" who returns to the work force after raising the children. She is beginning her career when her husband is in fact crystallizing his and directing his attention in other ways. Her position as a "novice"—to use Levinson's term—at the age of 40 may create even more difficulties in the workplace.

A final contribution of Levinson's work stems from its sensitizing us to the idea that socialization does not necessarily end with childhood but may continue throughout the adult years. At the end of the last chapter, we saw how occupational socialization typically begins during one's youth. Such socialization contains two components. On the one hand, youths must learn to fulfill a role within a particular organizational setting (e.g., they must learn how to be a second-year medical student). On the other hand, they begin to learn some of the attributes of a role they are to play in the future (e.g., doctor). As an adult, these dual roles should gradually be fused. Such a fusion is in part represented by Levinson's notion that one becomes one's own person.

Becoming one's own person involves continuing socialization. This is particularly significant with respect to one's job or occupation. This socialization may take place in a variety of ways. Identification and modeling of the behavior of significant others may be an important part of adult occupational socialization. The role of the mentor is crucial in this regard. Like other forms of socialization, the novice may have to be disabused of romantic idealizations of his or her job. A novice detective may learn that a good portion of the job entails boring paperwork. Some positions may require the novice to go through a hazing period, during which time he or she is required to perform some of the less desirable tasks associated with a particular job. Socialization processes such as these may continue throughout one's occupational life—as one comes to take on new jobs in different settings.

Such changes can affect one's personality and self-concept. Sociologist Donald T. Hall describes what he terms a pattern of "spiraling success" in this regard. Persons with higher self-esteem take on and succeed in completing more challenging tasks. Such success, in turn, leads to a further enhancement of their self-esteem and a willingness to approach more difficult and challenging tasks.[38] Recent studies have shown that the nature of one's job can have a significant impact on personality structure. People who have jobs that require autonomy and self-direction tend to maintain such values in other areas of life. Work roles that require dealing with complex problems also lead to greater intellectual flexibility. These studies indicate that occupational characteristics may affect personality and that it is not simply the self-selection of more creative and autonomous individuals to such positions.[39]

Occupational floundering and failure also has an effect on personality and self-concept. This may be true not only for the Hugh McCloud's of the world, who never succeeded in initiating a career trajectory, but also for people who have been successfully launched, but have reached impasses on their career ladders. As opposed to spiraling success, such individuals may be faced with a "career ceiling." Being "stuck" in this way can lead to a sense of emptiness and apathy.[40] During this time, people may come to redefine their aspirations and dreams and in some ways to redefine themselves as well. Energies may be redirected from work to family, community, or other pursuits. Such redefinitions may have an important bearing on one's understanding of oneself as a member of society. One study, for example, has shown that older careerists tend to measure their success in terms of the progress made from the start rather than the distance to the goal.[41]

ADULTHOOD AND THE NOTION OF COMPETENCE

When the term "adult" is used, there seems to be at least one underlying assumption. To be treated as an "adult," one must not be mentally or physically "deficient"—one should be in some sense "normal." When the focus of attention is an individual person, the term used to discuss the difficulty is borrowed from medicine. To be regarded as a full-fledged adult, one must be in "good health." Persons who are incapacitated for either physical or mental reasons may be excluded from some of the responsibilities as well as the privileges of adulthood.

But being a competent adult may entail much more than not being either physically or mentally incapacitated. For example, to be regarded as a competent adult in contemporary Western society, one must be considered as competent in social interaction. The phrase, "Don't act like a baby," among other things implies that adults are to be more reserved, considerate, self-sacrificing, and less demanding in their interactions with others. Indeed, from a dramaturgical perspective (see Chapter 2), competency is marked by the ability to respond appropriately in social situations and to preserve the image that one is in control of one's self.

Beyond demonstrating that one is adept in social interaction, competent adults also expected to manage social relationships according to established rules. The proper management of social relationships requires that adults fulfill the obligations and entitlements attached to the roles they come to play. Any specific role may have multiple obligations and entitlements. As a college student, you are entitled to a certain degree of deference and respect from your professor. You are further entitled to expect that he or she will attempt to provide for you some kind of learning experience and to evaluate your progress in a fair and objective manner. Your professor is also entitled to a certain degree of deference and respect, and you are obligated to at least try to learn course material. These role expectations may not always be consistent. For example, your professor may find that he is more effective as a teacher if he adopts a friendly posture toward you and other students. This friendliness, however, may seem ingenuous if you fail to earn a good grade in the course. Managing such relationships may tax even the most competent adults.

This represents only one surface problem associated with managing social relationships that consist of different entitlements and obligations. Indeed, the problem and complexity expand geometrically once we realize that any individual may play many roles. From this perspective, a competent adult is one who can effectively manage the many roles he or she may come to play. As one social psychologist put it,

> The member of any organized society must develop more than a single role, or role behavior, if he is to reciprocate and cooperate effectively with his fellows.

To the behavior pathologist, this implies further that the person whose repertory includes a *variety* of well-practiced, realistic social roles is better equipped to meet new and critical situations than the person whose repertory is meager, relatively unpracticed and socially unrealistic. The skilled role-taker, like the skilled motorist, has a better chance than the unskilled of withstanding the sudden, unforeseen stress and the effects of prolonged, unremitting strain.[42]

According to this perspective, the more roles an individual is able to play, the better equipped he or she will be for social life. The idea that adulthood is a period in which an individual gains roles is central to much social psychological thought on adulthood. Indeed, as we shall discuss in more detail in the next chapter, one theory of adulthood and aging holds that emergence into adulthood entails an increase in roles and their complexity, where aging entails a "disengagement" from these roles.

In the following pages, we shall investigate some of the difficulties associated with role complexity in modern society. We will consider some of the implications of such complexity for one's identity and self-concept.

ROLE ENACTMENT

Competence in contemporary life may be gauged by an individual's ability to *enact* particular roles and performances in appropriate social circumstances. Role enactment refers to an actor's ability to act or "perform" in ways that are consistent with expectations related to his or her role or status in any particular social situation. Role enactment is of central concern to social psychologists, because, as one social psychologist puts it, the "focus on role enactment bridges the gap between the individual and the group, between personal history and social organization."[43] Any role enactment may be gauged by three criteria:

> *appropriateness*—Has the actor selected the correct role for the social circumstances?
> *propriety*—Does the performance meet the normative standards for the role? Is it good or bad?
> *credibility*—Does the performance lead one to believe that the actor is truly "engrossed" in his or her role?[44]

The enactment of any particular role may be facilitated through different cognitive skills. Social psychologists have shown that an individual's ability to "take the role of the other," to perceive social circumstances accurately and to empathize with another, facilitates role enactment. Role enactment thus requires the expression of appropriate emotional as well as cognitive responses.[45]

PROBLEMS OF ROLE ENACTMENT

Interesting circumstances may emerge when a particular performance or enactment does not meet desired standards or if one defines one's standards differently from those with whom one interacts. Role theorists have identified a number of difficulties in social interaction that may be related to the roles individuals are called upon to play. Problems may result from the fact that individuals may be unable to define situations appropriately as a prelude to enacting appropriate role behavior. A variety of untoward types of behavior may be associated with an inability to define the situation appropriately. Erving Goffman suggests that certain forms of mental illness and other types of deviance may be related to such difficulties.[46] For many women in the contemporary world, knowing what role to enact when in the company of men can be a serious problem. Do I act as a "sweet," "demure," "old-fashioned" girl, or as an assertive woman? Do I allow the man to pay for my dinner or do I insist on paying my share? Uncertainty of this sort may begin by being little more than a mild discomfort. It can lead to a serious question, "Who am I?"

A range of problems may arise when an actor does not know a role appropriate to the social situation at hand. Such situations are more likely to occur for novices who are in situations where mechanisms of anticipatory socialization were not available. Although formal training may be available for such individuals, such "in-service" socialization may not always adequately prepare individuals for dealing with their new circumstances.[47] The example of "non-mentored" female cadets at West Point discussed in the previous chapter illustrates this point. Uncertainty as to role performance may, on the other hand, require a certain innovativeness in fashioning a performance to suit the situation. From a social learning perspective, Albert Bandura has discussed "creative modeling." This occurs when individuals piece together components of different roles to create an amalgamated role appropriate to the situation at hand.[48] Through such innovations, roles may be created in ways to facilitate social interaction. It is interesting to note that a number of social psychologists have commented on the role of the "stranger" in this regard. Strangers are typically in a marginal position: not quite "insiders" but not "outsiders" either. This requires them to make explicit what others on the social scene may take for granted, leading them to be perceptive observers as well as participants.[49]

Finally, an interactional difficulty may arise when there is a lack of consensus between actor and others about appropriate role behavior. Here role dissensus does not stem from an inability to meet role expectations, but from the fact that at least one party to the interaction defines those expectations differently from others. Most social psychologists believe that role dissensus needs to be minimized if social interaction is to proceed smoothly.

A number of mechanisms exist to smooth over and, hence, minimize the consequences of role dissensus. Negotiation is seen as one key mechanism. However, for negotiation to take place, the following conditions must hold:

1. There must be the possibility of compromise. Even if the definition of the situation of one of the participants prevails, the rules and procedures must not preclude consideration of other definitions of the situation.
2. It must be possible to make provisional offers and counteroffers. Issues must remain open, and conditional offers must be considered by participants.
3. Both participants must be permitted to reject unacceptable proposals.[50]

Certain social situations are designed to provide an opportunity for such negotiations. University faculty meetings, for example, are often designed to allow participants to present differing definitions of the situation. On the other hand, negotiations may in some ways pervade everyday life. We may compromise on how much we are to be paid, what time we are to meet, where we are to go, and with whom we are to associate.

Beyond negotiations, a number of other interactional devices exist to either justify or explain untoward behavior. "Accounts" may be used to justify what normally would be considered unacceptable behavior. Aggression, for example, may be justified on the grounds that the recipient is receiving his "just due." An obnoxious person may "deserve" a slap on the face or a punch in the face to balance the books, as it were. For such accounts to succeed, however, they must be perceived as being both legitimate and credible. Excuses admit that an action is untoward but claim that the actor is not totally responsible for the action. Actors may claim that their behavior was caused by events beyond their control, that they were forced to behave in such a manner, or that the consequences of their actions were unknown to them. Excuses must also be credible and legitimate. If accompanied by an apology, excuses must also be perceived as being sincere.[51]

ROLE CONFLICT AND SOME RELATED PROBLEMS

Problems related to role conflict are more persistent than are those related to role enactment. They may have enduring consequences for individuals. Social psychologists L. Sarbin and V. Allen cite research linking role conflict to a number of emotional problems, including frustration and depression.[52] One form of role conflict that the authors call *status incongruence*—as when a person is high in terms of one form of social ranking (e.g., education) but low in terms of another (e.g., income)—appears to be related to symptoms of physiological distress such as loss of appetite and dizziness.[53] According to this view, role conflict produces a stressful psychological state—role strain—a felt difficulty in meeting the multiple obligations of different roles.

Living in a complex society requires individuals to play a variety of different roles. Sociologist Robert Merton uses the term "role set"[54] to refer to the complex of roles that any individual may play. In most cases, individuals may be able to maintain multiple roles. One role, for example, may remain latent, whereas the other is active. The "hard-nosed" business executive may be a loving father at home. In other cases, roles may be merged or alternated. Role conflict may be said to exist when two or more roles that make up this complex entail conflicting obligations and expectations. It refers to that condition in which "an actor finds himself/herself in two or more positions requiring contradictory role enactments."[55]

A further distinction may be drawn between interrole and intrarole conflict. Interrole conflict refers to a situation in which an individual simultaneously occupies two positions that contain incompatible role obligations. The "man-in-the-middle" is often cited as the classic example of interrole conflict. A supervisor in a factory is one of the workers, yet he or she is responsible to the management for worker production. Such positions have been noted to produce considerable role strain. Intrarole conflict exists when relevant others hold incompatible expectations for the occupant of a specific role. In her study of college women in the 1940s, sociologist Mira Komarovsky notes that the requirement to be both brilliant and beautiful was a source of serious role strain.[56]

One can readily think of the working mother as a potential example of role conflict. The working mother is often expected to be a professional on the job. This may require that she be formal, impersonal, unemotional, and rational. At home, she may switch to a radically different behavioral repertoire. She may become highly affective with respect to her family. However, the contradictory expectations of each role may intensify the situation. Imagine coming home from work, cooking dinner, caring for children, and receiving a phone call from the office requiring you to deal with a problem at work. Such "role overload"[57] can create substantial strain.

There are a number of ways of dealing with role strain. Conflicting roles may be "segregated."[58] Our working mother may be a cool professional on the job and a loving housewife at home. Roles may be redefined. Traditional conceptions of "housewife" may be given new meanings. New roles may be created. In this instance, the creation of a role of "house husband" may help the working mother adjust to the demands associated with the multiple roles she has come to play.

SELF AND IDENTITY

The relationship of role, self, and identity is one of the most central issues in social psychology. Where some social psychologists argue that self can be defined in terms of role (i.e., that who we are is a function of our social position), others stress creative aspects of "role-making,"[59] noting that individuals may fashion new roles in response to unique circumstances. The relationship between self and role is very complex. To gain a better understanding of how diversity and complexity in the structure and organization of roles affects self and identity, it is necessary to take a closer look at social psychological conceptions of self and identity. We shall then discuss some current studies of role-self interconnection.

From a symbolic interactionist perspective the self is social. This does not necessarily mean that there is no true or authentic *you*. Rather, the social self refers to the idea that how you become who you are is a result of the social experiences in which you participate. Your identity, in this regard, is then a social identity.

Imagine someone asking you the question, "Who are you?" Beyond saying your name, how might you go about answering this question? One social psychologist, Morris Rosenberg, suggests that you are likely to select a noun from one of six different categories.[60]

In simple societies, *social status* might suffice as a basis for classification.[61] Your social status may determine your membership in other social organizations. In more complex societies, however, *group membership* may be based on a variety of factors: voluntary association, shared beliefs and interests, subculture, religion, and so on. Membership in such groups constitutes a second component of one's social identity.

Rosenberg's third category of social identity is *social labeling*. Labels are used to capture notable aspects of our behavior. Typically, these are negative. For example, if you think you drink too much alcohol, you might call yourself an alcoholic. Such labels may be positive as well. If you think you generally behave in a fair and positive manner toward others, you may categorize yourself as a "nice guy."

A fourth category of identity is called *derived statuses*. These identities emerge from one's personal history or biography. If you graduate from Harvard, for example, you would likely classify yourself as a Harvard graduate. Should your spouse divorce you, you might consider yourself on the way to becoming a divorcee.

Social types comprise a fifth category of social identity. Assume that you are walking down the street and someone approaches with orange hair, cut in a "Mohawk" fashion, jeans, a leather vest, and spiked bracelets. You might turn to your companion and refer to such an individual as a "punker." It is not unlikely that our passerby thinks of himself as a punker as well. Although social types may be ambiguous, they provide a basis for meaningfully categorizing others when other bases for making inferences about an individual's identity are unavailable. That a person appears to represent a particular "type" provides some cues on how one might interact with that individual.

Rosenberg calls the sixth category *personal identity*. This refers to an individual's unique identity, that which distinguishes him or her from all others. Two examples of your personal identity are your name and your fingerprints.

As can be readily seen, one's social identity can be derived from diverse sources. Moreover, combinations between different categories are infinitely complicated. There is nothing to suggest that our punker is not also a Harvard graduate who, besides being an extremely nice guy, is also a member of the Republican party. Such combinations, though seemingly unlikely, tend to be more widely distributed than expected in complex societies. Consider, for example, the happily married parent, who may occupy a position of responsibility in society—like a senator or a congressman—but whose sexual escapades, should they become known to others, could have serious negative consequences.

SELF-PROCESSES

An important idea underlying symbolic interactionist as well as other approaches to self and identity is the notion that the self is a process. As we have seen (see Chapter 4), social psychologists have differing views on the extent to which the self is most profitably thought of as an object (i.e., as a relatively stable collection of traits and personal assessments) or as a process (i.e., as a more continuous flow, responding differently to new life circumstances and situations). Unlike some Freudian social psychologists, who stress the importance of early childhood for personality formation, symbolic interactionists view the self as continuing to develop and change throughout adulthood and the life cycle. In the following pages, we shall discuss certain self-processes that enable us to respond to new and different situations as well as to maintain continuity throughout these situations.

Social psychologist Morris Rosenberg discusses four "principles" he considers to be essential to self-concept formation.[62] The first is *reflected appraisals,* which refers to our perceptions of how others view us. As Rosenberg puts it, "this principle holds that people, as social animals, are deeply influenced by the attitudes of others toward the self and that, in the course of time, they come to view themselves as they are viewed by others."[63] Reflected appraisals may fall into one of three categories: (1) *direct reflections,* which refer to the responses of others to our actions; (2) *perceived selves,* which refer to our perceptions of others' responses to our actions and; (3) *the generalized other.* Rosenberg uses this term to refer to a community's response to our action. This includes our sense of how we, as selves, fit into some larger collectivity.

As should be apparent, the concept of reflected appraisals is derived primarily from a symbolic interactionist perspective. A second concept—*social comparison*—is drawn primarily from reference group theory (see Chapter 4). According to this, we learn about ourselves by comparing ourselves to others. Based on such comparisons, we form positive, negative, or neutral self-evaluations. Clearly, those with whom comparisons are made must be comparable in relevant ways. If you are a fledgling runner, it will make little sense to compare yourself with experienced runners like Mary Decker or Alberto Salazar. Similarly, if you aspire to be a college professor, it would probably not be informative to compare your income to a banker's or brain surgeon's.

A third self-process concept is *self-attribution.* Self-attribution means that we make inferences about ourselves based on our objective performances. As discussed in Chapter 7, students who do well in school tend to have a high self-esteem with respect to academics. If you are a sales representative and sell a large number of your company's products, you are likely to consider yourself a good salesperson. In similar ways, life may be considered as a variety of "self-tests" in which different self-images and conceptions may either be verified or contradicted.

A final self-process concept is *psychological centrality.* According to this idea, the self is not merely a collection of different conceptions, images, and valuations; it is also an organizer of one's traits and assessments. Psychological centrality refers to the coordination of the different dimensions of self-concept and self-esteem. For example, you may have known certain unpopular and even rather obnoxious individuals who nevertheless held themselves in high esteem. Popularity may not be highly valued by such individuals. Hence, being unpopular, or even recognizing that they might even appear to some to be obnoxious, would not affect the self-esteem of these individuals who may value other traits and characteristics.

MULTIPLE IDENTITIES

Complexities related to role and self provide for complexity of identity. Social psychologists have called this the *problem of multiple identities.*

Initially, social psychologists viewed the problem of multiple identities as a problem of time and energy. According to this idea, people have a limited amount of time and energy. Our investment in different identities is a function of available time and energy.[64]

Identities may, however, be prioritized according to different principles. Some social psychologists have used Merton's concept of role set to understand how identities may be prioritized. From this perspective, we are likely to behave in accordance with a specific identity to the extent that we have a number of reciprocal role relationships that affirm that identity. Others have viewed identity prioritization as a function of rewards; we select courses of action consistent with specific identities to the extent that we are rewarded for such decisions.

The concept of self-esteem also has been applied to how we select courses of action in specific circumstances. According to this idea, we are likely to behave in ways that enhance how well we think of ourselves. A number of psychological mechanisms such as projection (i.e., attributing one's own undesirable characteristics to others), displacement (scapegoating), and repression (pressing undesirable characteristics from one's conscious mind) can, from this perspective, be viewed as mechanisms for maintaining self-esteem.[65]

The notion of self-consistency also is relevant to prioritizing identities. This refers to the desire to act in accordance with qualitative aspects of one's self-concept and to resist contradictory definitions. According to this idea, people act in a manner that is consistent with the "pictures" they hold of themselves.[66]

IDENTITY SALIENCE

People usually can choose to do many different things in any given social situation. They can define each situation in a variety of ways. Depending on which definition they select, they may find it necessary to have different identities and assume alternate aspects of their own selves. How one makes choices on different courses of action in such complex and ambiguous circumstances is the heart of what Sheldon Stryker calls *identity theory.*[67]

According to Stryker, identities can be understood as "reflexively applied cognitions in the form of answers to the question 'Who am I.' " Any one of us can imagine answering this question in multiple ways (e.g., I am a boy, son, student, athlete). From the point of view of identity theory, the collection of responses (which Stryker calls "role identities") to this question may be said to constitute the self.

Identity salience refers to one way in which these discrete identities may be organized. Stryker suggests that our different identities are organized hierarchically in terms of their salience for us. The position of any specific identity in this hierarchy is, theoretically speaking, determined by the probability that it will be consistently invoked within the same situation and across different situations. For example, you may consider yourself to be a competent computer programmer, a devoted parent, and a rather competitive racquetball player. If, while playing racquetball and programming computers, you would respond to the question "Who am I" with the word "parent," we might conclude that that identity is the most salient for you.

Stryker goes on to argue that the salience of particular identities is a function of one's *commitment* to those identities. Commitment refers to the extent that one's social relationships reinforce role identities. As Stryker states, "By this usage, a man is committed to the role of "husband" in the degree that the number of persons and the importance to him of those persons require his being in the position of husband and playing that role."[68] According to Stryker, role commitment is positively related to identity salience, which, in turn, is related to the probability that you will behave in a role appropriate manner in any social situation. An application of identity theory to the salience of religious identities has shown that occupying a variety of roles unrelated to religion tends to decrease the salience of religious identity.[69]

MULTIPLE IDENTITIES AND PSYCHOLOGICAL WELL-BEING

What are some of the consequences of having multiple identities? What kinds of complications might this have for our psychological well-being? From role theory, one might assume that multiple roles would produce multiple identities that would necessarily lead to role strain. Indeed this is one approach taken by a number of social psychologists.

From another perspective, multiple identities may have certain benefits. More privileges and resources may be associated with occupancy of different roles.[70] From this view, multiple identities may be thought of as the obverse of social isolation, and social isolation has been linked to a variety of psychological maladies.

In 1934, Robert Faris published a classic article linking schizophrenia to social isolation. According to Faris, "any form of isolation that cuts the person off from intimate social relations for an extended period of time may possibly lead to this form of mental disorder."[71] Although Faris's own research can be criticized on a number of grounds,[72] the idea that weakening social relationships through the loss of social support networks or social isolation can result in various kinds of stress and unhappiness has become central to the thinking of many social psychologists. According to this idea, occupying social roles provides for a meaningful existence. As recently expressed by one social psychologist,

> Identities are claimed and sustained in reciprocal role relationships. Role relationships are governed by behavioral expectations, the rights and duties of each interactant are normatively prescribed. Thus, if one knows who one is (in a social sense), then one knows how to behave. Role requirements give purpose, meaning, direction, and guidance to one's life.[73]

People who may be, in one way or another, deprived of such reciprocal role relationships, are consequently deprived of a sense of identity, which may in turn lead to psychological stress and a general lack of well-being.

Recently, sociologist Peggy Thoits has reformulated the social isolation hypothesis in terms of what she calls the identity accumulation hypothesis.

This states that individuals who have a number of different identities that are supported in reciprocal role relationships will have a generally better sense of psychological well-being than will those who lack such identities. Accordingly, individuals who take on new identities should be more psychologically healthy than those who suffer an identity loss. Thoits believes that a lack or loss of identity can lead to anxiety, depression, and seriously disorganized behavior.[74] As an illustration, Thoits cites the example of a man who "loses himself" in his work after being left by his wife. The existence of his role of work provided an alternative source of meaning for his life. Had this role not been available, the loss of his wife would likely have had more serious psychological consequences.

To test this hypothesis, Thoits examined the relationship between multiple identities and signs of psychological distress. Using a random sample of 1,095 adult men and women in a northeastern metropolitan area, Thoits was able to show that individuals who possessed a greater number of identities reported less psychological distress than did their more isolated counterparts. Because the panel had been interviewed at different points in time, Thoits also was able to explore the relationship between identity loss and gain and psychological well-being. Her results in this regard are very interesting. While integrated individuals (those with many reciprocal role relationships) benefited more from identity gain, they also tended to experience more psychological distress from identity loss than did isolated individuals. Thoits speculates that integrated individuals have both more to gain and to lose from identity changes because of their location within a relatively cohesive network.

For example, assume that your family members and friends all regard you as being a loving husband and father. If you leave your children and run away with another woman, your identity will likely undergo a substantial change in your own eyes as well as in the eyes of your friends and relatives. If, however, your identities are segregated (e.g., family members regard you as a loving father and husband, co-workers regard you as a competent computer programmer, and friends see you as a better than average racquetball player), the social and, as a result, psychological impact of leaving your wife and children will be less severe. One might then reasonably hypothesize that the consequences of identity loss will be more severe for highly integrated individuals whose identities overlap than for those whose roles are more segregated and identities more independent.

THE MODERN PREDICAMENT: A SOCIAL
PSYCHOLOGICAL PERSPECTIVE

A common theme in sociology and social psychology, as well as in art, literature, and philosophy has focused on what sometimes is referred to as the predicament of the modern or contemporary person. According to this idea, individuals in the modern world have somehow lost themselves; they are no longer sure of who they are or of how they stand in relation to others. This sense of loss, for artists, philosophers, and writers as well as for social psychologists is often associated with increased industrialization and urbanization. According to some, the modern person lives in a world that is impersonal and unemotional. The contemporary individual is taught to respond to others in terms of specific and often bureaucratically defined roles. Little effort is spent on attempting to relate to others as "total persons." Some would claim that the modern person's outlook is "me" oriented with little concern for the larger collectivities to which "we" may belong. For still others, the modern person has become estranged from himself and, as a result, estranged from others as well. The modern person is no longer a part of making the world; hence, the world is not made to satisfy his or her "true" needs.[75]

In the remainder of this chapter, we shall review some of the thoughts that social psychologists have had on this predicament. Such a consideration may highlight the often complicated but nevertheless important interconnections between the individual and society. We shall first discuss some of the social psychological conceptions of the modern predicament. We shall then discuss how such concepts as self, identity, and role may enhance our understanding of some of the problems of adult life in contemporary society.

The idea that industrialization and urbanization caused a breakdown in interpersonal relationships was a common theme for many nineteenth and twentieth-century social theorists. This theme was expressed in a variety of ways. Ferdinand Toennies distinguished between *Gemeinschaft* (community) and *Gessellschaft* (association).[76] Toennies argued that "communities" are characterized by intimacy, social solidarity, and tradition, whereas societies are more impersonal and individualistic. Similar ideas are evident in Charles Horton Cooley's distinction between "primary" and "nonprimary" groups. The former are typically composed of a small number of people who interact in a direct, personal, and intimate manner; the latter are larger and are composed of individuals who interact for specific purposes that are rational rather than emotional in nature.[77] More recently, the American anthropologist Robert Redfield has distinguished between "folk" and "urban" societies. An important difference between the two concerns the fact that in the latter, people are treated as "things" rather than as "persons." As Redfield puts it,

> A "person" may be defined as that social object which I feel to respond to situations as I do, with all the sentiments and interests which I feel to be my own; a person is myself in another form, his qualities and values are inherent within him, and his significance for me is not merely one of utility. A "thing," on the other hand, is a social object which has no claim upon my sympathies, which responds to me, as I conceive it, mechanically; its value for me exists in so far as it serves my end. In the folk society all human beings admitted to society are treated as persons; one does not deal impersonally ("thing-fashion") with any other participant in the little world of that society.[78]

These conceptions are not unlike Emile Durkheim's distinction between mechanical and organic societies. Durkheim used the term "mechanical" to refer to those types of societies in which most individuals perform similar roles and share essentially the same values. Organic societies on the other hand have a greater division of labor; the roles individuals play are more specialized and interdependent. The transition from mechanical to organic societies for Durkheim entailed a pathological state that he called "anomie." As discussed previously (see Chapter 3), anomie may be described as a breakdown in social norms resulting in a state of "normlessness." In this state, the constraints on human action are weakened. People are no longer sure of who they are or how they are to behave. The guideposts for life, in a sense, are no longer relevant.[79]

COMMUNITY LOST, SAVED, AND LIBERATED

How accurate are various images of societal change? What are their implications for individuals? These questions have underpinned a substantial portion of social psychological thought.

Perhaps the most prevalent theme in social psychological thinking about the modern predicament is the "community lost" idea.[80] This view holds that urbanization in particular has severely strained interpersonal relationships in ways that have had primarily negative consequences for individuals. The modern, urban individual is no longer a member of a solitary community. Rather, he or she belongs to multiple social networks. Membership in these networks is limited by specific interests. Hence, the total person has no place in any of these specific associations. The "community lost" idea contains an image of the individual located in the context of a number of cross-cutting circles. She or he may touch upon many of these circles, but is encompassed by none.

A second view of this problem is the "community saved" idea. This idea highlights the fact that many community-oriented types of social institutions may persist in the context of urbanization and industrialization. Urban ethnographies have often pointed out how informal structures of association may persist in neighborhoods located within urban centers, and especially within kinship units within those neighborhoods.[81] According to this idea, aspects of a more communal or *Gemeinschaft* life may continue in the midst of urban and industrial complexity.

The "community liberated" perspective constitutes a third approach to this issue. The community liberated theme is best expressed by one of its proponents. According to Charles Kadushin,

> this view emphasizes multiple cross-cutting circles or regions of solidarity which coexist with an otherwise loose and incompletely knit system of relations. The individual is offered a "do-it-yourself kit" of primary-like relations based on . . . interest, occupation or past history. The "kit" can be constructed in a variety of different ways using a wide combination of relationships.[82]

Rather than stressing the negative aspects of modern, urban life, the community liberated perspective highlights some of its more positive aspects: diversity, innovation, and the ability to mobilize resources from different networks. Social psychologist Claude Fischer has described what he terms the "unconventional urbanite." Urbanites tend to be more politically radical, less tied to established institutions such as religion, more innovative with respect to marital and familial relationships, and more in tune with recent developments in art, music, and literature.[83] From the perspective of some, all these may appear to constitute "deviant" behavior; from the perspective of others, they are the manifestations of creativity.

As with all social theories, it is difficult to assess which of these perspectives is "correct." Each may have some validity. All sensitize us to the existence of intervening factors in the relationship between individuals and large-scale social change. For example, in a recent study Charles Kadushin examined the role of what he calls social density (i.e., "the proportion of persons in the interpersonal environment who are connected to one another in various ways")[84] in reducing stress among Vietnam war veterans. Kadushin found that association with heterogeneous groups leads to reduced stress in small communities; for those veterans living in larger cities, however, association with a more homogeneous group of others who share their experience appeared to be more beneficial. Among its other implications, this study points to the complex relationships between what sociologists call macrolevel variables (e.g., city size), intervening factors (e.g., the density of one's interpersonal environment), and individual variables such as mental health and stress.

ALIENATION

Some years ago a distinguished panel of social scientists prepared a document issued by the U.S. Department of Health, Education and Welfare *(Toward a Social Report)*. It represented a serious effort to have the federal government issue a yearly social report made up of a number of "social indicators" that, in effect would describe the "social health" of the society. As James Rule has observed, the idea seems to be excellent, since who can possibly be against "social health"? Interestingly, however, one of the "pathological conditions" for which it was felt a social indicator was required was something called "alienation." It was expressed in the following terms:

> People need a sense of belonging, a feeling of community, in some small group. If such associations are lacking, they will feel alienated: they will have a tendency either to "cop out" of the central life of the society, or else try to reverse the direction of the society by extreme or even violent methods. The more numerous and stronger the social ties that bind an individual to the social order, the more likely he is to feel an attachment to the society, and work within existing rules to improve it.[85]

Rule points out that according to these authors, unwillingness to work within existing rules to improve a society is a manifestation of individual or social ill health. "But why," he asks, "not the other way around? Why not bracket those unwilling or unable to face up to the need for drastic change in America as 'sick'? Certainly, for anyone who mistrusts the intentions of those who hold power in America, and who sees little hope for improvement short of major changes in our basic political forms, disaffection from the present regime is reasonable and proper."[86]

This is not the place to attempt to settle the larger issues of who is "correct" in this dispute. Indeed that is probably an inappropriate way of phrasing the issue. To label either side as "sick" seems to involve one in an inappropriate use of the medical analogy.

More relevant for our present purpose is an examination of the term "alienation" and how it is related to "adulthood."

In the words of one distinguished sociologist, "in all the social sciences, the various synonyms of alienation have a foremost place in the studies of human relations. Investigations of the 'unattached,' the 'marginal,' 'the obsessive,' 'the normless,' and the 'isolated' individual all testify to the central place occupied by the hypothesis of alienation in contemporary social science."[87]

The concept has a long history not only in sociology and social psychology but in philosophy, theology, and political theory as well. Linguistically, the term is derived from the Latin noun *alienatio*, which comes from the verb *alienare*, "to take away" or "remove." Latin usage in different contexts, however, led to two different meanings. One of these comes from the usage in the context of transfer of ownership of property. In this context alienation meant "transfer of ownership of something to another person." This usage was quite common in the fifteenth century, and even in our contemporary world the term is often used in political, economic, and legal contexts to mean the transfer of property from one person to another. The second meaning of the term stemmed more directly from the verb *alienare* in the sense of "to cause a separation to occur." In this sense, alienation refers to "a state of separation or dissociation between two elements."[88]

In Christianity, Hinduism, and Buddhism, spiritual alienation has been interpreted as a state of separation or dissociation from God. This was seen as being caused by involvement in worldly (i.e., material and sensuous) affairs. To avoid this, alienation from the physical and social world was encouraged.[89]

Contemporary usage in the social sciences relies heavily upon the work of Hegel, Ludwig Feurbach, and Karl Marx.

For Hegel, alienation was in some ways another term for "growing up"[90] or, as we might put it, for becoming an adult. He saw it as a necessary step in the process of man's spiritual development. If human beings were to become *more* than they are by nature, they must become something *other* than what they are. They cannot simply remain as they are originally. This otherness is alienation. It is achieved by training, culture, education—in short, by becoming what their original nature does not specify them as being.[91]

For Feurbach, human beings have a constant tendency to project outside themselves qualities that properly belong to human nature. Human beings, however, idealize and place these values in a God who becomes everything that have searched for but did not find in themselves. Thus, for Feurbach, religion becomes the very essence of alienation. "It is man's refusal to become all he is capable of being, his unwillingness to find the perfection of human being in being human, relinquishing that responsibility in favor of submission to an alien God who is the idealization of those qualities which in their essence are properly human."[92]

Thus in the work of Feurbach, the concept of alienation has changed from the developmental process or becoming an adult process, which it was in Hegel, to virtually its opposite—a degradation of human beings from what they truly are or should be. In a sense, he was saying that to be alienated is to be *unlike* an adult—in some ways to be childlike. Feurbach, however, did not regard Christianity or other religions as degradations. "He did, however, look upon the failure to recognize the projection involved, precisely as degrading. Man can return to himself only if he realizes that in adoring God he is adoring the ideal in man."[93]

For Marx, religion is a significant manifestation of human alienation but not a *cause* of it: "the sources of that alienation are to be sought elsewhere, and if the uncovering of these sources will permit alienation to be eliminated, it will not be necessary to attack religion. Disalienated man will simply have no need for it."[94]

For Marx, the idea of alienated labor stressed the extent to which individuals have control over their labor and its product. For him, work ideally should be a goal in itself. To the extent that it becomes strictly instrumental— not done for intrinsic satisfaction but for other purposes (making money, etc.)—it becomes alienated labor. "This is most likely to occur in economic systems where labor is bought or owned (that is, where there is a distinction between owners of the means of production and workers, such as in capitalism, feudalism, and slave economies) and where the work is highly mechanized (as in industrialized societies). These conditions are conducive to the alienation of workers."[95]

Perhaps the basis for this analysis is Marx's assumption that the most distinctively human activity is productive labor. Other animals essentially must restrict themselves to what is found in nature; human beings *produce* the satisfaction of their needs. "Man is truly himself only to the extent that through the activity whereby he transforms nature he continues to create himself. But this he cannot do, if either the activity of producing or the product of the activity belongs to another than himself."[96]

In an article that has become something of a classic in the field of social psychology, Melvin Seeman tried to identify the logically distinguishable uses of the concept of alienation. The dimensions he outlined have, with some modification, become the basis for an enormous amount of social-psychological research on alienation in the modern world.[97]

The revised categories are as follows:

Powerlessness—This is the sense of low control versus mastery over events. Seeman, in his original article, saw this as the notion of alienation as it originated in the Marxian view of the worker's condition in capitalist society. The point here was that the worker was alienated to the extent that the prerogatives and means of decisions were appropriated by those who owned the means of production. Specifically, what Seeman saw as this distinctively social-psychological view of alienation could be seen as "the expectancy or probability held by the individual that his own behavior cannot determine the occurrence of the outcomes or reinforcements he seeks."[98]

Meaninglessness—This type is derived from Karl Mannheim's description of the increase in what he called "functional rationality" in the contemporary world and the concomitant decline of "substantial rationality." Mannheim felt that as society increasingly organized its members for the purpose of most efficiently realizing its ends (i.e., when functional rationality increased), there was a parallel decline in the capacity of people to act intelligently on the basis of one's own insight into the interrelations of events. Thus, on this dimension, we can speak of a high degree of alienation when "the individual is unclear as to what he ought to believe—when the individual's minimal standards for clarity in decision-making are not met."[99]

Normlessness—This comes from Durkheim's description of "anomie" (see Chapter 3). Seeman's short definition says "a high expectancy that socially unapproved behaviors are required to achieve given goals."[100]

Cultural Estrangement (called "value isolation" in the original article)—This refers to an individual's rejection of values that are commonly held in the society or a subsector of the society. The opposite pole of the continuum is complete commitment to the standards of the dominant society or subsector.

Self-estrangement—This is Seeman's effort to codify a concept of alienation used by such writers as Erich Fromm and C. Wright Mills. For Fromm, alienation referred to "a mode of experience which the person experiences himself as an alien. He has become one who is 'estranged' from himself. He does not experience himself as the center of his world, as the creator of his own acts—but his acts and their consequences have become his masters, whom he obeys, or whom he may even worship."[101]

C. Wright Mills observed that "In the normal course of her work, because her personality becomes the instrument of an alien purpose, the salesgirl becomes self-alienated."[102] In more general terms, he felt that "Men are estranged from one another as each secretly tries to make an instrument of the other, and in time a full circle is made: One makes an instrument of himself and is estranged from it also."[103]

In Seeman's words, this dimension of alienation referred to "the individual's engagement in activities that are not intrinsically rewarding versus involvement in a task or activity for its own sake."[104]

Social Isolation—This refers to "the sense of exclusion or rejection vs. social acceptance."[105]

Seeman has reviewed the extensive research done on each of these dimensions. Alienation continues to be an active area of research for social psychologists. One effort by another sociologist to redefine the concept may have some important implications for research in this area. Claude S. Fischer has formulated another definition of alienation in an effort to bridge what he sees as the still remaining gap between the theoretical and empirical sides of alienation. It reads as follows: "alienation is the state in which the actor fails to perceive a positive interdependence between himself and social relationships or other objectifications."[106]

Empirical research has associated alienation with what are considered to be a number of modern-day problems, ranging from alcoholism to paranoia. From a societal perspective, however, alienation may be a phenomenon that most all of us come to deal with in our adult lives. In this regard, it perhaps is Erich Fromm who many years ago best characterized the nature of alienation. Alienation is modern society, he told us, is almost total.

Man has created a world of man-made things as it never existed before. He has constructed a complicated social machine to administer the technical machine he built. Yet this whole creation of his stands over and above him. He does not feel himself as a creator and center, but as the servant of a Golem, which his hands have built. The more powerful and gigantic the forces are which he unleashes, the more powerless he feels as a human being. He confronts himself with his own forces embodied in things he has created, alienated from himself. He is owned by his own creatures and has lost ownership of himself.[107]

In a later discussion, Fromm observed that the prevailing high degree of alienation was reflected in a characteristic style of speech—essentially the substitution of nouns for verbs. For example, People speak of *having* a problem, *having* insomnia, *having* a happy marriage rather than saying, "I *am* troubled," "I *cannot* sleep," I *am* happily married." By making these substitutions, Fromm feels, subjective experience is eliminated: "The *I* of experience is replaced by the *it* of possession."[108] The point here is that a problem is not a thing that can be owned; therefore, I cannot *have* a problem. As Fromm puts it, "I have transformed *myself* into a 'problem' and am now owned by my creation. This way of speaking betrays a hidden, unconscious alienation."[109]

From Fromm's perspective, all adults could and indeed *should* have a set of characteristics in common. The qualities they should share include

Willingness to give up all forms of having to fully *be*

Security, sense of identity, and confidence based on faith in what one *is*, on one's need for relatedness, interest, love, and solidarity with the world around one, instead of on one's desire to have, to possess, to control the world and thus become the slave of one's possessions

Making the full growth of oneself and of one's fellow beings the supreme goal of living

Developing one's imagination, not as an escape from intolerable circumstances, but as an anticipation of real possibilities, as a means to do away with intolerable circumstances[110]

The extent to which these possibilities may be truly anticipated in modern society is a question that social psychologists and others might profitably examine.

NOTES

[1]William Blackstone, *Commentaries on the Laws Of England*, quoted in Winthrop D. Jordan, "Searching for Adulthood in America," in Erik H. Erikson, ed., *Adulthood* (New York: W. W. Norton, 1978), p. 191.

[2]Ibid., p. 191.

[3]Joseph Goldstein, "On Being an Adult and Being an Adult in Secular Law," in Erikson, ed., *Adulthood*, p. 249.

[4]Ibid., pp. 250–251.

[5]Tu Wei-Ming, "The Confucian Perception of Adulthood," in Erikson, ed., *Adulthood*, pp. 113–127.

[6]Ibid., p. 113.

[7]Ibid., p. 116.

[8]Ibid., pp. 116–117.

[9]Winthrop D. Jordan, "Searching for Adulthood in America," Erikson, ed., *Adulthood*, p. 189.

[10]Ibid., p. 189.

[11]Stanley Sue and James K. Morishima, *The Mental Health of Asian Americans* (San Francisco: Jossey-Bass, 1982), pp. 70–71.

[12]W. Caudill and H. Weinstein, "Maternal Care and Infant Behavior in Japan and America," *Psychiatry*, Vol. 32 (1969), pp. 12–43, quoted in Thomas P. Rohlen, "The Promise of Adulthood in Japanese Spiritualism," in Erikson, ed., *Adulthood*, p. 130.

[13]Daniel P. Moynihan, *The Negro Family: The Case for National Action* (Washington, D.C.: U.S. Department of Labor, Office of Planning and Research), March 1965.

[14]James E. Blackwell, *The Black Community: Diversity and Unity* (New York: Harper & Row, 1975), p. 53.

[15]Ibid., pp. 53–54.

[16]See George P. Rawick, *The American Slave: A Composite Autobiography*. Vol. 1: From Sundown to Sunup The Making of The Black Community. (Westport, Conn.: Greenwood, 1972) More than 20 additional volumes of edited interviews with ex-slaves have been published in this series.

[17]Ibid., pp. 11–12.

[18]Ibid.

[19]Barbara Sinclair Deckard, *The Women's Movement*, 2nd ed. (New York: Harper & Row, 1979), pp. 402–403. Also, see Betty Friedan, *The Feminine Mystique* (New York: Dell, 1963).

[20]Ibid., p. 403.

[21]Ibid.

[22]Ibid., p. 3.

[23]Ibid.

[24]Ibid.

[25]Ibid.

[26]Ibid.

[27]Sara Delamont, *The Sociology of Women* (Boston: George Allen & Unwin, 1980), p. 97.

[28]Ibid. The experiment referred to was reported by T. K. Broverman et. al., "Sex-Role Stereotypes: A Current Appraisal," *Journal of Social Issues*, Vol. 28, no. 22 (1972), pp. 59–78.

[29]Daniel Levinson, *The Seasons of a Man's Life* (New York: Ballantine, 1978).

[30]Ibid., p. 39.

[31]Ibid., p. 74.

[32]Ibid., p. 41.

[33]Ibid., p. 144.

[34]Robert R. Faulkner, "Coming of Age in Organizations: A Comparative Study of Career Contingencies and Adult Socialization," *Sociology of Work and Occupations*, Vol. 1 (1974), pp. 131–173.

[35]For a review of this research, see Jeylen T. Mortimer and Roberta G. Simmons, "Adult Socialization," *Annual Review of Sociology*, Vol. 4 (1978), pp. 421–454.

[36]Carol Gilligan, *In a Different Voice: Psychological Theory and Women's Development* (Cambridge, Mass.: Harvard University Press, 1982), pp. 159–160.

[37]Ibid., p. 160.

[38]Donald T. Hall, "A Theoretical Model of Career Subidentity Development in Organizational Settings," *Organizational Behavior and Human Performance*, Vol. 6 (1971), pp. 50–76.

[39]Melvin L. Kohn, and Carmi Schoder, *Work and Personality: An Inquiry into the Impact of Social Stratification* (Norwood, N.J.: Ablex, 1983).

[40]John Steiner, "What Price Success," *Harvard Business Review*, Vol. 50 (1972), pp. 69–74.

[41]Mortimer and Simmons, "Adult Socialization," p. 444.

[42]N. A. Cameron, *The Psychology of Behavior Disorders* (Boston: Houghton Mifflin, 1947), p. 465, quoted in Theodore R. Sarbin and V. L. Allen, "Role Theory," in Gardner Lindsey and Elliot Aronson, eds., *The Handbook of Social Psychology*, 2nd ed. (Reading, Mass.: Addison-Wesley, 1968), Vol. I, p. 491.

[43]Quoted in ibid., p. 490.

[44]Ibid.

[45]Ibid., pp. 514–517.

[46]See Erving Goffman, *Stigma: Notes on the Management of Spoiled Identity* (Englewood Cliffs, N.J.: Prentice-Hall, 1963).

[47]Jerold Heiss, "Social Roles," in M. Rosenberg and Ralph H. Turner, eds., *Social Psychology: Sociological Perspectives* (New York: Basic Books, 1981), p. 111.

[48]A. Bandura, *Social Learning Theory* (Englewood Cliffs, N.J.: Prentice-Hall, 1977), pp. 48–49.

[49]See Georg Simmel, "The Stranger," in Kurt Wolff, ed., *The Sociology of Georg Simmel* (New York: The Free Press, 1950), pp. 402–409, and Alfred Schutz, "The Stranger: An Essay in Social Psychology," in Arvid Brodersen, ed., *Collected Papers* (The Hague: Martinus Nijhoff, 1964), Vol. II, pp. 91–106.

[50]Heiss, "Social Roles," pp. 121–122.

[51]Lyman M. Stanford and Marvin B. Scott, *A Sociology of the Absurd* (New York: Appleton-Century-Crofts, 1970), pp. 111–144.

[52]Sarbin and Allen, "Role Theory," p. 544.

[53]Ibid., p. 544.

[54]Robert K. Merton, *Social Theory and Social Structure* (New York: The Free Press, 1957).

[55]Sarbin and Allen, "Role Theory," p. 541.

[56]M. Komarovsky, "Cultural Contradictions and Sex Roles," *American Journal of Sociology*, Vol. 52 (1948), pp. 184–189.

[57]Heiss, "Social Roles."

[58]Sarbin and Allen, "Role Theory," p. 541.

[59]R. H. Turner, "Role-taking: Process vs. Conformity," in A. M. Rose, ed., *Human Behavior and Social Processes* (Boston: Houghton Mifflin, 1962), pp. 20–40.

[60]M. Rosenberg, *Conceiving the Self* (New York: Basic Books, 1979), p. 10.

[61]Ibid., p. 10.

[62]Ibid., pp. 62–77.

[63]Ibid., p. 63.

[64]Sarbin and Allen, "Role Theory," p. 539.

[65]Rosenberg, *Conceiving the Self*, pp. 540–557.

[66]Ibid., pp. 57–62.

[67]S. Stryker and Robert T. Serpe, "Commitment, Identity, Salience and Role Behavior," in William Ickes and Eric S. Knowles, eds., *Personality, Roles and Social Behavior* (New York: Springer-Verlang, 1982), pp. 199–218.

[68]Ibid., p. 207.

[69]Ibid., p. 217.

[70]P. Thoits, "Multiple Identities and Psychological Well-being: A Reformulation and Test of the Social Isolation Hypothesis," *American Sociological Review*, Vol. 48, No. 2 (1983), pp. 174–187.

[71]R. Faris, "Cultural Isolation and the Schizophrenic Personality," *American Journal of Sociology*, Vol. 40 (1934), pp. 155–169.

[72]Thoits, p. 174.

[73]Ibid., "Multiple Identities," p. 175.

[74]Ibid.

[75]Herbert Marcuse, *One Dimensional Man* (Boston: Beacon Press, 1964).

[76]Ferdinand Toennies, *Gemeinschaft and Gesellschaft* (East Lansing: Michigan State University Press, 1957).

[77]Charles H. Cooley, *Social Organization* (New York: Scribners, 1909).

[78]Robert Redfield, "The Folk Society," *American Journal of Sociology*, Vol. 52 (1947), pp. 293–308.

[79]Emile Durkheim, *The Division of Labor in Society* (New York: The Free Press, 1964).

[80]See Charles Kadushin, "Mental Health and the Interpersonal Environment," *American Sociological Review*, Vol. 48 (1983), pp. 189–198.

[81]See Herbert Gans, *The Urban Villagers* (New York: The Free Press, 1962).

[82]Kadushin, "Mental Health," p. 190.

[83]Claude S. Fischer, *The Urban Experience* (New York: Harcourt Brace Jovanovich, 1976), pp. 192–197.

[84]Kadushin, "Mental Health," p. 190.

[85]Quoted in James B. Rule, *Insight and Social Betterment* (New York: Oxford University Press, 1978), p. 15.

[86]Ibid.

[87]Robert A. Nisbet, *The Quest for Community* (New York: Oxford University Press, 1978), p. 15.

[88]Rabindra N. Kanungo, *Work Alienation* (New York: Praeger Publishers, 1982), p. 9.

[89]Ibid., pp. 9–10.

[90]Quentin Lauer, S.J., "Alienation: Marxist Social Category," In William C. Bier, S.J., ed., *Alienation: Plight of Modern Man*, p. 12 (New York: Fordham University Press, 1972). For Hegel's detailed treatment, see G. W. F. Hegel, *Phenomenology of Mind*, translated by J. B. Baillie (New York: Harper & Row, 1957). (Note: The original German is probably more accurately translated as *Philosophy of Spirit*).

[91]Ibid., p. 12.

[92]Ibid.

[93]Ibid. For a more detailed presentation of Feurbach's view, see Ludwig Feurbach, *The Essence of Christianity*, translated by G. Eliot (New York: Harper & Row, 1957). The original edition was published in 1841.

[94]Ibid., p. 15.

[95]S. I. Lauer, "Alienation: Marxist Social Category," p. 15.

[96]S. J., Lauer, "Alienation: Marxist Social Category," pp. 16–17.

[97]The original article is Melvin Seeman, "On the Meaning of Alienation," *American Sociological Review*, Vol. 24, (December 1959), pp. F83–F91. A revision of the initial categories appears in Melvin Seeman, "Alienation and Engagement," in A. Campbell and P. E. Converse, eds., *The Human Meaning of Social Change* (New York: Russell Sage, 1972). A comprehensive review of social psychological research in this area will be found in Melvin Seeman, "Alienation Studies," in Alex Inkeles, James Coleman, and Neil Smelser, eds., *Annual Review of Sociology*, Palo Alto, Calif.: Annual Reviews, 1975), Vol. I. This article has been reprinted as "Current Research Findings," in R. Felix Geyer and David R. Schweitzer, *Theories of Alienation: Critical Perspectives in Philosophy and the Social Sciences* (Leiden: Martinus Nijhoff Social Sciences Division, 1976), pp. 265–305.

[98]Seeman, "On the Meaning of Alienation," p. 784.

[99]Ibid., p. 786. For a more complete discussion of Mannheim's ideas in this connection, see Karl Mannheim, *Man and Society in an Age of Reconstruction* (New York: Harcourt Brace & World, 1940).

[100]Ibid., p. 788.

[101]Erich Fromm, *The Sane Society* (New York: Holt, Rinehart and Winston, 1959), p. 120.

[102]C. Wright Mills, *White Collar* (New York: Oxford, 1951), p. 184.

[103]Ibid., p. 188.

[104]Seeman, "Alienation Studies," pp. 93–94.

[105]Ibid., p. 94.

[106]Claude S. Fischer, "Alienation: Trying to Bridge the Chasm," *British Journal of Sociology*, Vol. 27, no. 1 (March 1976), p. 43.

[107]Erich Fromm, *The Sane Society* (New York: Holt, Rinehart and Winston, 1955), pp. 124–125.

[108]Erich Fromm, *To Have or to Be* (New York: Harper & Row, 1981), pp. 21–22.

[109]Ibid., p. 22.

[110]Ibid., pp. 171–172.

CHAPTER TEN
GROWING OLD—
Problems of Aging

CULTURAL VARIABILITY

If you live long enough—anywhere in the world—eventually you will enter the ranks of "the aged" and be perceived as being "old." In the idiom of anthropology, "All societies have some system of age-grading which classifies individuals by age and ascribes different statuses and roles in terms of this classification."[1]

Among the Igbo people of eastern Nigeria, you are considered "aged" when you become chiefly a recipient rather than a furnisher of goods and services. This happens when your children have become mature and have established their own households. It also helps to have gray hair and to have accumulated some possessions. The respect and status accorded aged men in this society is justified largely on religious grounds. These men are intermediaries between ancestors and various spiritual beings whose good graces are required by all. It has been suggested, however, that as traditional religious controls disappear under conditions of "modernization," aged persons in this society will lose much of the status, power, and respect they had under more traditional conditions.[2]

In Samoa, we are told,[3] both old and young seem to view old age as a desirable stage of life. The aged are not threatened with economic insecurity; on the contrary, they seem to be more secure than ever and to enjoy the benefits of a higher status in society. They do not "retire" but engage in any kind of work they feel capable of performing. Since, for example, Samoans feel that the aged have more patience than younger persons, they often perform work that is more tedious but less demanding physically than others. They may also be asked to fill various honorific but relatively undemanding positions in the community. The high status of the aged in this society appears to be unrelated to property rights. Unlike older folks in some other societies, aged Samoans do not maintain their position by threatening to disinherit younger family members. All land is owned communally by an entire extended family and cannot be disposed of by a family head without the consent of the entire group, which may number hundreds of individuals.

This family structure seems to have been maintained even after the introduction of strong Western influences. Traditionally, Samoans were all required to contribute the products of their labor to the family head whose responsibility it was to distribute these among family members according to their needs. For years after, during which time Samoans earned their livings by working at such places as tuna canneries established by large Western corporations or on government jobs, informal surveys suggested that most of them continued to give at least a portion of their earnings to family heads to be distributed in the traditional manner.[4]

It is, however, in "old" China that respect for the aged assumed perhaps its most extreme form (in the eyes of "modern" Americans).[5]

There, we are told, people literally *wanted* to be old or at least to appear old because of the privileges enjoyed by older people. When two people of different ages met, the older one could speak freely while the younger one was expected to listen respectfully. As men grew older, their authority (we are told less about the experience of women) increased enormously. The significant unit of social life was neither an individual person nor the nation-state; it was what Lin Yutang has called the "great stream of family life."[6] Age, in itself, seems to have brought with it authority. "Man himself passes through the stages of childhood, youth, maturity and old age: first being taken care of by others; first obeying and respecting others, and later being obeyed and respected in proportion as he grows older."[7]

A sensitive Chinese scholar, Francis L. K. Hsu[8], has noted some of the more salient differences between attitudes of Americans and Chinese toward old age. Thus, he observes, at middle age, Americans tend to turn toward regimes that give them a sense of continuing youthfulness. Men find awakened interests in sports while, it seems to him, that American women seek out beauticians and masseuses who promise to maintain some of the glamor that appears to be slipping away.

To the average Chinese, however, old age has historically marked the beginning of a loftier and more respected status. Unlike Americans for whom old age often means the likelihood of a lowered standard of living, older Chinese have characteristically had no fear of unemployment or economic hardship with the onset of old age. Long before the Chinese become unable to work because of physical difficulties associated with old age, they tended to retire and live on the fruits of the labor of their children. If older persons do wish to continue working, they are not seen as handicapped by reason of age. On the contrary, if equally qualified, they may be preferred to younger persons. Beyond this relative degree of economic security, older persons in Chinese society have traditionally enjoyed an enhanced social importance. Older Chinese men and women do *not* tend to restrict their associations to persons of their own age. Younger persons of all ages tend to seek their counsel and company; they do not exclude their elders from recreational activities (such as gambling). Within the home, older persons living under the same roof as younger members of their family tend to exercise full control of significant decisions even if they do not continue to be "breadwinners." Even when children live apart from their parents, the advice of older members of the family continues to be sought on important affairs.[9]

In short, as one moves about the world examining various cultures, there seem to exist marked variations in the social psychology of aging. Aged people in different societies seem to think of themselves and to be regarded by others quite differently. Perhaps the central issue has to do with varying modes of dealing with the problem of power or status. Thus among Burmese villagers, we are told, older persons tend to lose their interest in worldly affairs, leave mundane, everyday tasks to younger members of the family, and devote their time to religious activities (that will help them to acquire merit for existence after death) and to meditation. Similarly, in Thailand, despite great deference to the aged, real power in the society tends to be held by middle-aged rather than older persons. Many older Thai men, having relinquished worldly power, enter the priesthood.[10] In several traditional societies of the Middle East and Africa, it is the task of younger men to deal with threats from enemies in this world whereas older men retain their power by dealing with threats from supernatural sources.[11]

In societies where the aged have not managed to retain power through their relationship with supernatural beings, they seem to have many more difficulties. Thus, among Indians of Mexico and the American Southwest, men who had become too old to serve as a warrior or hunter were characteristically forced to perform menial tasks. They were placed under control of women and were compelled to help the women do their work. In this sense, they occupied approximately the same status as children. One study of a Mexican village reported that while men were typically more exuberant than women, they were also more anxious and insecure. The researcher concluded that as men grew older, they lost their dominant position in society and appeared to be more disturbed, impulsive, and anxious.[12]

Interestingly, it would appear that while men, in most societies, begin from a position of power and lose this as they grow older, the reverse seems to be the case with respect to women. Thus Japanese men have been found to be more highly extroversive than women until age 60, after which their scores decline and they become less so than the average female. In Bali, older women often succeed to the power previously held exclusively by males and may become active heads of households. Samoan older women, it is reported, can say things that no other group in society would dare. Among Hindus in Indian society, older men retain legal status as heads of the households, but their wives see to it that their orders are carried out.[13]

CHANGES IN CULTURAL PATTERNS OF AGING

An important question to raise with respect to these cultural characteristics is, "To what extent are these traditional cultural patterns relating to age changed as a by-product of more broadly engineered social change?"

In many "underdeveloped" societies, we have seen evidence of modifications of traditional views toward aging and other matters as "industrialization" becomes more prevalent and as the daily life in these societies tends to approximate more closely the patterns found in the United States and Europe.

China, however, represents a markedly different situation. Here, a massive effort has been made to establish a communist society (although many communists as well as socialists throughout the world would deny that this is in fact what has been done). In any event, it is clear that massive social changes have occurred over a relatively short period of time, and it seems appropriate to inquire about the impact these changes have had on the role and status of older persons in Chinese society. Historically, age has been, as we have previously suggested, an important and even a central source of authority within Chinese society. Parents had absolute authority over their children and could go so far as to commit infanticide without fear of being punished by the legal system. Marriages were arranged by parents, and children were expected to acquiesce in these decisions.

After the revolution, of course, all remnants of legislation that required children to obey parents in the traditional manner were eliminated. Initially, the emphasis after the revolution was on the young. Young workers were given awards for productivity in industry and agriculture; young leaders took charge of political campaigns against those who opposed the revolution. Parents were increasingly portrayed as relics who opposed land reform or chose the wrong kind of marriage partners for their children. Young people, on the contrary, were described increasingly as progressive and leaders of social change.[14]

This pattern seems, however, to have undergone several successive changes. A study of stories published in China between 1962 and 1966 reported a "resurgence of stern parental authority."[15] During the Cultural Revolution that followed this period, on the other hand, criticism of older persons became fashionable and received official sanction. Young people were encouraged to regard virtually everyone over the age of 40 as a counterrevolutionary. This form of prejudice and discrimination was rejected again after the coup in 1976 that deposed the "Gang of Four." Among the sins if not the crimes with which the Gang was charged was their rude and disrespectful treatment of older officials in the government.[16]

In the countryside, these shifts of attitude have apparently been much less dramatic. Here, the traditions of respect, deference, and even obedience to older persons have remained strongly entrenched. Thus, in the rural villages where it has been estimated that 85 percent of the Chinese population continue to live, support of the aged continues to be a family tradition. Older persons live with their children when they are too old to engage in conventional work activities. Characteristically, it is only those older persons who do not have children, or those whose children for one reason or another are unable to support them, who receive what we might regard as welfare from common funds. In some countryside areas, old-age homes (Houses of Respect) are operated for the indigent, childless aged.[17]

As compared with the position of virtually complete power traditionally held by older persons in China, it would appear that their status has declined considerably. Legal restrictions have been placed upon parental power, and young people have been allowed to hold some leadership positions. The position of the aged, however, continues to be quite high. This has been attributed not exclusively to a continuation of old cultural attitudes, but to have come about in connection with some structural changes in Chinese society. Thus older persons continue to hold power not only in the central government (where their status is derived from their participation in the original revolution) but in local urban residential neighborhoods as well. Here, retired persons who have plenty of time available are organized to serve as agents of the state and furnish free administrative, social, and police services to the local community. Performing these tasks gives them a degree of authority, which, along with the traditional respect accorded older persons, solidifies their position. All this has inevitable consequences for how the aged view themselves, how they are viewed by others, and how society deals with problems of aging.[18]

AGING IN THE UNITED STATES: AN HISTORICAL OVERVIEW

Old age awaits most of us. Death, however, seems to be a much more definite state of affairs—for all practical purposes, you either are or you are not dead (despite some lively debates among some physicians, philosophers, and theologians about the precise requirements of death). Old age is a much more elusive phenomenon. Changes occur not only from society to society but even within the same society, despite the powerful forces that work to maintain traditional attitudes and practices.

Historians tell us that in American society old age has always been perceived as a distinct phase of the life cycle. What makes this at least somewhat remarkable is that human beings, during perhaps most of their recorded history, did not view "childhood" as a special period of human development, and the concept of "adolescence" does not appear to have arisen until the end of the nineteenth century (see Chapter 6).[19]

Although the concept of "old age" seems to have been with us throughout American history, there apparently has never existed a definition of the exact age when this stage begins. Although the Social Security system and other government programs have made age 65 fashionable, other definitions have from time to time included the ages of 55, 60, 62, 63, 64, 67, 70, 72, and 75. Moreover, throughout American history, there have always been many who insist that old age cannot be defined precisely in chronological terms.[20]

In the period before the Civil War, longevity was frequently used as an ideological weapon to demonstrate the advantages of the climate and social arrangements found in the United States. Impressive efforts were made to "prove" that life expectancy in the United States was greater than it was in

Europe or elsewhere. The life-styles of older persons were examined in an effort to derive hints about which were most effective for promoting a long and healthful life. "Scientists and popular commentators alike emphasized that the elderly proved the efficacy of temperance, moderation, industry and exercise in prolonging life and promoting health. In so doing, they underscored the value of the aged's example."[21]

The aged were used as exemplars in another sense. Prior to the Civil War, the old members of society were regarded as worthy models of virtuous and moral behavior. Aged persons could provide effective moral counsel and instruction to younger persons because their insights and experience had presumably been proven successful. Beyond this, they were seen to possess useful insights about virtually all aspects of farming and the details of any other trade, profession, or job they practiced. Older persons were frequently elected to high public office. In the private sector, mandatory retirement for the "aged" did not exist: "the idea that a person automatically stopped working at a pre-scribed age is absent from pre–Civil War definitions of the word."[22]

Despite what appears to be the favorable light in which older persons were regarded in this country prior to the Civil War, growing old was accompanied by many serious problems. Chronic illnesses and physical disabilities among the aged were much more prevalent than they were late in the twentieth century. When these difficulties made it impossible for older persons to continue working, economic difficulties increased enormously. Since formal retirement programs did not exist either in the private or public sector, older workers forced to stop working had to rely on their savings or assets to survive. Aged farmers might sell part of their land; laborers tried to obtain jobs that were less demanding in terms of physical activity. In general, however, many, if not most, people entered the ranks of the poor as they became "old"—however that was defined. Thus it has been estimated that more than 25 percent of all elderly men during the period of the Civil War had estates worth less than $100; women were even more poverty stricken. Slaveowners often freed slaves to avoid the responsibility of caring for them when they were too old or too disabled to work.[23]

These difficulties seemed to encourage the development of unpleasant personality traits among older persons. They seemed to complain excessively about their physical difficulties; uncertainties about their economic condition seemed to make them greedy; feeling useless and neglected seemed to increase their indifference to people and things about them and to their own physical appearance as well.

After the Civil War, negative attitudes toward the aged became much more pronounced. Instead of seeing older persons as stately and healthy, popular writers increasingly portrayed them as ugly and disease ridden. Instead of being praised for the practical and moral wisdom associated with old age, they were described in terms suggesting they were incapable of making useful contributions to society.[24]

The development of large-scale corporations and government bureaucracies reduced the need to tap the wisdom of "old fogeys." Since presumably society was changing at a rapid rate, wisdom based on outmoded social conditions was no longer relevant. "Youth" was the stage of life that could best adapt to these conditions and ensure continued "progress."[25]

Interestingly, research by natural and social scientists in the period between World War I and World War II served to confirm the then popular view that "old age was a period of pronounced physical decay, mental decline, undesirable psychological and behavioral traits, economic uselessness, personal isolation, and social segregation."[26]

More recent research has raised serious doubts about the scientific basis for such a judgment. Thus, more recent investigators have criticized early studies of the physiological and pathological manifestations of the aging process. Earlier studies exaggerated the degree of degeneration of old age because most of those studies were based on observations of older persons who were either institutionalized or disabled. Since more than 95 percent of elderly Americans are *not* institutionalized, and since the most severely incapacitated older persons are over the age of 75, it has been charged that the earlier studies were seriously biased. More recent studies are concentrating on aging processes among "normal" and "healthy" persons as well as those who have been studied traditionally. Thus contemporary survey research data indicate that 57.7 percent of all persons over the age of 65 are not prevented from performing basic work tasks because of physical limitations. Some 5.2 percent are restricted to some extent, while an additional 20.7 percent have chronic physical conditions that raise major limitations. It is the remaining 16.4 percent that are unable to carry out primary work activities. It scarcely seems reasonable to use the infirmities of the 16.4 percent to characterize the entire population of aged persons. Beyond this, studies have indicated that compensatory mechanisms and capacities often develop among aged persons. Thus, although older people characteristically work more slowly than do younger persons, the quality and accuracy of their work seems to offset this difficulty.[27]

With respect to intellectual acuity, a great deal of new evidence has virtually destroyed some early studies that postulated a curvilinear relationship between age and intelligence and suggested that older persons, in effect, became less intelligent as they grew older. "It now appears clear that earlier studies were actually measuring differences in educational levels and cognitive processes among various age groups, but were not proving that physiological changes in old age diminish mental capacities."[28]

On the contrary, recent studies indicate that people who remain in good health and continue to use their skills either maintain or improve their intelligence until the age of 70 and beyond. With respect to personality traits, research indicates significant variations among older persons with respect to general life satisfaction and overall psychological well-being. There seems to exist a considerable amount of variability among old people with respect to these factors. Individual differences among persons do not decrease as people become older. Differences between older and younger generations are increasingly being explained not in terms of age but rather on the basis of differences in the respective socialization processes each generation has experienced and because of differences in life conditions associated with being at different points of the life cycle. Old and young people share similar sets of values, goals, fears, and needs—at least these do not vary by reason of age alone.[29]

This, however, is not completely accurate. Some shifts in value orientation among aged persons as well as others do seem to be necessary for various reasons. The proportion of persons who live beyond their mid-seventies seems to be steadily increasing. As Martin B. Loeb and Edgar F. Borgotta have pointed out in a highly perceptive article,[30] our culture has become accustomed to addressing various physical and social problems from the perspective of providing "cures." Others have referred to this propensity as the "medical" model of dealing with problems. The point made by Loeb and Borgatta, however, is that "our service system is not tuned properly because our value system has not yet moved to the idea of reducing discomfort. As a matter of fact, within our value heritage, there is still some strength in the notion that one should learn to live with discomfort and adversity."[31]

Thus they cite the hospice movement as an approach that shocks many persons in the United States. Since the aim of the hospice is to make persons who are about to die as comfortable as possible during their last weeks or days on this earth, many techniques used violate all the precepts of "good practice." Thus in England heroin may be provided to dying patients, whereas American physicians, or at least their advocates, insist that such drugs are addictive and, therefore, should not be used. But this, as Loeb and Borgatta point out, seems to stem from a value orientation that places curing above caring.[32]

From the perspective of older persons, a shift in fundamental value orientation often seems to be what is demanded of them. In the United States, the work ethic is still widely pervasive. People are expected work at *something* throughout most of their lives. Even those who have independent financial means usually find it convenient to establish some role in society in which they can perform at least nominally "useful" tasks. Upon reaching that vague state popularly referred to as "old age," they are expected to adopt a set of values that, in their younger years, would have earned them such epithets as "lazy," "good-for-nothing," "worthless," "tramp," and worse. Since persons socialized in these cultures have spent lifetimes deriving their satisfactions from work, the prospect of entering into this new arena understandably poses severe problems for persons who feel that they must continue to work to maintain their basic identity.

How to deal with these shifts in value orientation represents an area of research that is still in its early stages in this country.

THEORIES OF AGING

Answers to such questions as "What does it mean to an individual person to be 'old'?" "Are old people 'well-adjusted'?" "What is it about old age that makes a person either happier or unhappier or well adjusted or maladjusted?" have probably been asked in one form or another throughout recorded history and in every nonliterate society as well. Many "commonsense" answers to questions such as these have been incorporated in more sophisticated theoretical statements that undertake to provide comprehensive explanations for them and for related questions as well. Some of these theories have emerged from extensive research undertakings; others represent codifications of knowledge and insight presumably either verifiable or already verified in some measure by completed research. At this point in time, it is fair to note that there still exists a considerable amount of controversy about the "truth" of each of these theories or at least about the level of general applicability that can be claimed for them. It is also fair to note that many additional theoretical formulations exist beyond the ones for which formal names are available. We shall try to suggest the nature of these throughout our discussion.

Activity Theory

This is an old, "commonsensical" orientation that was first formulated explicitly several decades ago by the authors of an extensive study of older people. How can older people be made happy? In a word, by keeping busy—active. "It may be expected that personal adjustment will be related to activity in such a way that the more active people—mentally, physically, socially—are the better adjusted."[33]

In these terms, the statement is more of a simple hypothesis. The researchers undertook to test it in "Prairie City"—described as a typical Corn Belt town. Personal adjustment was measured in two ways: (1) with an "Attitude Inventory" designed to measure the respondent's feelings of happiness, usefulness, and satisfaction with his or her activities, health, and economic status, and (2) with the "Cavan Adjustment Rating Scale," in which three raters decide about the general level of adjustment based on responses to an extensive questionnaire and additional information obtained about the respondent through observations made during the interview itself or at various organizational meetings.

"Activity" was measured through the use of a "role instrument" made up of a set of 13 role areas. Respondents were rated by four judges on a scale from 0 to 9 to reflect the degree of activity in each role area. The areas included activities in family relationships and in group or individual relationships (e.g., clubs, church activities, peer relationship), participation in community affairs including civic and work activities. The scale was called "Home Responsibilities," and it consisted of the following items:

0. Lives in an institution where care is given by others. Has no responsibility.
1. Lives in boarding or rooming house. Has no responsibility.
2. Lives with children or relatives. Has no responsibility.
3. Lives with family or in institution. Does odd tasks.
4. Assists children with upkeep or work in the home.
5. If in institution, takes care of self. Shares home with children. Also assumes some responsibility.
6. Is nominal head of household. Responsibility is carried by children or others.
7. Is head of house. Children or others take few responsibilities.
8. Shares responsibility for home with spouse or others, but has own tasks. Is independent; takes full responsibility for home.[34]

The researchers concluded that while age and socioeconomic status are only slightly related to personal adjustment, activity and social approval are closely related to it. In short, "what a person *does* is more important to his happiness than what he *is*."[35]

From a social interactionist perspective, activity theory can be viewed as a logical derivative of how one obtains a conception of his or her self and the social roles in any given society through which this self-conception is derived.[36]

Thus in any society, some self-conceptions and roles are more highly regarded than others. In the United States in the twentieth century, presumably the ideal male self-conception is that of a mature adult man who is at the height of his powers in a work role or "position" he has reached competitively through his own efforts. At the time of retirement, such a man has a well-developed self-image as a person who is competent, successful at some kind of work, self-supporting, and able to provide for his family. This self-image has been constructed over a period of years through the favorable reactions of family, friends, co-workers, and others in the society whose opinions he values. After retirement, however, the means for carrying on with this social role and this self-perception tend to disappear. The man is "a lawyer without a case, a bookkeeper without books, a machinist without tools."[37] Moreover, he is excluded from his former co-workers and, as a retired person, begins to find a different evaluation of himself in the minds of other people than the evaluation he enjoyed as an employed person. "He no longer sees respect in the eyes of former subordinates, praise in the faces of former superiors, and approval in the manner of former co-workers. The looking glass composed of his former important group throws back a changed image: he is done for, an old timer, old fashioned, on the shelf."[38]

Not surprisingly, our hero cannot accept this new evaluation. He has had the old self-image for many years, and it is no longer dependent upon current reflections of himself in the expressions and manners of others. "Any movement toward solving the conflict is made difficult because the new self-image offered by those around him is of lower valuation than his internalized self-image."[39]

To deal with this problem, according to activity theory, three things are necessary: (1) a culturally approved set of values for old age that can be used as the basis for a new self-conception by older persons, (2) the general acceptance of these values by the larger society as well as the specific groups to which the older person belongs or finds important, and (3) the construction of new roles (activities) through which the retired person can give expression to his or her new self-image."[40]

Activity theorists have provided similar analyses to deal with the roles of women in American society. It is probably true that in both cases the "typical" roles described are considerably "out of date," but activity theorists would insist that the general points made are sound even if the specifics of role and self-conception undergo changes as they do in any society through time and in different societies. In short, activity theory asserts that

> except for the inevitable changes in biology and in health, older people are the same as middle-aged people, with essentially the same psychological and social needs. . . . the decreased social interaction that characterizes old age results from the withdrawal by society from the aging person; and the decrease in interaction proceeds against the desires of most aging men and women. The older per-

son who ages optimally is the person who stays active and who manages to resist the shrinkage of his social world. He maintains the activities of middle age as long as possible and then finds substitutes for those activities he is forced to relinquish: substitutes for work when he is forced to retire; substitutes for friends and loved ones whom he loses by death.[41]

Disengagement Theory

Disengagement theory was first expressed in an article that appeared in 1960. Since then, it has become perhaps the most widely discussed theory in this field and has often been put forward as an alternative to activity theory.

The original article began with a complaint: "We have no social-psychological theories of aging—which is surprising when we consider the number of our theories of development and maturation."[42] It then proceeded to describe an "implicit" theory to which it would offer an "explicit alternative." The implicit theory was activity theory that assumed that older persons required new activities. The new theory—disengagement theory—would hold that older individuals cooperate in the disengagement occurring between themselves and society. In effect this was natural and good.

The article went on to report on the formulation and testing of hypotheses about social psychological changes "inherent" in the aging process. These hypotheses were focused on the central idea that the "freedom" of old age results from a decreasing amount and variety of interaction. They dealt with the process involved in this change of interaction pattern and suggested that it is preceded by a changed perception of the self. A final hypothesis stated that there is a change in the quality of interactions engaged in by older people.[43]

These hypotheses were tested in a study of 211 persons who were interviewed successively three times at intervals of about six months. Some of the subjects were drawn from a panel of healthy adults between the ages of 50 and 70; the remainder were drawn from a special study of ambulatory old people between the ages of 70 and 90.

On the basis of this study, a "tentative" theory of aging was formulated. This theory pictured individuals as participating, along with others, in a process of mutual withdrawal rather than being deserted by others. This seemed to begin during the sixth decade of life, with a shift in self-perception that reflected a beginning of anticipatory socialization to the state of being aged. The shift in perception was accompanied by a reduction in the number of interactions in which individuals undertook to become involved and by a subsequent reduction in the number of hours each day spent in the company of other persons. In addition, it was concluded that a shift in the quality of interaction with others took place. The aged chose a wider variety of "relational" rewards than did middle-aged persons. This resulted in a more "self-centered and idiosyncratic style of behavior among the ambulatory aged.[44]

A more detailed report of findings from what was called the "Kansas City Study of Adult Life" appeared the following year in a book authored by Elaine Cumming and William E. Henry called *Growing Old: The Process of Disengagement*.[45]

Both Cumming and Henry have subsequently revised the theory, but the early formulation still seems to capture its essence:

> In our theory aging is an inevitable mutual withdrawal or disengagement, result-ing in decreased interaction between the aging person and others in the social system he belongs to. The process may be initiated by the individual or by others in the situation. The aging person may withdraw more markedly from some classes of people while remaining relatively close to others. His withdrawal may be ac-companied from the outset by an increased preoccupation with himself; certain institutions in society may make the withdrawal easy for him. When the aging process is complete, the equilibrium which existed in middle life between the individual and his society has given way to a new equilibrium characterized by a greater distance and an altered type of relationship.[46]

As others have explained it, in every culture and historical period, both the society and individual prepare for the ultimate disengagement of death by an inevitable, gradual, and mutually satisfying process of social disengage-ment. The individual withdraws from society, and the society withdraws from the individual. Individuals want to disengage and do so by reducing the number and variety of roles they play and relationships in which they are involved. They also reduce the intensity of those that remain. The new or remaining sets of relationships are qualitatively different from those in which the individ-uals were formerly engaged. They tend to be more socioemotional and ex-pressive. Society offers the individuals freedom from various structural constraints and in effect gives them permission to withdraw. This process, once set in motion, is irreversible. Individuals withdraw from their customary social world and are to a considerable degree relieved of the usual controls that society imposes on its members. Thus the older persons become "desocialized" and can proceed with the process of disengagement. All this has the function of giving the aging person high morale and on the other hand of removing older persons from roles that can then be filled by younger per-sons. Although variations in this process may occur depending upon the in-dividual's physiology, personality, and life situation, the process itself is universal and inevitable.[47]

If one returns to the original article, it is interesting to observe the ex-tent to which the authors of disengagement theory were inspired by the work of Emile Durkheim and specifically his book *Suicide*. The researchers had noted that interviewers of healthy older persons frequently observed more spontaneity, less concern about approval in the interview situation, and in general a more "carefree" manner than was the case with younger respondents. The researchers summed up these features by calling them "eccentricity," "freedom from sanctions," and "egocentricity." They called this constellation of characteristics "permitted deviance" because they saw them as traits that would be considered "deviant" for middle-aged persons. They then reasoned that this appearance of deviance must have its source in decreased social con-trol and then developed the notion that the difference between middle-aged and older persons would be found in the degree to which they each were in-volved socially. Here the thought developed that middle-aged persons were fully engaged in life outside themselves whereas the aged were relatively dis-engaged from it.[48]

To provide more of the "flavor" of what they meant, the researchers then quoted the following passage from Durkheim's *Suicide*: "society is still lacking in [the child] . . . it begins to retreat from the [aged] . . . or, what amounts to the same thing, he retreats from it."[49]

In effect, Durkheim[50] was suggesting that *the social bond was much less strong on the very young and the very old.* The very young had not yet been sufficiently socialized, and the very old had begun the process of desocialization or disengagement.

Disengagement theory, however, seems to assume the continuation of social control well beyond the onset of the "disengagement" years. Disengagement is not so much a decision or inclination of older persons themselves as it is, in effect, a socially prescribed rule—one formulated for the "good" of the social system. Furthermore, like other "functionalist" theories,[51] the requirements of the social system apparently are regarded as fundamental rather than the needs of individual persons. Finally, disengagement theory insists upon what is essentially its universal character—what the social system must do if it is to maintain its equilibrium.[52]

It has become part of the folklore about modern American society and other industrial or incipient postindustrial societies that "achievement" is the most important goal for individual persons. This involves performance of socially acceptable tasks in a highly "efficient" manner. The proponents of disengagement theory assume, for example, that "In American life where achievement is perhaps the highest value, its abandonment has always been tinged with failure."[53] It is thus to be anticipated that giving up the quest for achievement would constitute a crisis in the lives of older persons who are more or less suddenly confronted with the necessity for giving up this goal (i.e., when faced with retirement). In dealing with "typical" or "modal" behavior in this connection, disengagement theory often seems to rely upon culturally bound stereotypes and inaccurate generalizations. Thus in discussing the relative problems of older men and women, we find statements such as the following: "Most married couples with children, no matter what secondary roles they may hold, have a basic division of labor in which the husband plays a core instrumental role vis-à-vis his family by working, and the wife a core socio-emotional one by maintaining their home and caring for their children."[54]

The point is that men are seen as having no clear-cut roles upon retirement, and it is presumably more difficult for them to adjust to retirement than it is for women who tend to do the same sort of thing they have been doing throughout their lives. In an era in which women increasingly are trying to eradicate the deep prejudices and discriminatory practices broadly referred to as "sexism," stereotyped thinking of this sort is, at the very least, most unfortunate. Throughout the years, there have been a variety of other criticisms of disengagement theory. These include the following:

1. Disengagement is not a process characteristic only of older persons. Thus some studies have indicated that disengagement seems to be more a function of individual subjective factors and the previous life history of the individuals involved. "Whether for research or policy issues," we are told, "to treat the aging population as a homogeneous class of persons does violence to the facts of the matter."[55]

2. Disengaged older persons are not necessarily the happiest ones, and there is some evidence to suggest that the reverse is more true (i.e., engaged elderly persons are more satisfied with their lives and are happier than are those who are disengaged.)[56]

3. Disengagement, to the extent that it does occur among the elderly, is a "function of American culture in this phase of its organization, not a universal for all time. American culture accords a low status to the elderly; we have youth-centered society. Many other societies accord special prestige and power to the elderly, do not disengage them from adult roles, or create new age-graded roles of importance for them."[57] Here, again, the thrust of the criticism is against the functionalist nature of disengagement theory. "The functionalists' assumption that 'whatever is, must be' merely ruins an initially valid observation by exaggerating it and denying any possibility of counter trends by declaring its inevitability."[58]

Role Exit

In view of the enormous amount of evidence and arguments available to contradict disengagement theory, its persistence for so many years becomes an interesting social-psychological question in itself. Zena Smith Blau has tried to explain this phenomenon by referring to the *Zeitgeist* of the 1950s and 1960s in this country. She characterizes the 1950s as a "regressive period" in American history. Americans, after the upheavals of the Great Depression and World War II, wearied of reform, social change, liberalism, and internationalism. The dominant mood of the country seemed to be one of conservatism. "A Republican general occupied the Presidency, there was a fear of political and ideological subversion. A preoccupation with the acquisition of material goods was aided and abetted by the saying, 'Buy now, pay later.' "[59]

Beyond this, Blau tells us, the Feminine Mystique continued to provide an excuse for middle-class white women to remain outside the labor force while they continued to bear more children. Younger workers resented the protection given by the seniority system to older workers in industry. This helped to induce managements and unions to set up private pension plans. These, together with the reduced minimum age requirement under Social Security (age 62), encouraged early retirement.

Blau sees all this as heightening the appeal of disengagement theory:

> If indeed disengagement is "normal and inevitable" then surely the incentive offered workers to retire, the pressure exerted on workers reluctant to retire, and the penalties inflicted on workers over sixty-five by the Social Security system could all be justified as being in the best interest of older workers and society in general. Resisting retirement could be construed as somehow abnormal and inappropriate in face of the inevitable and inexorable process of disengagement that purportedly characterizes old age.[60]

In her search for an alternate theoretical explanation of the social-psychological difficulties facing older persons, Blau introduces the concept of "role exits" that occur

> whenever any stable pattern of interaction and shared activities between two or more persons ceases. Loss, separation, departure, and ending are terms that

signify exit from a social role. They are events that engender a sense of loss, sadness, depression, and uncertainty analogous in character to the state of bereavement precipitated by the death of a beloved person. The bereavement process is precipitated not merely by the actual death of a significant other but also by the termination of any significant enduring pattern of activity shared between two or more people.[61]

The point is that many problems of old age are not direct results of the aging process but rather the results of the role exits that occur in old age (e.g., retirement or widowhood). Both according to Blau, are "roleless" statuses. They do not carry, as is usually the case with other statuses, a set of culturally prescribed rights and duties toward others in the social system.[62]

Role exits occur throughout the life cycle; they are not the sole possession of older persons. Divorce, graduation from school or college, entering school for the first time, becoming unemployed—all are illustrations of role exits that may occur at varying ages. For children, continuing membership in a family characteristically provides a support mechanism that helps them to deal with the strains of successive role exits in school and with peer groups. Blau sees adolescence as a difficult period precisely because it is a time at which young people are required to exit from the role set that provided their security during childhood. They try to deal with this instability and uncertainty by tying themselves to another role set (e.g., with their own sex peers or a younger person of the opposite sex). It is only those role exits that occur "out of phase" with one's own age-sex-class peers that have the result of isolating persons. Thus widowhood and retirement have negative effects on friendships for people in their sixties because at that age most of an individual's age contemporaries may still be married or employed. The same role exits are much less traumatic for persons in their seventies because at that age level the peers presumably will, for the most part, be faced with the same set of conditions (e.g., retirement or widowhood).[63]

Role exit theory thus begins with examining the problem of "demeaning of the self" that occurs when a person has a significant loss (such as a role) and the sense of depression and the diminished self-concept that usually accompany this. What is required is some form of "restitution" to restore one's sense of identity after significant role exits. Blau sees three analytically distinct social mechanisms that can help to provide such restitution. The availability of each depends upon the stage of life at which the role exits occur:

1. *Role Succession.* As we have suggested, people tend to proceed throughout life according to more or less well-defined culturally prescribed timetables. Going to school, dating, beginning a job, getting married, having children all provide new roles to replace the roles from which individuals exit. To be "out of phase" thus places a person in a deviant position with respect to his or her peers and can have, at the very least, disturbing consequences for the individual involved. Children who are left back when their age group is promoted, young people who delay marriage beyond the age when their peers marry, homosexuals who do not marry in any conventional sense, or heterosexuals who simply refuse to conform to customary practices often face difficulties because of the lack of a well-defined succession to new roles while their peers go on to do the "normal," "usual" thing that "everyone" is expected to do.

2. *Role Repetition.* This refers simply to the process of repeating a former, familiar role. Remarriage, transferring to a new job, converting to a new religious faith, joining a different political party, immigrating to a new country all involve repetition of roles that were formerly enacted even though the specifics are different. Thus people who have been divorced or who have lost a marriage partner through death are often eager to remarry because marriage is a familiar and comfortable status.

3. *Involvement Reallocation.* This is the process of intensifying a person's involvement in one or more of the roles remaining in his or her repertoire after a role exit has occurred. For example, recently divorced or widowed persons may devote increased energy and time to their jobs or children. Adolescents, breaking away from ties to parents, may spend much more time with and devote much more energy to a set of friends or to a single person of either the same or opposite sex. New immigrants try to find fellow immigrants from the old country by participating in appropriate organizations or living in appropriate neighborhoods.

Blau reports on several studies that show a cumulative decline in morale among older persons according to the number of major role exits experienced by the individual. For example, "The proportion exhibiting low morale is highest among those who are both widowed and retired, and lowest among those both still married *and* employed."[64]

In short, Blau sees the number of roles in a person's repertoire as a reserve of social resources that can be called upon in time of need. This seems to be true throughout the life cycle but becomes exaggerated for older persons because they usually have fewer opportunities to gain new optional roles.

RESEARCH ON AGING

Interest in research on problems of aging and the aged has increased enormously in recent years. The reasons for this interest are not completely clear, but one observer may have raised a central point when he observed that the same Americans who constituted the post–World War II baby boom, "those young people described as 'greening' America, will 'gray' America."[65] The fact seems to be that the aged are rapidly changing from a small minority group that could safely be ignored by the people who "count" to a political force of significant dimensions. They threaten to change established perceptions of others about the meaning of age as they modify their own perceptions about the implications of reaching "the golden years." Accordingly, it seems safe to predict that future research will differ in important ways from what has been done in the past. One pair of perceptive researchers, after noting some matters that they feel require immediate research attention, observe that they have emphasized the extent to which values are intimately related to what they call change and to what they and others expect in the present and the future:

> The values of the society are not clearly defined and singular, and so policies of the government often are stated in generalities that have to be interpreted by bureaucracies. The whole process requires study, and more specifically, the actual values that come into play in the implementation of policies now requires study. What is required is not only the study of the needs of the aged, of the

population in general, or the current status of the aged, but of what the values are that are currently determining policy and the values that are being determined by policy.[66]

We have attempted, in the "sampler" that follows, to trace the outlines of some currently available research in this field.

How Can One Prolong Life?

A study[67] of octogenarian veterans of the Spanish-American War focused on the social correlates of longevity. The following factors seem to be significant:

1. *Parental longevity.* Note, however, that it was difficult to sort out the relative effects of genetic inheritance and those due to a stable home environment.

2. *Senior birth order in a large family.* This seems to contradict the notion that, as a group, children of long-lived parents are also long-lived—but it does help to be a first or older child. As a group, children of long-lived parents are also long-lived. The researchers suggest that senior birth order may encourage the early formation of adaptive skills.

3. *Intelligence, education, and occupation.* These three, the researchers felt, led to a social position that has important consequences for the maintenance of health.

4. *Status group membership.* The subjects in this study were all "Spanish-American War veterans," a status that gave them a special social prestige. The researchers felt this membership provided resources and morale that contributed to longevity.

5. *Small number of children.* This seemed to limit the economic and emotional burden on the breadwinner.

6. *Maintenance of "with-spouse" status.* This provided physical and emotional support. Being married was advantageous as far as longevity was concerned, and being single was disadvantageous. As married people get older, however, the risk of losing a spouse by death increases. This seems to neutralize the advantage of being married.

7. *Maintenance of occupational role or its equivalent into the elder years.* The subjects in this study did not, as a group, stop working at the age of 65. Some 78 percent of them continued at least part-time employment after this age. The average age of complete cessation of work was 70. At least 6 percent were still doing remunerative work at the time of the interview. The subjects were mostly involved in nonmanual occupations and could more easily continue to do the same sort of work as they aged.

The researchers felt that it was the combination of these factors that helped their subjects to become octogenarians.

How Do Older Persons Function Intellectually?

A longitudinal study of 96 men who were originally tested on the Army Alpha test of mental abilities at age 19 were retested with the same instrument at age 50 and 61. Results? Total scores and verbal scores increased significantly between the ages of 19 and 50 and remained relatively constant from age 50 to age 61. Reasoning scores showed slight increases between the ages of 50 and 61 while numerical scores declined during this period. The researchers note, however, that the subjects were mostly engineers who may have reached the peak of quantitative sophistication at college graduation since many of them subsequently moved into less technical work that lessened their need to maintain quantitative knowledge and skills.[68]

An interesting study[69] addressed itself to some methodological problems involved in cross-sectional versus longitudinal studies of aging and intellectual functioning. The researchers observed that most cross-sectional studies report peak performance occurring in the early twenties or thirties with a steep decline thereafter. Most longitudinal studies, on the other hand, report a slight decline, no decline, or a slight increase at least until the mid-fifties. They observe that in *cross-sectional* studies, the differences between various age groups can be (1) a function of actual age differences, (2) a difference between cohorts (i.e., generations), or (3) a function of both age and cohort differences. In *longitudinal* studies, however, the differences can be due to (1) age changes, (2) environmental effects over time, or (3) both age and time differences. In short, the cross-sectional method tends to confound age and cohort differences whereas the longitudinal method confounds age changes and time differences.

To examine this problem, the researchers designed a study to differentiate components of developmental change that are a function of differences in the *initial* level from those that are attributable to *maturational* processes. They concluded that much of the variance attributed to age differences in past cross-sectional studies must properly be assigned to differences in ability between successive *generations*. Within the same person, age changes over time were much smaller than were differences between cohorts. They suggest that reported declines in intellectual functioning with age may be nothing more than the effects of increased environmental opportunity and/or genetic improvement. Furthermore, the findings on longitudinal age changes indicate that the levels of functioning reached at maturity can, with few exceptions, be retained until late in life.

How Long Do Older People Think They Are Going to Live? Do Their Estimates Affect Their Behavior?

John Steward Sill recalled that a central factor in disengagement theory was the aging person's awareness of his or her impending death. Most studies investigating the phenomenon of disengagement, however, have seemed to ignore this and have attempted simply to correlate age with activity level. Sill felt that, if what he called "awareness of finitude"[70] is an important cause of disengagement, it should be more useful than chronological age in predicting the level of disengagement. He studied 120 residents of eight residential facilities with high concentrations of elderly residents, using a structured interview. The subjects ranged in age from 55 to 98. The median age was 79.7. When asked about how long they expected to live, 30 percent gave no answer. Those who did reply tended to give one or the other of two extreme responses. Either they expected to live 10 years or more or thought they might die at any time. Sill found a significant relationship between awareness of finitude and activity count. This relationship was stronger than age or physical incapacity. As a matter of fact, when the effect of awareness of finitude and physical incapacity were subtracted, the older persons in the sample were actually more active than were the younger ones. Sill felt that his work demonstrated that disengagement is "more a social than a biological process."[71] Others have suggested that elderly persons may degenerate both mentally and physically after being labeled, in effect, "as good as dead." Sill feels that his study suggests that aging persons themselves, rather than those about them, may initiate the labeling process. Those aged persons seeing themselves as very near to death may begin to constrict their life space and withdraw from various forms of activity. Others, however, may perceive themselves as having much more time and therefore remain much more engaged in life and activities. He sees questions such as the following as still being unanswered and awaiting further research: "What interventions are possible to change the self-labeling process" (i.e., the one in which people label themselves as very close to death)? "What aspects of the social or physical environment may modify the aging person's feeling that 'This is the place I have come to die'?" "What factors in the subculture of a residential community have an impact on this feeling? What can professional staff persons do to change it?"[72]

What Does "Growing Old" Mean for the Elderly?

Andrea Fontana, in a fascinating little study,[73] has used ethnographic data, in-depth interviews, and participant observation to examine the process of growing old from the perspective of old people themselves. Fontana studied elderly persons in three different settings; a senior citizen center for middle- and upper-class older persons, a metropolitan senior citizen center for lower-class older persons, and a convalescent institution for older persons.

Fontana found that individuals grow old in a variety of fashions. He has assigned labels to some of the most distinctive of these. Thus there are the "relaxers," the "do-gooders," the "joiners," and the "waiters."[74]

The *relaxers* have succeeded in freeing themselves from the characteristic concern with time that pervades contemporary American society. They view old age as a time of life in which it is appropriate to relax. They have been successful during their working years and do not regret the loss of roles that are productive from the perspective of society. They go fishing, read books, watch television, play golf, take walks, talk to people, visit museums—all with no or at least relatively little thought about being "useful" or "productive" in any conventional sense.

The *do-gooders* have retained the work ethic that has been such an important part of their earlier existence. They try to maintain an identification with activities and roles that correspond more or less closely to conventional perceptions of work. Characteristically, they take part in a range of unpaid volunteer activities to help other older persons. This can involve anything from being a coordinator for dances or other festive occasions to serving as librarian, typist, travel consultant, income tax expert, or general program planner.

The *joiners* tend to be those who receive the benefit of the planning done by the do-gooders. They are the persons who have only partially divested themselves of the conventional work ethic. They do not regret the cessation of their work activities and do want to enjoy themselves—to have fun. But they find themselves curiously ambivalent. They have been "busy" for most of their lives, and "activity has become synonymous with success."[75] There seems to exist for them (perhaps unconsciously) an identification of activity with success. They seem to feel that they will be successful to the extent that they join a large number of organizations or engage in a large number of activities. For them, the meaning of old age is not to be found in the content of what is done but, perhaps, in some cases, in the sheer number of things done—the number of trips taken or the number of clubs belonged to—the number of activities in which they have participated. The "quality" of this participation, the depth of these experiences, tends to be essentially of secondary importance as compared with the sheer volume of activity.[76]

The *waiters* seem to be composed of several different kinds of people. All seem to be confronted with realities that make the niceties of what to do with one's leisure time and how to avoid boredom largely irrelevant. Some—the "waiters in crisis"—are confronted with a profound life crisis that has "sapped their will to continue a meaningful existence or even to attempt to find surrogate meaning in activities aimed at filling time. These individuals wander about as spectral souls in a Dantesque Inferno."[77]

Others tend to be those suffering from poverty. They include (1) "Sitters" who keep glued to a chair either because they suffer from a crippling illness or because they simply do not have anything better to do. They survive on a financial pittance and fill their days with small tasks to keep from being bored but know that no change will occur in the future. (2) The "drifters" who "choose a different way to keep boredom and despair at bay. They move on trying to keep one step ahead of the emptiness of their lives; lost pioneers of a frontier, old age which for them is nothing but a wasteland."[78] (3) The "waiting-for-God" subgroup. These are sitters who, though in a wasteland, are walking toward an oasis, the afterlife. "Thus whatever calamity life has in store for them can be endured with a smile; no matter how trivial the ways in which they fill their days there will be something better at the end."[79]

In addition to these subgroups, Fontana identifies other waiters such as those older persons who essentially are prisoners in convalescent centers. These resemble the sitters in most respects except that they are not free to leave. Additional groups and subgroups can probably be identified endlessly. The central truth that seems to emerge from this study of older persons is not so much the inevitability of growing old but "the enormous differences in what growing old can mean to different people and how these meanings regulate the elders lives and can lead to happiness, despair or just apathy."[80]

CASE HISTORIES

Sex and the Elderly: Fictional Case Histories

One of the more pervasive stereotypes about older persons is that after a given age (never specified precisely), these individuals lose interest in sex and do not engage in sexual activities. Many studies have confirmed the fact, however, that sexual activity does continue into advanced old age for many persons—into the eighties and beyond. In some cases, sexual interest and activity has reportedly *increased* with advanced age. The point is that age alone is not the decisive variable. Sexual behavior in older persons seems to be influenced by a variety of considerations ranging from sexual behavior in early life to a complex combination of physical, psychological, and social factors.[81]

Among the more important social factors are the social taboos with respect to sex and older persons. In the United States and in some other Western societies, many of these taboos are gradually being removed. Many behavioral science studies have done much to clarify the situation, but it has been charged that these have been concerned "primarily with physical aspects of sexuality and have not considered sufficiently the deeper human motives and relationships that affect behavior."[82]

Literature is a fruitful source of relevant case histories that, by dramatizing individual reactions and behavior, convey "human insights that are lacking in norms and statistics."[83] Celeste Loughman, in an interesting article entitled "Eros and the Elderly: A Literary View,"[84] has examined several short stories in an endeavor to obtain some relevant insights.

Thus in Eudora Welty's "Old Mr. Marblehall,"[85] the author's satire is "directed principally at an undiscerning society which can offer its old only indifference or ridicule."[86] The story describes the experiences of Marblehall, a 66-year-old man who is seen by people around him as a different sort of creature—as someone who in a sense is half-dead. This, despite the fact that, when speaking to him, they often tell him how "well-preserved" he is and perhaps even "how young" he looks. Marblehall married for the first time at age 60 and now has a 6-year-old son. The townspeople find this difficult to accept. They are simply overwhelmed, however, when they learn that Old Mr. Marblehall has been leading a double life and in fact has *two* wives and two sons!

In a story by V. S. Pritchett, "The Spree," [87] the author's central concern seems to be the question, "When does old age begin?" Loughman notes that the author here is questioning the conventional application of "old" to all persons who have lived a given number of years. From that perspective, the central character in this story, Mr. Dawson, is viewed as being old and is treated as an "old" person by his children. If age means repudiating the present and living by a withdrawal into the past, then Dawson is not old. His resistance to old age takes the form of an appetite for life. This is expressed in a variety of modes, including taking trips to London to get his haircut while enjoying the scent of the barber shop, visiting shops where he is stimulated by the sight of women's dresses, cosmetics, and jewelry to say nothing of the women themselves.

In general, these and other stories "extend to the elderly the liberal sexual attitudes that other segments of the population have been experiencing. More than that, they challenge long-standing myths that have become codified into rigid social norms that have effectively severed old age from other stages of life. As behavioral science confirms, the persistence of the sexual impulse gives evidence that life is a continuum and that behavior tolerated in the young should not be censured in the old. Above all, the authors demonstrate that the tension between the old and society is less significant than are the tensions within the old themselves. More than a physical drive, the erotic impulse is an expression of fundamental desires—for human contact, for love, for life itself—desires of an essentially unchanging self that are contradicted by the dying body."[88]

Retirement and Depression

Mr. J, a retired legal adjudicator, was diagnosed as having an adjustment reaction to old age—in this case, to retirement. He was irritable, sad, anxious, fearful, and perplexed. He described himself as always having been fidgety, but this trait had increased since retirement. Time dragged heavily, and he missed feeling useful. He had voluntarily retired four years ago at (66), having done little planning for his old age or the future. He tended to deny his aging state and felt frightened and depressed about the future. He had shown no previous adjustment or personality problems.[89]

In commenting on this case, two mental health specialists observe that for many men in our society, retirement is a concern that can affect the very essence of their lives. Many men (and presumably many women as well) develop virtually a single-minded identity with their work, with few if any diversified interests outside their formal work role. "Work and life become so interconnected that the loss of a job can demolish the reason for living."[90]

They note that there is considerable research as well as commonsense evidence that people adjust better if they can choose when and how completely they wish to retire. Unfortunately, in a social system oriented toward production, on the one hand, and youth, on the other, this evidence tends to be disregarded in the work-a-day world. They suggest the need for a redefinition of work itself and propose the alternation of work, leisure, and study throughout the life cycle rather than having these activities parceled out according to age groups. They also suggest that men should be encouraged to take a more active part in other aspects of life—including more involvement in the care of children and the home and sharing of financial responsibility for financial support with their wives. Both spouses should find more leisure time throughout life for rest, study, and involvement in cultural and social activities—these should not be reserved exclusively or predominantly for the retirement years. "A call for male as well as female liberation is in order if men are to escape the crushing burden of overidentification with work and the problems of stress, coronary, retirement shock, and shortened life expectancy that are associated with it."[91]

This advice seems to be based on a more traditional society rather than on one that is rapidly in the process of change. Women in enormous numbers now find that they share the financial responsibilities of men and presumably can in increasing numbers anticipate difficulties similar to those encountered by the Mr. J's of this world.[92]

Maggie Kuhn, Gray Panther

The following material is taken from an interview conducted by Jane Seskin with Margaret Kuhn who, with five friends, established an organization originally known as the Consultation of Older and Younger Adults for Social Change. In 1972, the group became known officially as the Gray Panthers, and by 1980, the organization had a nationwide membership of about 35,000. It is concerned broadly with social justice, but high on its priority list is what has become known as the problem of ageism: "age discrimination and age stereotyping—and its relationship to racism, sexism and other oppressive, dehumanizing forces within our society."[93]

At the time of the interview, Maggie was 74 years old and was engaged in an extensive lecture and travel schedule. In one recent month, it is reported, she traveled to eight states and gave 19 talks.

Maggie was born in Buffalo but grew up in different parts of the country including Memphis, Louisville, and Cleveland. Her father was a hard-driving businessman whose company transferred him to many places.

She feels that her social consciousness developed from many sources but at least in part from an adolescent revolt against her father who was very authoritarian and who oppressed her mother in what was then (and now?) a socially acceptable fashion. That is, Maggie's mother was required to account for every penny her husband gave her, but she never received any *spending* money (i.e., money for her own personal needs).

Maggie eventually obtained a position with the Y.W.C.A. that at that time (1930s and 1940s) was helping women organize in the labor movement. She subsequently went to Boston to organize and work with Unitarian women and eventually went to the Presbyterians where she stayed for 22 years.

She, and some friends she had made in connection with her involvement with the Vietnam antiwar movement, were required to retire at the same time. They formed the organization or movement that later adopted the name "Gray Panthers."

"I think my generation was programed to keep quiet," she says, "to accept things the way they were, to comply. We're trying to challenge that thinking."[94]

She thinks people are afraid to grow old because of the rigid segregation by age that is so characteristic of our society. She feels the media have conditioned older persons to believe they are no longer attractive persons and certainly not lovers. But these perceptions, she feels, are gradually disappearing.

"My generation of women still depends on men. I have no regrets that I've never married. I've been engaged three times. I've had lovers. But I've been very devoted to my career. If there was a man who really interested me, who could become part of my life, we would live together. But marriage would take too much energy and time. I was the only one of my class in college who didn't immediately marry. They're all widowed now, they're all alone."[95]

She tells older people who feel lonely and depressed to stop thinking about themselves and reach out to an ever-widening community. If they do not find circles that continue to expand, then in old age when the primary circle contracts, people find themselves alone. "If all through your life you've been wrapped up in your family, and then they die, and you've never developed any facility or any feeling of competence, you're stuck with yourself—stuck with your own memories, your own anger. You think you have no future, only a lonely, miserable present. And you make everyone else around you miserable too."[96]

Richard Johnson's Father—and His Depression

Richard Johnson's father had always been a placid, uncommunicative man. At the age of 82, he lost the sight of his right eye. Shortly thereafter, Richard visited him. Immediately, Richard sensed that his father was quite depressed. The cause for his depression was not difficult to find: the father had become listless and depressed as a result of losing the eye. It was relatively easy to see the emotional difficulty as a consequence of a physical problem.

A year before this incident occurred, however, Richard had arranged to have brunch with his father on a beautiful spring day. He found his father deeply depressed and was unable to account for the father's bad mood. As it happened, earlier that day, the father had been reliving the memory of another spring day when he had enjoyed the camaraderie of friends on a softball diamond. That memory apparently stood for a loss that was every bit as real to him as the subsequent blindness. Richard, however, was not aware of the reason for this depression and could only be distressed at his father's unaccountable behavior.[97]

In commenting on this case, the authors observe,

> It may not normally occur to us that our aging parents' social identities, personal histories, and emotional needs are fully as much a part of them as are the physical aspects and needs of their bodies. We tend to make a distinction between these two spheres. Generally we consider the social-emotional sphere to be less "real" than the physical sphere. Such a distinction often leads us to react one way to a father's irritability if it seems to center around his arthritis and another way if he becomes irritable "for no reason" during our daily phone call. Many sons and daughters may not realize what a costly distinction this is or just how it can make then unwitting victims of unnecessary stress.[98]

Thinking about aging from a social psychological perspective requires that one go beyond a purely physical consideration. Like other phases of life, growing old entails not only the loss of roles, but also the accumulation of new roles. Role loss and accumulation involve a concomitant redefinition of identity. As with any other stage of life, understanding one's self involves an implicit evaluation of one's self worth. The development and maintenance of a sense of self-worth and dignity are as important in "growing old" as they are in "growing up."

NOTES

[1]Donald O. Cowgill, "A Theory of Aging in Cross-cultural Perspective," in Donald O. Cowgill and Lowell D. Holmes, eds., *Aging and Modernization* (New York: Appleton-Century Crofts, 1972), p. 4.

[2]Austin J. Shelton, "The Aged And Eldership Among the Igbo," in Cowgill and Holmes, eds., *Aging and Modernization*, pp. 31–49.

[3]Lowell D. Holmes, "The Role and Status of the Aged in a Changing Samoa," in Cowgill and Holmes, eds., *Aging and Modernization*, pp. 73–89.

[4]Ibid., p. 83.

[5]Albert R. Chandler, "The Traditional Chinese Attitude Toward Old Age," *Journal of Gerontology*, Vol. 4 (July 1949), pp. 239–244.

[6]Lin Yutang, *The Importance of Living* (New York: Reynal and Hitchcock, 1937), p. 188.

[7]Ibid., p. 189, quoted in Chandler, "The Traditional Chinese Attitude Toward Old Age," p. 239.

[8]Francis L. K. Hsu, *Americans and Chinese*, 3rd ed. (Honolulu: University Press of Hawaii, 1981), pp. 335–351.

[9]David Gutmann, "The Cross-cultural Perspective: Notes Toward a Comparative Psychology of Aging," in James E. Birren and K. Warner Schaie, eds., *Handbook of the Psychology of Aging* (New York: Van Nostrand Reinhold Co., 1977), p. 304.

[10]Ibid.

[11]Ibid., p. 305.

[12]Oscar Lewis, *Life in a Mexican Village: Tepoztlan Restudied* (Urbana: University of Illinois Press, 1951), cited in ibid., p. 305.

[13]Gutmann, "The Cross-cultural Perspective," pp. 309–310.

[14]Judith Treas, "Socialist Organization and Economic Development in China: Latent Consequences for the Aged," *The Gerontologist*, Vol. 19, no. 1 (February 1979), pp. 34–35.

[15]Ibid., p. 35.

[16]Ibid.

[17]Ibid., pp. 35–36.

[18]Ibid., pp. 41–42.

[19]W. Andrew Achenbaum, *Old Age in the New Land: The American Experience Since 1790* (Baltimore: Johns Hopkins University Press, 1978).

[20]Ibid., p. 2.

[21]Ibid., p. 15.

[22]Ibid., p. 22.

[23]Ibid., pp. 28–31.

[24]Ibid., p. 39.

[25]Ibid., pp. 53–54.

[26]Ibid., p. 153

[27]Ibid., pp. 153–154.

[28]Ibid., p. 154.

[29]Ibid., pp. 155–156.

[30]Martin B. Loeb and Edgar F. Borgatta, "Values and Future Needs for Research," in Edgar F. Borgatta and Neil G. McCluskey, eds., *Aging and Society: Current Research and Policy Perspectives* (Beverly Hills, Calif.: Sage Publications, 1980), pp. 195–212.

[31]Ibid., p. 196.

[32]Ibid.

[33]Robert J. Havighurst and Ruth Albrecht, *Older People* (New York: Longmans, Green, 1953), p. 54.

[34]Ibid., p. 377.

[35]Ibid., p. 289.

[36]Ruth Shonle Cavan, "Self and Role in Adjustment During Old Age," in Arnold M. Rose, ed., *Human Behavior and Social Processes: An Interactionist Approach* (Boston: Houghton Mifflin, 1962), pp. 526–535. Also see Ruth S. Cavan et al., *Personal Adjustment in Old Age* (Chicago: Science Research Associates, 1949), for the report of a study generally agreed to be the first to state activity theory implicitly.

[37]Ibid., p. 528.

[38]Ibid.

[39]Ibid.

[40]Ibid., pp. 528–529.

[41]Robert J. Havighurst, Bernice L. Neugarten, and Sheldon S. Tobin, "Disengagement and Patterns of Aging," in Bernice L. Neugarten, ed., *Middle Age and Aging* (Chicago: University of Chicago Press, 1968), p. 161.

[42]Elaine Cumming et al., "Disengagement Theory—A Tentative Theory of Aging," *Sociometry*, Vol. 23 (March 1960), p. 23.

[43]Ibid., p. 24.

[44]Ibid., p. 35.

[45]Elaine Cumming and William E. Henry, *Growing Old: The Process of Disengagement* (New York: Basic Books, 1961).

[46]Ibid., pp. 14–15.

⁴⁷Arlie Russel Hochschild, "Disengagement Theory: A Critique and Proposal," *American Sociological Review*, Vol. 40, no. 5 (August 1975), p. 553.

⁴⁸Cumming et al., "Disengagement Theory," pp. 24–25.

⁴⁹Ibid., p. 25.

⁵⁰Emile Durkheim, *Suicide: A Study in Sociology* (Glencoe, Ill.: The Free Press, 1951), pp. 208–216.

⁵¹See Jaber F. Gubrium, *The Myth of the Golden Years: A Socio-Environmental Theory of Aging* (Springfield, Ill.: Charles C Thomas, 1973), pp. 17–27, for a critique of disengagement theory as a functionalist approach.

⁵²Ibid., pp. 20–21.

⁵³Elaine Cumming, "Further Thoughts on the Theory of Disengagement," *International Social Science Journal*, Vol. 15, no. 3 (1963), p. 381.

⁵⁴Ibid., p. 386.

⁵⁵Richard Videbeck and Alan B. Knox, "Alternative Participatory Responses to Aging," in Arnold M. Rose and Warren A. Peterson, eds., *Older People and Their Social World* (Philadelphia: F. A. Davis, 1965), p. 48.

⁵⁶Arnold R. Rose, "A Current Theoretical Issue in Social Gerontology," in ibid., p. 363.

⁵⁷Ibid.

⁵⁸Ibid., p. 366.

⁵⁹Zena Smith Blau, *Aging in a Changing Society*, 2nd ed. (New York: Franklin Watts, 1981), p. 4.

⁶⁰Ibid., p. 4.

⁶¹Ibid., p. 184.

⁶²Ibid., pp. 20–21.

⁶³Ibid., pp. 183–192.

⁶⁴Ibid., p. 95.

⁶⁵Robert N. Butler, "Overview on Aging," in Gene Usdin and Charles K. Hofling, eds., *Aging: The Process and the People* (New York: Brunner/Mazel, 1978).

⁶⁶Martin B. Loeb and Edgar F. Borgatta, "Values and Future Needs for Research ," in Borgatta and McCluskey, eds., *Aging and Society*, p. 212.

⁶⁷Charles L. Rose, "Social Correlates of Longevity," in Robert Kasterbaum, ed., *New Thoughts on Old Age* (New York: Springer, 1969), pp. 76–91.

⁶⁸W. A. Owens, "Age and Mental Abilities: A Second Adult Follow-up," in Irene M. Hulicka and B. R. Bugelski, eds., *Empirical Studies in the Psychology and Sociology of Aging* (New York: Harper & Row, 1977), pp. 7–11.

⁶⁹K. Warner Schaie and Charles R. Strother, "A Cross-sequential Study of Cognitive Behavior," in ibid., pp. 11–15.

⁷⁰See John Stewart Hill, "Disengagement Reconsidered: Awareness of Finitude," *The Gerontologist*, Vol. 20, no. 4 (August 1980), pp. 457–462.

⁷¹Ibid., p. 461.

⁷²Ibid., p. 461.

⁷³Andrea Fontana, *The Last Frontier: The Social Meaning of Growing Old*, preface by Fred Davis (Beverly Hills, Calif.: Sage, 1977).

⁷⁴Ibid., pp. 172–182.

⁷⁵Ibid., p. 173.

⁷⁶Ibid., p. 173.

⁷⁷Ibid., p. 174.

⁷⁸Ibid., p. 174.

⁷⁹Ibid., p. 174.

⁸⁰Ibid., p. 174.

⁸¹Celeste Loughman, "Eros and the Elderly: A Literary View," *The Gerontologist*, Vol. 20, no. 2 (April 1980), p. 182.

⁸²Ibid., p. 182

⁸³Ibid., p. 183.

⁸⁴Cf. Ibid., pp. 182–191.

⁸⁵In E. Welty, *A Curtain of Green* (Garden City: Doubleday, Doran, 1941).

⁸⁶Celeste Loughman, "Eros and The Elderly," p. 184.

⁸⁷In V.S. Pritchett, *The Camberwell Beauty* (New York: Random House, 1974).

⁸⁸Celeste Loughman, "Eros and the Elderly," p. 184.

[89]Ibid., p. 186.

[90]Robert N. Butler and Myrna I. Lewis, *Aging and Mental Health*, 2nd ed. (St. Louis: C.V. Mosby, 1977), p. 37.

[91]Ibid., p. 37.

[92]Ibid., p. 37.

[93]Jane Seskin, *More Than Mere Survival: Conversations with Women over 65* (New York: Newsweek Books, 1980), pp. 123–134.

[94]Ibid., p. 123.

[95]Ibid., p. 128.

[96]Ibid., p. 131.

[97]Ibid., p. 132.

[98]Stephen Z. Cohen and Bruce Michael Gans, *The Other Generation Gap* (Chicago: Folcett, 1978), pp. 109–110.

CHAPTER ELEVEN
MASS COMMUNICATION

SNAPSHOTS

1. The Arapesh of New Guinea

For this small group of mountain people, communication is seen primarily as a way of arousing the emotions of the audience. Food is scarce. People constantly move about individually or in small groups to find food. When any unusual event occurs (a birth, death, quarrel, or visiting strangers), the people are likely to be widely scattered. A system of calls and gong beats is used to attract the attention of those at a distance. The signals convey only the information that something important has happened. The point of the communication is simply to attract attention and assemble a group of people who will respond emotionally to whatever event has occurred. This behavior has been explained as being consistent with the lack of precision that characterizes Arapesh thinking. The Arapesh have a short attention span, and their tendency is to respond "emotionally" rather than "logically." It is only after an initial emotional response has been received that attempts are made to communicate more refined concepts.

2. Manus of the Southern Coast of the Admiralty Islands

A hard-headed trading people who live near lagoons, the Manus are interested in material things and economic activity. Unlike the Arapesh who seldom count as high as 100 and use units with a very low level of abstraction, the Manus count into the hundred thousands. In communicating, they use drum signals that have formal openings that set the stage in terms of content rather than emotion. One beat may mean "I am about to announce a date on which I will give a feast." This has the effect of establishing an intellectual readiness in the audience to listen for a piece of relevant information. Household heads have special patterns of beats to serve as individualized beats.

3. Bali

This was not a preliterate society but one very different from ours and comparable in political and economic organization to the early Middle Ages in Europe. The Balinese lived in small village communities in which all residents were tied together by a large number of shared ceremonial and economic tasks. They maintained an elaborate irrigation system, temples, roads, forces of watchmen, town criers, and messengers. Living in a given village, and having a given caste, sex, or marital status, provide the context for what an individual will do on a given day of the week. People do not have to remember what they have to do—this is the assigned task of special officials who take turns performing various duties. It is assumed that if people have the necessary information, correct behavior will be forthcoming. When, on occasion, individuals do not perform as expected, small fines may be levied. If the fine is not paid, the amount is increased. If a person is perceived as unwilling to pay the fine, it is increased at a greatly accelerated rate, and the individual is virtually isolated from the community until it is paid. In no case, however, is anger ever shown. The system is impersonal; no exceptions are allowed and no changes are permitted.

In this society the mass communicator (e.g., a rajah, or village council) acts as if the audience were already in a state of suspended, unemotional attention needing only specific words or phrases to move them into action. These words or phrases have been compared with red or green lights in a modern traffic system where no police officer is needed and where pedestrians and drivers accept the signals as part of the world. Even communications from the gods that may be forwarded through the mouth of a possessed person have a quality that is unemotional and unhurried. People listen to these and other communications with an attitude of finding out what the time or weather is and what must be done about it.

4. Modern Singapore

This is a small, independent state having a population somewhat in excess of 2 million persons of which more than 75 percent are Chinese, about 15 percent are Malays, about 7 percent are Indians, and less than 2 percent are "others," including Eurasians, Europeans, and Americans. Each major ethnic community has a number of dialect speech groups. Thus there are five major languages (Malay, English, Mandarin, Tamil, and Hokkien) and three minor languages (Teochew, Cantonese, and Hainese). Each of the three major ethnic communities retains sentimental attachment to its ethnic mother tongue and cultural tradition.

When Singapore achieved independence in 1965, it was decided to use four official languages: Malay, Chinese (Mandarin), Tamil, and English. So the official language policy is multilingualism or linguistic pluralism.

In Singapore, the policy of multilingualism states that all four official languages are, in principle, equal. Nevertheless, the English language has become dominant. It is the language of the government bureaucracy and is used for authoritative texts of legislation and court records. It is not, however, a native language. It is accepted as a means of furthering Singapore's national development—to attract foreign capital, promote international trade, and serve as an instrument of foreign technical knowledge and skills. Mass communication is conducted in English when issues of economic and technical concerns are involved. For issues involving moral concerns, character building, and leisure-time activities, reliance is placed upon the so-called "vernacular" languages. One might say that the population thinks in English and feels in Chinese, Tamil, or Malay.

FUNCTIONS OF MASS COMMUNICATION

The preceding "snapshots" illustrate important functions of mass communication in societies where, according to some conceptions, mass communication did not exist. After all, according to one conventional view of mass communications, "In the beginning," there was the printing press and the Gutenburg bible; then came the telegraph, typewriter, telephone, phonograph, motion pictures, radio, and television; and finally the crowning achievement of the twentieth century, color television along with weekday soap operas and Sunday afternoon football telecasts. This is the story of the "progress" of mass media and mass communications.

In another sense, however, members of all societies need to communicate with each other on a societal basis. This may be to announce an unusual event (as among the Arapesh), to provide information (as among the Manus), or to move people into action (as among the Balinese). Each society must "choose" a particular language through which mass communication messages are to be presented. Such choices may often have important political, social, and even economic ramifications.

This chapter is concerned with mass communication in the contemporary world and the contribution that social psychology can make toward increasing our understanding of society-wide communication patterns. First, however, a word on a social-psychological perspective of mass communications.

MASS COMMUNICATION: A SOCIAL PSYCHOLOGICAL PERSPECTIVE

A wide variety of topics may fall under the heading of mass communication. For some, the study of mass communication includes art, literature, music, and other aspects of what they call high culture. For others, mass media means popular culture. It may include rock and roll but not classical music. For still others, mass communication means information presented to the public that is concerned with news and public affairs. This information may be presented through media such as television, radio, or newspapers or through personal appearances of individuals before large audiences. For some researchers, everything presented on television, radio, or in the newspapers counts as mass communication. Mass communication thus may entail a wide variety of phenomena.

As we saw in Chapter 2, a number of social scientists think that the most important thing about communication in general is the information it conveys. A good deal of theory in this area has attempted to develop methods to distinguish "noise" from "information." However, one may question whether all mass communications are designed to provide information. As we discussed in Chapter 2, communications may be designed to do a variety of things *other* than provide information. They may be designed to convince or persuade individuals to think or act in particular ways. Information may be part of this process. However, it is not the only component of such activities, nor is it always the most important part. Beyond this, communication contents may be multileveled, and as a result, they may contain multiple meanings. This does not mean that one meaning is information and the other is noise. Different components of communicative acts may work in harmony to produce a coherent meaning. On the other hand, however, they may work in a contradictory manner—as with the parent who tells his child he loves him while pushing him into a corner—to produce confusion.

Mass communications are certainly as complex as ordinary communications. As such, they may be designed to convince, persuade, bolster, frighten, insult, cheer-up, sadden, and so on. Moreover, the preceding types of communicative acts may be complexly interrelated within any specific communicative episode. As we shall see shortly, for example, fear may be an important component of persuasion. Like ordinary communication, mass communication messages are multidimensional and, thus, may have complex implications for individuals and society.

Second, the consequences of mass communications are similarly complex. This results from the fact that many communications may operate in serendipitous ways. For example, a great deal of concern with television violence was based on the notion that violence on television would produce violence in society. Indeed, some research, as we shall see, supports this proposition. Other research, however, has shown that violence on television produces fear among viewers and that this fear may result in subservient attitudes toward authority. It is hazardous to ascertain whether such an effect is contemplated or not. In any event, such findings highlight the idea that mass communications may have multiple effects that may not always be anticipated by either researchers or practitioners.

From this perspective, the study of mass communication is of enormous interest to social psychologists. Mass communication reflects the ways in which societywide messages are distributed and what communications are available to large numbers of individuals in society. How does mass communication affect individuals? What are the patterns through which these communications are disseminated? What are the processes through which such communications come to be understood and internalized by individuals? How do they exert influence on groups and individuals?

TRANSPORTATION VERSUS RITUAL MODELS¹

Within the field of communications research, there are two different theoretical frameworks for understanding the impact of mass communication. The first of these has been referred to as the *transportation model*. According to this idea, a communication may be thought of as an event transported or carried through time and space that affects others in a discernible manner. Mass communications may thus be thought of as communications produced by a relatively small number of individuals but carried to a relatively large number through mass media—newspapers, television, radio, and so on. The large number of persons are "affected" by these communications. The notion of "effects" has been a central concept in mass media research, though, as we shall see shortly, the idea that mass communication in and of itself directly changes people in powerful ways has been substantially modified.

The second of these frameworks has been called the *ritual model*. This conception, though a bit more difficult to understand than the transportation model, may in some ways capture the more subtle workings of mass communication. According to this idea, mass communication provides a symbolic environment in which we participate as social beings. Specific communications do not necessarily affect us in discrete ways. Rather, we learn a particular vernacular and way of thinking from the totality of mass communication messages. This then affects our behavior in subtle ways that may be difficult to detect.

In this chapter we shall not argue for either of these two perspectives. We shall attempt to show how each has been applied in the study of mass communication in particular areas: politics, television, entertainment, and advertising. We hope to show how each of these perspectives may help us to understand different implications that mass communications have for us as human beings.

SOME BASIC RESEARCH

Initially, many social scientists feared that the development and proliferation of mass communication, particularly through electronic media, would lead to instability in the social world. They feared that people would be easily swayed by the powerful images and symbols that certain elites could promulgate through the media. Early studies conducted on propaganda use during World War I showed how enemies portrayed one another as beings who were less than human, perverse, and vile and how such portrayals provided a context in which the generally inhumane act of killing another human being could appear both reasonable and justified.² Mass arousal in Nazi Germany, which centered on specific symbols (e.g., the swastika) and images (e.g., Aryan superiority), contributed to a concern that mass media might lead to irrational mass behavior. Many social scientists feared that the mass media would facilitate mass arousal, converting people to ideologies they would not normally adopt.

During and following World War II, social psychologists in the United

States studied the effects of mass communication on individuals. Two of the more important of these research endeavors were panel studies (see Chapter 3) of voting behavior during the 1940[3] and 1948[4] election campaigns. In the first study, the intentions of approximately 600 voters were ascertained in May, prior to the beginning of the campaign. These voters were then reinterviewed after the election. For most of the people, mass media exposure tended to reinforce rather than change their precampaign decisions. Although a substantial number of individuals changed from "undecided" to one party or another, or from one party or another to being "undecided," only 5 percent of the sample "converted" from allegiance to one party to another party, and mass media exposure did not turn out to be an important factor in that decision. The 1948 study found a similar pattern. Interestingly, the researchers found that those individuals who had the greatest amount of exposure to campaign information were the least likely to change from one party to another, leading them to conclude that mass media "exposure crystallizes and reinforces more than it converts."[5]

Social psychologists were somewhat surprised by these and other studies that indicated that mass communication did not appear to be as powerful in changing attitudes and behavior as had been supposed. Based upon a detailed review of studies conducted over a 20-year period, Joseph T. Klapper[6] has identified a number of social and psychological factors that "mediate" the effects of mass communications. Among Klapper's "mediating factors," the following are most interesting from a social psychological standpoint:

1. Preexisting interests and opinions that lead to selective exposure, perception, and retention of mass communication messages
2. Membership in groups that have norms that contradict mass communication messages
3. The interpersonal context through which mass communications are disseminated and the role of opinion leaders in shaping individual's approaches to mass communications[7]

Selective Exposure, Perception, and Retention

Imagine that there is a heated debate on your campus surrounding an issue that you consider to be quite important—the presidency of the student union. Two candidates, who have very different views, are running for the office. One (candidate A) feels that student union fees should be increased to provide better and more varied student activities; the other (candidate B) believes that students are already financially burdened and opposes any increase in student fees. If you believe in an active student union providing a large number of varied activities, you are likely not only to support the first candidate, but also to listen with greater attention to his or her speeches, read his or her campaign material, and attend to information about this candidate when it is presented in the mass media. You are not unlike others in this regard. A number of studies have shown that people are more likely to pay attention to communications with which they already agree than to those with which they disagree.[8] Social psychologists term this phenomenon "selective exposure."

Selective exposure is not that surprising. It is much more interesting to note that people will not only selectively pay attention to messages that are in accord with their views, but that they will selectively *perceive* messages so as to interpret even contra-attitudinal messages as being consistent with their views and opinions. In what is now regarded as a classic study of rumor, Gordon Allport and Leo Postman[9] showed white subjects in an experiment a picture of an altercation on a train involving a white man and a black man. The white man had a rather large and menacing razor. Then, subjects who were shown the picture were asked to describe what they saw to other subjects, who then described it to still others. At some point in these successive narrations, the razor almost always was described as being held by the black man. Other studies present similar results. In one study, for example, cartoons intended to ridicule racial and religious prejudices were perceived as glorifications of the "American way" by highly prejudiced individuals.[10] One very interesting early study demonstrated a curious interaction between selective exposure and retention. As expected, pro-Soviet individuals tended to read newspapers favorable to the Soviet position. They considered these newspapers to be much less pro-Soviet however than did their anti-Soviet counterparts.[11] A more recent study has shown that those persons most favorably affected by the television drama "Roots" were those who already were sympathetic to the ideas expressed by that program.[12]

Finally, a number of studies have shown that people will tend to remember information consistent with beliefs they already hold. In one study, for example, researchers presented pro- and anti-Communist messages to college students with different sympathies. The students were then tested at weekly intervals to determine how much information they retained from the presentation. Persons in the pro-Communist group retained more of the pro-Communist messages whereas those in the anti-Communist group retained more of those sympathetic to their view.[13]

Group Membership

Back on the campus now. As a student, you do not spend all your time studying. You may devote some time to extracurricular activities. Let us say that you are a member of the dance club and the drama club. As a political science major, you also try to stay involved in campus politics and, in fact, write an occasional column for the student newspaper. All these activities are funded in part by student union fees. The person across the hall, let us call him Jim, has a rather different life. He is an engineering major, and, although he has a definite aptitude for engineering, the courses are far from easy. Jim also has a strong desire to excel, which leaves him little time for extracurricular activities. As a result, he may have little interest in the student union and little desire to pay increased fees.

From one standpoint, you and Jim can be seen as belonging to different interest groups. You have a certain rational interest in having an active student union; Jim has little reason for spending his money on extracurricular activities. More important, you and Jim are likely to have different friends who may share your different interests. Like you, your friends are probably interested in dance and drama and may spend a considerable amount of time discussing campus politics through the student newspaper. You and your friends may be said to form a group that values the student union highly as well as the kinds of activities it supports. To be opposed to the student union might violate group norms and severely strain your friendships and your acceptance in this group.

Research has shown that individuals, under most circumstances, are unlikely to be affected by mass communication messages that contravene group norms. In the 1940 voting study, it was found that only 4 percent of the respondents who voted said that someone in their family had voted differently from themselves.[14] Experimental studies have shown that individuals who value group membership will be more resistant to media than will those for whom group membership is not as important.[15]

Groups may operate in a variety of ways to reinforce existing attitudes and opinions. Group membership may intensify selective exposure. Discussions with friends or other group members may increase one's awareness of media presentations consistent with group norms and values. Subsequent discussions may highlight relevant norms and reinforce basic values. In some cases, group exposure in the form of rallies and mass meetings may provide special occasions for the presentation of sympathetic messages. It is not unlikely that you and your friends may attend a rally for candidate A *en masse*. After the rally, you may even get together to discuss the many ways in which he and his policies are superior to candidate B's. In this context, it is easy to understand why you may not be convinced by candidate B's press conference later that evening.

It is interesting to note, however, that groups can serve to facilitate change as well as to reinforce existing attitudes and opinions. Individuals are likely to be more susceptible to mass media influences if important members of the groups to which they belong have changed their positions.[16] If membership ties to a group are broken or if the group is dissolved, then members may become more easily swayed by counterattitudinal mass communication messages. Research conducted during World War II showed that Allied propaganda directed at German prisoners of war often became effective only after the dissolution of the military units to which soldiers belonged. The dissolution of group ties, according to this research, facilitates communication effectiveness by leading individuals to search for a new reference group. Having lost contact with a group that has supported a particular ideology, individuals may now be exposed to radically different norms and values. These norms and values are now accepted in that they appear to accord with the individual's new reference group. Social scientists have called this shifting from one group to another a "motivated move."[17]

Individuals who are members of groups advocating conflicting positions are more susceptible to mass communication appeals. Assume that there is another political science major on campus (Barbara). She and you have similar interests in dance and drama. Unlike you, however, Barbara is a staunch fiscal conservative and, in fact, is a member of a political organization that reflects this position. Barbara may experience certain "cross-pressures" resulting from her membership in different groups. While her political friends may urge her to vote for candidate B, her drama and dance friends would likely support candidate A and would probably urge Barbara to do so as well. Barbara is likely to be more susceptible to mass communication messages precisely because she is receiving contradictory messages from her reference groups. Individuals subject to such cross-pressures seem to be more likely to change their voting intentions during the course of a campaign than are those who are not. Respondents whose families or friends consist of both Republicans and Democrats are more likely to delay their voting decision until late in the campaign. They are also more likely to change their voting intentions during the campaign. The more cross-pressures an individual is subject to, the more indecisive he or she is likely to be and the more receptive to mass media information. For you, listening to candidate A may become a kind of ritual in which you reaffirm values shared by you and members of your reference groups. Barbara may listen both to candidates A and B because her membership is conflicting groups makes her choice more difficult. For this reason, the content of the communication is likely to be more salient for her than it is for you.

Interpersonal Dissemination and Opinion Leadership

It is Thursday evening and you are sitting in your room diligently studying social psychology. Suddenly, Ralph, a senior and president of the Drama Club, bangs on your door and informs you that candidate A will be speaking on the campus television station to deliver an important message. You rush downstairs to listen to his statement. Afterward, Ralph and you discuss the significance of candidate A's remarks. Your attention to this particular media event results, in part, from the fact that you are friends with Ralph—that you respect him, that he knew of candidate A's public statement, and that he thought to inform you of the event. If your support of candidate A had been wavering, it is likely to have been reinforced through your interactions with Ralph.

Mass communication does not necessarily flow directly from a source to discrete individuals. Rather, it is mediated by others who direct attention to specific messages. Voting studies have led to the formulation of a "two-step flow" theory—the influence of mass communication is mediated by personal contacts who operate as opinion leaders. These opinion leaders are generally more attentive to mass media than are most others.

Opinion leaders may exercise influence in a variety of ways. Like Ralph, they may direct your attention to specific media events. Later, through discussion, they may help you to interpret the salient points of the message. Other, more subtle, factors may facilitate the effectiveness of opinion leaders. Because they themselves are more exposed to relevant media, they may appear to be more informed. Recent studies have found that opinion leaders tend to be specialized; that is, there are fashion leaders, movie leaders, public affairs leaders, and so on. Also, opinion leaders tend to exhibit valued gro᠁p characteristics. This may further facilitate their effectiveness.[18]

Generally, opinion leaders tend to reinforce rather than change existing attitudes and opinions. In the voting studies, such leaders were found to have played an important role in ensuring that "deviates" and "waverers" conform to group norms. People who made up their minds late in the campaign often mentioned the role of opinion leaders as a significant factor in their decisions to "return to the fold." In this sense, opinion leaders actually counteracted the effect of campaign information and propaganda.[19]

The extent to which mass media serve to reinforce rather than change existing attitudes and opinions is a matter of continuing debate and investigation. As we shall see in following sections of this chapter, there may be conditions under which mass media can be very effective in shaping attitudes and opinions. Some researchers believe that the "effects" model may underestimate the actual impact of mass communication and that other conceptualizations are necessary to explain the role of mass communication in contemporary society. Nevertheless, the early research conducted on the effects of mass communications is significant in two respects.

First, this research highlights the social character of our knowledge and opinions. Mass communication messages are components of stocks of knowledge in which individuals already have certain shares. Mass communications do not affect all of us in the same way. Rather, their impact will be mediated by what we have been exposed to, what we know, what we believe, and what we want to believe.

Second, this early research highlights the importance of the interpersonal context of mass communications. We approach mass media as social animals; we go to political rallies in large groups, we go to movies on dates or with friends, we watch television with family members and football games with "the guys."

Given these considerations, one may question the value of pitting mass communications against interpersonal factors. The interplay between the two may be a more important concern. Two recent studies highlight this. They show that mass communication may be effective in and of itself. Mass communication is more effective, however, when reinforced by interpersonal contacts. In a field experiment,[20] researchers attempted to improve healthful behavior in different communities through a multimedia campaign. In one community, the media campaign was supplemented by personal contacts. The persuasive effort was more successful in the latter community. Similar results were found in a study of a public television campaign to change children's sex role stereotypes by showing women performing mechanical, scientific, and athletic types of activities.[21] Some children simply watched the program while others watched the programs and participated in a discussion group focused on the programs. Again, the attitudes regarding sexual stereotypes of both groups of children changed. The change was more substantial, however, for those children who viewed the programs *and* participated in the discussion groups.

Persuasion

Assume that you have decided to work very hard for candidate A's election. After studying the matter in some detail, you have decided that you would like not only to show your support for candidate A and the issues he supports by voting for him yourself, but that you would like to convince others to do so as well. Your job then is to figure out a way to persuade your fellow students that candidate A is the better choice. Luckily, you are taking social psychology and social psychologists have conducted a number of experiments on persuasion that may be of use in your efforts for candidate A.

As a first step, you may attempt to solicit certain individuals to speak on the merits of your candidate. Even before thinking about the content of what you would like these speakers to say, you need to consider the speakers themselves as sources of information and how they might affect the students you want to persuade. Common sense tells you, first, that you want a speaker who will be credible (i.e., one whom your fellow students will be likely to believe). But what are the dimensions of credibility? What makes some sources more credible than others?

The source   First, you probably want a source who appears to be competent (i.e., who knows what he or she is talking about). A number of studies have shown that individuals are more likely to be persuaded by a communication from a source viewed as knowledgeable than from one who is viewed as having little expertise in a particular subject matter.[22] However, a knowledgeable source is not ipso facto a credible one. Experts may have hidden agendas that may lead you to be suspicious of their messages. An expert physician who works for a cigarette company is not likely to be very persuasive if he tells you that cigarette smoking is not harmful to your health.

With respect to persuasion, then, trustworthiness may be as important as expertise. What, however, makes one source more trustworthy than another? Prestige and image may be important. One early study, for example, found that subjects who held Catholic priests in high esteem learned more from their messages and underwent greater attitude change.[23] However, you do not know in what esteem your audience holds Catholic priests or other officials for that matter, and therefore, you should look to other factors.

Perhaps you should ask the chairperson of the drama department to speak on behalf of your position. First, she is both attractive and well known on campus. Social psychological experiments have shown that both attractiveness and familiarity can be an asset in persuasion.[24] Second, she has a high degree of prestige among both students and faculty. Are there any liabilities to such a selection?

Thinking back to your social psychology class, you remember a study conducted at the University of Massachusetts. Students were presented with a speech attacking the industrial pollution of a river. One group of students were told that the speech had been given by a pro-environment speaker. The other group was told that the speaker was pro-business. The students considered the pro-business speaker to be more sincere and were more persuaded by his arguments.[25] Speakers who can be presented as having little to gain themselves from a particular cause are likely to be more convincing than are those who are perceived as having much to gain. Luckily, you know a biology professor who also feels strongly about the student union. He might be a better selection since he has little to gain from funding the arts. Beyond this, the biology professor is known for his staunch fiscal conservatism. That he would advocate higher spending in this area would lend further credence to the cause. Students in another experiment were persuaded more by arguments for generous compensation to a plaintiff suing for damages in a mock trial when the arguments were said to have come from a person portrayed as selfish than when they came from one portrayed as generous.[26]

The biology professor may be the best choice. He is attractive and familiar to many of the students. He is knowledgeable about university affairs and is trustworthy. He himself has nothing to gain if the student fees are increased.

The presentation   What ought he say and how should his presentation be organized? What kinds of arguments should he use? You may first want to consider whether you would prefer a rational or a more emotional type of appeal. Would it be better if he told a heart-rending story of how student union fee cutbacks spelled an end to an aspiring dancer's career? Or should he argue that dance and drama enrich university life for everyone? Your decision in this matter will depend in part on your estimation of your audience. Rational appeals are more effective for well-educated audiences and for those that have a high degree of interest in the topic.[27] It seems plausible that individuals for whom an issue has a great deal of significance and who have the skills and resources to analyze fully the relevant concerns will be less swayed by emotionalism than by logic. Given that your audience consists of college students who are both well educated and have a strong interest in the topic, you may decide to present a rational type of appeal.

Fear appeals   You may want to consider whether it might be worthwhile to try to scare people into following your position. Perhaps you could argue that a failure to support the student union is somehow connected with other educational matters, that without a strong student union students will no longer be adequately represented to the faculty and administration. New requirements will be added. Courses will become more difficult and less relevant to student concerns. Perhaps you could argue that dissipation of the student union is part of a larger plan to disenfranchise students.

Social psychologists have shown that fear appeals can be successful under certain conditions. In general, studies have shown that the more people can be frightened, the more likely they are to be persuaded by a particular communication.[28] Such appeals, however, are not always successful. Research has shown, for example, that fear appeals are more successful with individuals who think well of themselves (i.e., who have high self-esteem) than they are with individuals with low self-esteem.[29] Presumably, the latter are overwhelmed by the fear. Lacking a sense of self-confidence, they may feel that there is nothing they can do about the situation. For their more self-confident counterparts, the fear appeal may act to motivate an appropriate response. Some studies lend credence to such speculation. When individuals are given specific instructions on how to deal with a situation, they are more likely to respond in a positive manner. Students subjected to a high fear communication on the dangers of smoking were more likely to stop smoking for a longer period of time if they were given specific recommendations on what to do when they had an urge to smoke (e.g., drink a glass of water).[30]

One-sided versus two-sided arguments   Once you have selected a speaker and know something about the type of argument he is going to present, you may want to think about how that argument should be organized.

Perhaps you want to present both sides of the issue. Perhaps a debate would be most convincing.

Again, some early research in social psychology may be of assistance. During World War II, certain U.S. officials were concerned that support for the war effort would decrease after Germany's defeat. The war against Japan still continued, and military officials did not want people to become overconfident about the conflict in the Pacific theater. Two radio broadcasts were recorded. Each contended that the war in the Pacific was likely to be prolonged. One broadcast presented both that argument and contradictory claims that Japan was close to defeat. The other broadcast presented only the argument that war was likely to continue for two or three more years.

The findings in this case are interesting. Both communications were effective but for different types of audiences. The two-sided explanation was more effective for more highly educated members of the audience; the one-sided communication worked better on less educated members of the audience.[31] Perhaps the highly educated group had anticipated some of the counterarguments. By dealing with those arguments, the two-sided communication may have addressed the concerns of the more educated listeners while it may have confused the less educated group. If you are attempting to persuade a highly educated group of college students, you may want to use a communication that presents both sides of the argument.

There is, however, one further matter you may want to consider before deciding on whether to use a one-sided or two-sided presentation. Research has shown that one-sided presentations are more effective in strengthening the attitudes of individuals who already share the viewpoint that you may be espousing. Accordingly, if your purpose in making a speech in favor of the student union is to convince students who already support the union to become more active and committed, then you may want to choose a one-sided appeal. Two-sided appeals, on the other hand, are more effective in reducing the strength of the opposition to your position. If your purpose is to convert opponents to your side, a two-sided appeal would be preferable. Individuals who already believed that the Pacific war was likely to be prolonged tended to be even more convinced after hearing the one-sided appeal, while those who thought the war would be short lived were less convinced after hearing the two-sided appeal.[32]

If you have decided to use a two-sided approach, you need to consider which message ought to go first. Common sense is confusing on this point. On the one hand, you may reason that it would be better to place your message first. "First impressions are lasting," someone told you once long ago. Social psychologists call this the "primacy effect." On the other hand, you may think that people will be more likely to remember your point if it is presented last. They will leave the presentation with your side of the issue freshest in their minds. Social psychologists call this the "recency effect."

To determine the conditions under which these effects operate, two social psychologists devised the following experiment.[33] Subjects were presented with a condensed transcript of a jury trial. All the arguments for the plaintiff were presented together as were all the arguments for the defendant. Subjects were then exposed to both arguments. The length of time between the presentation of each argument and that between the presentation of the second argument and some decision point (i.e., agreeing with either the plaintiff or the defendant) was systematically varied for each experimental group. The researchers found a primacy effect when there was a small gap in time between the presentation of each of the two arguments and a large gap between the second argument and the decision point. A recency effect was found when there was a large gap between the arguments and a small gap between the second argument and the decision point.

The implications of this study for your particular campaign are interesting. If the vote for the student union follows quickly on the heels of your presentation, you may want to schedule an intermission or break between the two arguments and present your position last. That would heighten the chances of a recency effect. If, however, the vote on the student union is not scheduled for some period of time after your presentation, you would want to present your position first with no break or intermission before presenting the other side.

You can see that understanding mass communication's effect is very complicated. This results in part because of the complex relationships between mass communications and interpersonal communication networks. We will need to keep this in mind as we move to consider some of the other implications of mass communication in society. At the same time, we shall consider whether the "effects" model is the best way of conceptualizing the role of mass media in society.

TELEVISION: PROGRAMMING AND ADVERTISING

Television programming and advertising has long been subject to criticism from a variety of sources. In this section, we shall explore some of these critiques and relevant social psychological perspectives that may help us to understand television's effect on individuals somewhat better.

Violence and the Media

If you come home one evening, kick off your shoes, and sit down to watch three hours of prime-time television, it is quite likely that you will see at least one violent episode. Someone is likely to be shot, killed, beaten, harassed, or at least threatened with a fatal weapon such as a knife or gun. Indeed, according to some estimates, you may see as many as 18 violent episodes per hour during adult viewing hours (9–11 P.M. EST). The amount of television violence is not that much less during family viewing hours (8–9 P.M. EST) or during children's viewing hours.[34]

Many people are concerned about the amount of violence presented on television. Some people feel that the presentation of violence leads to violence in life. Violent crimes, in particular, are often thought to be stimulated by television portrayals. The immolation of a woman in Boston in 1974 was preceded by a television show in which a similar event occurred.[35] One social psychologist notes that the number of bomb threats to airlines increased following the airing of a show featuring such a disaster aboard an airplane.[36] Exotic and dangerous robbery attempts often are blamed on television violence.

Research conducted in Boston, Massachusetts, during the tumultuous years in which that city was attempting to implement a school desegregation plan suggests that media reports of violence in one setting may have served as a provocation for subsequent violence in another. For example, white students at one school, having seen a news report of a white student being injured at another school, may then have selected a black student at their school for retribution. Much of the violence appeared to have a retributive character, and the media, particularly television, appeared to be the vehicle through which stimuli for retribution were carried to different parts of the community.[37]

It is, of course, difficult to conclude anything about the relationship between television and violence on the basis of a few unique events. However, such occurrences certainly warrant more systematic inquiry on television violence and its potential impact.

The relationship between television and violence is not unlike the sports and violence issue addressed in Chapter 7. Some social psychologists have hypothesized that television violence, like sports violence, can have a cathartic effect, serving as an outlet for people's emotions. However, as the research reviewed in connection with sports and violence (see Chapter 6) indicates, there is very little basis for such a conclusion. Indeed, research on the effect of television violence suggests that viewers are likely to imitate violent role models especially when such models are rewarded for having engaged in violent behavior. Moreover, the presence of violence-related stimuli in the environment (e.g., a gun) further enhances the likelihood of violent response. As discussed in Chapter 7, children who were shown a film containing a violent episode were more likely to enact such behavior themselves. The likelihood of violence was increased when the protagonist was presented as justifiably engaging in violence and was then rewarded for his actions.

Such experimental findings gain added validity from surveys that have found that young people who tend to engage in violence also tend to watch a great deal of television violence.[38] The causal connections, however, are complicated. According to a major study of television violence,[39] there *appears* to be a relationship between heavy viewing of television violence and actual participation in violent activities for *some types* of individuals. Both violent behavior and heavy television viewing of violence may thus be produced by some underlying condition. In short, this research suggests that television may play more of a contributory than an independent causal role.

This is not to suggest that a frustration-aggression approach to television and violence is totally inappropriate. Vicarious participation in aggression does not reduce aggressive tendencies. As we have seen, however, frustration is likely to increase aggression. One theorist thus hypothesizes that mass media, particularly television, may contribute to the existence of violence in society by contributing to people's frustrations. According to James D. Halloran,

In these circumstances, deprived groups in society are reminded, by a daily bombardment, of what is available to others, what is said to be theirs for the asking, yet what they certainly do not possess and, moreover, are not likely ever to achieve. There are, of course, other powerful agents of frustration operating at a variety of levels, from the interpersonal to the environmental, but it would be foolish to ignore the possibility that the media, in their normal day-to-day operations, by the presentation of these norms and values, may increase expectations unrealistically, aggravate existing problems, contribute to frustration and consequently to the aggression and violence that may stem from this.[40]

Research has yet to be completed to support such a conclusion. However, we ought not to close our minds to the possibility that mass media may operate in such complex and enigmatic ways.

Another approach to the question of the impact of television violence has been developed by George Gerbner and his colleagues at the Annenberg School of Communications at the University of Pennsylvania. According to Gerbner, television communications are more important for what they *imply* about the nature of the world in which we live than for what they state explicitly. All societies contain myths and rituals that serve to demonstrate to individuals accepted constructions of reality. Such constructions produce views of how things are, how they should be, and what needs to be done to "make things right." Such constructions tell us what is right and wrong or proper and improper in terms of social relationships; they tell us how we should relate to one another. One theorist refers to such constructions as "a kind of grammar which rules the conduct of its members, which decides what is compulsory, forbidden and allowed and what is seen as right, reasonable, and wholesome."[41] As Gerbner and Gross state

> Common rituals and mythologies are agencies of symbolic socialization and control. They demonstrate how society works by dramatizing its norms and values. They are essential parts of the general system of messages that cultivates prevailing outlooks (which is why we call it culture) and regulates social relationship. This system of messages, with its story-telling functions, makes people perceive as real and normal and right that which fits the established social order.[42]

Taken as a whole, mass communications, especially television, implicate us all in a world view that is both coherent and structured. In this sense, the media "cultivates" among its viewers a particular view of reality that may then have consequences for behavior. "Commercial television . . . presents an organically composed total world of interrelated stories," which are viewed regularly and ritualistically (i.e., "by the clock rather than by the program") by its audience.[43]

According to Gerbner, violence is one of the central elements in television's message system. As he states,

> Violence plays a key role in television's portrayal of the social order. It is the simplest and cheapest dramatic means to demonstrate who wins in the game of life and the rules by which the game is played. It tells us who are the aggressors and who are the victims. It demonstrates who has the power and who must acquiesce to that power. It tells us who should be feared—and by that achieves the goal of real-life violence. The few incidents of real-life violence it incites only serve to reinforce this fear. In the portrayal of violence there is a relationship

between the roles of the violent and the victim. Both roles are there to be learned by the viewers. In generating among the many a fear of the power of the few, television violence may achieve its greatest effect.[44]

For heavy television viewers, violence may be an important part of their perception of reality, even if it is not actually as real as it may appear on television.

To assess the extent to which heavy television viewing cultivates a different world view among its audiences, Gerbner and his colleagues interviewed both heavy and nonheavy television viewers. Both groups were asked to answer questions concerning the amount of "actual" violence they think exists around them.

They conducted phone interviews in four urban areas.[45] Based on this study, the researchers concluded that the world for very heavy television viewers was a good deal more frightening than it was for people who do not watch much television. For example, heavy viewers overestimated the amount of violence in their neighborhoods and their own chances for becoming involved in violence. Heavy viewers also tended to view the amount of both police and criminal activity as being much more prevalent than nonheavy viewers. Beyond this, heavy viewers of television violence tended to have a greater mistrust of others than did those who did not watch a lot of television violence.

Gerbner's early conclusions were criticized by two researchers at the University of Toronto.[46] They claimed that Gerbner failed to control for certain important variables in his analysis. Most important, urban areas are likely to contain both safe and dangerous neighborhoods. Anthony Doob and Glenn MacDonald hypothesized that the actual incidence of crime existing in a particular neighborhood would be a more powerful predictor of the extent to which an individual felt that he or she was likely to become a victim of crime in the future. Door-to-door interviews were conducted in both high-crime and low-crime Toronto-area neighborhoods. Doob and MacDonald found that neighborhood did make a difference for the extent to which an individual felt that he or she was likely to become a victim. Individuals living in high-crime sections of Toronto, however, were significantly affected by heavy television viewing. The researchers speculated that police crime dramas dealing with inner-city crime would likely be very salient for this segment of their sample who would then tend to be more strongly influenced by such shows. The authors also note that other relationships postulated by Gerbner and Gross were confirmed in their study. For example, like Gerbner and Gross, Doob and MacDonald found that heavy television viewers tended to overestimate the amount of violence taking place in their neighborhoods even if they themselves did not expect to be victimized.

In fairness to Gerbner and his colleagues, it should be pointed out that they expected television viewing to operate as "part and parcel" of a complex of variables, including lower education. Television would be a more important source of information for individuals with limited access to other sources. In a subsequent study,[47] Gerbner et al. sampled students from two schools: a public school in a suburban New Jersey community and a school in New York City. Students were questioned about their perceptions of their chances of becoming involved in violence, their fear of walking alone at night, the extent of police activity in their respective communities, and their trust and mistrust of others. Overall, the researchers concluded that heavy television viewing was associated with increased fear, mistrust, and heightened perceptions of police activity for both groups of students. Lower-class New York City youths tended to have more exaggerated perceptions than did the suburbanites of the number of people involved in crime and violence. The authors cite another study of 2,200 7- to 11-year-olds that found "a significant relationship . . . between amount of television viewing and violence-related fears even with controls for age, sex, ethnic background, vocabulary and the child's own reports of victimization."[48] Based on such studies, the authors conclude "that one correlate of television viewing is a heightened and unequal sense of danger and risk in a mean and selfish world."[49]

Based on the available research then, it does appear that violence as it is presented in the media may affect individuals in different ways. Exposure to violence may serve to instigate subsequent violence. There is a continuing debate about whether the media are a "cause" of the high level of violence in American society or whether they merely reflect and reinforce existing violent tendencies. Such "chicken and egg" questions may be difficult if not impossible to answer. As part of a general pattern, however, media violence certainly appears to contribute to an atmosphere of danger and fear.

This suggests a further ramification of media-presented violence. Perhaps a crucial question is not whether the media directly instigate violence, but whether they create a psychological atmosphere that may have other consequences. Gerbner and his colleagues argue, for example, that the sense of fear, danger, and vulnerability promulgated through the media may lead to a general subservience to authority. Television violence, in this sense, serves to validate certain power relationships in which the proper use of violence is the prerogative of the state through police, soldiers, and other officials. This may serve as a warning to those who would challenge such authorities. One researcher characterizes the media's role in this regard as one of "labeling amplification."[50] Television "amplifies" the idea that in general police and other officials are "good" and that it is all right for them to use violence. The media also tell us who are deviants and how they should be treated.

Such considerations have wider implications for how we regard the role of media in society. Rather than looking for direct effects, we may need to pay more attention to their more subtle contributions in creating and promulgating general conceptions about social life and social relationships. We shall keep such considerations in mind as we approach other aspects of mass communications.

Advertising

It is always possible that you might come home one evening, sit down, kick off your shoes, and begin to watch television and not see any violence at all. Perhaps a "special" or sporting event (like track rather than hockey or football) will capture your attention. Such an occurrence may not be the norm, though it is certainly a possibility. One event is not very likely. If you come home and turn on one of the commercial television stations, you are very unlikely to escape commercials. Some television critics, as we have seen, have criticized television entertainment, particularly the preponderance of violence in such entertainment; others, however, have focused their critiques on television advertising.

Although the "reality" presented by television entertainment, according to its critics, may be "ruled by violence," the medium itself, some claim, is ruled by commercials. In the following pages, we shall review some of the complaints that have been made about advertising on television and in other media. We shall then discuss the relevance of different social psychological perspectives for understanding the role of advertising in society and, in particular, its impact on children.

Some complaints about media advertising   Advertising has been criticized from a variety of perspectives. Some critics complain that commercials depict men and women in a sexually stereotypical way. According to this view, women are presented as either "sexual objects," who passively accept male sexual aggression, or as near idiots, who have a passionate concern with cleanliness. The first image, according to this critique, may be exemplified by a perfume ad in which a woman may be portrayed in a sexually inviting position; the second image is exemplified by the number of commercials directed at housewives, often designed to tell how to get sparkling floors, shiny furniture, clean windows, and immaculate dishes and clothes, as well as the potential embarrassment should something not be perfect (e.g., should a husband be caught with "ring around the collar"). Commentators have claimed that the media in general present unrealistic and demeaning stereotypical images of women.[51]

Others have claimed that media advertising is deceptive. What does it mean, for example, to hear that nine of ten doctors recommend brand A aspirin? Does this mean that they would not recommend other brands? Does this mean that brand A is superior? What about the doctors? How were they selected? Most important, what about the doctor who did not recommend brand A? The questions one may ask about such claims are infinite, though on its face, the claim appears to be a strong endorsement of brand A.

Another way in which advertising is said to be deceptive concerns misleading associations and implicit promises. Will eating a particular brand of cereal necessarily help you to become an Olympic-class athlete? Will driving a specific sport car result in your having a beautiful woman in the passenger seat? Will wearing a particular shirt make you handsome and slim? Will using a particular brand of perfume result in tall dark strangers being magnetically attracted to you? How will a particular aftershave turn you into a sea captain? Most ironically, perhaps, how will consumption of beer enable you to "dunk" a basketball, hit home runs, catch long football passes, score goals in soccer, run long distances, ski treacherous terrains, and ride horses not to mention hang glide and sky dive. Some critics claim that the association of particular products (i.e., cereal, cars, clothes, cosmetics, and beer) with romantic and exciting activities contains an implicit promise that using the product will enable one to perform those activities. Such a promise is not likely to become a reality.

Others have claimed that advertisements often contain subliminal messages.[52] Sexual images may be hidden in pictures, and sexual verbal messages may be contained in the background of tapes and recordings. Such techniques, critics argue, are especially pernicious because they pander to unconscious drives and desires.

Still others argue that advertising is, if not deceptive, at least confusing. Advertising contains its own language, which often inverts conventional English usages. For example, due to regulations and possible lawsuits, advertisers are reluctant to make direct comparisons between their product and the competition. However, one may claim that one's product is "the best" without implying such comparisons. To claim that one's product is "the best" is apparently no different from saying that one's product is "one of the best." Hence, the advertiser is not claiming that his or her product is necessarily superior to any other. In the language of advertising, therefore, it is easier to claim that one's product is "best" than it is to claim that it is better. Where, in common English, "best" is superlative, in advertising English, "better" tends to become the superlative. At least one research study has shown that such usages may create considerable confusion for children.[53]

Some advertisements fail to present sufficient or relevant information; others may present information that seems to be highly informative and technical but in fact is incomprehensible to most nonprofessional readers or viewers. Consider the following excerpt from a recent magazine advertisement: ". . . our latest technical development. A promotion stabilization system to give maximum motion control. . ." One must be thoroughly versed in technological jargon to make an intelligent decision about purchasing a pair of running shoes these days.

Finally, some people object to advertisements because, according to them, commercials trivialize life and make people look stupid. One theorist, Herbert Marcuse, has argued that advertisements, as a form of modern culture, present persons as though they are one-dimensional, preoccupied with the material aspects of life. Marcuse argues that advertising and other forms of media create "false needs." People become concerned with "affluence." This distracts them from other more meaningful aspects of existence and limits the possibilities and alternatives that people may seek in social life.[54] Interestingly, people who have had a long-term exposure to large amounts of advertising may indeed tend to be more materialistic than a comparable group with less advertising exposure.[55]

As a part of our culture, we may think of advertising in broader terms. Has it contributed to the development of a kind of consumer culture in which products are purchased not because of their need, but because of their capacity to communicate something about the individuals who own them? But how valid are these media-created identities? A shirt with a small animal on the pocket may say you are a "preppy," whether or not you can afford a private preparatory school education. Has advertising contributed to the kind of conspicuous consumption discussed in Chapter 1?

One theorist[56] has argued that the larger intentions behind advertising are not to encourage people to buy specific products, but to motivate them to buy in general. This may become more apparent if we look at the different senses in which one may "shop." You may, for example, need a car, and shopping may mean going from one dealer to another to "get the best deal." On the other hand, you can imagine yourself going to a shopping center to "shop" without any idea of what you "need." Shopping (i.e., buying) is an activity in and of itself. For some people, buying something may provide them with a sense of well-being. If you are feeling "blue," buying something may cause you to feel a bit better. Such an idea is implicit in certain commercials that tell you, for example, that buying a hamburger and a shake can make it a "great day."

The reader may want to keep considerations like these in mind as we go on to review some of the research on advertising and its effects. In particular, we shall focus on advertising's impact on children. But, first, let us consider television and the worlds of children.

Television, commercials, and the worlds of childhood   In a recently published popular book, author Marie Winn has articulated the opinion that watching television has a singularly negative impact on children's cognitive and social development. In *The Plug-in Drug*,[57] Winn argues that children attend to television in a passive manner and that viewing television has a narcotic-like effect, chilling children's senses and hindering cognitive development.

Young children think differently from adults. Reality is different for them in many ways. Hence, television and television advertisements in particular may be different for young children than it is for adults. As children grow older, their approach to reality changes; they become less restricted perceptually and begin to develop a capacity to see the world from different physical and social perspectives. Children begin to "take the role of the other."

These developing abilities have implications for how children come to understand television in general and television advertising in particular. As we shall see, the idea that children watch television in a "drugged" state may not be totally appropriate. In the following pages, we shall review some of the research on how children of different ages approach television reality. We shall then discuss the role of advertising in the reality of childhood. Finally, we shall consider some of the findings on the impact television advertising appears to have on children.

Research conducted from a cognitive perspective[58] suggests that children are not as passive in their viewing of television as some of the critics claim. It is interesting to note that although a kind of "attentional inertia" (i.e., a state in which viewers continue to watch for a period of several minutes, seeming to be engrossed in the object) has been observed among college students viewing television in a laboratory setting, younger children pay attention to television in a more cyclical and, in some ways, more sporadic manner. Young children have little interest in messages that are not comprehensible to them. Beginning at about age 2 or 3, children begin to monitor the television, attending to different messages. Some television images (e.g., moving images, puppets, and female adults) may be more successful in capturing a child's interest than others. Children are thus selective in their attention to television, although their patterns of attention may be manipulated with certain techniques.

Watching television may even enhance the development of certain kinds of cognitive skills. In a recently published essay, psychologist Ellen Wartella[59] has reviewed the relevance of such cognitive activities with respect to three aspects of television's reality: plot lines, characters, and filmic techniques.

Most of us have been watching television so long we have forgotten that we may have had to learn something to understand ordinary programming. Television is second nature to us; we can turn on a game show, a drama, or a soap opera and figure out what is going on even if we have not seen the show from the beginning. Although we do not always realize it, we are capable of such feats because we have implicit knowledge of the structure of television plot lines, television characters, and the organization of television presentations. We were not born with such tacit knowledge. Rather, it evolved through our experience with television as children or adolescents.

For young children, understanding a plot line is no easy task. It requires memory and, more important, the ability to select information relevant to the story. This is almost impossible for young children, who tend to focus on the more surface characteristics of television presentations (e.g., visual information). The ability to piece together a story increases with age.[60] A number of studies have shown that overall memory of what has taken place in a particular television drama as well as memory "of information" essential to the plot line increases with age. This results from basic maturational processes, although some researchers speculate that the kinds of selective processes that children develop in watching television may facilitate other kinds of learning. According to one researcher in this area:

> as children grow older, their ability to understand what is important in the plot increases and they acquire greater control in allocating their attention and focusing on what is important. This increased *attention control* has been found in other types of information-processing tasks.[61]

This is not of course to suggest that watching television will make your child more intelligent. Watching television, however, does appear to require some cognitive operations relevant to other forms of learning.

This can be seen with respect to the child's development of an understanding of television characters. Younger children are much less likely than older children to describe television characters in terms of internal characteristics (e.g., personality characteristics and motivational states) than they are in terms of surface characteristics (e.g., what a character "looks like").[62] For the young child, television may appear as a kind of "magic window" on the world. Very young children may believe that television characters are like living puppets who reside inside the set. Kindergartners and first graders have difficulty in distinguishing television characters from actors portraying events. Is "Archie Bunker" real or is he a fictional character created by an actor named Carroll O'Connor? It is interesting to note that many of the characters designed for children's television have ambiguous identities in this regard. When one of the authors of this text was in kindergarten, Roy Rogers and Gene Autry were two very important television cowboys. In "real life," they also were named Roy Rogers and Gene Autry. Young children today may experience a similar ambiguity with respect to the popular Mr. Rogers.

The child's ability to understand the reality of television characters, to distinguish them as actors portraying parts rather than as "real people," and to understand their portrayals in terms of relevant plot lines, increases with age. We should not close our minds to the possibility that there may be an interaction between the natural development of cognitive abilities and television viewing itself. Television drama in particular may provide an opportunity for children to identify with specific characters. Some research has shown that young children in particular are likely to adopt fictional characters whom they may consider to be real and with whom they identify.[63] Such identification may lead them to emphasize with these and other characters. Among other things, then, television may be one medium that contributes to a child's developing abilities to "take the role of the other."

Television techniques also may pose problems for young children. One child, for example, when questioned about the "Six-Million-Dollar Man," expressed concern about "Steve Austin's" ability to always catch the villain while he ran slowly.[64] The child obviously did not understand that slowing the film while Steve Austin was running was supposed to indicate that he was running at exceptionally fast speeds. Television uses a number of production techniques that young children do not understand. The use of "flashbacks," for example, may be difficult for a young child who may be having difficulty following a straight plot line.

Like understanding plot lines and characters, understanding filmic techniques appears to increase with age. Although research in this area is in an early stage of development, some studies have shown that mastering television techniques can help to facilitate cognitive development. One researcher, for example, has examined the use of the zoom lens that focuses on parts of objects as well as the whole object in teaching children part-whole relationships. Exposure to zoom techniques appeared to enhance understanding of part-whole relationships among Israeli children; similar findings were not reported for an American sample. The researcher noted, however, that the Israeli children were much more serious television watchers. This, they speculate, may account for the discrepancy. In any case, further research is required.

To summarize, children do not approach television as totally passive recipients. Rather, watching television for young children requires cognitive activity, and some research suggests that television may even contribute to the development of some cognitive operations. Researchers do not claim, however, that television is a substitute for other activities or that it facilitates cognitive, social, and emotional development as well as direct involvement in reading, play, and other childhood activities.

Television advertising and children   Media advertising may have a significant impact on all of us. However, researchers and policymakers are most concerned with the impact of television advertising on children. Although there are large individual differences, the average child between the ages of 2 and 11 may watch as much as 4 hours of television per day. In 1961, researchers concluded that:

Throughout the preschool years, television time far exceeds other media time; in fact, it usually exceeds the total of all other media time. . . . Two-thirds of all children are already television viewers before they have much experience with movies. Even at the end of 10 years, when they are making some use of all media, television is the only one they are using day after day. At age 10, three-fourths of all children, as we discovered, will be likely to be watching television on any given day. This is more than twice the percentage for any other medium at that age.[65]

Such observations are even more valid today. If children watch about 4 hours of television per day, then we may estimate that they see 3 hours of television advertising each week or, roughly, 20,000 commercials each year.[66] Will these commercials be mainly those presented during children's programming hours (i.e., on Saturday mornings and after school)? Research indicates that this is not necessarily the case. Children watch a considerable amount of television in the evenings and during adult viewing times.[67] Hence, they are almost as likely to see former athletes advertising "lite" beer and beautiful women advertising cosmetics as they are to see Ronald McDonald "pushing" hamburgers or Captain Crunch selling cereal. Some people are concerned about exposing children to adult products. There is concern that cumulative exposure to drugs and medicines may create a tendency for children to rely too heavily on such medicines.[68] Others worry that exposure to beer and wine ads leads to increased use of these substances among children.

How children approach commercials City water and sewer systems directors have noted sharp drops in water pressure during commercials for programs that typically have many viewers (e.g., the Super Bowl). Apparently, most adults understand that there is a time-out on the field of play and that all they stand to miss by making a quick trip to the kitchen or bathroom is someone trying to sell them something. Commercials do not necessarily mean the same thing to children. Up until the age of 5 or 6, many children are unable to distinguish commercials from regular television programming. Between kindergarten and third grade, children begin to develop a notion that television advertising is different from programming in that someone is trying to sell a product. It is not until they are 9 or 10, however, that most children begin to take an advertiser's "intentions" into consideration when making sense out of commercials.[69] Hence, most children are likely to have between 5 and 7 years of exposure to commercials before they begin to understand that Ronald McDonald says burgers are good not because he really cares whether children will like their lunch but because it is his job to sell hamburgers.

Many people are concerned about the effect that television advertising may have on children. In the following pages we will review some of these concerns and some of the relevant research.

Concerns have been raised about the use of program characters in advertisements. Critics claim that this contributes to the child's confusion about what constitutes an advertisement and what constitutes regular programming. Certain studies have provided tentative support for this idea. In one study, for example, children who saw Pebbles (a Flintstone character) advertising cereal during a Flintstone cartoon were more likely to think that the ad was part of the cartoon than did children who saw the same ad during a Bugs Bunny cartoon.[70] Research such as this has led some social scientists to recommend that commercials using program characters not be placed adjacent to programs in which those characters appear.

A more salient concern, however, has to do with the idea that children, who are basically unsure and confused about the reality of television characters to begin with, are likely to be strongly influenced by such characters. Researchers have termed this the "endorsement effect." Children may place a great deal of "trust" in television characters. For this reason, certain officials have objected to products such as "Spiderman" vitamins, on the grounds that the advertisers are exploiting the child's trust in the character to make the vitamin appealing.[71]

Research suggests that both direct endorsements (i.e., those in which a character explicitly recommends a product) and indirect endorsement (i.e., those in which a character is shown to be passively associated with a product) can have powerful effects on children. Not all characters are successful, however. One study, for example, demonstrated that Mohammed Ali, former President Ford, and Captain Kangaroo were successful in promoting a variety of different products but that Lucille Ball was less so and, in one instance (in which she was presented as promoting a gun), even had a negative effect.[72] Evidence suggests an interaction between product and endorser. Generally, findings suggest that as endorsers, adults are more effective than are children; that, as children grow older, same-sex endorsers are more effective than are endorsers of the opposite sex; and that black endorsers are more effective for black children and white endorsers for white children. The race effect, however, appears to be contingent on the child's prior socialization with respect to race attitudes and prejudice.[73] Peer endorsers also tend to be more effective for older than for younger children. It is hypothesized that older children are more concerned with social acceptance than are their younger counterparts.[74] It is interesting to note that ads portraying women in counterstereotypical roles changed children's sex role stereotypes.[75] Since many ads portray men and women in stereotypical roles, one may hypothesize that this can have a similar effect on a child's social stereotypes.

Television endorsers thus appear to be quite effective in making their products attractive to children. This seems to be the case for fantasy characters (e.g., Pebbles Flintstone) as well as for real actors and celebrities. As one researcher points out, however, such distinctions may be blurred by characters such as Ronald McDonald and the Burger King who have both a fantasy status (i.e., they appear "in role" at public events) and are, at the same time, actors impersonating characters. Such confusion has provided problems for researchers (i.e., How do we categorize such characters?).[76] If understanding such characters is difficult for researchers, imagine the confusion they can create for young children.

So what, if advertisements sell products? Isn't that what they are supposed to do? Yes. The concern, however, is that they may have other consequences—possibly undesirable ones. We have already seen that advertisements can have an impact on sex role stereotyping. What about other effects?

Children go through a stage when peers are quite important to them. Consider, now, the type of advertisement promising that ownership of a particular product will make one "the most popular kid on the block." Among other things, such advertisements may promote a kind of "materialism." Specifically, such ads may lead children to believe that possession of a particular item is sufficient to make them popular. Studies have shown that children exposed to large amounts of advertising do tend to be somewhat more materialistic than a comparable group without sustained and heavy advertising exposure.[77] Beyond this, the reader may wonder whether such advertisements may produce a more general belief that happiness is somehow connected with particular products. Policymakers have been concerned about such "social status appeals," which are now prohibited by advertising regulation. More general appeals that associate happiness with product usage are not regulated. Nor is there sufficient research on their impact.

In addition, some researchers have been concerned with the effect that television commercials may have on family life. It is hypothesized that commercials can produce strains in family relations by creating desires among children for items that, for one reason or another, may not be desired by parents. Generally, surveys indicate that most parents do not feel that commercials create familial problems. Other studies have indicated that children's disappointment with parental denials of requests for television-advertised Christmas toys can lead to conflict. The nature of such conflict is difficult to discern through the use of conventional social psychological methods. One unanticipated consequence of parental denials, however, may be learning. Children tend to remember parental reasons for denial (e.g., "expense" and "poor value"). In this way, commercials may contribute to consumer socialization.[78]

Finally, concerns have been expressed about the extent to which advertising contributes to antisocial behavior—particularly alcoholism. Generally, studies show that children do tend to imitate and model social behavior but that parents and peers are more important influences than are the media in this regard.[79] It should also be pointed out that rates of alcoholism are high in some cultures that have no commercials at all.[80]

In short, commercials, in general, and television advertising, in particular, have mixed implications. On the one hand, they may detract us from what some may consider more fundamental concerns. They are, if not deceptive, at least devious, relying on a number of social psychological tricks (i.e., trust, identification, role modeling) to promote a product. On the other hand, advertising may not be as potent as some suppose. Advertising effects appear to be mediated by social factors and may in fact contribute to consumer socialization. A more complete understanding awaits a consideration of advertising in a social structural and interpersonal context.

Political communications: a reconsideration   The idea that mass media have limited effects (i.e., effects that are mediated by social and psychological factors) has become somewhat of an axiom among many social psychologists. This idea may, however, seem odd to journalists and lay observers who note that the mass media receive a great deal of attention. The reader may wonder why, if the effects of mass communication are so limited, politicians worry so much about their television images and why advertisers spend millions of dollars on making their products look attractive. Media critics are not likely to be convinced by arguments that politicians are attempting to persuade only the 5 percent of voters who are "waverers" or that advertisers are simply concerned about "market shares" (i.e., attempting to convince a higher proportion of product users to buy their brand as opposed to other brands). For many people, then, the idea that mass media have limited effects may seem a bit naive at best.[81]

As we have suggested earlier, one of the problems in assessing the actual importance of mass communication in society stems from the idea that the effects model does not sufficiently capture the subtleties of the social psychology of mass communications. Any communication may contain both a manifest (explicit) and a latent (implicit) message. (See Chapter 2.) As we have seen, much early research attempted to assess the impact of a particular communication's manifest content on some relevant attitude or behavior (e.g., a nonsmoking film on attitudes toward smoking). Such an approach is based on the idea that there is a direct corespondence between the manifest content of a particular communication and relevant attitudes and behavior. Research on television and advertising has suggested that content alone may not provide a sufficient explanation of mass communication's impact. Mass communication may operate through other more subtle social psychological processes. Imitation, modeling, identification, trust, and fear are among a number of social-psychological processes through which mass communications may influence individuals. Such influence may not always entail a direct correspondence between the manifest content of a communication and a related attitude or behavior. Violent television programs, as we have seen, may lead people to become more violent. They also may cause them to become more fearful and more subservient to authority.

Political communication may operate in an equally subtle manner. According to one view, political communications define political reality. Mass communications perform an agenda-setting function; if they are not totally successful in telling people what to think, they may be extremely successful in telling people what to think about.[82] Mass communications, in this sense, may define issues and set the contours of public debate by telling us about the important concerns of our time.

A number of social psychologists have used the concept of myth to characterize mass media transmitted political communication. According to Murray Edelman, "The word 'myth' signifies a belief held in common by a large number of people that gives events and actions a particular meaning; it is typically socially cued rather than empirically based."[83] The terms of political communication—political language—are based on shared conventions rather than empirical realities. As Edelman elaborates, "Political language can evoke a set of mythic beliefs in subtle and powerful ways." Symbolic cues and code words, in particular, can serve to define the "geography and topography of the political world."[84]

Suppose that a "disturbance" takes place on your campus. What do you call it? If you call it a "riot," you imply that it was spontaneous and unplanned.

One might surmise, from your language, that the perpetrators are irresponsible. For someone else, however, the riot may more appropriately be characterized as a "rebellion," signaling a more serious effort to challenge authorities. Edelman points out, for example, that a survey of blacks' opinions about the riots in the late 1960s indicated that those who were sympathetic to the disturbance tended to prefer the term "rebellion" or some other word denoting a planned movement toward a social goal.[85] The language of politics thus plays a role in "ordering" political relationships. It tells us whom we may trust and identifies those individuals whom we ought not to trust. Such code words place us in specific groups and identify other members. They also implicitly define nonmembers; they tell us who is wrong or right, victim or victimizer, friendly or unfriendly, and so on.

In some cases, particular groups may engage in symbolic struggles aimed at defining public controversy in strategic ways. Berg and Ross[86] suggest that understanding the Boston school integration conflict as one of "busing" or "forced busing" rather than "desegregation" harmed public acceptability of the desegregation plan. Edelman and others argue that government largely controls the promulgation of political myths in ways that sustain existing power relationships.

Social psychologists in both the United States and the United Kingdom have been interested in news as a form of socially constructed knowledge. As such, news is a form of socialization as well as information. In this sense, "news has the capacity to create meaning independent of the specific events to which the stories refer."[87] Consider, for example, a news story about a State Department spokesperson who asserts that U.S. military aid to friendly countries is needed in Central America to avoid "Communist takeovers" and the influx of large numbers of immigrants (labeled "feet people"). Such a statement is hardly a simple prognostication. It we probe deeper, it becomes clear that such statements implicitly define not only Latin American but also Asian immigrants ("boat people") as undesirable. Such statements also appear to pander to fears that large waves of immigrants will take jobs away from "Americans" already beleaguered by unemployment. In a round-about way, then, the statements imply that keeping one's job may be tied to support of military spending in Latin America. Beyond this, such news events imply that the State Department officials possess special knowledge, which makes them "expert" in such areas and that we ought not question their decisions.

According to Peter Dahlgren, television news in particular is designed to socialize viewers to be "nonreflexive." A nonreflexive consciousness, according to Dahlgren.

> does not see itself as a participant in the construction of the social world; it sees itself as merely acted upon by the social world. . . . Consciousness is solidified and frozen, structuring a relationship of domination. Some examples of this form of consciousness include unquestioned authority patterns within the family, reified social structures of hierarchy in bureaucracies, labor's acceptance of its subordination to capital, and uncritical acquiescence to the legitimacy of "experts."[88]

Television news generates a nonreflexive consciousness in three ways. First, it typically situates the viewer in a subordinate position with respect to various officials, experts, administrators, and so on. These agents are portrayed as being in possession of valuable and important knowledge. The viewer is thus implicitly "dependent" on the news for such knowledge. Second, viewer consciousness distinguishes between newsmakers—those who actively shape major events—and the news recipients, who, as a consequence, also are the recipients of the realities shaped by others. With respect to the political world, the viewer is essentially "inefficacious." Finally, television news presents an historically static view of reality. Viewers are not informed about how events came to develop. According to Dahlgren, nonreflexive consciousness as promulgated by television news is consistent with the need for mass loyalty in capitalist societies.

Mass media may perform a similar function in communist and socialist societies as well. V. S. Korobeinikov describes the role of Soviet mass communications in the following terms. His account is worth quoting at length.

> In Soviet society the mass media have become an instrument for the building of socialism and communism. The task of strengthening the material base of the new society and of raising labour productivity called primarily for the upbringing of a conscious toiler full of initiative . . .
>
> Under socialism the impact of the mass media on economic development is observed, primarily, in the broad coverage of socialist emulation, in the establishment of the relations between people as free creative toilers full of initiative. This task is solved by giving wide publicity to socialist emulation and by constantly informing the working people of its goals, conditions, progress and results.
>
> The mass media take under their control the implementation of plans by enterprises and help to bring out the production reserves. They develop and propagate diverse forms of emulation and exchange of experience including friendship meets, contest of best workers, rallies of innovators, inter-branch, inter-republican and international forms of emulation. For instance, several national newspapers have taken diverse industries and branches under their "guardianship". . . . The newspapers keep watch over the emulation in their respective branches and regularly sum up the results. In this connection checking-up raids are held, economic surveys, commentaries and feature stories about innovators and front-rank workers are published.
>
> Similar forms are used by the local press. They often publish "Rolls of Honour" with the names of the emulation winners for each month and quarter of a year. Sociological studies show that representatives of different trades give an exclusively high appraisal of the social recognition of their work through the mass media.
>
> Socialism raises high the social prestige of labour and not little credit belongs here to the mass media which, by their own peculiar methods, glorify man the toiler, forming a positive attitude to representatives of diverse trades. (Sociological surveys show that among professions covered most extensively by the Soviet press, radio and television, leadership belongs to researchers, engineers, tractor drivers, foremen and steel founders. . . .) As noted by L. I. Brezhnev . . ., our most respected people are "front-rank workers. Many of them are known all over the country, they figure in the press, they are elected to government bodies."[89]

In the Soviet Union, then, mass communications are more openly designed to promote specific values and ideals.

A similar process has been observed in China. According to Godwin C. Chu, postrevolutionary China has undergone a change in cognitive structure. At the instigation of their leaders and as promulgated through mass communications, the Chinese, according to Chu, have begun to think in a more "dynamic action"–oriented manner. This is reflected in postrevolutionary interpretations of traditional Chinese phrases:

TRADITIONAL MEANING	POSTREVOLUTIONARY MEANING
Proceed	Vigorously stir up
Enquire	Feeling the bottom
Deal with	Resolutely grasp
Take a long view	Ruthlessly criticize
Provide aid	Support mightily[90]

Chu also notes that where prerevolutionary Chinese thought categories are primarily family oriented and based on ancient traditions, postrevolutionary categories are oriented toward the collectivity as whole and the future.

Finally, it is important to keep in mind that mass communications provide a forum in which elites not only communicate with the public, but also one in which different elites may communicate with each other about concerns relevant to different publics. Complex interactions exist not only in communication between elites and publics but in those between different elites as well. These interactions continue to be insufficiently studied but may have a substantial bearing on world events. For example, the difficulty that NATO leaders have in convincing their respective publics to support deployment of nuclear weapons could be construed by Warsaw Pact leaders as either instability rendering any agreement questionable or as a demand for "sanity," which would increase the possibilities for concluding an agreement. For this reason, a number of theorists have recently suggested that worldwide communications must take place in the context of open and honest discussion, facilitated by a reflexive rather than a nonreflexive discourse. Such discussion needs to take place in an atmosphere of trust and stability. It would also require an examination of the meanings of the terms of debate and their significance for different publics.

NOTES

[1]Horace Newcomb, "Assessing the Violence Profile Studies of Gerbner and Gross: A Humanistic Critique and Suggestion," in G. Cleveland Wilhoit and Harold DeBock, eds., *Mass Communication Review Yearbook* (Beverly Hills, Calif.: Sage, 1980), pp. 450–469.

[2]Harold D. Lasswell, *Propaganda Technique in the World War* (New York: Peter Smith, 1938).

[3]Paul F., Lazarsfeld, Bernard Berelson, and Hazel Gaudet, *The People's Choice* (New York: Columbia University Press, 1948).

[4]Bernard Berelson, Paul F. Lazarsfeld, and William McPhee, *A Study of Opinion Forma-tion in a Presidential Campaign* (Chicago: University of Chicago Press, 1954).

[5]Ibid., p. 248.

[6]Joseph T. Klapper, *The Effects of Mass Communication* (Glencoe, Ill.: The Free Press, 1960).

[7]Ibid., pp. 18–26.

[8]Ibid., pp. 19–20.

[9]Gordon Allport and Leo J. Postman, "The Basic Psychology of Rumor," *Transactions of the New York Academy of Sciences*, Vol. 8, Series II (1945), pp. 61–81.

[10]Patricia L. Kendall and Katherine M. Wolfe, "The Analysis of Deviant Cases in Com-munications Research," in Paul F. Lazarsfeld and Frank N. Stanton, eds., *Communications Re-search* (New York: Harper and Brothers, 1949).

[11]Herbert H. Hyman and Paul B. Sheatsley, "Some Reasons Why Information Campaigns Fail," *Public Opinion Quarterly*, Vol. 20 (1947), pp. 412–423.

[12]Kenneth H. Hur and John P. Robinson, "The Social Impact of Roots," in Wilhoit and deBock, eds., *Mass Communication Review Yearbook*, pp. 491–508.

[13]Jerome M. Levine and Gardner Murphy, "The Learning and Forgetting of Controversial Material," *Journal of Abnormal and Social Psychology*, Vol. 37 (1943), pp. 507–517.

[14]Lazarsfeld, Berelson, and Gaudet, *The People's Choice*, p. 142.

[15]Klapper, *The Effects of Mass Communication*, p. 27.

[16]Ibid., p. 65.

[17]Ibid., p. 67.

[18]Ibid., pp. 32–37.

[19]Ibid., p. 37.

[20]Nathan Maccoby and J. Alexander, "Use of Media in Lifestyle Programs," in P. O. David-son and S. M. Davidson, eds., *Behavioral Medicine: Changing Lifestyles* (New York: Brunner/Mazel, 1980).

[21]Jerome Johnston, James Ettema, and Terrance Davidson, *An Evaluation of FREESTYLE: A Television Series to Reduce Sex-Role Stereotypes* (Ann Arbor: Institute for Social Research, Univer-sity of Michigan, 1980).

[22]Klapper, *The Effects of Mass Communication*, p. 102.

[23]John Kishler, "Prediction of Differential Learning from a Motion Picture by Means of Indices of Identification Potentials Derived from Attitudes Toward the Main Character," *Ameri-can Psychologist*, Vol. 5 (1950), pp. 298–299.

[24]Robert Zajonc, "The Attitudinal Effects of Mere Exposure," *Journal of Personality and Social Psychology Monograph Supplement*, Vol. 9 (1968), pp. 1–27.

[25]Alice Eagly, Wendy Wood, and Shell Chaiken, "Causal Inferences About Communicators and Their Effect on Opinion Change," *Journal of Personality and Social Psychology*, Vol. 36 (1978), pp. 424–435.

[26]J. Wachtler, and E. Counselman, "When Increasing Liking for a Communicator Increases Opinion Change: An Attribution Analysis of Attractiveness," *Journal of Experimental Social Psychology*, Vol. 19 (1981), pp. 386–395.

[27]Carl I. Hovland, A. A. Lumsclaine, and F. Sheffield, *Experiments on Mass Communica-tion: Studies in Social Psychology in World War II*, Vol. III (Princeton, N.J.: Princeton University Press, 1949). Also, see S. Chaiken, "Communicator Physical Attractiveness and Persuasion," *Journal of Personality and Social Psychology*, Vol. 37 (1979), pp. 1387–1397.

[28]Howard Leventhal, "Findings and Theory in the Study of Fear Communications," in L. Berkowitz, ed., *Advances in Experimental Social Psychology* (New York: Academic Press, 1970), pp. 119–186.

[29]Ibid.

[30]Ibid., p. 185.

[31]Hovland, Lumsdaine, and Sheffield, *Experiments on Mass Communication*.

[32]Ibid., p. 178.

[33]Norman Miller and Donald Campbell, "Recency and Primacy in Persuasion as a Func-tion of the Timing of Speeches and Measurement," *Journal of Abnormal and Social Psychology*, Vol. 59 (1959), pp. 1–9.

[34]George Gerbner et al., "The Demonstration of Power: Violence Profile No. 10," in Wilhoit

and deBock, eds., *Mass Communication Review Yearbook*, pp. 403-405.

[35]J. Michael Ross and William M. Berg, *I Respectfully Disagree with the Judge's Order: The Boston School Desegregation Controversy* (Washington, D.C.: University Press of America, 1981), p. 88.

[36]Albert Bandura, *Aggression: A Social Learning Analysis* (Englewood Cliffs, N.J.: Prentice-Hall, 1973).

[37]Ross and Berg, *I Respectfully Disagree*, pp. 318-324.

[38]George Comstock, "Television and Its Viewers: What Social Science Sees," in Wilhoit and deBock, eds., *Mass Communication Review Yearbook*, pp. 495-499.

[39]Surgeon General's Scientific Advisory Committee on Television and Social Behavior, *Television and Growing Up: The Impact of Televised Violence*. Report to the Surgeon General, U.S. Public Health Service (Washington, D.C.: Government Printing Office, 1972).

[40]James D. Halloran, "Mass Communication: Symptom or Cause of Violence," in Wilhoit and deBock, eds., *Mass Communication Review Yearbook*, p. 437.

[41]Luc Van Poecke, "Gerbner's Cultural Indicators: The System Is the Message," in Wilhoit and deBock, eds., p. 424.

[42]George Gerbner and Larry Gross, "Living with Violence: The Violence Profile," *Journal of Communication*, Vol. 26, no. 2 (1976), p. 173.

[43]Gerbner et al., "The Demonstration of Power," p. 406.

[44]Ibid., p. 406.

[45]Gerbner and Gross, "Living with Violence," pp. 173-179.

[46]Anthony N. Doob and Glen E. MacDonald, "Television Viewing and Fear of Victimization: Is the Relationship Causal?" in Wilhoit and deBock, eds., *Mass Communication Review Yearbook*, pp. 479-488.

[47]Gerbner et al., "The Demonstration of Power," pp. 403-422.

[48]Ibid., p. 422.

[49]Ibid., p. 422.

[50]Halloran, "Mass Communication," p. 444.

[51]For a collection of interesting articles on this point, see G. Tuckman et al., eds., *Hearth and Home: Images of Women in the Mass Media* (New York: Oxford University Press, 1978).

[52]Wilson B. Key, *Media Sexploitation* (Englewood Cliffs, N.J.: Prentice-Hall, 1976).

[53]John R. Rossiter, "Source Effects and Self-concept Appeals in Children's Television Advertising," in Richard P. Adler et al., eds., *The Effects of Television Advertising on Children* (Lexington, Mass.: D. c. Heath, 1980), pp. 85-86.

[54]Herbert Marcuse, *One Dimensional Man* (Boston: Beacon Press, 1964).

[55]John R. Rossiter, "The Effects of Volume and Repetition of Television Commercials," in Adler et al., eds., *The Effects of Television Advertising*, p. 72.

[56]Stuart Ewen, *Captains of Consciousness: Advertising and the Social Roots of the Consumer Culture* (New York: McGraw-Hill, 1976).

[57]Marie Winn, *The Plug-in Drug* (New York: Viking, 1977).

[58]Ellen Wartella, "Children and Television: The Development of the Child's Understanding of the Media," in Wilhoit and deBock, eds., *Mass Communication Review Yearbook*, pp. 516-533.

[59]R. Krull and W. Hudson, "Children's Attention: The Case of Television Viewing," in E. Wartella, ed., *Children Communicating: Media and the Development of Thought, Speech, Understanding* (Beverly Hills, Calif.: Sage, 1979).

[60]Wartella, *Children Communicating*, pp. 516-553.

[61]Ibid., p. 519.

[62]Ibid., p. 532.

[63]Ibid., p. 533.

[64]Rossiter, "The Effects of Volume and Repetition of Television Commercials," p. 87.

[65]Quoted in Richard P. Adler and Ronald J. Faber, "Background: Children's Television Viewing Patterns," in Adler et al., eds., *The Effects of Television Advertising*, pp. 16-17.

[66]Ibid., p. 16.

[67]Ibid., pp. 18-21.

[68]Thomas S. Robertson, "The Impact of Proprietary Medicine Advertising on Children," in Adler et al., eds., pp. 111-222.

[69]Wartella, *Children Communicating*, p. 555.

⁷⁰ Laurence K. Meringhoff and Gerald S. Leper, "Children's Ability to Distinguish Television Commercials from Program Material," in Adler et al., eds., *The Effects of Television Advertising*, pp. 29–42.

⁷¹Reported in Rossiter, "The Effects of Volume and Repetition of Television Commercials," p. 71.

⁷²Ibid., p. 65.

⁷³Ibid., p. 75.

⁷⁴Ibid., p. 87.

⁷⁵Ibid., p. 83.

⁷⁶Ibid., p. 78.

⁷⁷Ibid., pp. 76–77.

⁷⁸For a review of this research, see Thomas S. Robertson, "Television Advertising and Parent-Child Relations," in Adler et al., *The Effects of Television Advertising*, p. 197.

⁷⁹D. Strickland, "Advertising Exposure, Alcohol Consumption and Misuse of Alcohol," in M. Grant et al., eds., *Economics and Alcohol: Consumption and Control* (New York: Gardner Press, 1983), pp. 201–222.

⁸⁰D. S. Pittman and M. D. Lambert, "Alcohol, Alcoholism and Advertising: Preliminary Investigation of Asserted Findings" (St. Louis, MO: Washington University, Social Science Institute, 1978).

⁸¹See G. Tuckman, "Myth and the Consciousness Industry: A New Look at the Effects of Mass Media," in Elihu Katz and Tamas Szecsko, eds., *Mass Media and Social Change* (Beverly Hills, Calif.: Sage, 1981), pp. 83–100.

⁸²Murray Edelman, *Politics as Symbolic Action: Mass Arousal and Quiescence* (Chicago: Markham, 1971), p. 14. For a detailed and critical assessment of such a view, see Gay Tuckman, "Television News and the Metaphor of Myth," *Studies in the Anthropology of Visual Communication* (Fall 1978), pp. 56–62, and Gay Tuckman "Myth and the Consciousness Industry: A New Look at the Effects of the Mass Media," in Elihu Katz and Tamas Szecsko, eds., *Mass Media and Social Change* (Beverly Hills, Calif.: Sage, 1981), pp. 83–100.

⁸³Murray Edelman, "Language, Myth and Rhetoric," *Society* (July 1975), pp. 14–21.

⁸⁴Ibid., p. 14.

⁸⁵Edelman, *Politics as Symbolic Action*, p. 30.

⁸⁶William M. Berg and J. Michael Ross, "The Partisanship of Silence: Symbolic Politics of School Desegregation in Boston," *Qualitative Sociology*, Vol. 5, no. 1 (1982), pp. 3–32.

⁸⁷Peter Dahlgren, "TV News and the Suppression of Reflexivity," in Katz and Szecsko, eds., *Mass Media and Social Change*, pp. 101–114.

⁸⁸Ibid., pp. 104–105.

⁸⁹V. S. Korobeinikov, "Mass Intercourse and Mass Information in the Process of Social Development," in Katz and Szecsko, eds., pp. 59–60.

⁹⁰Godwin C. Chu, "Revolutionary Language and Chinese Cognitive Processes," in Wilhoit and deBock, eds., *Mass Communication Review Yearbook*, p. 631.

CHAPTER TWELVE
ORGANIZATIONS
A People Perspective

THE MEANING OF "ORGANIZATION"

Everyone knows what the word "organization" means. There are business organizations, labor union organizations, hospital organizations, universities, and public organizations on various levels ranging from the United Nations to village volunteer fire-fighting organizations. Indeed, in the contemporary world, it is difficult to find any significant action of any kind that does not seem to be taken by or in conjunction with an organization of one sort or another. Organizations produce automobiles, breakfast cereals, strikes, college graduates, roads, telephone services, baseball games, and even (with the aid of sperm banks, donors, and social acceptability) human babies. They are defined as "an arrangement of interdependent parts, each having a special function with respect to the whole."[1]

This, like most other definitions, is ultimately confusing because it includes many things that are "organized" without being what we think of as "organizations." The human heart, stomach, and lungs, for example seem to be interdependent parts each of which has some special function with respect to the whole human body, but we do not normally think of them as being parts of an organization.

To "organize" something, it seems that one must first decide what the whole is to be like and then fashion a set of parts. Each part must have a special function with respect to the whole—it is all somewhat like assembling an automobile from a set of component parts.

HUMAN BEINGS VERSUS COMPUTERS AS WORKERS
IN ORGANIZATIONS

One difficulty is that in organizations—even those characterized by a high degree of automation—at least some of the parts are human beings. (In the contemporary world, there are, of course, increasing numbers of "completely automated" factories, but somehow we do not feel comfortable about calling them "organizations".)

A second difficulty is virtually a corollary of the first: human beings always seem to do things for "reasons"—they are "motivated." And so it is that organization builders always have some set of nonorganizational concerns that may relate to power, control, personal profit, or even simple intellectual satisfaction.

If I am setting up a business corporation that I am to head, I may construct "roles" for president, chairman of the board, and mail clerk. Do I formulate these roles in terms of what is most effective with respect to the needs of the corporation or in terms of what is most congenial with my wishes to maintain control or to obtain personal rewards of various kinds?

In organizations, presumably the various roles are defined independently of the people who are to occupy them. "The roles, and the formal organization, can survive replacement of any or even all of its members."[2]

Actually, these organizational roles are what we prefer to call "statuses" or simply "positions." Organizational designers often like to believe, or at least pretend to believe, that organizations consist of a relatively fixed set of positions that the personnel department then proceeds to fill with human beings whose talents and experience best qualify them to accomplish the tasks assigned to these positions. In return, the human beings receive the rewards the organization can provide.

But why human beings?

Recent dramatic advances in the field of computer technology continually raise questions about the ultimate or even the present necessity for human beings in the work process. There is a long tradition in the field of systems engineering in which efforts are made to determine the relative strengths and weaknesses of human beings and computers for various kinds of work assignments. Thus we have been told that

> the most important respect in which men excel computers is in the accessibility of the items in storage. Men can get at a single memory in many different ways; in particular, they can recover memories on the basis of similarity alone; computers, by contrast, have no such efficient cross-indexing. If they did, it would be possible to write programs which rely on the computer to locate and produce any item in memory without specific instructions concerning where that item is. At present, no such procedure is possible.[3]

But various memories can readily be programmed for computer use, and this kind of argument can easily be reversed or modified to show not only the shortcomings of computers but the relative inadequacy of human memory as well. Thus computers can engage in comprehensive searches in a matter of moments or use a variety of hints that successively increase the probability that an elusive item is the one for which one is searching. Unaided human beings are simply not equipped to engage in such searchings.

The simple truth seems to be that when the conditions and requirements of work have been spelled out completely—when an organization assumes the format of an idealized bureaucracy in which all actions have been rationalized, then it is probably the case that computers are invariably better workers than are the most efficient of human beings.

Why, then, do organizations continue to employ human beings?

An organization is a collaborative or cooperative enterprise formed to do something that one person working alone cannot do. But if one person working alone with only a computer for assistance can operate a business, school, trade union, hospital, or army, then why are organizations necessary? Why do they continue to exist and even seem to increase in importance everywhere?

One of the most perceptive books we know on the subject of computers and their relationship to human beings was written by a professor of computer science at the Massachusetts Institute of Technology, Joseph Weizenbaum. In his book, *Computer Power and Human Reason*, Weizenbaum argues that an organism is defined, to a considerable extent, by the problems it faces. "Man faces problems no machine could possibly be made to face. Man is not a machine . . . although man does most certainly process information, he does not necessarily process it the way computers do. Computers and men are not species of the same genus."[4]

Not many years ago, most persons confronted with a statement like this would probably say something like, "How absurd to raise the question! Of course, computers are different from human beings; one needn't be an MIT professor to see that!"

The point is there exists a growing and influential body of opinion that insists that the differences, in principle, can be made to disappear. "Artificial intelligence" has become a subdiscipline of computer science addressed to the problem of the relationship between human and computer intelligence and dedicated to the proposition that computers can ultimately be constructed that will not only equal what the brains of human beings can accomplish but exceed them by many orders of magnitude: "the extreme, or hardcore wing of the artificial intelligentsia, will insist that the whole man, . . . is after all an information processor, and that an information-processing theory of man must therefore be adequate to account for his behavior in its entirety."[5]

The claim that human beings can be described adequately as "information processors" can scarcely be called "true." Human beings do, of course, process information. They seem, however, to do much more than that. And although it may well be the case that existing computers can perform some tasks more rapidly and efficiently than can human beings, this is a long way from the assertion that human behavior can be or *should* be replaced in entirety by "artificial intelligence." Even the assertion that it *is possible, in principle*, to simulate all human behavior through artificial means is, at *this time in history, simply an unproved hypothesis.*

Beyond this, however, there seems to be an increasing body of neurological evidence that suggests that existing computer technology may be addressed to the simulation of some parts of only one hemisphere of the brain. Years ago, in a seminal article, Joseph E. Bogen suggested that one way of interpreting a considerable body of available neurological and other evidence was to postulate two different ways of thinking.[6] Briefly, he concludes that the cerebrum is double. Evidence from various sources, especially from hemispherectomy (the removal of one hemisphere of the brain), seems to establish the fact that one hemisphere is sufficient to sustain a personality or mind

> We may then conclude that the individual with two intact hemispheres has the capacity for two distinct minds . . . . In the human, where *propositional* thought is typically lateralized to one hemisphere, the other hemisphere evidently specializes in a different mode of thought, which may be called *appositional*.[7]

In short, Bogen suggests that there are two quite different modes of thought. One mode, the propositional, it associated with the left hemisphere of the brain. It involves the manipulation of symbols, the use of logical, analytic, or digital processes; it is the embodiment of conventional "rationality." The other mode, the appositional, is associated with the right hemisphere of the brain. The term "appositional" implies "a capacity for apposing or comparing of perceptions, schemas, engrams, etc., but has in addition the virtue that it implies very little else."[8]

The point to be made in connection with all this is simply that the rules or methods involved in *propositional* thought have been subjected to detailed analysis for many years. This "left-brain" function is the side that speaks, reads, and writes. It has been analyzed through the use of such aids as syntax, semantics, and mathematical logic for many years. The rules by which *appositional* thought is elaborated in the other hemisphere of the brain, however, have yet to be studied or codified.

For example, the right hemisphere of the brain has been described as essentially the seat of intuition, and intuitive thought, although logical, uses standards of evidence that are very different from those ordinarily associated with logical thought. "In ordinary discourse, for example, when we say that two things are the same, we mean that they are identical in almost every respect; the standard of evidence we demand to justify such a judgment is extremely demanding. But when we construct a metaphor (e.g., the overseas Chinese are the Jews of the Orient), we pronounce two things to be the same in a very different sense. Metaphors are simply not logical; when taken literally, they are patently absurd. The RH (right hemisphere), in other words, has criteria of absurdity that are far different from those of the logical LH (left hemisphere).[9]

Thus, to return to our initial question—Why human beings?—perhaps Professor Weizenbaum's answer will serve. After reviewing the many debates that have taken place on the issue of "computers and mind," he concludes that

> the relevant issues are neither technological nor even mathematical; they are ethical. They cannot be answered by asking questions beginning with "can." The limits of the applicability of computers are ultimately statable only in terms of oughts. What emerges as the most elementary insight is that, since we do not now have any ways of making computers wise, we ought not now to give computers tasks that demand wisdom.[10]

Professor Weizenbaum is unquestionably aware of the extent to which human decisions both inside and outside of organizations tend to fall short of what he and we and many others would agree constitutes "wisdom." As optimists, however, perhaps we all subscribe to the "intuitive" notion that ultimately it may be possible for human beings to develop some consensus about what would constitute "human" rather than some form of nonhuman or inhuman wisdom. From a very pragmatic perspective, it seems likely that human beings prefer to reserve to themselves answers to questions such as the following: "What is the boundary line between sound business practice and sharp deals that must be called cheating?" "What are the relative costs and benefits to members of a labor union and to business executives of a potential strike?" "How much pressure can be placed upon employees of an organization to increase their productivity?" "To what extent ought this organization feel free to pollute the environment with the by-products of its manufacturing processes?" "How much money and effort should this organization devote to lobbying efforts that will ensure government regulations favorable for this organization however unfavorable they may be for others in this society?" "To what extent ought this hospital to specialize in patients and activities that will maximize its profitability rather than maximize its service to its local community?" "To what extent should this university serve the research and special technical needs of local corporations rather than the broad educational needs of its students or the larger society?"

SOME REALITIES OF ORGANIZATIONAL LIFE

Everyone in the contemporary world knows or should know why organizations are important—people spend so much of their time in them. As two distinguished organizational theorists noted a long time ago, most of the adult members of modern societies spend more than a third of their waking hours in the organizations that employ them. Beyond this, children spend almost an equal amount of time in the environment of school organizations, and both children and adults spend large amounts of their leisure time with a wide variety of voluntary organizations as well. "In our society, preschool children and nonworking housewives are the only large groups of persons whose behavior is not substantially 'organizational.' "[11]

From the perspective of the social psychologist, however, more is involved. Questions such as the following arise: "What influences impinge upon individual human beings from their environment?" "Since organizations represent a major part of the environment of most people in the contemporary world, what effects do they have on the behavior of these (and other) people?" "To what extent do organizational environments influence behavior more *specifically* than do other aspects of human environments?" With respect to this last question, it has been observed that, for example, there is a strong contrast between organizational communications and communications through mass media.

The audiences to whom newspapers and radio address themselves possess no common technical vocabulary; there is no subject about which they have any special shared knowledge; there is no good way of predicting what they will be thinking about when the mass communication reaches them. In principle at least, the recipient of an organizational communication is at the opposite pole. A great deal is known about his special abilities and characteristics. This knowledge is gained from considerable past experience with him and from a detailed knowledge of the work environment in which he operates.[12]

Conventionally, social psychologists have considered a wide range of topics related to organizations and behavior within organizations. Prominent among these topics are matters of "leadership" and "supervision," "morale," "employee attitudes," "work motivation," and "the effects of communication patterns on behavior within an organization." In more general terms, conventional theory and research from the perspective of individuals can be subsumed under such topics as "employee selection," "socialization" (i.e., training and related experiences), "motivation," and "employee satisfaction." From the perspective of the organizational entity itself, topics such as leadership, modes of decision making, problems of control, and conflict within the organization have been considered.

In addition to conventional academic and scholarly research, however, there have been innumerable studies conducted by various public and private agencies often addressed to quite specific concerns within a particular organizational context. These studies are often carried out by consultants or, in any event, persons not employed within the organization being studied. Moreover, most large organizations, in their personnel or industrial relations departments, often employ persons with social psychological training to investigate ongoing matters of organizational concern.

Beyond this, however, there is an enormous literature of books written by successful organizational officers, consultants, academicians, and others who titillate readers with nuggets of insight based on actual cases they have observed, heard about, or thought about in connection with organizational life. It is from these that we have selected a few extracts and present them here. We urge the reader to compare them with some of the theory and research findings presented later in this chapter. Which material is more relevant or "important"? Which is probably more "true"? What difference will any of this material make in the way *you* might behave or be affected by organizations?

Extract 1: A Simile

The African witch doctor wisely indulges the unconscious needs of his clientele. Instinctively he knows that most diseases are psychosomatic and can be treated with a chant, dance and a three-piece suit.[13]

The simile, of course, is intended to be humorous. It evokes images of a consultant who goes into a "song and dance," that is, does not deal with substantive organizational problems but with the anxieties and susceptibility of the client. It reminds us that not all efforts to resolve organizational difficulties are "sincere." There is a discrepancy between the definition of situation implicit in the mind of the client and that within which the consultant may operate.

A consultant's primary task in a money-oriented society is to make money—for himself or herself. We like to assume that this goal can be achieved as a reward for valuable services provided to an organization. Unfortunately, what is often *not* mentioned in conventional academic treatments is the extent to which these services often are addressed to the personal needs or idiosyncrasies of the client rather than to "real" organizational problems. All of which raises a larger issue: To what extent can the problems of an organization be completely separated from the "personal" difficulties of the people who work in it or manage it?

Extract 2: A Generalization

When we begin to communicate, whether as a society or as individuals, our efforts are initially confused by our desire to express ourselves. We have an emotion and we want to give it outlet. A lion roars (one would guess) because it feels like roaring, not because it has any profound thought to express . . . . The first thing to realize, therefore, is that *most people want to talk but few have anything to say.* Anyone who doubts this should watch someone in a glass-sided telephone kiosk. Note the gestures and expressions, the pointing finger, the clutched fist, the smile, the tapping foot. All these signs are wasted on the telephone. We realize, in fact, that they are not seriously meant to convey anything to anybody . . . . What is true of the individual is often true of the organization. Those who sit in head offices may relieve their feelings in letters, telegrams, notices and memoranda, but these are often as meaningless as the gestures made when we are on the telephone. What people say or write or print often means nothing at all and is not even meant to mean anything. It is merely the bureaucratic equivalent of breaking wind.[14]

This generalization shifts the field rather sharply. One could spend enormous amounts of time engaging in a content analysis of letters, telegrams, and other forms of written or oral communication in any organization and pinpoint any number of apparent areas of difficulty without realizing that many, and perhaps even most, of the communications were not really meant to mean anything. Experienced organizational practitioners seldom accept any form of internal communication at face value.

Extract 3: A Piece of Advice

And then there is the administrator who is on the way up and knows it. He had best not form too close a relationship with his peers who one day will be his subordinates. Ever fire a friend, discipline a buddy? Personal involvement with one's subordinates inserts an element into the decision process that warps the results. The able administrator must select his peer-group friends carefully. Pick the winners, avoid the losers: You are judged by the company you keep. Associate with the people who are going places, doing things.[15]

One difficulty with giving advice is that often the people who give it assume that their own values are shared by the persons who receive it. In this case a fundamental assumption is made about what is most important to the people who presumably will act upon the advice: it is more important to ascend the organizational hierarchy than it is to have friends whose friendship is valued intrinsically. This, of course, is a valid assumption to make about many people: it is *not* a valid assumption for many others. The extract illustrates a more general problem involved in giving advice: often those giving it may not be aware of all the circumstances within the context of which actions must be taken or decisions made. In this case, it is a matter of possible ignorance about values; in other cases, there may be ignorance about basic facts that are either withheld or simply not presented for a variety of reasons.

Extract 4: The Art of Management—Chinese Baseball

The unique art that sets all great leaders and executives apart from the rest is Chinese baseball, a game played almost exactly like American baseball .... There is one and only one difference. And it is this: after the ball leaves the pitcher's hand and as long as the ball is in the air, anyone can move any of the bases anywhere.

The polished manager, therefore, does not complain that people are not following the rules or are changing their minds while the program is underway. He does not expect that Nature is going to hold the Universe constant, while he goes about making up his plans and pursuing his projections. ... There is no such thing as a "labor problem," for instance, which can be attacked and settled once and for all. There are only labor issues—never fully defined, gyrating in constant chameleonic flux and defying even semipermanent dispositions.

So leave the scientific models, Occam's razor, and other simplifying temptations to the scholastic sirens to sing . . .[16]

"Chinese baseball" bears a remarkable resemblance to what J. L. Moreno, many years ago, called "spontaneity." As Moreno tells it, when God created the world, He began by making every living being a machine (or what we might today call a "robot"). The machines acted upon each other, and the entire universe ran like an enormous machine. This seemed to be safe, sane, and comfortable. But then He thought about it for a while. "He smiled and put just an ounce of spontaneity into each of the machines, and this has made for endless trouble ever since—and for endless enjoyment."[17]

Moreno had many more specific things to say about spontaneity. For example, "Spontaneity operates in the present, now and here; it propels the individual toward an adequate new response to a new situation. ... it is the least developed factors operating in Man's world; it is most frequently discouraged and restrained by cultural devices,"[18] and:

Spontaneity is difficult to define but this does not relieve us from asking what its meaning is. An important source of information are the experiences from one's personal, subjective life. I discovered the spontaneous man for the first time at the age of four when I tried to play God, fell and broke my right arm. I discovered him again when at the age of seventeen I stood before a group of people. I had prepared a speech; it was a good and sensible speech but when I stood before them I realized that I could not say any of the fine and good things I had prepared myself to say. I realized that it would be unfair to the moment and to the people surrounding me not to share the moment with them and not to express myself as the situation and the present needs of the people required. . . ."[19]

For Moreno, this quality of spontaneity could be improved through various forms of "spontaneity training" that essentially consisted of exposing people to a variety of new situations and insisting that they deal with them effectively. His primary instruments in this connection were various forms of role playing and psychodrama.

One may wish, however, to think about the extent to which managers in contemporary corporations are indeed free to be "spontaneous" or the extent to which players in the game within which they find themselves are completely free to move the bases about at will. Organizations and their environments characteristically have well-developed cultural restrictions (ranging from legal inhibitions to simple matters of habit) that effectively circumscribe the viable alternatives available to managers and others who must act within them.

Extract 5: A Warning

The major criticism directed at the corporation throughout these pages is its inability to deal with the whole human being. The corporation defines the individual by a single function that has meaning to it—work. To the corporation, the individual is simply a rather erratic, easily decalibrated machine with excessive maintenance requirements needed to perform a few necessary services that no nonhuman machine can duplicate, unfortunately. Everything else about the individual is irrelevant in the organizational view.

The principal warning directed to individuals here has been that if you permit the organization to dictate your values and plan your life, it will eventually take over both.[20]

The author of this extract reveals some fascinating details of his own life that perhaps account for his subsequent warning. As a successful employee of a large organization, he felt rather self-satisfied with the way his life was progressing, until he became aware of some disturbing features of his own existence. For example, while chuckling at the way another employee kowtowed to the senior vice-president, he realized that he had engaged in virtually identical behavior a few days earlier. He also noted that he had adopted the standard organizational dress code without protest and no longer considered raising an objection when his boss called him on a Saturday night to insist that he be in a city across the country by Sunday evening. "I tried to make a list of possible orders I was certain I would refuse to obey. It was humiliatingly short."[21]

He found that the corporation game meant making many sacrifices he now felt he was unwilling to make. Thus the job required that he spend a great deal of his time away from home and away from his family. Beyond this, he discovered that in the corporation game, success seemed to relate not to productivity but to such things as style of dress, social compatibility, contacts, influences, and status. "Many employees spend their careers plotting the next move in the game: which executives to invite to their party, whether to call the attention of their superiors to what they have done lately, or to work a particular weekend because the boss is expected to drop in."[22]

The subtitle of Jerry Koehler's book is "How to Win the War with the Organization and Make Them Love It." One wonders whether in a contest with a large-scale organization there truly is as much hope for individual, alternative life-styles as this subtitle would lead us to expect. For possible answers to such questions as this, an examination of organizational theories and relevant research may be helpful.

ORGANIZATIONAL THEORY

Frederick W. Taylor and "Scientific" Management

Frederick W. Taylor, the man whose name has become virtually synonymous with "scientific" management, was born in Philadelphia in 1856. His parents were well-to-do "proper Philadelphians." He spent a couple of years at the Phillips Exeter Academy, but instead of continuing on to Harvard for a traditional collegiate education and an eventual career in law, he became an apprentice machinist and patternmaker and subsequently received a mechanical engineering degree from Stevens Institute of Technology (in 1883).[23]

The American Society of Mechanical Engineering had been founded in 1880. The early mechanical engineers were not graduates of engineering schools but mostly skilled craftsmen and mechanics who had worked their way up to become shop managers or owners of their own shops. Mechanical engineering thus became as much a business as a profession.[24]

By 1886 a paper had been presented to the society entitled "The Engineer as Economist," which insisted that the engineer employed in industry could no longer concern himself solely with mechanical efficiency—it was necessary to recognize efficiency criteria other than those derived from traditional engineering. Economic criteria expressed in terms of costs and revenues were required. It was necessary for mechanical engineers to analyze and systematize management practices and discover what worked and what did not. The author of this paper (Henry R. Towne) suggested that the ASME serve as a clearinghouse for the best available information on managerial practices.[25]

From a traditional mechanical engineering perspective, the basic problem was to design and operate machines efficiently. What Towne had added was the injunction that efficiency was not only a matter of energy loss but dollar costs as well. A machine could, in theory, produce x units of output during a given period of time. When human beings operated the machines, somehow they did not produce up to this theoretical standard. "The reason for this was not a technological one; it involved, in the words commonly used at the time, 'the human aspect.' Workers apparently did not wish, and could not be induced by any normal methods, to work at the paces of which the machine was capable."[26]

Thus the problem was not defined as "technological" but "psychological," and "The mechanical engineers who tackled it fell back on the cruder versions of the crude psychological knowledge of their day. The worker, like every other human being, was motivated by self-interest. Self-interest, in this case, meant the monetary reward received for work done. To get the individual to work harder, all that was necessary was to offer more pay on condition that he or she do so. This resolved itself into the problem of designing incentive payment schemes—systems of buying labor that would make the total daily pay received by the worker depend on daily output. This was a problem by no means uncongenial to those with engineering training and experience: it was quantitative and mathematical; it was susceptible to refinement in detail; and by its apparent practical adequacy, it made superfluous any attempt to explore more comprehensively the factors that influence motivation. A problem of considerable psychological complexity was to be disposed of by a mechanical linkage of pay to productivity."[27]

In 1895 Taylor presented his first formal paper to the society entitled "A Piece-Rate System, Being a Step Toward Partial Solution of the Labor Problem." Eight years later he read his paper entitled "Shop Management." This was received enthusiastically by members of the society. Henry R. Towne called it the most valuable contribution to the subject yet made.[28] The paper was published and attracted an enormous amount of attention.

In what he called an "index" to this paper, Taylor tells us that his chief objective in writing it was to "advocate the accurate study of 'how long it takes to do work' or Scientific Time Study as the foundation of the best management."[29] The other important reason for writing the paper is "advocating the coupling of high wages for the workman with low labor cost for the employer."[30]

To achieve these objectives, Taylor insisted that it was necessary to apply the following principles:

1. *A large daily task.* Each worker should have a clearly defined task each day. The task must be circumscribed carefully and completely and should not be easy to accomplish.

2. *Standard conditions.* Each worker's task should call for a full day's work. Workers must be given the conditions and appliances that will allow them to accomplish the task with certainty.

3. *High pay for success.* Workers should be assured of high pay when they accomplish their tasks.

4. *Loss in case of failure.* Workers who fail to accomplish their tasks should be convinced that sooner or later they will lose something (presumably either wages or the job itself).

5. When an establishment has reached an advanced state of organization, in many cases a fifth element should be added: the task should be made so difficult that it can be done only by a "first-class man."[31]

Taylor himself referred to his technique of management as the "task system"; his associates learned to call it the "Taylor system." Everyone else soon began to call it "scientific management." The explanation conventionally given about the genesis of this system is approximately the following.

When Taylor first became a gang boss, he tried to increase output by putting pressure on his workers. A serious struggle soon developed between them. Taylor eventually won the struggle, but the experience troubled him. He thought about the matter and finally concluded that the cause of such conflicts was ignorance on the part of management. If managers knew exactly what a day's work was, they could obtain the necessary output simply by showing how it could be done. He therefore started to try to discover methods for specifying a proper day's work for every job in the shops he worked as manager or consultant. The technique he developed had two major elements: (1) discovery by trial and error of the best way of doing and the proper time for accomplishing every operation and suboperation—the best material, tool, and machine manipulation of the tool or machine by a human being—and the best flow and sequence of unit operations and (2) a new division of labor between management and the workers. Management had the responsibility for discovering the best ways of doing the units of operation, planning operations, and making available at the proper time and place the necessary tools, instructions, and other facilities required by the workers. None of these decisions and actions was to be left in the hands of the workers. The great increase in productivity that would come about under this system was due not to greater exertion on the part of the workers but to elimination of wasted effort and delays occurring through misapplied efforts.[32]

In attempting to characterize scientific management before a special committee of the U.S. House of Representatives in 1912, Taylor insisted that scientific management

> is not any efficiency device, not a device of any kind for securing efficiency; nor is it any bunch or groups of efficiency devices. It is not a new system of figuring costs; it is not a new scheme for paying men; it is not a piecework system; it is not a bonus system; it is not a premium system . . . it is not holding a stop watch on a man and writing things down about him; it is not time study; it is not motion study, not an analysis of the movements of men . . . . The average man thinks of one or more of these things when scientific management is spoken of—but what I am emphasizing is that these devices in whole or in part are not scientific management; they are useful adjuncts . . . . Now in its essence, scientific management involves a complete mental revolution on the part of the working man engaged in any particular establishment or industry—a complete mental revolution on the part of those on the management's side . . . a complete mental revolution as to their duties toward their fellow workers in the management, toward their workmen, and toward all of their daily problems. And without this complete mental revolution on both sides scientific management does not exist.[33]

The scientific management movement encountered many difficulties. Between 1905 and 1912, there were many recorded instances of workers who refused to cooperate with the "time and motion" people. Trade unions saw it as a direct threat to worker control of their own trades, and in 1911 a serious spontaneous strike occurred at Watertown Arsenal, a government arsenal that employed civilian union labor. This led to a full-scale government investigation.[34]

After extensive hearings, it was concluded that scientific management, although an effective means for "working out details" of production and administration, was not designed to ensure the best interests of workers. The abuses uncovered by the investigation, along with widespread labor opposition to scientific management, led to the banning of the Taylor method in Navy shipyards and in all government agencies.

The investigations of scientific management had indicated that "time and motion" experts often simply guessed at the optimum rates for various operations. This, of course, undercut the entire rationale of scientific manage-ment. It meant, in effect, that "the arbitrary authority of management had simply been reintroduced in a less apparent form."[35]

The ASME refused to publish Taylor's *Principles of Scientific Manage-ment* essentially because of widespread sentiment that the system was not "scientific." For example, it was charged that Taylor had used arbitrary defini-tions for "average" and "first-class" worker in standardizing his results. More-over, it was charged, the large percentages added to the time calculated for a job to compensate for unavoidable production delays had been determined arbitrarily.[36]

For engineers concerned with these matters, the rejection of Taylor's "scientific" pretensions seemed to have two consequences:

> First, it meant that the methods already developed required further refinement, to eliminate room for error and arbitrary judgment. Second, it indicated that the mere transfer of traditional engineering techniques to the social problems of management would not suffice; the new human focus of engineering required that the discipline of engineering itself had to expand, to include the new methods of the social sciences. The rejection of the pretensions of scientific management, like scientific management itself, had been based on too narrow a conception of "science."[37]

Later organizational theorists had many criticisms of Taylor's understand-ing of human behavior and comments about the limitations of his method. For example,

1. He assumed that workers were motivated solely by wage payments. He did not appreciate adequately the fact that wage payments constitute only one of a number of rewards in a work system; others include achievement, acceptance, recognition, and the experience of personal effectiveness. He did not appreciate the fact that definitions of appropriate wages are largely a matter of group norms, traditions, group structure, and individual judgment.[38]

2. He was not sensitive to the "subjective side of work, the personal and interac-tional aspects of performance, the meanings attributed to his work by the in-dividual, and the significance for him of his social relations while at work.[39]

3. He did not take into account "the constructions that workers would put on to the new procedures, their reactions to being timed at work and closely super-vised."[40]

4. "He had an inadequate understanding of group factors—of the relation of in-dividual incentive to interaction with, and social dependence on, a group of im-mediate work associates. Study after study has now shown that motivation and performance are intimately affected by norms set by colleagues and that these norms compete with those set by employers, and that economic aspirations are modified because of dependence on social rewards and punishments emanating from and developed in interaction with colleagues."[41]

Elton Mayo and the "Human Relations" Approach

Despite the range of criticisms directed at "scientific management," in-dustrial managers persisted in their efforts to use "science" to help increase productivity of workers and the profitability of their enterprises. "Science," in this context, seemed to refer largely to the physical aspect of production. In 1927 an elaborate research program had been started at the Hawthorne Works of Western Electric (a branch of the American Telephone & Telegraph Company that, in addition to other activities, manufactured telephones and other kinds of communication equipment). This program had been preceded by another set of experiments begun in 1924 under the auspices of the National Research Council.[42] The council was interested in the precise relations between physical illumination and individual work efficiency. The illumination experiments had gone through three separate stages. In the first phase, a group of employees was put into a room where the illumination was altered experimentally. A control group whose light remained unchanged was also observed. The researchers concluded that illumination was only one factor affecting productivity and that other factors (as yet unmeasured) also influenced productivity. They decided to eliminate or control these other factors.

In the second set of experiments, the researchers were startled by the results. As the lighting for the test group was increased, production increased, *but production also increased for the control group* whose lighting had remained *unchanged.*

In the final stage, lighting intensity in the test room was *decreased.* Production, however, *increased,* not only for the test room group but for the control group as well.

What did the experimenters learn from these initial experiments? In the first place it was clear that "Nothing of a positive nature had been learned about the relation of illumination to industrial efficiency."[43]

Some of the investigators were not willing to draw this conclusion. They felt that it was exceedingly difficult to test for the effect of a single variable in a situation in which there were many uncontrolled variables. Others, however, began to suspect their basic assumptions with respect to human motivation. It occurred to them that the trouble was not so much with the results or with the subjects as it was with their notions about the way in which their subjects were supposed to behave—that there existed a direct, simple cause and effect relationship between certain physical changes in the workers' environment and the responses of the workers to these changes.[44]

Following this preliminary set of studies, a research program was carried out at the Hawthorne works in Chicago for about five years beginning in 1927. The studies were carried out by the company itself and a research group at Harvard University under the leadership of Elton Mayo.[45] We shall describe some of these studies in the next section of this chapter (under "Organizational Research").

At this point we wish to note the general nature of Mayo's ideas, the significance they have had for organizational social psychology, and the nature of the controversies they have stimulated in the field.

To begin,

Mayo's emphasis on the contemporary failure 1) to study the social aspects of industrialization, and 2) to develop social skills to match the technical skills of a rapidly changing society, drew attention to the possible contributions of sociology to industry and industrial management. His own gradual progression from a psychological/physiological approach to one with more of a sociological perspective was widely believed to demonstrate the desirability of this perspective. The first point to note, therefore, is that it was chiefly on the basis of Mayo's work that the case for the sociological study of industrial behavior was advanced.[46]

Mayo insisted that every group of organized human beings must deal with two fundamental administrative problems. It must somehow manage to obtain for its members (1) the means to satisfy material and economic needs and (2) the means to ensure spontaneous cooperation throughout the organization. He felt that the material successes of recent industrial societies have demonstrated that we (i.e., our engineers) know how to organize to achieve material efficiency. But we do not know how to ensure spontaneous cooperation. Evidence for this is to be found in such widespread problems as absenteeism, labor turnover, and wildcat strikes. This ability to obtain cooperation between individuals and groups is what Mayo calls "social skills," which are very much undeveloped, he felt, in modern societies. "I believe," he wrote, "that social study should begin with careful observation of what may be described as communication: that is, the capacity of an individual to communicate his feelings and ideas to another, the capacity of groups to communicate effectively and intimately with each other. The problem is beyond all reasonable doubt, the outstanding defect that civilization is facing today."[47]

Parenthetically, he observed that individuals usually described as psychoneurotic, but free from any organic pathology, are unable to communicate easily and intimately with other persons. This was a difficulty that beset not only individuals, but governments, which had great difficulty in communicating with each other, and of course, in industrial societies in general, an outstanding illustration of this defect was the continuing difficulties between managements and workers.[48]

Although, as we shall see, Mayo and his "human relations" followers have been severely criticized as essentially partisans of a conservative ideology that viewed industrial relations from what was essentially a management perspective, it was Mayo who provided a cogent critique of classical economic theory—the basic theoretical underpinning of this ideology. He begins his critique by observing that in the days of the original classical economic theorists, the economic system was made up chiefly of small industries and businesses. When one business of this type shut down, it did not bring on a significant community problem—some rival business was often available to hire the persons who had become unemployed. In contemporary industrial society, however, business organizations had grown to the point that failure often resulted in the unemployment of thousands of workers in a single community. "A problem of this kind" he said, "cannot be left to 'individualism' or 'enlightened self-interest'; that nineteenth-century track is closed."[49]

In short, he maintained, a primary assumption of nineteenth-century economic theory was no longer tenable. It was no longer possible to believe that the pursuit of individual interest was the basis of economic organization. Although

> this assumption is still voiced by economic and political theorists, it is perfectly clear that business and political practice are based nowadays upon a vitally different conception of human society. This divergence between theory and practice is perhaps the source of at least part of the confusion that prevails in politico-economic discussions of the present. Whereas the economic theorist of the university still assumes individual interest as a sufficient basis for theory and the development of economic insight, the administrator with actual experience of handling human affairs bases his action upon a contrary, but empirically derived assumption.[50]

Specifically, Mayo disputed three postulates or "limiting concepts" that served as the basis for classical economic theory:

1. The implicit notion that natural society consists of a horde of unorganized individuals
2. The assumption that every person acts in a manner calculated to obtain his or her own self-preservation or self-interest
3. The assumption that all persons think logically, to the best of their ability, to achieve this purpose (i.e., self-interest or self-preservation)[51]

Mayo insisted that the field studies of modern anthropology made the first notion fundamentally untenable. Here Mayo was essentially insisting upon the universality of social organization. It was only under highly exceptional circumstances that societies might temporarily disintegrate into a horde of individuals each of whom would desperately search for the means of self-preservation. Thus it was essentially only under conditions of crisis or emergency that the second point could be justified to any degree. With respect to the third point (i.e., that every individual always thinks logically), Mayo points to a variety of industrial studies to demonstrate his point that the assertion is completely misleading:

> The economists' presupposition of individual self-preservation as motive and logic as instrument is not characteristic of the industrial facts ordinarily encountered. The desire to stand well with one's fellows, the so-called human instinct of association, easily outweighs the merely individual interest and the logical reasoning upon which so many spurious principles of management are based.[52]

Strangely enough, it was Mayo's argument against classical economic theory that seems ultimately to have provided the basis for some of the attacks later made against his own work and more generally against the work of the human relations school that he initiated.

A central issue revolved about the matter of motivation. Managers and social scientists wanted to understand what it was that made workers work hard or "goof off." Classical economic theory, of course, as well as Taylor and managers, both "scientific" and "unscientific," had assumed that money was the basic motivator for workers. The theories of Mayo and his human relations followers, however, seemed to point in another direction. If motivation was a more complex phenomenon—if workers were motivated not only by money but by other factors ranging from the customs of their work groups to how "happy" they were in their work—then perhaps managers could save money by providing cheap frills of various kinds. "Human relations" could readily become a means for cutting labor costs. Many social scientists, union leaders, and workers developed strong antagonisms toward the human relations movement. The most obvious alternative was a return to the theory of money as the prime or sole motivator. A typical argument was stated in the following terms: "Human-relations programs are never a substitute for sound economic relationships. Geraniums in the plant windows and a turkey for Christmas do not make up for substandard pay."[53]

In a penetrating critique of the theoretical basis of the human relations school, Harold L. Sheppard pointed out that human relations devotees called for cooperation or spontaneous cooperation without specifying the *basis* for *cooperation among the parties involved.*

> It is not the same problem as getting a football team to cooperate, or a corner gang, or a family, to cooperate. Cooperation for what? Toward what goals? At what price to each side? This brings us inevitably into the matter of power issues, values and interests in the sphere of labour-management relations. And the sociologist is of very little value or use if he attempts to tell employers and workers alike that they really are arguing over nothing important, or over intrinsically non-existent matters, that in reality they are simply manifesting a break-down in communication, or excessive ego-involvement.[54]

Management Science and the Systems Approach

Taylor's scientific management and Mayo's human relations approach had some marked similarities, although superficially they appeared to be quite different orientations. Both approaches tended to emphasize the necessity for increasing the productivity of individual workers or small groups of workers. Both seemed to operate on the basis of an implicit assumption that the whole is fundamentally the sum of its parts—that if you want to increase the total productivity or efficiency of an organization, the way to begin is with its component persons or groups.

The contemporary alternative to these approaches is broadly referred to as the "systems" approach. Its advocates have given themselves many different labels including "management scientists," "operations researchers," "systems engineers," "systems designers," or more simply "systems analysts." Perhaps the central feature of this approach as it relates to organizations is its emphasis upon the efficiency of the whole organization rather than the efficiency of its individual parts. Underlying this, of course, is the assumption that the performance of the whole may be quite different from the sum of its parts.[55]

All this is by no means to suggest that this approach, as it is practiced, is addressed to the concerns of all persons working within the organization. In the words of one perceptive critic, "It [management science] incorporates Taylor's principles of efficiency and Mayo's theories of motivation into a body of knowledge that seeks to maximize the efficiency of the organization as a whole while minimizing the problems of worker resistance."[56]

Management science practitioners or systems theorists would not, of course, agree with this characterization. C. West Churchman, for example, tells us that there are five basic considerations to be kept in mind in connection with systems:[57]

1. The total system objectives or more specifically data that provide performance details for the entire system (or organization). Trying to discover precisely what these are can become a formidable undertaking. From the perspective of Churchman,

> it is no easy matter to determine the real objectives of a system, anymore than it is an easy matter to determine the real objectives of an individual person. We all hide our real objectives because in some cases they are hardly satisfactory ones from the point of view of other people; if they are widely publicized, they may be harmful in terms of attaining various kinds of support in our lives."[58]

2. The system's environment. This is what lies outside the system, and it again is quite difficult to determine. For example, if the organization being considered is an automobile factory, what is its environment? Clearly, it is not the physical space beyond the factory's walls. Churchman observes that not only may the organization have agents outside the factory building itself who buy raw materials or sell the factory's products, but on a more subtle level, managers of the organization may belong to various political organizations that can exert various degrees of political pressure on behalf of the organization. These political activities belong to the system, although they do not take place within the physical or even the formal social framework of the organization. This, he feels, is analogous to the observation of Marshall McLuhan that in the age of electric technology, the telephone has become part of individual persons; that is, the telephone is part of the "system" that is called the "individual person." The decisive feature about a system's environment is simply that the system can do little or nothing about its characteristics or behavior. Thus to the extent that a system operates under a fixed budget, the budgetary limitations are in the environment of the system. If, however, it is possible for the system to influence the budget, then the budgetary process is regarded as being *within* the system.

3. The resources of the system. Here Churchman insists that the traditional corporate balance sheet omits many of the important organizational resources. The balance sheet lists such things as building, equipment, accounts receivable, and other things that, in principle, can be converted directly into dollars. It does *not* list a detailed account of the people available to the firm, their education, training, and ability to accomplish various tasks. This, Churchman feels, should be represented by a more or less "fictitious" entry on the balance sheet roughly comparable to the intangible notion of "goodwill."

Beyond this, however, management scientists have an even stronger objection to traditional income statements of corporations. Such statements should describe not only how resources were actually used, but how they might have been used as well. "For the management scientist, the systems approach entails the construction of 'management information systems' that will record the relevant information for decision-making purposes and specifically will tell the richest story about the use of resources including lost opportunities."[59]

Central to the application of management information systems is the use of computer technology, which, for management scientists, often seems to be the most valuable resource available to an organization. We shall discuss these systems (often abbreviated as MIS) shortly.

4. The components of the system, including what they do, what their objectives are, and how well they perform.   Components are the subsystems or parts of the system. They characteristically are *not* the conventional departments or other bureaucratic units of organizations. They are the people or machines whose performance is related to the performance of the overall system. Very often, however, there is an irregular or even an inverse relationship between conventional performance measures of a component and the productivity of an entire system. Churchman provides the example of a production unit that institutes various kinds of cost reduction policies that result in a reduction of inventories. As a result of this, the unit's cost for each item produced may decrease, but the performance of the entire firm may go down because the reduction in inventories may lead to shortages and the possibility of loss of sales.

5. The management of the system.   The management of the system, from the perspective of management science, must see that plans for the entire system are made. It must decide upon overall goals, recognize the environment, and decide how resources and components are to be utilized. It must also take steps to see that the plans are carried out in accordance with its original ideas. If they are not, management must be able to discover why they have not. This process is called "control." It does not necessarily involve physical coercion, but it does mean that if components deviate beyond certain more or less specified limits, correction of some sort will be taken. The management part of the system must, therefore, receive information that tells it not only about the performance of the system within the framework of existing criteria, but presumably when the basic framework is inadequate for some reason and fundamental changes are required.

In this connection, Norbert Weiner's use of the Greek word for "steersman" has suggested the term most widely used in contemporary management science—"cybernetics." As Churchman explains it, the captain of the ship has the responsibility for making sure that the ship arrives at its destination according to schedule. This is one way of describing the objective of the ship. Its *environment* includes not only such physical features as the weather, wind, and wave patterns but the performance characteristics of the ship's machinery and personnel as well. The ship's *resources* are its personnel and machinery (here Churchman might have added the *procedures* used to get things done by either the ship's personnel or its machinery or both working together). The ship's *components* are its various missions (engineroom mission, maintenance, etc.). The captain is the ship's management. He sees that plans for the ship's operations are made and carried out. Basic to this management role is the development of various kinds of information systems throughout the ship that will tell the captain what "deviations" from the plan have occurred and why they have occurred. Finally, it is management's task to decide when the plan must be changed if the information received indicates the desirability of doing so.

Churchman tells us that "Weiner and his followers developed a theory of cybernetics which has mainly been applied to the design of machinery. But it is only natural for the management scientist to attempt to apply the theory to the management control of large organizations."[60]

Management Information Systems (MIS)

Anyone living in the contemporary world can scarcely have failed to notice the widespread effect on all sorts of things that modern computer technology seems to have had. It will come as no surprise to learn that such developments as large mainframes, mini- and microprocessors, stand-alone and graphics terminals, chip technology, bubble memory, more powerful software, and better communications equipment have made easier the collection, storage, processing, retrieval, and display of data. "Such improvements in computerized information systems are changing the way both managers and organizations perform."[61]

Fortunately (or perhaps unfortunately), we have a definition for MIS. Actually, several definitions are available, but this one will do to begin our discussion:

> A computer-based management information system (MIS) is a computerized procedure for providing managers with immediate access to the knowledge, information and data they need to make decisions, direct people, and regulate operations in order to better attain organizational goals. This is accomplished by remote-access, time-sharing computers and graphic display devices that give the system its intrinsic capacity to input, process, store, transform, transmit, and output data internal and external to the organization into appropriate formats for use by decision makers.[62]

It has long been recognized[63] that "people problems" arise long before an MIS is actually installed; they begin as soon as the management of an organization begins to consider the feasibility of installing one. Among the difficulties that seem to arise are the following:

1. Managements often try to convince employees that no serious changes will occur in individuals' jobs and conditions of employment. When these assurances are shown to be false, a credibility gap occurs, leading to morale problems and many other related difficulties.[64]
2. Under the best of circumstances, initiation of a computerized system often leads to increases in anxiety among employees who fear the possibility of unemployment or loss of job security or experience a feeling of inadequacy in performing

the redefined job resulting from installation of the system. In addition, job failures or inadequacies may be highlighted by the MIS system itself, leading not only to increased pressure from supervisors but from peers as well who can detect more readily employees who fail to "pull their share."[65]

3. Related to the matter of increased visibility of activity is the loss of personal privacy experienced by many persons working within an MIS environment. Individuals often perceive their own participation in organizational activities as simply that of a "cog" in a larger process that is unconcerned with the personal needs of the employee.[66]

4. Introduction of an MIS can be quite traumatic not only to rank-and-file employees but to managers as well. The radically new situation within the organization may lead some managers to feel that their personal relationships with top management no longer constitute a protective security blanket. The previously familiar environment becomes strange and even threatening. The managers may suffer from "MIS-created alienation."[67] Systems personnel within an organization may become something of an internal technical elite or "technology priesthood." The apparent power held by this group may cause further alienation among "old-line" managers.[68]

Underlying the design of the typical MIS are several assumptions that have long been known to be erroneous:[69]

1. The notion that the informational deficiency from which managers suffer is the lack of relevant information. As Russell E. Ackoff pointed out years ago, managers seem to suffer more from an overabundance of *irrelevant information*. The major problem, in short, is *not* how to give managers more information, but how to help filter or evaluate and condense available information so that it can be used effectively.

2. The assumption that managers need the information they want. MIS designers tend to "determine" what information the system must provide by asking managers what information they wculd like to have. Managers characteristically "play it safe" and ask for "everything." The MIS designer who understands even less than the manager also tries to provide "everything." (Parenthetically, it should perhaps be noted that if the designer is also interested in selling a complex computer system, there is an even greater incentive to do this.)

The moral, Ackoff tells us, is simple: it is not possible to specify what information is necessary for decision making until an explanatory model of the decision process and the system involved has been constructed and tested. "Information systems are subsystems of control systems. They cannot be designed adequately without taking control in account."[70]

3. The idea that if managers have the information they need, their decisions will improve. Here Ackoff insists it is necessary to determine how well managers can use needed information. When they cannot use it well, they should, he feels, be given decision rules or feedback on their performance so that they can identify their own mistakes.

4. The unexamined "truism" that "more communication means better per-formance." Ackoff tells us this is not only not necessarily the case but indeed is *seldom* the case. For example, it is scarcely to be expected that two competing organizations will become more cooperative because they each receive better information about the other: "when organizational units have inappropriate measures of performance which put them in conflict with each other, as is often the case, communication between them may hurt organizational performance, not help it."[71]

5. The comforting assurance that a manager does not have to understand how the MIS works but must simply know how to use it. This assurance often leaves managers with the sense that they are unable to evaluate the MIS as a whole because they do not understand its underlying design. They often are afraid to try to evaluate the system for fear of displaying their ignorance publicly.

Here Ackoff may be underestimating somewhat the "courage" of organizational managers, but as many practitioners in this field have learned, it is relatively easy to impress even the most "hard-headed" businessperson with the glamor of impressive technology. The cost of new computer equipment in many ways often resembles the cost of a new automobile, a piece of jewelry, or a fur coat—it is chargeable (on the psychic level) to conspicuous consumption (i.e., in general, the higher the cost, the greater the prestige).

The Future of Organizational Theory

In many ways Douglas McGregor summed up the significant history of organizational social psychology in his classic distinction between Theory X and Theory Y.[72]

Theory X is based on a view of workers that sees them as creatures who fundamentally are opposed to work. To get them to perform, it is necessary for managers to induce them somehow to engage in the disagreeable tasks that must be done. It is possible to do this by rewarding them when they produce well, punishing them when they do not, and in general using both the carrot and stick in an effort to make them work. Workers have little in the way of ambition and do not wish to assume responsibility. It is, accordingly, necessary for managers to specify every detail of every task and ensure that the work is done according to these specifications.

Theory Y was presented as the fundamental alternative to Theory X. Theory Y begins with the assumption that people are not "naturally" passive, irresponsible, and unresponsive to organizational requirements. They have become that way as a consequence of the manner in which they have been treated traditionally in organizations. All persons are potentially capable of assuming responsibility at various levels and of being highly motivated to do the things that require doing. The fundamental task for management is to arrange the structure of organizations in such a fashion that people can best achieve their own goals by doing what the organization wants them to do.

Superficially, these two theories may seem to correspond to the orientation of scientific management, on the one hand, and to some extent to the human relations school, on the other. Management science from this perspective would appear to be scientific management dressed up in human relations clothing; that is, the robotlike tasks of organizations are ultimately assigned to bona fide robots whereas presumably managers and other necessary human employees are free to be creative, that is, to do what they want to do so long as that fulfills organizational objectives.

Many workers in this field, however, are finding all this much too simplistic. Quite apart from the complexities of human motivation that are scarcely dealt with by either of these theories, many professionals have for some years now felt that psychology has been focused too narrowly within the organization itself, ignoring "organizational-environment relationships."[73]

> Psychologists working on organizations seem to us to have been the worse culprits, perhaps because training in that discipline has taught us to work from the individual outward; and to concentrate, therefore, on the microcosmic insides of the organization, on individual and small-group behavior. And those of us with an applied bent have been so deeply preoccupied with interorganizational change that we have tended to fend off "external" issues that might muddy up our analysis of internal processes.[74]

What does all this mean specifically?[75] It can mean a greater awareness of political activity as an approach to the problems of people inside and outside of organizations. Organizational structures, people, products, and markets change in response to events occurring "out there" in the environment. Related to this is the phenomenon of organizations established by people who wish to change other organizations. These can range from labor unions and business associations to reform organizations such as those set up by Ralph Nader and Saul Alinsky.

Concern with organizational environments can have at least two major consequences. One of these is a change in the language and syntax of organizational thought. It has been observed that organizations (especially in the era of high-speed computer technology) seem to overvalue rational, analytic styles of thinking.

> Organizations act as though their goals are knowable and specifiable; as though long-range planning is unequivocally good, and nonplanning is irrational and bad; as though it is obvious that the design of the organization should proceed analytically from the task backward to the logically most appropriate structure. All these beliefs are to some degree being questioned. . . . Perhaps it is time for our organizations to include thinking styles much more like those Western males generally ascribe, deprecatingly, to females. Perhaps organizations have to respond to their impulses as well as to their intellects; to be freed of supporting today the proposal they made last week; to behave more intuitively.[76]

A second major consequence of interest in organizational environments is an increased concern about organizational values:

> To what extent are organizations there to do work and to what extent to satisfy the needs of their members? To what extent are the two mutually exclusive? . . . it is not only the growth and self-actualization of organizational members of other organizations, and of society at large. The organization's interest in providing

a satisfying internal environment becomes more than a matter of improving intra-organizational effectiveness. It also becomes a matter of acceptance by the community, indeed of active efforts to curry community favor.[77]

Finally, there is another old issue that is raised in connection with concern about organizational environments. This is the issue of interpersonal trust. It now seems necessary to examine the issue of interorganizational trust:

High trust, though difficult to achieve, holds promise (as it always has) as an alternative means of organizational control—a long shot that promises a triple payoff of more socially relevant organizations, more effective organizational decision-making, and a less-alienated organizational life for the individual.[78]

ORGANIZATIONAL RESEARCH

Early research in this field was, as we have indicated, heavily influenced by the engineering and physical science background of its early researchers and practitioners. For Taylor, an early research problem could be defined in terms of a question such as, "What is an ideal load for a shovel if you want to maximize the productivity of the human being who carries it and minimize fatigue?"

Taylor's research for such a problem would begin by selecting of the "best" workers he could find. These were his research subjects. He varied the load on their shovels as they moved various kinds of material. He concluded that the highest rate of productivity occurred when the shovel load was 21.5 pounds. This led to the recommendation that shovels of different sizes be provided workers as they worked on different materials—to retain the optimum weight of 21.5 pounds per shovel load to the greatest possible extent.

This essentially single-dimensional view of workers as physical objects that had to be cared for with approximately the same level of concern with which one handled sensitive machinery persisted, as we have previously pointed out, until the puzzles of the Hawthorne studies led to a reexamination of this perspective.

The Relay Assembly Test Room Study

To determine where the previous illumination studies had gone wrong, the Hawthorne researchers designed a new study in which six workers were placed in a separate room. In this room the workers could be observed carefully and their output could be measured exactly. The task assigned to these workers consisted of assembling small "relays" that consisted of 35 separate parts. The experimenters initially recorded temperature, humidity, the kind and amount of food consumed daily by each worker, and the number of hours of sleep each worker had each night. This was done to establish the basic physical data related to each subject (the analogy to examining a motor for the purpose of recording gas and oil consumption, hours of operation, etc., is not very far-fetched). As time went on, output increased steadily, but the experimenters could find no significant relationship between any physical factor and variations in productivity.

The Hawthorne Effect

The Hawthorne experimenters continued with their efforts to "improve" the environment in the relay assembly test room. The workers were made a separate group for pay incentive purposes, were provided scheduled rest periods for varying periods of time, and were given snacks during midmorning and midafternoon breaks, and the length of their workday was reduced. Saturday work was discontinued. Throughout the 26-month period of this "experiment," measured productivity continued to rise. No significant relationships were found between productivity and variables ranging from changes in work methods and materials to physical fatigue, monotony, room temperature, hours of sleep, fluctuations in weather, or physical conditions of the workers.

After about 18 months had passed, the researchers removed all the improvements they had provided the subjects. Rest periods were eliminated, Saturday work was restored, and so on. The prediction, of course, was that productivity would revert to the initial level. On the contrary, however, productivity rose to an all-time high.

> The group itself became important to the experiment. Feeling part of a team and consulting with the researchers about the changes to be made, the girls(i.e., the workers) developed pride in their work, in themselves, and in one another. The planned experimental innovations were not found to be particularly important, and cumulative fatigue was not shown to be present at any time. The impact of the girls' behavior on the outcome of the experiments has often been called the *Hawthorne effect*. From the standpoint of good research, the Hawthorne effect is undesirable, since it precludes control of experimental conditions and contaminates research results. Experimenters working with human beings are now aware of the effect and try to exclude it from their research work.[79]

The Bank-Wiring Experiment

This part of the Hawthorne studies was made during the period November 1931 to May 1932. In this experiment 14 male workers were brought together in one room and were observed by a researcher in the same room. The workers included three occupational specialties: "wiremen," "soldermen," and inspectors. The task involved wiring "banks." The output of the subjects was observed before they knew that they were going to be studied. They had been paid on the basis of a group incentive plan that presumably would encourage the workers to maximize their total output and to encourage faster workers to put pressure on the slower workers to increase their productivity. It was learned, however, that the workers had developed their own standard for a day's work: wiring two banks per day. The men seemed to feel that, if they were to exceed this rate, it would be dangerous (presumably because the rate of pay per bank would be decreased by management). The workers had coined their own terms for individuals who deviated markedly from this implicit rate: "rate-buster" was someone who produced *more* than the norm, and "chiseler" was one who produced *less* than the norm. In addition, a practice had developed among the men called "binging"—a painful blow to the arm of a deviant.

The bank-wiring experiment was directly concerned with the implications of group membership. The researchers observed the relationships of the workers to each other and to the supervisor. They also made detailed records of conversations. In the words of one commentator, the study "showed that primary groups among workers, where they do not have amicable relations with management, restrict output in accordance with an elaborate system of rules and sanctions."[80]

In short, the Hawthorne studies pointed up the implications for industrial productivity of elaborate relationships established among workers, the development of *group* norms for productivity, and how these norms were maintained through sanctions available to the workers themselves. "This contrasted both with person-centered industrial psychology and with the management assumption that their workers were 'simply individuals working next to one another.' "[81]

Small-Group Research

The focus on interpersonal behavior in small groups that emerged from the Hawthorne studies has developed into a centrally important specialty within the field of social psychology. Interestingly, the issue of "group bogeys" (i.e., the pressure to conform to standards of work set by a work group) was an issue faced by the pioneers of scientific management. When Taylor was asked by the steel industry to help raise individual productivity, he found that men carrying pig iron or unloading coal from coal cars were much more productive if they could be encouraged or allowed to escape these group constraints— the standards of work set by the group were characteristically lower than management would wish them to be.

The "heyday" of small-group research[82] seemed to have begun in the middle 1930s, at the time when Hitler and other authoritarian rulers achieved world prominence. Much of the research in social psychology done just prior to, during, and after World War II was carried out by European scholars who came to the United States to escape this authoritarianism. They hoped to use their knowledge to promote the theory and practice of democratic forms of group process and to combat the influence of authoritarianism. The two men who had the greatest influence on the development of small-group research were Kurt Lewin, who came from Germany, and J. L. Moreno, who came from Austria.

Beginning with the late 1920s, three main schools of small-group research dominated the field: (1) sociometry (Moreno), (2) group dynamics (Lewin), and (3) small group (R. Freed Bales).

Moreno (who died in 1974) used the term "sociometry" to include not only the sociometric test (which he developed) (see Chapter 3) but the full range of other methods, ideas, techniques, theories, and philosophy that for him constituted the corpus of sociometry.[83] These included such things as psychodrama, sociodrama, role playing, sociometric tests, spontaneity tests, and a staggering variety of other ideas and group methods.

Kurt Lewin was a contemporary of Moreno but died much earlier (in 1947). Along with a group of colleagues, he carried out basic research on the influence of authoritarian and democratic leadership on groups. Lewin popularized the term "group dynamics," which began as an identifiable field of inquiry in the United States toward the end of the 1930s. In 1945, Lewin established the first organization devoted explicitly to group dynamics research. Two authoritative social psychologists in this area have defined group dynamics as

> a field of inquiry dedicated to advancing knowledge about the nature of groups, the laws of their development, and their interrelations with individuals, other groups, and larger institutions. It may be identified by its reliance upon empirical research for obtaining data of theoretical significance, its emphasis in research and theory upon the dynamic aspects of group life, its broad relevance to all the social sciences, and the potential applicability of its findings to the improvement of social practice.[84]

In practice, most of the research labeled "group dynamics" has tended to concentrate on small, informal, or primary groups, but we are cautioned that it would be unwise to define the field as the study of any particular type of group just as it would be unwise to define it in terms of any particular research method or adherence to a single theoretical orientation.[85]

Despite this, group dynamics in organizational settings has perhaps become best known through its identification with "sensitivity training groups" or "T-groups," which have been widely used by management consultants and others concerned with training executives in industrial settings. Broadly speaking, T-groups refer to more or less structured (perhaps "unstructured" is a more accurate term) group experiences designed to foster and develop what is referred to as interpersonal and social effectiveness among participants.

> The trainers, as educators, are concerned that the members learn from the group experience how to be productive and effective member-leaders in their back-home work and community settings. The participants tend to come to the T-group experience as members of organizations in which they hold supervisory, managerial, or instructional positions. They hope that the experience will help them become more effective in their work roles, so that their contributions will enhance the overall effectiveness of their organizations and communities.[86]

Robert Freed Bales is a Harvard sociologist who was initially best known for his development of the "interaction process recorder" (see Chapter 3), a device to be used behind one-way mirrors useful in the recording of the behavior of members of small groups. Subsequently, he gave up this observer role and "now takes his place inside the classroom as a trainer in a self-analytic group. His primary concern is no longer to provide a set of categories for professional social scientists to use in their laboratory studies of groups; rather, it is to provide the group member with a way of evaluating his own behavior and that of his peers."[87]

RESEARCH IN ORGANIZATIONAL SOCIAL PSYCHOLOGY

Liking or Disliking Other People

A phenomenon of which virtually everyone is aware at one level or another is the attraction that some persons feel toward other persons and the sense of actively disliking or being repelled by others. This phenomenon is, of course, central to Moreno's concept of sociometry and is the basis for sociometric tests. Social psychologist Theodore M. Newcomb decided to study this phenomenon many years ago in a "real-world" setting. He rented a house near his university campus. The house was large enough for 17 persons. He then offered free rent to students transferring to the university from other universities and selected 17 male students who did not know each other. Each student was offered free rent on the condition that he agree to spend four or five hours each week being interviewed by Newcomb or his assistants, filling out questionnaires and participating in experiments.

After analyzing the data he received, Newcomb concluded the following:

1. Roommates seemed to like each other more than they did other people in the building. Furthermore, the men seemed to prefer other persons who lived on the same floor than they did persons living on other floors.

2. The men liked others who, they felt, liked them or who in fact did like them (as determined by reports).

3. The men were very accurate in guessing who liked them and who did not. The degree of accuracy did not change much after the fourth day, although some persons came to be better liked and others less well liked.

4. Each man tended to prefer those persons who saw him approximately as he saw himself—especially when they saw his weaknesses as well as his strengths.

5. The men who liked each other tended to agree (i.e., to be similar to each other) in their liking for other men and in their attitudes toward important and relevant objects, such as the house, values, and other kinds of objects.[88]

Communication Networks and Leadership

A classic problem posed by group dynamic investigators is the relationship between communication channels in organizations and efficiency in group performance. The problem was first raised by Alex Bavelas late in the 1940s,[89] and many researchers have since devised what sometimes appears to be an endless variety of experiments devoted to studying it. The usual method of research that developed was to impose various communication networks upon groups to determine their consequences for effective performance. Group members are placed in cubicles connected by slots in the cubicle walls. Through these slots written messages can be passed. When all slots or channels are open, every person in the group can communicate directly with every other group member. Other patterns of communication can be formed simply by closing the appropriate channels. Instead of written messages, telephone lines or messengers can be used.[90]

The prototype of these experiments compared the relative effectiveness of several different communication patterns: the five-person wheel, chain Y, and circle (see Figure 12-1). The group was asked to identify which of several

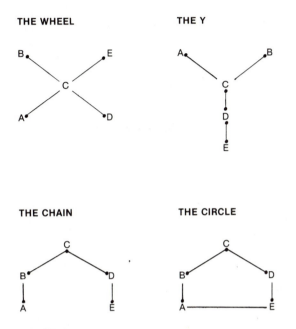

FIGURE 12-1
Five Person Communication Patterns (For persons A, B, C, D and E)

symbols (stars, triangles, circles, etc.) appeared on each card held by all members of the group. Each group was given 15 trials. After the conclusion of the final trial, each person was asked, "Did your group have a leader? If so, who?"

The researchers concluded that

1. Different communication patterns resulted in differences in accuracy, total activity, satisfaction of group members, emergence of a leader, and organization of the group.
2. The positions that persons occupied in a communication pattern affected their behavior while occupying those positions. The chances of becoming a leader, one's satisfaction with one's job and with the group, and the quantity of a person's activity were all affected by position in the communication pattern.
3. Persons who occupied *central* positions in a communication network were most likely to emerge as leaders. Persons whose positons were peripheral or low in centrality compared with other group members tended to become followers; they became dependent upon the leader and fell into roles that allowed little opportunity for prestige, activity, or self-expression.

These basic findings have been verified in a number of subsequent studies.[91]

Complexity and Decision Making

Many people seem to agree that a major characteristic of modern organizations and societies is the increasing complexity of their environments. On the other hand, there have been many studies that conclude there are severe limitations on the ability of human beings to process information. Thus it would appear that our allegedly complex social environments should make it difficult or even impossible for people to process all information required to make intelligent decisions. In short, it seemed to be generally agreed that increases in complexity result in increasing difficulty in controlling, managing, operating in, or adapting to such systems.[92]

An interesting study conducted in Australia raises some intriguing questions with respect to all this. An experimental situation was constructed to study how people interact with complex, changing systems and to examine the effect of increasing complexity on the ability of decision makers to guide the behavior of the system.

A simulated welfare administration project was developed in which the experimental subjects were required to make a variety of decisions that would optimize total welfare in a series of computer models of a welfare administration project over time. Complexity was studied on three dimensions: (1) the number of elements in the system, (2) the number of connections between the elements, and (3) The presence or absence of random variations.

It was found that performance in the more complex systems was not always poorer than performance on the simpler systems. The results of the experiment were not clear cut, but in some cases, they were opposite what one would expect if one believed that increasing complexity resulted in poorer performance.

The researchers conclude (1) that some revisions of current theories of the effects of complexity are called for as they apply to human interaction with social systems and (2) that they have demonstrated the difficulty of predicting behavior in complex real-life situations on the basis of simple laboratory experiments, that is, that "We cannot expect to synthesize an understanding of everyday human decision making from an aggregation of experiments focusing on only one or two aspects of this subject."[93]

NOTES

[1]Dorwin Cartwright, "Influence, Leadership, Control," in James G. March, ed., *Handbook of Organization* (Chicago: Rand McNally, 1965), p. 1.

[2]Murry Webster, *Action and Actors! Principles of Social Psychology* (Cambridge, Mass.: Winthrop, 1925), p. 110.

[3]Ward Edwards, "Men and Computers," in Richard M. Gagné, ed., *Psychological Principles in System Development* (New York: Holt, Rinehart and Winston, 1965), p. 94.

[4]Joseph Weizenbaum, *Computer Power and Human Reason: From Judgment to Calculation* (San Francisco: W. H. Freeman, 1976), p. 203.

[5]Ibid., p. 213

[6]Joseph E. Bogen, "The Other Side of the Brain: An Appositional Mind," reprinted in Robert Ornstein, ed., *The Nature of Human Consciousness* (New York: Viking, 1974), pp. 101–125 (originally published in the *Bulletin of The Los Angeles Neurological Societies*, Vol. 34, no. 3, July 1969, pp. 135–162).

[7]Ibid., p. 119.

[8]Ibid., p. 111.

[9]Weizenbaum, *Computer Power and Human Reason*, p. 215.

[10]Ibid., p. 227

[11]James G. March and Herbert A. Simon, *Organizations* (New York: John Wiley, 1958), p. 2.

[12]Ibid., p. 3.

[13]John Wareham, *Secrets of a Corporate Headhunter* (New York: Atheneum, 1980), p. 36.

[14]C. Northcote Parkinson and Nigel Rowe, *Communicate: Parkinson's Formula for Business Survival* (Englewood Cliffs, N.J.: Prentice-Hall, 1972), p. 9.

[15]Qass Aquarius, *The Corporate Prince: A Handbook of Administrative Tactics* (New York: Van Nostrand Reinhold, 1971).

[16]R. G. H. Siu, *The Master Manager* (New York: John Wiley, 1980), pp. 2–3.

[17]J. L. Moreno, *Who Shall Survive: Foundations of Sociometry Group Psychotherapy and Sociodrama* (Beacon, N.Y.: Beacon House, 1953), p. xvii.

[18]Ibid., p. 42.

[19]J. L. Moreno, *Psychodrama* (Beacon, N.Y.: Beacon House, 1959), Vol. II, p. 137.

[20]Jerry W. Koehler, *The Corporation Game* (New York: Macmillan, 1975).

[21]Ibid., p. xii.

[22]Ibid., p. xiv.

[23]Daniel Nelson, *Frederick W. Taylor and the Rise of Scientific Management* (Madison: University of Wisconsin Press, 1980), pp. 21–35.

[24]David F. Noble, *America by Design* (New York: Alfred A. Knopf, 1977), pp. 36–37.

[25]Hugh G. J. Aitken, *Taylorism at Watertown Arsenal* (Cambridge, Mass.: Harvard University Press, 1960), pp. 35–37. See, also, Henry R. Towne's paper "The Engineer as Economist," in *Transactions*, A.S.M.E., Vol. 7 (1886), pp. 428–432.

[26]Aitken, *Taylorism at Watertown Arsenal*, p. 38.

[27]Ibid., pp. 38–39.

[28]Nelson, *Frederick Taylor and the Rise of Scientific Management*, pp. 118–120.

[29]Frederick W. Taylor, *Shop Management* (New York: McGraw-Hill, 1911), p. 1337.

[30]Ibid.

[31]Ibid., p. 1368.

[32]Harlow S. Person, "Foreword" to Frederick Winslow Taylor, *Scientific Management* (New York: Harper and Brothers, 1947), pp. x–xi.

[33]F. W. Taylor, in "Taylor's Testimony Before the Special House Committee," Ibid., p. 26–27.

[34]Noble, *America by Design*, p. 272.

[35]Ibid.

[36]Ibid., p. 273.

[37]Ibid., pp. 273–274.

[38]Cyril Sofer, *Organizations in Theory and Practice* (New York: Basic Books, 1972), p. 37.

[39]Ibid.

[40]Ibid.

[41]Ibid., pp. 37–38.

[42]In the following summary of the National Research Council studies, we have relied heavily on the work of Loren Baritz, *The Servants of Power* (Middletown, Conn.: Wesleyan University Press, 1960), pp. 78–95, and J. H. Smith, "Foreward to Elton Mayo," *The Social Problems of an Industrial Civilization*, 1975 ed. (London: Routledge & Kegan Paul, 1975), pp. ix–xl.

[43]F. J. Roethlisberger, *Management and Morale* (Cambridge, Mass.: Harvard University Press, 1941), p. 10.

[44]Ibid., pp. 10–11.

[45]The classic description of these studies appears in a work coauthored by F. J. Roethlisberger (an academic colleague of Elton Mayo) and William J. Dickson (chief of The Employee Relations Research Department at the Works), *Management and the Worker* (Cambridge, Mass.: Harvard University Press, 1956).

[46]J. H. Smith, "Foreword," ibid., p. xxxv.

[47]Mayo, *The Social Problems of an Industrial Civilization*, pp. 20–21.

[48]Ibid., p. 21.

[49]Ibid., p. 33.

[50]Ibid.

[51]Ibid., pp. 36–37.

[52]Ibid., p. 39.

[53]Arthur Kornhauser et al., eds., *Industrial Conflict* (New York: McGraw-Hill, 1954), p. 511. Quoted in Baritz, *The Servants of Power*, p. 173.

[54]Harold L. Sheppard, "Approaches to Conflict in American Industrial Sociology," *The British Journal of Sociology*, Vol. 5 (1954), pp. 339–340.

[55]For an explanation of the systems approach by one of its most distinguished practitioners, see C. West Churchman, *The Systems Approach*, revised and updated edition (New York: Dell, 1981). For critical analyses, see Robert Boguslaw, *The New Utopians: A Study of System Design and Social Change*, enlarged edition (New York: Irvington, 1981), and Robert Boguslaw, *Systems Analysis and Social Planning: Human Problems of Post-Industrial Society* (New York: Irving, 1981). For excellent studies of the impact of this approach in the field of data processing, see Joan M. Greenbaum, *In the Name of Efficiency* (Philadelphia: Temple University Press, 1979), and Philip Kraft, *Programmers and Managers: The Routinization of Computer Programming in the United States* (New York: Heidelberg Science Library, Springer-Verlag, 1977).

[56]Greenbaum, *In the Name of Efficiency*, p. 38.

[57]Churchman, *The Systems Approach*, pp. 29–48.

[58]Ibid., p. 31.

[59]Ibid., p. 39.

[60]Ibid., p. 47.

[61]Pat Anthony Frederico et al., *Management Information Systems and Organizational Behavior* (New York: Praeger Publishers, 1980), p. v.

[62]Ibid.

[63]Ibid., p. 113.

[64]Ibid., p. 114.

[65]Ibid.

[66]Ibid., p. 115.

[67]Ibid., pp. 25–26.

[68]Ibid., p. 26.

[69]Russell E. Ackoff, "Management Misinformation Systems," in Peter P. Schoderber, ed., *Management Systems*, 2nd ed. (New York: John Wiley, 1971), pp. 179–185.

[70]Ibid., p. 181.

[71]Ibid., p. 182.

[72]Douglas McGregor, *The Human Side of Enterprise* (New York: McGraw-Hill, 1960).

[73]Harold Leavitt, Lawrence Pinfield, and Eugene Webb, eds., *Organizations of the Future: Interaction with the External Environment* (New York: Praeger Publishers), p. v.

[74]Ibid.

[75]Our "answer" to this question relies heavily on ibid., pp. 191–196.

[76]Ibid., p. 194.

[77]Ibid., p. 195.

[78]Ibid.

[79]Earl F. Lundgren, *Organizational Management* (San Francisco: Canfield Press, 1974), p. 52.

[80]Cyril Sofer, *Organizations in Theory and Practice* (New York: Basic Books, 1972), p. 20.

[81]Ibid., p. 70.

[82]For an authoritative history of small-group research, see A. Paul Hare, *Handbook of Small Group Research*, 2nd ed. (New York: The Free Press, 1976), pp. 384–395. Our discussion of this history is based largely on this source.

[83]For three perspectives on Moreno's concept of Sociometry, see Edgar F. Borgatta, Robert Boguslaw, and Martin R. Hashell, "On the Work of Jacob L. Moreno," *Sociometry*, Vol. 38, no. 1, (1975), pp. 148–161. For an unconventional biographical perspective, see Robert Boguslaw, "J. L. Moreno-Obituary," *American Sociological Association (Footnotes)* (November 1974), p. 3

[84]Dorwin Cartwright and Alvin Zander, eds., *Group Dynamics: Research and Theory*, 3rd ed. (New York: Harper & Row, 1968), p. 19.

[85]Ibid., p. 40.

[86]Rory O'Day, "The T-Group Trainer: A Study of Conflict in the Exercise of Authority," in Graham S. Gibbard et al., eds., *Analysis of Groups* (San Francisco: Jossey-Bass, 1974), p. 388. For a more complete discussion, see L. P. Bradford et al., eds., *T-Group Theory and Laboratory Method: Innovation in Re-Education* (New York: John Wiley, 1964), and E. H. Schein and W. G. Bennis, *Personal and Organizational Change Through Group Methods* (New York: John Wiley, 1965).

[87]Hare, *Handbook of Small Group Research*, p. 75.

[88]Clovis R. Shepherd, *Small Groups: Some Sociological Perspectives* (San Francisco: Chandler, 1964); the study was originally reported in the *American Psychologist*, Vol. 11 (1956), pp. 575–586. Figure 1 is adapted from Figure 4 on p. 42 of that study.

[89]See Alex Bavelas's, "A Mathematical Model for Group Structures," *Applied Anthropology*, Vol. 7 (1948), pp. 16–30, and his "Communication Patterns in Task-Oriented Groups," *Journal of the Acoustical Society of America*, Vol. 22 (1950), pp. 725–730.

[90]Marvin E. Shaw, *Group Dynamics*, 2nd ed. (New York: McGraw-Hill, 1976), pp. 137-141.

[91]Ibid., p. 140. For the original study, see H. J. Leavitt, "Some Effects of Certain Communication Patterns on Group Performance," *Journal of Abnormal and Social Psychology*, Vol. 46, no. 1 (January 1951), pp. 36–50.

[92]Andrew J. Machinnon and Alexander J. Wearing, "Complexity and Decision Making," *Behavioral Science*, Vol. 25, no. 4 (July 1980), pp. 285–296.

[93]Ibid., p. 296.

CHAPTER THIRTEEN
CRITIQUE IN LIEU
OF A CONCLUSION

When the study of a new field begins with a definition, it seems appropriate to end it with a "conclusion." Since we did not begin this book with a definition, however, it would seem that we do not really require a "conclusion." Instead we believe that it is more appropriate to provide something of a critique—an assessment not only of our own efforts but of the field of social psychology itself.

It should be clear by now that to formulate a definition of a field almost inevitably involves taking a particular position among what may be strongly competing frames of reference. Since this book is intended as an introduction to the field of social psychology, we felt it important to present a range of methods, theoretical orientations, and substantive issues that continue to be used by or are of interest to practitioners. But we have by no means presented the full range of conflicting intellectual and substantive concerns that trouble the contemporary social psychologist.

Take, for example, a simple statement such as "Social psychology is the science of . . . ."

Surely everyone would agree that this field is a *science!*

Not so.

Kenneth J. Gergen, a respected member of this profession, years ago, in an influential paper[1] noted that thinking of social psychology as a science is a direct descendant of eighteenth-century thought. At that time, the physical sciences had produced great advances in knowledge, and people were optimistic about the prospects of applying the "scientific method" to human behavior. This general orientation (which sociologists and some philosophers refer to as "positivism") held out the hope that if "scientific" principles of human behavior could be established, it might be possible to reduce social conflict, eliminate mental illness, and create social conditions in society that everyone would approve. People like Bertrand Russell hoped that these principles could be converted into mathematical form and that ultimately one could develop a mathematics of human behavior that would compare favorably in precision to the mathematics of machines.

In contrast to this orientation, Gergen argued that social psychology was quite different from the natural sciences and indeed was "primarily an historical inquiry."[2] He insisted that, unlike the natural sciences, social psychology deals with facts that are largely nonrepetitive and that fluctuate widely through time. Moreover, he maintained, knowledge cannot accumulate in the usual natural science sense because the knowledge that is found is restricted by historical boundaries. One important reason for this, he tells us, is that in the social sciences, knowledge held by the scientist can affect the behavior of persons being studied. This is not true in the natural sciences. Thus, in psychological experiments, it is common research practice to avoid communicating one's theoretical premises to the subject before or during the research. Even the most subtle clues of expectation on the part of the experimenter have been shown to alter the behavior of the subject. This is not only the case in formal experiments, it happens in so commonplace an area as parent-child relationships as well. Thus parents may use direct rewards to influence the behavior of their children. Over time, children become aware of the fact that the adult assumes the reward will lead to the desired results. They may then become "obstinate" and refuse to behave in the predicted manner. The adult may then pretend to "not care" whether the activity is engaged in or not. The child may then do it but also indicate his or her sophistication by saying something like "You are just saying you don't care because you *really* want me to do it."[3]

Gergen also notes the inconsistencies that have been found in studies like those that have tried to discover predictors of political activism. "Variables that successfully predicted activism during the early stages of the Vietnam War are dissimilar to those which successfully predicted activism during later periods."[4]

Shortly before Gergen gave us his critique, two other workers in this field devoted a serious book to consideration of the "possibility of a scientific study of those psychological states, conditions and powers which are to be attributed to individual people when they are engaged in social activity."[5] They called for a comprehensive theoretical treatment of social psychology and a reformed methodology that they felt to be an urgent need recognized by persons within the profession. "The underlying reason for this state we believe to be a continued adherence to a positivist methodology, long after the theoretical justification for it in naïve behaviorism has been repudiated."[6]

They insisted that an adequate social psychology could be developed "only as a cooperative enterprise among psychologists, philosophers, and sociologists. No one of these groups seems to be able to be successful alone."[7] They argued that psychologists had often been concerned with too narrow a conception of social action and severely handicapped by "conceptual naiveté." Philosophers, on the other hand, have not lacked conceptual sophistication but often have been simply ignorant of social and psychological facts. Sociologists, they insist, while often having great breadth of conception have been unable to develop satisfactory theories of individual social action. Along with psychologists, sociologists often suffer from conceptual naiveté.[8]

This seems to suggest that disciplines exert an overwhelming influence upon their members, but it does not begin to explain why or how changes occur *within* disciplines. Thus many writers have pointed to the changes that have occurred or are occurring within the field of social psychology itself. According to one perceptive account of the history of American social psychology, "social psychology became much less groupy in the 60's than it had been in the 40's and 50's . . . this change was manifested not only by the diminished concern for larger social systems, but also an increasingly individualistic treatment of other social psychological phenomena."[9]

In an "individualistic" treatment, an organism is seen as a relatively self-contained unit. The actions it takes reflect its own internal state or processes. From this perspective, the universe is seen as being composed of individuals who are acted upon by external events. In turn, the external world is modified or may be modified by what the individuals do. Universal scientific laws, however, always relate to single organisms.

The "groupy" approach, on the other hand, sees the individual as an element in a larger system such as a group, organization, or society. What the individual does is presumed to reflect the state of the larger system and the events occurring within it. Explanations are sought outside the individual person and in the collective actions of others or in the constraints imposed by the larger system.[10]

The difference between these two approaches is illustrated by an event that occurred during the early days of the civil rights struggle in this country. One Sunday morning someone threw dynamite against the door of a church in Birmingham, Alabama, while Sunday School was in session. Three black children were killed. How does one explain the behavior in this event? For many newspaper editors and radio commentators, the explanation was framed in such terms as "warped mind" or "psychotic character." Reverend Martin Luther King viewed matters differently. He concluded that *all of us* were guilty. People throw dynamite because society approves of it, defines it as a reasonable act, or at least tolerates it. Thus the true explanation of the deed lay in what all of us were doing or failing to do.[11]

As you will have observed by now, this book, written by two sociologists, emphasizes a "groupy" approach rather than an "individualistic" one. Since it has treated a range of theories and methods, however, it can in some ways be regarded as "pluralistic." It is not, of course, exhaustive, and there are many methods and theories that have been dealt with either in a cursory fashion or not at all. This is the case not only with those on the "individualistic" end of the continuum (if indeed it is a "continuum") but for those at the groupy end as well. For example, we have not examined the implications of a forthright historical approach to social psychology, although our organization in terms of developmental processes is clearly related to such an orientation at least from the perspective of the life of an individual person. And we have not dealt at all, in direct terms, with what has been referred to as "dialectical social psychology."[12] Our conscientious readers will not be shocked to learn that there does not yet seem to exist a satisfactory definition of dialectical social psychology. An admittedly abstract account of what it is asserts that it would

> study persons and groups as (1) changing historical entities in changing historical circumstances who (2) experience contradictions within themselves as well as in relation to their circumstances, and whose activities are (3) only likely to be better understood by a discipline that can properly recognize and represent the complex, illogical absurdities of real social life: interpenetrating opposites, qualities and quantities transforming into one another, and all the various magic tricks performed by language.[13]

Clearly an historical perspective is related to such an orientation, but it is scarcely the equivalent of one. As another scholar has put it,

> Calls for purely technical solutions to our present dilemmas (e.g., more field research or complex experiments) may be quite irrelevant given the historical forces that shape our science. Until we overcome our historical perspective, we will not come to grips with the dialectical interrelationship of data, theory and social context which is the past and present of social psychology.[14]

We have elected to refrain from burdening newcomers to social psychology with the heavy choice of deciding between a dialectical orientation and more conventional forms of method and theory. Positivism still reigns supremely, if somewhat uneasily, these days over a field that in recent years has seen significant inroads made by methodological and theoretical alternatives provided by orientations such as symbolic interaction and psychoanalysis.

Nevertheless, it is probably still the case that "If the dialetic orientation is to be taken seriously, its adherents must be prepared to confront the realities of an inimical institutional structure."[15]

This is a more genteel way of asserting that to be "successful" in the profession, one must learn to do one's work in a fashion acceptable to the existing "establishment." Thus, beginning with entrance into graduate programs and proceeding through the rigors of obtaining tenure as a university professor, it is helpful to be known as one who works within the framework of currently fashionable paradigms. "Anyone concerned with the exigencies of continued employment would be wise to avoid the dialectical perspective or to seek ways of altering the existing structure."[16]

For some critics, even a dialectical approach does not deal with the underlying problems of our discipline. Thus Philip Wexler lumps dialecticians with pluralists and sees them both as separating the question of method from the

> substantive content of social psychological theory, to say nothing of its cultural history and current uses. The pluralists want to adopt more conventional methods of social science, like field studies, surveys and abstracted quantitative longitudinal macrostructural analysis. The dialecticians abstract dialectics as a logic from

any social materialist dialectics which does indeed include a theory of social relations and social change.[17]

The more general point being made here has to do with the limited value of changes or "improvements" that are restricted to methodological or theoretical matters without taking into account the broader context of the "real world" within which they occur. This point was perhaps made most cogently by Karl Marx in his critique and subsequent adaptation of Hegel's dialectical approach. Marx understood and accepted the part of Hegel's work that noted that human beings created themselves in a continuous process in the course of their own work. He objected, however, to the abstract character of Hegel's analysis and concerned himself with "real people" and the concept of "Praxis." This refers to the activity of people aimed at fundamental social change as well as their own self-development.

> Man is not a passive product of external influences, but instead participates, through his own practical activity, in shaping the conditions for his existence. It is through these conditions that his personality is formed. The transformed environment does not . . . lose its determining influence on Man, even though it is at the same time the expression of his activity in the socio-historical process of self-development. Thus, practical transformation of the world includes shaping as well as *changing human mind and consciousness.*[18]

In a strange sort of way, this sentiment is reminiscent of something once written by the sociologist Emile Durkheim who was very much interested in understanding the social or societal influences on phenomena ranging from suicide to religion: "If a science of societies is to exist, we must expect that it will not consist of a simple paraphrase of traditional prejudices but rather that it will lead us to see things in ways diverging from views currently accepted."[19]

It has been suggested that new and unexpected ideas in science are not only due to the inspiration and the genius of an individual but also to the readiness of individuals to upset conceptions current in their own time and place.[20] But, of course, change is not always an unmixed blessing. Thus when social psychology began to see itself as a behavioral science, it was hoped that this would lead to a science with foundations as firm as those presumably existing in the physical sciences. The new orientation shifted the focus of attention from society to individual and interindividual phenomena seen from a quasi-physical rather than a symbolic perspective.

> But this change in terminology reflected a corresponding change in values and interests. Indeed, workers in the new social sciences restricted their ambitions to searching for palliatives for the dysfunctions of society without questioning either its institutions or its psychological adequacy in the face of human needs. This narrowing of horizons is closely related to the restriction of the subject to the "study of behavior." The close association with general psychology that this restriction represents conceals its social and political implications; it prevents us from viewing in their true perspectives the phenomena we are supposed to be studying and it even provides some justification for the opinion that we contribute to the alienation and to the bureaucratization of our social life.[21]

In our first chapter, we suggested that the multiplicity of definitions of social psychology (and the multiplicity of intellectual orientations among its practitioners) may be regarded as either a threat or an opportunity. It could imply either that the field is one characterized by a great deal of disorganization or that it is a field in which a great deal is happening and where an inquiring mind can make important contributions. Perhaps it is now time to remove the "either's" and the "or's." Universal conformity—slavish adherence to established doctrine—is clearly not an indication of intellectual maturity in any field. Perhaps a modicum of "disorganization" is ultimately necessary before progress can take place in any discipline. Perhaps the future of social psychology lies in becoming a forthright social science—one that examines the processes of communication, individual development, and human community not as rigid, physical truths, but as insights sensitive to changes in the concerns of human beings, to the constraints imposed by their traditions, and to their continuing efforts to change the social fabric—to fashion a "better" world. In a world that often seems increasingly to threaten the robotization of the human spirit, perhaps an ultimate test for the quality of being human is demonstration of the ability to engage in and accept a world (as well as a social psychology) of continual (and, it is hoped, progressive) social change.

NOTES

[1]Kenneth J. Gergen, "Social Psychology as History," *Journal of Personality and Social Psychology*, Vol. 26, no. 2 (1973), pp. 309–320.

[2]Ibid., p. 310.

[3]Ibid., p. 314.

[4]Ibid., p. 315.

[5]R. Harre and P. F. Secord, *The Explanation of Social Behavior* (Totowa, N.J.: Rowman and Littlefield, 1972), p. 1.

[6]Ibid.

[7]Ibid., p. 2.

[8]Ibid.

[9]Ivan D. Steiner, "What Happened to the Group in Social Psychology?" *Journal of Experimental Social Psychology*, Vol. 10, no. 1 (1974), p. 95.

[10]Ibid., pp. 95–96.

[11]Ibid., pp. 96–97.

[12]Leon Rappoport, "Symposium: Toward a Dialectical Social Psychology," *Personality & Social Psychology Bulletin*, Vol. 3 (Fall 1977), pp. 678–680.

[13]Ibid., p. 679.

[14]Steve R. Baumgardner, "Critical Studies in the History of Social Psychology," *Personality & Social Psychology Bulletin*, Vol. 3 (Fall 1977), p. 685.

[15]Kenneth J. Gergen, "On Taking Dialectics Seriously," *Personality & Social Psychology Bulletin*, Vol. 3 (Fall 1977), p. 718.

[16]Ibid.

[17]Philip Wexler, *Critical Social Psychology* (Boston: Routledge & Kegan Paul, 1983), p. 17.

[18]Jaromir Janousek, "On the Marxian Concept of Praxis," in Joachin Israel and Henri Tajfel, eds., *The Context of Social Psychology: A Critical Assessment* (New York: Academic Press, 1972), p. 279.

[19]Quoted by Serge Moscovici, "Society and Theory in Social Psychology," in Israel and Tajfel, eds., *The Context of Social Psychology*, p. 65.

[20]Ibid.

[21]Ibid., p. 50.

INDEX